Church: A Generous Community Amplified for the Future

ADVANCE PRAISE

"*CHURCH: A Generous Community Amplified for the Future* is, beyond any doubt, one of the most hopeful, realistic, enthusiastic, positive, informed, and empowering assessments I have seen to date of where we are today as Christians and as the Episcopal Church. As such, it constitutes a very emphatic, very episcopal call to all of us—lay and clergy—to get up off our anxieties and preconceptions and get about our appointed work in God's economy, both current and forthcoming. Bishop Doyle is part-cheerleader, part-practical architect, part-scold, but always, always a loving and credible counselor. Pray God we hear him well and effectually."

- **Phyllis Tickle**, *author of The Great Emergence: How Christianity is Changing and Why*

"This is one of the most hope-filled, articulate and visionary books on the future of the church that I have seen for many years. Andy Doyle offers us an intelligently-crafted, mission-minded and spiritually-focused account of what our churches are, and what they can become. Rooted deeply in the Episcopal tradition, this book will nonetheless appeal to a wide range of readers from across the mainline denominations. It is a refreshing and reasoned argument that has the potential and power to rejuvenate our churches. The author brings together his own rich experience of ministry with fresh and original theological insight, powerful imagination and rich wisdom. The result is a compelling and courageous book that deserves not only a full hearing, but also a wide amplification across our churches."

- **The Very Revd. Prof. Martyn Percy**, Dean of Christ Church, Oxford and author of *Anglicanism: Confidence, Commitment and Communion*

"'To hell with the warranty.' Andy Doyle casts of a vision of the Church unfettered from anxious premonitions of death and decline. Nimbly drawing inspiration from sources as diverse as quantum physics and 60's sitcoms, he paints a lively picture of the changing world we inhabit. From this landscape emerges an irresistible sketch of tomorrow's Church: twining its way up through our past to thrive, re-imagined, in our future. Doyle's characterization of the Episcopal Church as "a diaspora community that dwells on the edge of culture" rightly locates our tribe of Jesus-followers on the fringes and the margins, but vibrantly interconnected to the society around us. This book lays out, with clarity and hope, life-giving principals that will guide the future Church, a significant navigational tool for anyone who stand at the helm of a Christian community."
-    *Emily M D Scott*, *founder of St. Lydia's Dinner Church, Brooklyn*

"This is great work. Comprehensive historically, culturally, technologically, ecclesiastically, and motivationally. Historically because it covers all the 20 centuries, something not often the case; culturally because of the importance culture has as a driving force for all we do; technologically because you utilize the new realities of communication and links between people and groups; ecclesiastically because we need an identity piece to connect for the faithful the vast diversity we both have and which also we lack; motivationally because we need to hear good news about possibilities within our own tradition with a multiplicity of ideas of ways to innovate."
-    **The Rt. Rev. Claude E. Payne**, Bishop of Texas and author of *Reclaiming the Great Commission.*

"This book has the courage to ask gnawing questions about the future church in a world of volatility, uncertainty, complexity, and ambiguity. While constructively dissecting the Episcopal Church, his resulting insight will be disruptively useful for everyone seeking faith in the future. Andy Doyle is making the future."
-    **Bob Johansen**, distinguished fellow, Institute for the Future and author of *Leaders Make the Future and The Reciprocity Advantage*

"Andy Doyle clearly names the pressing issues that the Episcopal Church faces as we continue into the 21st century, and offers a treasure house filled with ideas and principles that will serve the future growth of the church. There is something in this book for Episcopalians across the broad spectrum of beliefs, practices, and positions—as well as for leaders of other denominations. This is a book that calls for deep reflection and generative thinking, and will serve everyone who cares about the present and future of the church."

- **The Rev Paul Fromberg**, rector of St. Gregory Nyssa, San Francisco

"We surely have more than enough literature on the crisis in and the future of the church. We do not need more of it...except that this book is wholly different. It really is about the future church by a churchman who has read and thought and prayed and imagined into a scary, hope-filled future. Full disclosure: I rarely read a complete manuscript in order to write an endorsement; I read enough to get the gist and offer of the book. In this exceptional case, however, I have read every page, because Doyle has led me boldly into a new world of connectedness that rings true both to fact and to experience. That 'ringing true' is like a daring leap from Newtonian static reality into the dynamism of Einstein, only now rendered theologically and ecclesially. Like me, other readers will find, in its imaginative probes, that this book rings true with both deep hope and hard work yet to come."

- ***Walter Brueggemann***, *Columbia Theological Seminary and author of* The Prophetic Imagination

"People often ask me why I am hopeful about the future of mainline Protestantism. It's because of leaders like Bishop Andy Doyle. His new book about the future of the church inspires realism and hope. It's full of specific choices mainline churches (and especially the Episcopal Church) can make, but equally powerful, it converts readers to an open, creative, and hopeful posture toward the church of the future. And in my opinion, Chapter 24 alone is worth twice the price of the book."

- ***The Rev. Brian McLaren***, *author of* A New Kind of Christianity *and* We Make the Road by Walking

CHURCH:

A Generous Community Amplified for the Future

C. Andrew Doyle

VTS PRESS

First Published in the United States by

VTS Press
3737 Seminary Road
Alexandria, VA 22304
www.vts.edu

ISBN-13:
978-1508952299

ISBN-10:
1508952299

Printed in the United States of America
June 2015

First Edition

For
My Friends Who Have Lost Faith
In The Future Of The Episcopal Church

"Any usable discussion of Great Emergence and what is happening in Christianity today must commence with yesterday and a discussion of history. Only history can expose the patterns and confluences of the past in such a way as to help us identify the patterns and flow of our own times and occupy them more faithfully."

—Phyllis Tickle, author, _The Great Emergence_

TABLE OF CONTENTS

PREFACE

A friend reminds me that publishing is like performing—it's never perfect. I am grateful for that reminder. This book is not perfect but I had fun writing it and am glad to have had many individuals walk along the writing path with me as friends and companions. They have been honest when in my exuberance I was too strong. They let me know when my hope was too subtle. With friends and colleagues such as these we will most assuredly steer our Church into the future faithfully.

The Rt. Rev. Neil Alexander reminded me of the movie *The Color of Money*, and pool hustler Fast Eddy Felson (played by Paul Newman) who says that, "pool excellence is not about excellent pool." It is about becoming someone. This is true in book writing too. This book is about me becoming a better bishop from having thought and dreamed about the future. We will become a better diocese and a better Church from having had this conversation. We are always on the road to becoming the person and Church that God dreams.

Let me begin by thanking the Rt. Rev. Claude Payne for his leadership. He was my first bishop and challenged us to reclaim the Great Commission. He challenged his clergy to be mission and vision oriented. He believed in a living and thriving Episcopal Church and inspired me to believe with him. I am grateful for his kindness over the years, his willingness to be a first reader, and his support of my efforts. He continues to challenge me to believe in God's desire to share the Good News of Salvation, to grow the church, and to believe in the future of the Episcopal Church.

I am grateful to conversation partners who, over the last two years, have helped me think about the future of the Church and how to take steps forward and march into it: Margaret Wheatley, Bob Johansen, and Rachel Hatch among many others. Their own imagination and foresight have given me space in which to think and imagine.

I am also thankful to colleagues The Rev. John Newton, The Rev. Matt Russell, The Rt. Rev. Neil Alexander, The Rt. Rev. Sean Rowe, The Rt. Rev. Nick Knisely, The Very Rev. Dr. Cynthia Kittredge, The Rev. Dr. William Danaher, The Rt. Rev. Michael Curry, and The Rt. Rev. Pierre Whalon for being advance readers. A special "thank you" goes to Dr. Jim Hollis. Jim was kind enough to help me think through a piece on the Church, its *shadow*, and Carl Jung.

Canon Mary MacGregor, who has been a collaborator on the future of congregational development in the Diocese of Texas for over 10 years, has my deep gratitude. I also give thanks to Carol Barnwell, who has been my technology partner, and who has helped me to completely rethink communications for the Diocese of Texas. For over ten years both Mary and Carol have allowed me to come into their offices, interrupt, and talk about the future and the ideas I had rolling around in my head; so to both of them I have a deep appreciation for their patience, willingness, and excitement about how God might want us to do our work.

I am thankful to The Rev. Canon Kai Ryan and Bob Biehl, my canon to the ordinary and chief financial officer/treasurer, who helped give me space in my work life to get this written. For Stephanie Taylor who cleared my calendar and protected me while I was on retreat.

I have many good friends who have been supportive during the writing of this book. There are three who deserve special mention. When I first publicly talked about the book it was at a lunch with my friend John Price. I realize now his interest and encouragement enabled me to have that first bit of faith to continue the work of thinking and writing. As I neared the halfway mark, that place where all good books go to die, I had drinks with a new friend Matt Russell. It was Matt's excitement that encouraged me forward. Finally as I worked on these footnotes, I realized that the two most important influences on my thinking are Daniel Kahneman and Nassim Nicholas Taleb. The Rev. Patrick Miller introduced me to both of these authors and their books. He also has been an excited conversation partner over the last year of writing and for his support, encouragement, and excitement I am thankful.

I was glad to have served on the Task Force for Re-Imagining the Church (TREC). It was a great gift to me to be placed in a room with committed leaders who believe we can do better as missionaries, and that God is inviting us into a new future. It was an honor to serve and to work towards a common reimagined future together. The outcome of that discussion will be transformational for the Episcopal Church. Though this book is of my own thinking, it was helpful to be in conversation with others about the future as I was writing.

I want to say a special thank you to The Rev. Dr. Ian Markham and his support of my writing, of this particular book and for his willingness to bring it to the public through the VTS Press. I am indebted to him for his friendship and for his encouragement. He even suggested I add a chapter! The Rev. Dr. J. Barney Hawkins and Mr. Curtis Prather put in the hours to make Ian's offer come to reality. I will forever be grateful for Barney and his detail oriented editing and Curtis for his layout mastery.

In the summer of 2014, I was blessed by The Diocese of Texas to be provided a time to reflect about the future of our diocese and the Church. This book is the culmination of that time away. I enjoyed many days in the mountains of Colorado thanks to friends The Rev. Kit and Rufus Wallingford, their children Halley and Thomas Ortiz. Janie and Jim Stevens were also gracious and giving during this time providing a hideaway to be with family. Their generosities allowed my family to rest and enjoy the outdoors with me. I spent the mornings writing, enjoying coffee, and looking out at brilliant painted skies. I could not ask for any better environment in which to write.

I am so happy that JoAnne married me. She put up with me during the writing of the book—in fact it is her special talent to put up with me all the time. She has forever been and continues to be my first reader—something saved for only the ones I love! She is the one who inspires me by taking interest in my writing, life, and ministry. In 2015 we celebrate 25 years of marriage. Our two beautiful girls, a great group of close friends, and a wonderful life together reveals our happiness in having found one another.

For these blessings and all the blessings of this life I am humbled and grateful.

<u>INTRODUCTION</u>

*"So we beat on, boats against the current,
borne back ceaselessly into the past."*
— The last line of <u>The Great Gatsby</u> by F. Scott Fitzgerald

August 2, 2014, a large semi-truck dropped off a gigantic dirt digger at the house across the street. Within 15 minutes, it was destroying the 1960's ranch house that had most recently been the home to a series of renters. It is a scene familiar in Houston. Old homes, and just about anything that is left standing without purpose, is torn down so that something new can be put up in its place. There is something that is both exciting and disturbing about this routine demolition. An architect friend once told me that not every house *should* be saved. Sometimes I think we think it is easier simply to discard the past and build a new thing.

The idea that we can start from scratch, unaffected, without the weight and baggage of the former life is perhaps a uniquely American lie. I have discovered there is no real starting over. We are always walking into the future with a key ingredient of the past—ourselves. There is no tabula rasa. Lessons learned and lessons unlearned all come with us. The only thing new that is taken into the future is the lie that it is untouched and disconnected from all that comes before it. Bill Bryson in his book *At Home*, writes: "Houses are amazingly complex repositories. What I found, to my great surprise, is that whatever happens in the world—whatever is discovered or created or bitterly fought over—eventually ends up, in one way or another, in your house. Wars, famines, the Industrial Revolution, the Enlightenment—they are all there in your sofas and chests of drawers, tucked into the folds of your curtains, in the downy softness of your pillows, in the paint on your walls and the water in your pipes."[1]

This book is about a house–God's house. It is about the Church; more specifically the future Church. That being said, I have no interest in pulling up with a giant dirt digger and going at it. That just isn't the way things work. Besides, I love our Church in all its complexity and idiosyncrasies.

In *At Home,* Bryson describes the timeworn former Church of England rectory that he and his wife purchased in Norfolk. Norfolk produces twenty-seven thousand archaeological finds a year, more than any other county in England.[2] The home they purchased is an old home, added onto, repurposed, used, and lived in well. He writes, "Victorian houses are often a collection of architectural bewilderments."[3] So he has the idea of walking around the house looking for the "evolution of private life" in the artifacts that are present inside the house.

The same is true for this Church in which we find ourselves. It is a storehouse of the past. It is filled with artifacts from the theology, liturgy, and Sunday Schools of our past. The culture has deposited here the Enlightenment, the Industrial Revolution, the 1950's, and all manner of musical tastes. If we take a walk and make our way through God's house, we will find some interesting truths about the past Church. If we look closer still, we will see the profound impact the last 200 years have had on who we think we are and how we use the buildings of our faith. Here is the fascinating part though; if we look closely and we look at the world around us...we will also see artifacts of the future.

CHURCH: *A Generous Community Amplified for the Future* is a book about taking a second look at our Episcopal Church. It is about seeing a living organism making its way in the world in space and in time. This book is about the future and the Church's place in it. It is also about what will be necessary for us to remain and grow, and what can fall away. It is about our future mission, prayerfully undertaken in stewardship, service, and evangelism. It is about taking up our ministry with excellence, unity, and connectivity. What I am proposing is a more diverse Christian community in mission, community size, economic model, service, and leadership which makes our ministry more antifragile.[4] What you have before you is the culmination of over five years of imagining and listening to the exciting future that is already making itself known in the present. As you walk around the church and the churchyard, and look out into the world around us you can see it, you can hear the future calling us to see and take note.

I offer this book as a hopeful futurist and theorist. I offer it as a person tasked with casting a vision for my diocese and the wider Church. I offer it as a participant in the past and a leader of its future. I am a chairman on many Church boards, I am the head of several governance structures, and I am responsible for the livelihood of many clergy, professors, teachers, and lay professionals of every kind. Therefore, I am invested in the future of the organization and helping the Church to thrive. This means asking difficult questions that will most certainly bring difficult answers along the way. Former Presiding Bishop and founder of Seminary of the Southwest, The Rt. Rev. John Hines, believed that we should be open to the world, should always look to the future, and raise up leaders that speak the language of social sciences, culture, and theology. This is the spirit that must drive the work of the future Church. This is the spirit that must drive our conversation. This is the spirit of this book.

My hope is that this book will be provocative in order to get people talking. I hope it will stimulate you to see a hopeful horizon that is out before us. I want us to have an eye there and talk about how we will reach the distant shore. There will be places where you agree and where you disagree. When disagreement comes I hope it will cause you to pause an think deeply about your position and what is important for you. There will be zealots among us. I am not one. The zealot will say, "This is the way it must be." They will want us to create a new kind of "fundamentalist future map." That is not the purpose of this book. I am hoping for a conversation wherein people listen, critique, and prepare carefully for what is coming as it comes, remaining strong and focused in the meantime. We cannot bury our head in the sand. Instead we must work together with anticipation and with patience so we can sort out the trends that will be manifest as time evolves. With this book in hand and brave conversation partners, I believe we can gauge the trends and capitalize on them for the health of Church, and for the sake of the future mission. We must always do this from a position of health and strength. When we move to the future out of weakness and faithlessness we will always steer into the ditch.

My hope is that this text will offer leaven to feed the Church's imagination. It is an offering to God and the Church. It is an offering to all those who have lost hope in their church over the last two decades. Most of all, it is an offering for those who deeply desire to be part of what God is doing in the world around us. It is you, the imaginative lover of Jesus, passionate missionary, and worldly pilgrim, whom I hope to engage in a discussion about the future.

While we beat on against the current of the past and its Church, I am here to tell you there is an exciting movement forward—into our future. True, the tide draws us forever back to the shore. Jesus however is in the boat ahead of us. He beckons to us. He invites us to put our backs into it, to beat against the past, and to come along. Jesus invites us to join him and to make our way across to the other side with him. Only in following God in Christ Jesus into the future kingdom will we find our way onto the shore of that distant shore. We must make our way from the past into the future, heads up, and eyes on Jesus. For it is there—on that distant shore—that Jesus is standing, waiting, the fire is burning. He stands there and he is eager to break bread with us and to hear stories of our passage.

CHAPTER ONE
Schrödinger's Church

Jerry Seinfeld: "Why are we always looking back?"
Joel Hodgson: "We know what to say about the past, not the future."
—From Comedians in Cars Getting Coffee,
Episode "A Taste of Hell from on High"

Do you believe in a dying Church? Or do you believe in a living vibrant church? I believe in a vibrant Church. I caution you to be careful how you answer; everything may depend on it. In most every field of study the modern conundrum of how one sees the world is a debate which is alive and well. The dispute about how one sees the world began a long time ago for scientists. It began when Isaac Newton and his fellow physicist Christiaan Huygens proposed competing theories of light: light was thought either to consist of waves (Huygens) or of particles (Newton). The debate continued for hundreds of years until the last century. Albert Einstein and his contemporary Erwin Schrödinger argued about it. Schrödinger eventually tweaked Einstein's theory in his own work improving it and moving the discussion forward. The reason why the discussion continued is that in science there is an odd paradox that has existed since the seventeenth century. Humans can look at the same thing and measure it differently, and even describe its behavior differently. Part of the trouble was that scientists were beginning to be able to measure and observe ever-smaller things. Atom smashers and the like brought about a new science of small things—*quantum*[5] science. For the scientific community the paradox is highlighted because the observance of nature and the behavior of matter at the microscopic level do not behave by the same rules as nature and matter behave at the macroscopic level, or so it seems. What the scientists saw through a microscope and what they could see with the human eye told them different things about how the universe works.[6] This is the theory of *superposition* also called the *observer's paradox*. The observation or measurement itself affects the outcome and, that outcome, as such does not exist unless the measurement is made. This all can really make your brain hurt. Thank goodness for Schrödinger.

Schrödinger was a physicist who was interested in offering a thought experiment that would illustrate the quantum theory of *superposition*. He wanted to show that the Quantum view of probabilities was stronger than his predecessor's views of the world as deterministic. He devised what today is a famous illustration of this principle. Schrödinger's theoretical experiment works this way: We place a living cat (forever to be known as Schrödinger's Cat) into a steel chamber, along with a device containing a vial of hydrocyanic acid—a radioactive substance. When a single atom of the substance decays during the test period, a relay mechanism will trip a hammer, which will, in turn, break the vial and kill the cat. We know that it will decay we just don't know when.

What the experiment illustrates is that the observer cannot know whether or not an atom of the substance has decayed yet, and consequently, cannot know whether the vial has been broken, the hydrocyanic acid released, and the cat killed. Since we cannot know, according to quantum law, the cat is considered both dead and alive, in what is called a superposition of states. There are yet to be discovered many probabilities and we will participate in them, shaping them and forming them. When we break open the box and learn the condition of the cat the superposition is lost, and the cat becomes one or the other (dead or alive).[7] The probabilities are shown to be true. This is of course an oversimplification of the experiment but I believe you understand my point. Please note there is no actual cat and no cats were harmed in the thought experiment in Schrödinger's brain.

If we look at the work of Howard Becker, an American sociologist, we see the *observation paradox* applied in what he called the "labeling theory." Becker put together the work of predecessors Frank Tannenbaum and Edwin Lemert in his popular 1963 book *Outsiders*. He was working on the idea of deviance. He believed that when society labeled, or tagged, an individual as deviant, that same individual would then take on behaviors that matched their label. He wrote, "...social groups create deviance by making rules whose infraction constitutes deviance, and by applying those roles to particular people and labeling them as outsiders. From this point of view, deviance is not a quality of the act the person commits, but rather a consequence of the application by others of rules and sanctions to an 'offender.'"[8] He continues, "Labeling places the actor in circumstances which make it harder for him to continue the normal routines of everyday life and thus provoke him to 'abnormal' actions."[9] Becker also applied the idea to the social interaction between culture and the artist in his 1982 book *Art Worlds*. No longer is art simply something one person produces for the enjoyment of others. Instead, in Becker's theory art is a collective action of materials, interactions, observation, shared meaning, and value. It was the community that defined and made art *art*.[10] Becker's idea was popular and his critics vehement. However, his theories have never been displaced. Instead they have been modified, amended, and "absorbed."

Margaret Wheatley, in her book *Leadership and the New Science: Discovering Order in a Chaotic World*, says it this way: "Reality is co-created by our process of observation."[11] "We participate in the creation of everything we observe."[12] Two realities are always in existence within a thing and how we observe or what we say about a thing changes the essence of it. How we look at Schrödinger's Cat actually shapes its fate, whether it lives or dies. In fact more than two realities may exist together at the same time. The way we observe art actually participates in making it art. Whether we classify a person as a *deviant* or *good* plays a part in their behavior. In quantum theory it is recognized that in any given moment two states exist and that the observer shapes the reality of that which is observed. This is true for art and people. This is true for light. This is true for Schrödinger's cat. And, it is true for the church. The way you see your Church has a direct effect on the Church itself.

The church that we observe is very much the church that comes into being. If we observe a church that is dying, then we will most assuredly affect growing entropy. If we observe a church that is alive and thriving, then our church will thrive and be alive. This is not simply a power of positive thinking lesson. Quantum physics teaches us that the observer shapes the reality of that which is being observed.

In the church we call that the power of the Living Word. In the same way that God creates by speaking God's word, we too co-create (although on a much smaller scale) our church and the world around us by *how* we perceive it and the kinds of stories we tell about it. The implication, I think, is that nothing is more threatening to the life and mission of the church than cynical and negative leadership. The inability to see God's hand at work in the world around us creates an environment where it gets even *harder and harder* to see God. Life in ministry then becomes a downward spiral.

So, the way we see and what we say about ourselves, the church, etc., matters greatly. Theologian the Rev. Dr. Paul Zahl once said, "We become as we are regarded."[13] These quantum thinkers are helpful: reality is co-created by our process of observation. How we observe the church will create the church we observe.

This is, of course, not the first time we have been offered an opportunity to think about this matter. There is a story in the Bible that goes like this . . . Jesus had been teaching and he was probably tired. He decides to get away for a bit. He and his friends—Peter,

James, and John—go away take some time away from the crowds of people and the daily routine of teaching and healing. They go up to the top of a mountain to pray. While Jesus is praying and the others are watching, Jesus begins to be changed. His face changes and shines bright. His clothes become dazzling white. "Wow," they think, "this is really awesome." Then as if it couldn't get any better, two great prophets appear: Moses and Elijah. They appear and they are as wild looking as Jesus—sparklingly and white. They are all there and they are talking about everything that is about to happen and how Jerusalem is going to be an important place in the story of Jesus. It is a transfiguring moment.

Peter says to Jesus, "It is good for us to see this and to be here with you." Then Peter says, "Let us make three dwellings, three booths, three boxes in which we can have you and Moses and Elijah dwell. It will be great because then people can come to the mountain like we did and be here with you." But Jesus doesn't accept their plan. Jesus is clear that their business is to leave the mountaintop and go back to the world preaching, teaching, and healing. This is the work of Jesus and he is clear that this is the work of those who follow him. (Luke 9:28-36)

The story is dynamic and about a living mission, God's mission. It is about being alive and in the world and not crammed into a box. It is a story about abundant life and abundant mission. I believe in a church that is alive and flourishing in the world. I believe in a Church that is ancient and new, multiplying and diverse, creative and so much more. This book is about the Church that I believe in. It is about the church I observe and believe is possible in a new missionary age. It is Schrödinger's Church with all its paradoxes and complexity.

It is our work to co-make this church. Certainly, God is even now creating this church and God's Holy Spirit is moving to bring it to completion. Yet we are the makers. We are the co-creators. What it will look like? Who leads it? How does it exist in the world? What does its mission look like? How is it organized? These are important questions to ask if we are the makers with God in this endeavor.

Regardless of the form that this missionary church takes, from the outset it is important to remember the words of King Solomon regarding the temple, "The highest heaven cannot contain you, much less this house that I have built!" (I Kings 8.27)

As individuals across a global community, we have a desire to make things and to build things. It is part of who we are, our very nature. We will continue to build machines like we have always done; but we also will invest in communities and in building networks. We will forever be about the work of co-creating by taking those things available to us and making something new from them; tinkering, or re-purposing parts from already existing things. We are in the end made to create and make. This reality is now making its presence known throughout the world through the *maker movement*. This movement has a motto: If you can't open it, then you don't own it.

If you can't open it, you don't own it. The idea is that if you can't open it and take it apart and use it and reuse it, then you really don't own it. It is somebody else's. Now I am going to give you an example from a company that I have evidently become dearly connected to and committed to, which is Apple. I love Apple products, so that is my disclaimer. If you by chance own any kind of smartphone—but especially the iPhone—you've bought it and you own it—so you think. Well, kind of. You see, you can't unlock it, and you can't use other things on it. You can only use the things that Apple says you can use. Now some of you are probably far technically superior than I am and know how to or who to go to for help in unlocking your iPhone; but for me—the poor iPhone owner—who does not know of these things, I am fearful that if I unlock my phone, I will void the warranty. My phone's ultimate potential is closed to me. I own it . . . but I don't own it. I can't really do with it everything that I might want to, so I can only use it—if you will—the way in which Apple wants me to use it. Or, to say it in another way, I can only use it in the manner my user agreement says I can. And there it is. I am a user, not an owner. This is amazing, given that Apple itself is one of the founding parents of the *maker movement* in computer technology.

Here's another example. Every year since 2006, a maker's conference called the Maker Faire has been held. Creative thinkers come from all over the world; they gather; and they show off their innovations. There's art and new technology, and everything is open and reusable. Well, a number of years ago, some artists came up with the idea of dropping a Mentos candy into a one-liter bottle of Diet Coke. Those of you who have teenage boys may have seen this already. Or you can go on the Internet and watch this "trick". Even better, you can do this in your own backyard. When you drop the Mentos in the bottle, it creates a chemical reaction with the Diet Coke. It explodes and a geyser-like explosion shoots out of the top! The Maker Faire artists were going around and capturing the image of the explosion as a form of art. Now, you and I can debate whether that is art or not; but that's not the point of this illustration. Here is the rest of the story. Mentos and Coca-Cola did not like this because their products weren't intended for such explosions; they were invested in a closed use of their products, and so they actually anteed up to sue these artists and keep them from re-purposing their product. Evidently, a ground swell of sixth graders all over the country stood up to them and said, "No." As the story goes, they begrudgingly gave in. Today both Mentos and Coca-Cola sponsor these artists at the Maker Faire. The companies had to come to terms with the fact that they could not control their products and that they were open to new applications or re-purposing.[14]

There is a passage in Mark's Gospel where the disciples are grumpy about people bringing their children to Jesus. In their opinion these children are really messing up the Gospel. These children are a problem to the disciples, who obviously are Very Serious Men. "There is no time for this," they thought. They decide that they are going to keep the children from coming to Jesus because they are interrupting all the other really good work that Jesus is doing. So, they say, "Look. We think the little ones should all go away—they can't be here." What's more, scholars have taught us that the first followers of Jesus were called the "Little Ones." This particular knowledge helps us to understand the all-encompassing meaning of the text. As we ponder what the disciples are doing, it becomes clear that they are invested in a closed system. They want to control how Jesus is used; how Jesus relates; with whom Jesus spends time; and who has access to Jesus. Who they think should have access to God is impacted by their desire for control. It is not the first nor the last time in the Scriptures that the disciples will think that they are able to control the Good News of Salvation and manage Jesus. Meanwhile, Jesus is busy opening up the kingdom to whoever would listen. In fact, that seems to be the purpose of his coming. He has come to glorify God, bring good news, and open up and give access to the reign of God for all people. This must have driven the disciples nuts! Just as they are figuring things out, creating a new power structure, and getting clarity on the best way to market the rock star Jesus... he is going around handing out backstage passes to everyone. The reign of God is open to everyone. "The heavens cannot contain this God or the house that I have built." (I Kings 8.27)

The God that we choose to follow is a God who is out and among the people. The God we follow bids us "make" a church where he is. We are to make a church that is out and among the people. Like God we are to make room for creativity and innovation. Our God cannot be contained. God's mission cannot be contained. God's mission has a church and that church is not to contain God.

The church must re-purpose, re-make, and make itself into a new creation— so that God may once again be accessed through its ministry. The church is a handmade vessel of God's grace. It can no longer choose to be a stumbling block for all those who long for a little measure of grace, mercy, and kindness, in a world that is cold and dark most days. The Church must choose to leap and take a step forward to find this God. Where the church is in the way, it must be changed. We must allow people to come forward and to find God, whether it is through the church doors or to sit and listen to somebody out in the world.

For many of us access to God and God's love is why we are in the church. We belong because it makes a difference in our lives. It changes who we are. It challenges us to be a better people. Such a God cannot be contained, even in you or me.

We must become a church generation of makers who play—who play in the waters of baptism and in the Scriptures and around God's altar. This is sacred and holy play where we reenact in our lives, inside and outside church buildings, the great story of God's creation.

. We are to be about making the world into a different place. We are to make it different with all the tools at our disposal. Most especially, we are to make it new by God's love, grace, forgiveness and mercy. We are to share and open up our church and walk out into the sweet smelling and lush garden of creation. We are to invite, welcome and connect with others. We are to share the message that God says to all people—"Come unto me all you who travail and are heavy laden and I will refresh you." God opens himself up and says to us we who are weighed down by the world—"Come unto me. I'll give you rest." Don't keep away the little children. Don't keep away those who have tried to follow Jesus and believe they have failed. Don't keep away those who have drifted away from the church and from God. Give God away! By all means let them all come. And let us go. Let us make the church together.

CHAPTER TWO
A New Missionary Age

"A pessimist sees the difficulty in every opportunity;
an optimist sees the opportunity in every difficulty."
— *Sir Winston Churchill, Prime Minister of Great Britain*

The Lemhi Pass[15] is at the border of Montana and Idaho. A wooden fence, cattle guard crossing, and logging road mark the pristine spot. One arrives there by following the Missouri River from Fort Benton to Fort Peck Lake along the Lolo Trail. When you stand there now, it looks in many ways as it looked when Merriwether Lewis stood there on the morning of August 12, 1805.[16] With friends nearby, he made his way to the top. That moment is described clearly in his journal: "We proceeded on the top of the dividing ridge from which I discovered immense ranges of high mountains still to the West of us with their tops partially covered with snow."[17] Meriwether Lewis was the first European American to look on the great northwestern range, the first to take a step out of the Louisiana territory onto the western side of the Continental Divide.[18]

Did the sight before Lewis suggest two great worlds colliding? Two thoughts occurring simultaneously, neither fully formed.

With the disheartening sight, the first thought would be "the shock, the surprise," as historian John Logan Allen mused, "For from the top of that ridge were to be seen neither the great river that had been promised nor the open plains extending to the shores of the South Sea . . . the geography of hope [gave way] to the geography of reality."[19] The journey to find a western portage to travel by boat from east to west across the United States was a failure. Everything Lewis was certain he would find not only was *not there*—it never would be. The dream, framed by a year of study and preparation and two years of travel across wild country, was over.

The second thought was in reaction to the view of the great empire of the Americas. Encircled by a grand panorama, Lewis might have envisioned a wealthy and abundant new territory with a spectacle of fertile land and the spirit that would become the United States. In an age with little change in transportation, energy, and food since the Greeks, Meriwether Lewis may have glimpsed in its raw form the rapid emergence of the bountiful nation we were destined to become. Yet he could not imagine what it would take to unify the land nor could he predict the tragic saga of tribal relationships that would be left in the wake of his discovery.[20]

Two thoughts not fully formed, yet coexisting, shaped who Americans are today. Today we are becoming a new people, transformed and forged in a fiery furnace of sweeping historic change. Not unlike that morning in August 1805, America's social and economic geography are giving way beneath our feet. The past falls away in the present while the future is yet to solidify. Our time requires clear vision and the ability to see beyond the chaos and incongruities of our time to a future others cannot see. If we look carefully, we may see the future and all God hopes for the whole world and us.[21]

Bob Johansen, distinguished fellow at the Institute for the Future (IFTF), reminds us that we live in a VUCA world: "volatile, uncertain, complex, and ambiguous."[22] As a church, we have a nagging knowledge that things are not as they were. We have had a view that things will remain the same. We have acted out of an understanding that if we simply did things better all would return to normal. As Margaret Wheatley says, "We grew assured of the role of determinism and prediction. We absorbed expectations of regularity into our very beings. And we organized work and knowledge based on our beliefs about this predictable universe."[23]

In the face of this VUCA world, we have consistently and stubbornly believed that:

- those who are called by God to be Episcopalians will find the Episcopal Church and walk through its doors;
- once they are inside the doors they will stay because of the awesome liturgy;
- one day we will grow again, and then we can take care of our deferred maintenance;
- all we need is the right clergyperson and everything will be okay;
- by solving the issue of the day, we would surge in growth;
- by clinging to the past we wait our revival;

But that is not so. Things have changed. When did the world change? When did the Church change? What happened? Many blame and scapegoat *this* fact or *that* fact. *When* it all changed is scientifically unknowable. The Church is a complex organism that is rooted in geography, cultural contexts and political worlds. Change was not the result of any one event nor did it happen at one particular time. We must admit that we have not been good at changing missionary strategy to keep up with this evolution. Rather, change crept in and is upon us, though we cannot yet fully comprehend its impact or what outcome it will bring.

We operate out of a model that depends upon assumptions about the culture from mid-century of the last millennium: People will come; they will bring their family; and they will bring their money. For many congregations the simple battle against inflation will create a never-ending cost cutting habit that will eventually put them out of business. We are holding on to an economically unsustainable model. In consideration of the church economy, the average Episcopal

Church (TEC) congregation hosts fewer than 60 people on any given Sunday. If it is fortunate enough to have had wealthy benefactors early in its life, it may still be able to afford a full-time seminary-trained rector. Even with endowments and investments, congregations and dioceses have faced reduced returns because of a weakened U.S. economy, forcing hard choices about funding.

The problem is that fewer people will seek out and react positively to the Church's business-as-usual demeanor. Meanwhile, we are outperformed by culture. No longer does the Church corner the market on community life, networking, social services, weddings, funerals or healthcare. Social media networks, bars, gyms, sports clubs, hospitals, friends, and even funeral homes outperform us.

Everything has changed but the idea of Church has not. The Church did not have much to do with the change, and it simply is powerless to stop it. People who gave a lifetime of faithful service and faithful ministry to the Church find in their last years that the Church can neither offer pastoral care nor bury them. Churches are closing and people are forced to look elsewhere for support. As a bishop, I can tell you stories about rectors who do not bury people they don't know, and do not do home/hospital visits except on Christmas and Easter—if that. This church economy leads only to greater loss, conflict and closures. If left unchanged, the demise will be slow, painful and sad.

In the 1990s the military began to use the term VUCA (volatile, uncertain, complex, and ambiguous) to describe the emerging world of the new millennium.[24] Bob Johansen has successfully used the term to describe the complicated way in which the world comes into contact with corporations and communities.[25] Johansen has been interested in how such organizations make sense of the world and make their way through it. As we think about and ponder each element, it is possible for us to see how our own church systems work and how we are constantly reacting to the forces at work in the world around us.

Volatility is clearly present in the world as we pause and consider for a moment the acceleration of change. The immense growth in technology and user interface has within a short amount of time changed the way in which individuals communicate. Today we see that immediate communication now travels globally and creates innumerable reactions. News of Christian troubles a world away can now be the topic of local conversations within minutes. On Sunday mornings a priest can be faced with questions spanning the horizon of local to global politics—church and secular. The average parishioner may well have reactions, both positive and negative, to events that only ten years ago would have gone unnoticed. It is easy to see how financial volatility in Asia or Europe has disrupted economies in America. The same is true for church life. Whether it is news or the economic climate of the local community, church life is impacted and invited to respond to growing chaos within the local and global culture. In positive and negative ways, volatility is part of our common experience in congregational church life.

Uncertainty, the second of Johansen's VUCA, is also a key factor that affects the life of the church. Predictability has long ceased to be a static value within the culture, our communities and the local church. In the last four decades alone there has been a great deal of change. From prayer book revision to women priest to blessings of same-gender relationships, the church has been trying to figure out how to speak the language of and engage in the cultural context that surrounds it. Conflicts arising from this attempt to sort out uncertainty have created a take-it-or-leave-it attitude by both the leadership and the parishioners. The mass retirement of the builder and boomer generations has also been a destabilizing factor within church life. Sunday mornings and programs have become as unpredictable as the rest. The massive amount of information and communication means that there is a growing complexity to understanding issues and events as they unfold. The Church has been behind in participating in the conversation. As individuals, we are energized by change and the excitement of discovery, and at the same time we long for some stability. This longing for stability means that Sunday morning has become a more segregated day when people huddle in like-minded silos, safe from the uncertain world around them. No mainline denomination has been untouched by the results of congregations living in these uncertain times.

Complexity, the third Johansen concern, is the rule of the day. The closer we look, the more complex everything gets! What was true as quantum physics wrestled with the Newtonian world is present in every part of our culture. Not even the church escapes the widening consensus that we are a complex organic community. This is most obvious in the results of the 1990's Decade of Evangelism. Most everyone will say that this missionary effort was a failure for the Episcopal Church. For those who found the Episcopal Church during the late nineties, I doubt they would say that is true. What is a fact is that we now know that voting on a resolution calling for evangelism and tinkering with church structures will not lead to growth. As we entered the new millennium, we had more questions about what makes a congregation tick and evangelism work than we did in the decade before. More and more competing ideas offered salvation to the church's downward spiraling numbers. Everyone was sure it was one thing or the other. If you, as a congregation, would just get your theology, orthodoxy, liberalism, liturgy, preaching, teaching, hymnody, vestments, or coffee correct, then your church would be a success. Today, after two decades of trying the quick fix program, the church is waking up to admit that each congregation, each diocese, and the wider church is more complex and organic in its life than ever imagined. We have more questions today than we do answers. Today, ministry is a complex art of finding a path through the maze of competing priorities. The complex nature of the world around us, our families, and our communities, results in our path looking more like a sailboat tacking across an open sea than the directions from an accurate GPS device. The world is only getting more complex as connectivity and information sharing increase.

The first three elements of the VUCA world lead to the last one: ambiguity. When I was in college, I used to say, "Ambiguity is the key to surprise." Little did I know this would become the mantra of the world in which we live. What is real anymore? Is a parishioner there to support you or get you kicked out? Your numbers are down but the community is exploring the Bible more deeply than ever before. You are reaching out and engaging your community and meeting needs unaddressed for years—but not everyone cares. Clergy care a lot and they want to be relevant. The people in the pews want to do good work and find meaning in the midst of life. But there is a lot of confusion out there about what is valuable and what is not. There are a lot of mixed signals and confusing messages being sent by the preacher from the pulpit and by the church in general to the world. Competing truths and competing for members have become the themes of a new millennium Christianity. Christianity today is literally consuming itself. Individuals throughout the world are trying to make a pilgrimage of meaning and find a bit of truth, instead they find in the Church a bickering community of self-interested and inwardly focused individuals. We have, as a Christian faith, attempted to offer our version of a competing truth in the hopes of finding followers instead of helping people live into a new world order. Confusion is the order of the day, and I don't believe the church at large has been much of a companion along the way.

Johansen's VUCA world is here to stay. The church that I hand over to my successor bishop will continue to offer the challenges of volatility, uncertainty, complexity, and ambiguity. How we understand our work, the plans we make, the policies we engage, and the budget decisions that are made must all take into account these themes. Somehow, we as a church organization must wrestle with the nature of a world that is no longer predictable with a known geography.

The VUCA kind of world situation is not new for the followers of Jesus. One of our sacred stories offers us a vision of the way we are to look at the world and how we are to engage with it. In the Gospel of

Luke we read about a couple of disciples who were confused by the events that had taken place in Jerusalem. Their leader had shared a final dinner with them and talked to them about leaving. Shortly thereafter, he had been arrested and then crucified by the authorities. Some of his followers, mostly women, had gone to the tomb where he was buried and discovered that the body was missing. Despite mixed messages about going to meet Jesus in Galilee and fear about their own potential death, some disciples headed home. As they were walking close to a town called Emmaus, Jesus came and met them on the road. They didn't know it was Jesus, but they accepted the stranger and walked along the road with him. He invited them to share with him their experiences and they did. He listened and they talked. They were very sad. Things had not turned out the way they thought. I imagine Jesus was a good listener.

They told the disguised Jesus that Jesus (their leader) was a great prophet. The Jesus they knew was mighty in power and preaching. He was recognized as a man of healing and freedom. They told the "stranger" that they were disappointed. They could not believe that this "stranger" did not know anything about the things that have occupied all of Jerusalem for these past weeks.

Jesus then told them that they were foolish. He said they were lacking heart. The prophets had spoken about these things. The disguised Jesus then told them the way the whole of Scripture attests that all will be well; that the chaos of the last days was part of the story; that the resurrection and re-creation of the world were now underway, even in the midst of great confusion. It was then the disciples' turned to listen. They listened to a story that was complex and stretched to the beginnings of creation itself. They walked, and as they walked together the time went by quickly. Soon it was time to stop and have a meal. They invited this remarkable man to stay with them.

As they broke bread and shared wine, the disciples recognized the risen Lord. Their eyes were opened and they saw Jesus before them. As quickly as Jesus had come beside them on the road, he was gone from them. It was in this moment that they saw the world differently. They understood how the ancient stories had come alive and how their current situation, while still chaotic, made a bit of sense. They must have been clearer about their vision of things and the world that surrounded them. Perhaps they understood what they were to do next and how they were to make their way in the world. First things first, they began their new lives by telling others and helping them to understand what new creation was being brought into being in the world around them. (Luke 24) The story that continued was not so much a story of how order was brought to a chaotic world—but rather how Christ was present with his disciples in the midst of a chaotic world. To this day we remind ourselves that Jesus has promised all those who follow him that he will be with them to the end of the age. It is no less true today in the midst of this seemingly new VUCA world.

We are living in a time when two worlds are colliding: the world of Newtonian physics and the world of quantum physics. The tug and pull between these two worlds is what makes it so difficult to lead a church today. While we have glimpses of the future church we are stuck in the present with the church of the past. We have struggled against the reality of a church organization that is based upon the finest science of the eighteenth century.[26]

Most individuals make a living within a corporation that works on principles found in Newtonian law.[27] If you have ever had your organization described as a set of interlocking cogs, then you know exactly what I am talking about. Newtonian physics describes how the macro universe works. It describes how big bodies and machinery, planets and stars, missiles and spaceships work.[28] When I was nine years old, I checked out a book from the library on scientists. Today I realize the book was about Newtonian physicists; Isaac Newton, Johannes Kepler, and Galileo are the names of the Newtonian physicists with whom I grew up. These laws work well as long as what is being examined is large. When the details in need of examination get small, then quantum physics is necessary. Things that are complex and move fast require a different set of rules to measure and understand the way they work. Most of our organizations are not able to deal with the complexity of the minute forces that are bombarding and creating fields of influences and causing unexpected results. Instead, organizations operate in the Newtonian world. The church is no different.

The church analyzes its life and ministry by breaking it into large manageable ministry areas. We believe that, if we control this area or make a seemingly major change in another area, we will have a positive impact on the organization. We plan ministry and objectives with the idea that the world will respond in the anticipated manner. We believe that if the church can simply figure out the correct tools by which to measure reality we can adjust and make everything right.[29]

A great example of this is the governance structure of The Episcopal Church. Some of the same individuals who influenced the framers of the then embryonic Episcopal Church influenced the framers of the Constitution. Jim Dator is a futurist and political scientist at the University of Hawaii. He explains, "Government and law were designed to run like a giant machine, leading to predictable, rational, and beneficial outcomes. People, as well, were expected to act by a rational calculus—that is, to determine 'what are the rewards and punishments of actions?"[30] The designers of our Episcopal Church applied their understanding of Newtonian mechanics to institutional life, as did those in the federal government, industry, and society in general. I can imagine that the way in which the hope of individuals operating in synchronicity like a well-oiled machine was an exciting prospect—and it worked for over 200 years.[31]

So what happened? VUCA. The global explosion of communications and interrelated economies would bring chaos and with it a volatility, uncertainty, complexity, and ambiguity. As Thomas Friedman would teach us all in a brief history of the twentieth century, the world is flat and we are all connected.[32] Dator described the effect this had on organizations in this way: "What happened in the twentieth century is that a new cosmology called quantum physics—and the new technologies of the electronic information and communications revolution—became out of sync with many social institutions and practices, specifically with government systems, which are still locked into technologies of 200 years ago."[33]

We are aware of these shifts and the inefficiencies of our church organization to navigate the chaotic world. For nearly two decades the reality of our predicament has made its way into our conversations as a church. Though we have not known quite what to do with the information, we are aware that things are not well.

We are aware that the number of churches and people in them has not kept up with population growth. The population has grown, and the number of people who attend church and the number of churches where they may find a home has not grown. In fact, the number of individuals who do not go to church has more than doubled in two decades. The expected notion that young adults will return to church after college has also become the unexpected reality that they do not. New methods have been designed to measure these effects by the Barna Group. According to this research firm which focuses on the intersection of faith and culture, the number of people who are completely unattached—having not attended church in the past year—equals to one in four Americans.[34] One-third of that number is individuals with no faith background.[35] The Barna Group now classifies another trend they call "intermittents."[36] One out of every seven adults has attended some kind of faith community once in the last year, and two thirds of those attended within the last six months.[37] Almost all clergy persons within an urban or suburban context will echo the findings of this report as they consider and think about their congregation's community.

We also know that things in our culture are affecting the ability for small congregations to remain economically viable. There have been real economic pressures simply based on the cost of doing business; these are multiplied if we consider shrinking attendance. The economic change has affected most of the congregations.

Consider for a moment that the average congregation in The Episcopal Church hosts fewer than sixty on any given Sunday with a budget of around $80,000—$100,000. The cost of electricity, water, and sewage alone has increased over the last three decades. The cost of gas and insurance for the priest's car has increased. The cost of telephone or mobile phone connectivity has increased. A truly fortunate congregation of fewer than sixty on a Sunday can afford a full time person; however, that is rare indeed. In the end, the average congregation has to have a new member, who gives more than the average pledge as soon as he or she walks in the door, added to their communicant list every year in order to keep up with inflation alone. Moreover, they can never lose a parishioner. It is an untenable economic reality that will continue to lead to the closure of small congregations.

Church work is difficult in small communities and it is difficult in urban areas. There is a mass retirement of clergy and in some places there is a shortage. The quality of preaching and teaching is an issue; finding the best people to lead communities is a challenge for diocesan leadership. Geographically what is happening is that clergy move to where the jobs are—meaning one area may have too many clergy and another area not enough. The growth of alternative seminaries training bi-vocational or worker-priests is an illustration of how the church is seeking to meet the pastoral needs in an economically trying era. A "tentmaker" ministry is currently helping to keep many congregations open.[38]

Churches have a cross section of generations, all of whom have different ideas about the church. Each generation is continuing to grow and to have new ideas. Each generation is responding in its own unique way to the cultural changes affecting the church. Personal stories and life events affect the ways each generation interprets both the cultural force and the church's response. Some of the loudest voices echo a refrain that the church is dying. Others are not sure but skeptically maintain a hopeless vision of the future. It is a false prophetic voice that echoes throughout every church, mainline and nondenominational, and the voice sounds like this: "If we don't (fill in the blank), then our church will die." You can fill in the blank with the following: return to traditional values, commit to progressive ideals, use guitars, get rid of the hymnal, use more vestments, use no vestments, etc. The problem is that each suggestion echoes the Newtonian mechanized view of church ministry: if we replace the broken cog, we can get the machine started again. Such ideas lack a vision that considers that cultural volatility and trends affect everything, including our mission and God's mission. The idea of the broken cog denies the impact actions will have on the uncertain and unpredictable responses of a discriminating community. Such an assumption ignores the complexity of the world and the interrelation of all things from liturgy to community life, to neighborhood, to connections, to message, and back again. And lastly, the idea of the broken cog does not consider the ambiguous and fickle nature of a quick-moving, trend-based culture.

The Church reminds me of Concorde in *Monty Python and the Holy Grail*. Concorde is Sir Lancelot's squire and is shot with an arrow and Lancelot is sure that his squire is dying, so he leaves him.

The scene goes like this:

CONCORDE: *"Uh, I'm-I'm not quite dead, sir."*
LANCELOT: *"Well, you shall not have been mortally wounded in vain!"*
CONCORDE: *"Uh, I-I think uh, I could pull through, sir."*
LANCELOT: *"Oh, I see."*
CONCORDE: *"Actually, I think I'm all right to come with you—"*
LANCELOT: *"No, no, sweet Concorde! Stay here! I will send help as soon as I have accomplished a daring and heroic rescue..."*[39]

The Church is a resilient organization. It is something that, for the believer, lives because God has a mission and God's mission has a church.[40] Our theology teaches us that the church is the earthly vessel of the Holy Spirit. God is continually making and remaking the church as the Church navigates history. The church, however, is made up of human beings, and we must ask ourselves if we are willing to be made well and figure out what God is doing. Sometimes it can be difficult to understand what God is doing because we are so tied to our tradition and understanding of the past.

In the Gospel of John, chapter 5, the author describes a festival and, along with crowds of people, Jesus and his disciples are drawn to Jerusalem. There is in Jerusalem a gate and by the gate, a pool. Along the edge of the pool are these little porticoes. In these alcoves are people. They are blind, lame, and paralyzed. The pool is a bubbling pool believed to have healing properties. So each time the water is stirred up, the ill and infirm make their way into the water in order to enjoy its healing properties. As Jesus is passing by, he encounters a man who has been there for 38 years! —38 years of trying to make it to the pool and hoping for healing, 38 years of infirmity, 38 years of paralysis. That is a long time for the body not to be working, to seek some healing balm in the water, and find nothing. Jesus sees this man and he goes to him and asks, "Do you want to be made well?"

The man then gives a long list of reasons why this is not possible. "I don't have people to help me get to the pool. People knock me down just when I am about to make it. There are always people ahead of me with better skills." Jesus says, "Stand up, take your mat and walk." Of course, the religious leaders of the day say, "WHAT?! You can't heal on the Sabbath! We have rules!" It's too late, the man is healed, he takes up his mat and he walks. This is one of the important stories in John's Gospel because it illustrates how the case against Jesus was made that he just wasn't religious enough; he just didn't quite get how things were done.

I always wonder if the man really wanted to be healed. He was so stuck. He was so sure he would be sick forever. For 38 years he had believed all the cards were stacked against him. He had no way of improving and lots of reasons why it wasn't worth trying. The religious authorities wanted to control the healing powers and wanted to make sure that it was clear you couldn't simply go around doing whatever you want; there is a form and a way and a means by which God works. Jesus proved both the man and the authorities wrong.

God is alive and his Holy Spirit is moving and making all things new. The church is not to die, nor is it to be ill forever. Even now the Holy Spirit is moving the waters, Jesus is coming near, and the opportunity for health is before us. The question is a good one. On this day in this hour, cost what it will, do you want to be healed? I hope the answer for the church and the religious leaders of our generation is "Yes." (John 5:1-18)

CHAPTER THREE
A Courageous Church

"Courage is found in unlikely places."
— *J.R.R. Tolkien, author*

What are we doing with this information about our Church? We
have attached our self-worth to the success of the church. If we were
growing and influential, we would be worthy. If people loved the
church, we would be worthy. If our church were exciting, we would
be worthy. If our church grew in number and its disciples grew in
spiritual depth, we would be worthy. For the leaders such success
would make them worthy. For the people who go to the "right"
church, attending the one with the "right" stuff makes the
parishioners worthy. If other people love our church, then we are
worthy.[41]

I think that members of the Episcopal Church, and members of
most mainline denominations, do not feel worthy because their
church is shrinking in numbers; takes stands that embarrass them
(both conservative and liberal); changes its liturgy; and the list can go
on and on. At the end of the day many of our members feel shame
because their self-worth is tied up in these things—these ideas about
church.

When our self-worth is tied to our church, to public opinion, and
people do not respond positively to it, we are as human beings less

inclined to offer it to others.[42] We are crushed when people make fun of our church; tease us about our church; speak hatefully about our church; and do not honor the Church like we do. So, we shut down. Like the man at the bubbling waters in the Jesus story in John 5, we give up even trying. As researcher, social worker, and professor Brené Brown says, "You shut down. Shame tells you that you shouldn't have even tried. Shame tells you that you're not good enough and you should have known better ... You're officially a prisoner of 'pleasing, performing, and perfecting.'"[43] The honest truth is that our church culture participates in this imprisonment and we are gifted in the art of sharing shame. We train people that God only wants perfection and only loves perfection. We tell people they are not good enough and no offering will ever be pleasing to God. This theology has turned to destroy us as we have used shame to manipulate the culture wars and our churches' participation in them. We have shamed those who are not like us and who don't follow the religious traditions we hold dear—others shame us for following the religious traditions they do not hold dear. We react to the VUCA world by feeling shame because we are no longer the strong and powerful Episcopal Church of the past.

But this is not the Gospel story. God chooses us in our imperfection. God reaches out and loves before we repent. God offers grace and mercy to the sinner. The whole of the Gospel story is about Christ Jesus who comes into the world to draw the world closer to a living, loving God, whose message is not for the ones who have it right, but rather for the ones who do not get it at all. Jesus comes to share food with the hungry. He offers love for the unlovable. He befriends the friendless. He spends time and eats dinner with the outcasts. He heals the broken and lame. He spends almost all of his time with those who have received more than their share of shame, and he offers them love and courage and hope. In the end Jesus risks his life for the sake of the unlovable and dies at the hands of the righteous.

The church must reinvest itself in a new era of community making. The future Church will be focused on community making that is filled with individuals who understand that their worth is greater than earthly things. We would even say their worth is their very being because they have been given life and breath from God. We are God's; we are all God's. This knowledge gives us strength and courage in the face of shame. It is still difficult when people do not like us or the things we are involved in—but our self-worth must not be tied to the things of this world.[44] This new community and the people who inhabit it will dwell in the assurance that self-worth is tied to God and God's love and mercy.

In order to navigate the world and deal with our own shame, we must begin by recognizing that it is actually the shame that is killing us! Shame undermines all innovation. When leaders hold back and do not risk a new idea because we have never done it that way before, we are practicing shame control. When we are not honest with one another and do not help others improve with honest and loving feedback, shame is at work. When we do not want to hurt a parishioner or priest's feelings with honesty or a creative idea, shame is the dictator. The fear of believing we do not know enough to be called to be a minister for Christ is shame. The inability to participate in making our communities healthy by our own participation is shame controlling the direction of our labors. One of our Eucharistic prayers says that Christ's work makes us worthy to stand before God; not feeling worthy to stand before God is shame at work. Not speaking to others about the faith that is in us for fear of what people might think is shame silencing us.[45] So much of what passes for Christian community today participates in a shame culture. This culture of fear keeps us from embracing the new missionary era as opportunity and believes that our church is dead. Peter Sheahan, CEO of ChangeLabs, says, "Shame becomes fear, fear leads to risk aversion. Risk aversion kills innovation."[46] A lack of innovation in the wake of a new world is like spending 38 years at the edge of a pool, hoping someone will help you in, hoping people will get out of your way, waiting for a miracle. (John 5)

Jesus Christ risks all the way to the cross; he offers himself to others; he continues on no matter what the stumbling blocks are ahead of him. In Christ we see ourselves differently. We see ourselves as people who are worthy and inspired to be vulnerable. In Christ we are willing to be creative and innovative. We will try and try again. This is the way of Jesus.[47] Brené Brown writes, "Shame keeps us small, resentful, and afraid. In shame-prone cultures, where parents, leaders and administrators consciously or unconsciously encourage people to connect their self-worth to what they produce, I see disengagement, blame, gossip, stagnation, favoritism, and a total dearth of creativity and innovation."[48] YIKES! I want to be part of a community that is open and offers itself to the world and to all kinds of people from all backgrounds. I want to be part of a church that takes risks for the good news of freedom that is found in Christ. I want to be part of a community that sees stumbling blocks as challenges to be overcome and presses on. I want personally to risk more to be more connected to other people; and as my grandmother used to say, "Resolve well, and persevere." This is a great vision for the church and for the people in it. I believe to risk is the vision of God and the vision of Christ Jesus. I believe it was the vision that Christ had being crucified, in the hope that among the many things that might be laid to rest on the cross, shame would be chief among them. Let us lay our burden down and bravely face the future.

Recently, the term *diaspora* has been used to describe communities that exist in the culture of the new millennium. A diaspora is a like an island. I recently introduced my twelve-year-old daughter to one of my favorite television shows: *Gilligan's Island*.[49] In every show just about the time the castaways are going to get off the island, Gilligan messes things up, at which point my daughter howls with peals of laughter. She has memorized the song and is now introducing her friends who spend the night to this lovable, funny show. As a proud parent, I feel as though my work is done. Sometimes the Church is like Gilligan on Gilligan's island.

The Christian Church is a large global web of communities. Regardless of what part we look at, what we see are islands in the sea of a culture that is quickly forgetting them. From the large denominations to the small nondenominational churches, we recognize that the world inside the church doors is vastly different from the world outside. A peer in ministry once described his work as continuing the ancient traditions like the ancient Israelites who found themselves in captivity in Babylon. For the ancient people carried off to a foreign land, the world outside is strange and irrelevant to the things that matter inside the church. To the people outside, the world inside these islands of faith seems odd and somehow disconnected from Christian life. My fellow minister is correct; Christian communities exist today as diasporas. *Diaspora* is a term describing the Babylonian captivity of the Jewish people and today it describes the many Jewish communities who exist as islands outside of the Holy Land.

You might remember what I said earlier about how the observer influences the thing studied and the nature of Schrödinger's Cat. This is true when it comes to these islands of Church life and the castaways who dwell inside. The Church is a diaspora community. It is a community which shares values and worldviews. Inside the diaspora things are clear. It is clear who you are, what you stand for, and who you are not.[50] The Christian Community large and small has primarily an inward focus. Our communities are so unlike the rest of the world that it is difficult for people to look in and understand what we are doing and why. Things just do not make sense when you look out and things do not make sense when you look in.[51] Your world view determines how the community lives and moves and has its being within the larger society.

I believe that right now, in large part because of the shame factor, the Christian Church has become an unhealthy diaspora. We categorize people in such a way as to shame those not like ourselves.

We put people into definable groups and navigate our relationships by who has it right and who has it wrong—despite the reality that no person's identity is never-changing and "static."[52] When groups do become static and isolated like an island and never changing, the diaspora begins to die.

We can see this in the story of the Shaker community. The Shaker community was a particular Protestant faith tradition that believed in Christ's imminent return and followed a prophet named Ann Lee. They are best known for their cultural contributions, communities, and furniture. Although there were six thousand believers at the peak of the Shaker movement, there were only twelve Shaker communities left by 1920.[53] In 2012 there were only three. The Shaker community was a diaspora. As went the Shakers, so goes all of Christianity, if our faith tradition remains an unhealthy community turned in on itself.

On the one hand, a diaspora can be a place where people who have similar beliefs congregate. A healthy diaspora knows who they are and why they exist. They have clarity about their purpose and what holds them together—just like the Shakers. The difference between a community that is a healthy diaspora and one that is not is simple: healthy diasporas are interested in communicating and intersecting with groups and communities outside of themselves. Healthy diasporas invite participation and the crossover of ideas. The sharing of life between those who are part of the diaspora and those who are not is essential in making the community stronger. On the other hand, an unhealthy diaspora will try to control everything and everyone. It won't be enough to share the common vision and core values and work on common goals; it will seek to control how those are achieved and the minutest detail of how the community works. An unhealthy diaspora cuts itself off from the rest of the world and then creates policy for every level of the community and eventually strangles innovation and creativity.

The Episcopal Church is a diaspora–an island far from home. It is a group that exists within a broader culture. For The Episcopal Church to remain healthy, it must strengthen its center—clarifying its vision and core values while at the same time encouraging engagement with the culture around it. This is the opposite of what our Newtonian business model suggests is normative behavior.

The Newtonian world imagined the cosmos as a perfectly created machine, an island in space, wound up and set in motion by God. It is a world where the Great clockmaker wound it up and walked away. It is a world that cannot be trusted and is filled with chaos when not ordered. We have interpreted our sacred scripture and created our organizations in light of this clockmaker's design. We believe that we are responsible, like little clockmakers, to keep the world moving, pressing forward and pushing the great cogs of industry. It is our work to create new machines.[54] We believe that if we can build the right machine from items on the island we will be able to leave it safely and return to our place of power and authority.

The future Church must claim its diaspora quality, but also be willing to be a risk-taker and innovator. The future Church sees the world differently. A healthy diaspora can have a place in the world that makes a positive impact on the culture around it, especially if we engage instead of hide; if we use different methods instead of trying to fix the old machines. Hope comes when we take a look at the chaos and see before us not barriers but opportunities. The world around us is a new world, ripe for experimentation and engagement. It is our world. It is our time. It is the world in which we are called to be missionaries. We want to open ourselves up to the themes, events, and technologies already emerging in the world around us. We want to build our capacity to see these as opportunities for creativity and innovation.

If we are going to talk about the future church we need to talk about the notion of time. Augustine of Hippo, a great church theologian of the fourth century, wrote in his book, *The Confessions,* that when it comes to the construct of time there is no past and there is no real future. There is only the present. In the present is the memory of the past, so that is what he calls a "present past." In the present is also the idea of the future, so that is the present future.[55] In some way then we might say that the present/ past Church coexists with the present/future Church. Embracing our world as a diaspora community means walking with clarity out into the brilliant sunlight of the present future. Bob Johansen and the folks at the Institute for the Future (IFTF) believe that we can see artifacts of the future in our society today.[56] We can see artifacts of our present future Church too. What we do with this information will determine our future.

In 2008, Bob Johansen, then president of the IFTF, sat down with leaders of endowed parishes to discuss what the future Episcopal Church might look like. Johansen challenged the group to see the bits and pieces of artifacts from the surrounding culture as "provocative" moments. He questioned, "Can we sift through the flotsam and jetsam of the future that even now is washing up upon our shores as we make our way through the perilous waves undaunted?"[57] Today, we are five years into those pregnant ideas having only begun to take our first steps. It seems prudent to look at the material once again and begin to see the re-imagined church emerge before us.

If we are going to speak about church communities, we need to look at what is happening in the context around us. If we are going to speak about whom we raise up as missionaries, we must look at how people are trained today. If we are to speak about stewardship, we need to look at how people use, spend, and network money. If we are going to talk about service and outreach, then we will look at how people are doing this today. In each scenario we are able to perceive the gap between where we are today and where the future lies. When we see the gap we are able then to move into it and begin to create the future church.

CHAPTER FOUR
Church Next

*"If you understand human nature's glacier-like character, and
at the same time realize the world's 'ever changing moods,'
then you won't go very far wrong as a prophet."*
— The Rev. Dr. Paul Zahl, theologian

Beginning in the late 1990s, I was asked to offer a bit of prognostication for those interested in ordination. So I began to offer a vision for the church that was yet before us. I believed then and I believe now that the future of The Episcopal Church will be driven by the Holy Spirit and co-created, co-made, by God's people. It will clearly need to be a church that builds digital and real commons with a goal of collaboration at every level. It will have to seek unity above all else, even above uniformity. The future Church will need to invest in a life that embraces randomness and creativity, allowing for locally led ministry in a variety of ever-diverse contexts. It will have to become comfortable with interchangeable parts and reusing old traditions in new ways. The organization will change.

The Episcopal Church of the future with its many and varied congregations, schools and institutions will have to change its manner of using authority; and it will have to engage all of God's people in ministry which calls for increased and expected participation at every level as the norm. It will be one that has clear values and is vision-oriented and vision-driven. It will be a diaspora but it will not become an island of castaways. To be a healthy diaspora the Episcopal Church will have to measure success in a new way, not using a 50-year-old model. The leadership of this future organization will have to be organic and contextual. It cannot afford to manage itself in the ways it has over the last hundred years and expect different results. As a church, we will need to embrace a new way of organizational thinking that is risk-taking.

The Church organization today is like a locked operating system. In order to unlock ministry, permission must be given to rip open the box; re-purpose anything necessary for mission; and to hell with the warranty. In the future, successful organizations will be those who allow members to open, rearrange, and play with the product. The contents must be easily accessible and the organization must be ready for people to use its resources in various ways.[58]

What does the future Church look like? The economy of this organization will need to be built upon sound stewardship principles which maintain that all things are God's things—and the question is how are we going to use God's stuff. Episcopal communities will have to look at new ways of building digital platforms and dispersing funds connecting the giver with the receiver. This will have to begin in the world of technology and on the Internet, but it will need to lead to mission immersion experiences where those who give are able to work with their own hands as well. The church must be about the work of inspiring generosity in giving and in action. It will have to become entrepreneurial and experimental in its funding of new communities and new congregations. It will have to understand that the new church will be formed with technology as a hub of life and not an addition to life. The church's website is more important than its address and its phone number because people will find it first in the cloud and only then geographically.

Leaders of the Episcopal Church will have to rethink how they present who we are and what we do. The age of religious sectarianism is over with a new trend clearly underway towards the individual's search for spiritual depth. Clarity about who we are as Episcopalians and how we talk about and experience God through spiritual practice will continue to be elemental in mission. Worship and worship-type experiences beyond Sunday morning and outside of the church will be essential edges for the church. Churches will need to find new forms in which to place our traditions and to use the depth of our tradition as Episcopalians to speak to a whole new generation of people ready to discover and go deep. It will become more and more important for Episcopalians themselves to do this seeking and to draw others closer to an intimate and loving God. This search for deeper spirituality and offering of spiritual experiences will challenge the church not to become a tourist site. The Episcopal Church will have to use its heritage of spiritual depth and ancient tradition and add it to the service of others. The more one interacts with a God of love, the more one will want to serve others. Therefore, the church will and must remember that these two things are linked both in our tradition and in the desire and hearts of the seekers—love of God and love of neighbor.

We must know our context well. We must understand the artifacts found in the society around us, and we must seek to engage those artifacts and ask how they are vessels for this mission community. We will need to pattern new rhythms of life and ministry around the ebbs, flows, and movements of the world, always reminding ourselves that our inherited traditions have ancient roots that have been reshaped through the centuries according to time, place, and context. Our context will have its own motion and resistance that needs not so much to be controlled but understood.

Contexts have their own boundaries. Contexts have their own relationships and interrelationships. Contexts interact differently with outside forces, and ours resists certainty and invites wonder.[59] In order for us to move into this new era and navigate it, we will need to become comfortable with a measure of chaos and complexity. "What is being sought," writes biologist Steven Rose, "is a biology that is more holistic and integrative, a science that is adult enough to rejoice in complexity."[60] We need to remind ourselves that God is a God of chaos and disorder and is always playing and molding and making. It is true for the church that comes next. It will have to mimic and invite God into co-creative work. Yet, not unlike the faithful people of Israel who believed in the Creator God, we may find God's hand is already creating in the world around us.

We must be willing to allow ourselves to become accustomed to volatility, uncertainty, complexity, and ambiguity. As Nassim Nicholas Taleb writes in his book *Antifragile: Things That Gain From Disorder*, we must allow our "fear to be transformed into prudence, our pain into information, our mistakes into initiation, and our desire into undertaking."[61] We must also realize that we are going to have emotions of anger about these changes and that we need to capture and harness that energy into action and invest in good works. As the author of Hebrews writes: "Do not neglect to do good and share what you have for such sacrifices are pleasing to God." (Hebrews 13.16)

It is not too late for The Episcopal Church to transform itself into the kind of vessel needed to navigate the waters of the new world of tomorrow. We are a church of tradition and innovation. We are a church of resources spread across seventeen countries. We are a church made up of every kind of human being; with every kind of gift; and with multiple resources. We are a church that has never been afraid of facing difficult tasks or asking hard questions.

The answer is that it is not too late. God has a mission and God's mission has The Episcopal Church helping to undertake God's reconciling work on earth. Our vision is clear and it is up to us to breach the gap between the vision God has of God's reign and the reality we experience. It is our work to think intentionally about the shape of the once imagined and future church that even now lies before   us.

Bob Johansen reminds future leaders that it is up to us to make the future.[62] Leadership, organizational vision alignment, and governance all must shift from being a locked system to an open and usable organism. On the one hand, we must be permission-giving; on the other hand, we must take initiative. The Church exists to invite people to interact with the God who has repeatedly sought to enjoy the diversity of God's creation. The Good News of Salvation, the love of God, and the unique witness of Christ are to be possessed by all God's people and not held captive by the Church.

We set our face firmly toward the vision of being a church fully engaged in God's mission. We cannot measure success based on accomplishments or numbers. Our success will be measured in the course of time as people look back on our generation as a people who picked up the banner of God in Christ Jesus and the Episcopal Church and carried it forward. We will be measured by the transformation that occurred on our pilgrim journey, even as by the witness of those changed by encountering us along the way.

Headway is marked, not with hopelessness about marginalization in an ever-secular culture, but with a spirit of joy and excitement about mission work. We will move forward not with a fear of failure, but with creativity, experimentation, and a willingness to learn from failure; not with suspicion, but with Christian fellowship shared in the common cause of Christ. Despite today's variety of congregations and dioceses and the diversity of cultural contexts and languages, we will focus on personal discipleship as Christians who are unabashedly Episcopalian and on serving Christ through evangelism and service of others.

We stand at the precipice of a new age of mission, our own Lemhi Pass. God has called us. We are the ones chosen to remake and rethink strategies for the undertaking of God's ministry. Together we take steps into the wilderness as the people of The Episcopal Church, whom Christ calls friends.

CHAPTER FIVE
Our "Believies"

*"Episcopal identity is a communal expression of living out the
Way of Jesus in the power of the Spirit. The Episcopal embodiment
of the Christian faith has Jesus Christ at its center, for in Jesus we see
God's vision for human flourishing. In Jesus we know the depth of the
Creator's love for a broken creation and we receive our calling to
participate in the restoration of the world. This is God's ongoing work in
which we share through the gifts and energy of the Holy Spirit, not
a project God delegates to us to accomplish on our own."*
— *Reimagining the Episcopal Church Identity Statement*

Faith is the quality of difference between an acculturated Church and a missionary Church.[63] Louis C. K. is an earthy comedian who stars in his own television show, *Louie*. It is for mature audiences only. In a stand-up routine he said the following about belief: "I have a lot of beliefs ... And I live by none of them. That's just the way I am. They're just my beliefs. I just like believing them—I like that part. They're my little believies. They make me feel good about who I am. But if they get in the way of a thing I want, I [sure as heckfire] do that." Let me say that I think we are in a time where you and I have come to know that we (and our people) have received some "little believies." Not unlike Louis C. K., I have my believies. It is perhaps part of the human condition to so relativize faith that it becomes only a few believies which we keep in our hip pocket.

As leaders and parishioners look out at the world, we could easily feel like one of Noah's animals cooped up in a smelly box adrift in a sea of competing truths. We look at our congregations, and we see that our churches are awash in individualistic, congregational, and local contextual theology, which can disconnect us from our language of believing, our culture of believing, and our ability to build and sustain transformational communities.

There has been a lot of discussion about the time we now occupy. Prophets abound and they call for a change and for transformation. A key piece of their understanding that leads to their prophecy is the historical axial age, and it looms large in their prediction. The axial age was a time between 800 and 200 BCE. It was a time when influences made their way across the globe via trade routes. Thinkers and cultural ideals had a profound influence on future philosophies and religions, identifiable characteristics common to each area, emerged as a global movement.[64] Perhaps you have heard this new axial age mentioned and words like "emerging" and "emergent" used to describe this time.

I do believe we are in a new axial age—an age wherein there swim competing arguments for truth and for the way society and church should be constructed. It is also my opinion that in some real way we as Christians, and in particular Episcopalians, have abandoned the field of philosophical discussion, of apologetics, of bearing witness to the faith that is in us. We are leaving behind our own inherited theological views in favor of picking up other views from various and sundry traditions which we find interesting. We are more likely to enter discussions on Sunday morning and during the week that engage the culture through different media, never bringing to bear our own Anglican and Episcopal tradition. When this happens, we simply become acculturated instead of seeking to find and explain the Gospel in the cultural media we engage. We are listening more to the culture narrative and leaving behind the narrative of the Episcopal Church.

I think this comes out of the goodness of our own hearts to try, in the midst of a great pluralism of discourse, to be relevant. However, it is exactly by doing this that we leave behind the tradition(s) (the language and culture of our inherited faith) that may best help us navigate the world in which we live and the conversation which we are having. It also abandons who we are as a corporate body, a larger organization. In some ways, we begin to whittle away the identity of the Episcopal Church, and we become something different. But the challenge (or paradox since you quote Merton) of the new missionary age is to engage faithfully in an ever-changing world and remain rooted in a never-changing God. As Thomas Merton explains, "The biggest paradox about the Church is that she is at the same time essentially traditional and essentially revolutionary. But that is not as much of a paradox as it seems, because Christian tradition, unlike all others, is a living and perpetual revolution." In other words, the only way the Episcopal Church can step confidently into the future is to get clear on what we cannot shed from our past.[65] These conversations are both an inner (with our heart and mind) and outer dialogue in conversation with community members and in our workplaces. Our confusion has become as much an individual confusion as a corporate one—especially for the Episcopal Church.

In an age where everyone can become an expert on just about anything, we have, in point of fact, become experts about very little. We find in our corporate life little time to translate the faith of Christianity as received by the Episcopal Church. We have for decades shied away from preparing people "to glorify God in this life and the life to come."[66] Our work as leaders is to pass on the faith inherited from the saints.

Robert N. Bellah, formerly Professor Emeritus of Sociology and Comparative Studies at the University of California, Berkeley, had one view of what has happened.[67] Bellah described the tension well between Christianity (Pauline specifically) and pluralism.

Recognizing the challenge of proclaiming the gospel in our Western culture, he writes:

> *We are getting our wires crossed if we think we can jettison defining beliefs, loyalties, and commitments because they are problematic in another context. Reform and re-appropriation are always on the agenda, but to believe that there is some neutral*

ground from which we can rearrange the defining symbols and commitments of a living community is simply a mistake—a common mistake of modern liberalism. Thus I do not see how Christians can fail to confess, with all the qualifications I have stated, but sincerely and wholeheartedly, that there is salvation in no other name but Jesus.[68]

The Good News of Salvation, and the uniqueness of God in Christ Jesus, is a Christian belief in which we have (especially as an Episcopal Church) a text, language, liturgy, and culture. Discipleship in the Episcopal Church is conveying this reality to our covenant, creedal community and to the world around us. We are not just another Christian Church. It is not up to us to decide what our corporate faith is; such things were defined and decided a long time ago. It is our work, as it has been from the time of the first disciples, to convey that faith, delivered to us, in new contexts and with new languages to the ends of the earth. (Matthew 28: 18-20)

A wise statement about our present situation of religious pluralism comes from Herbert Fingarette in his book *The Self in Transformation: Psychoanalysis, Philosophy and the Life of the Spirit*: "It is the special fate of modern man that he has a 'choice' of spiritual visions. The paradox is that although each requires complete commitment for complete validity, we can today generate a context in which we see that no one of them is the sole vision."[69] In reality, I find that many of us today and many of our parishioners do not hold Christianity as the sole vision, let alone the Episcopal translation of that faith as the sole vision. We have other allegiances, other "believies," which we apply to the Christian faith—mutating it for our own purposes. This happens both in the liberal and the traditional church groups who campaign for allegiance. Fingarette does not let us off the hook that easily. He writes: "Thus we must learn to be naïve but un-dogmatic. That is, we must take the vision as it comes and trust ourselves to it, naïvely, as reality."[70] In Mark's Gospel we are told by Jesus "trust" the good news. (Mark 1.14ff)

Christians have a "believing" that is part of their community life. We believe we are called to be missionaries. This is part of our ancient heritage. We are to be people who honor the stranger in our midst. (Exodus 2:22; Psalm 146; 147; 111; 112; 113; Hebrews 13:2-9) We are to be hospitable and kind. We are to remember that we are all strangers in a strange land. (Exodus 22:21) At the same time we are to be faithful, despite the strange land in which we live. We are to have a place where we dwell and have our being, a spiritual home. Robert Bella says it this way, "One may be a sensitive and seasoned traveler, at ease in many places, but one must have a home. Still, we can be intimate with those we visit, and while we may be only travelers and guests in some domains, there are our hosts who are truly at home. Home is always home for someone; but there is no Absolute Home in general."[71] This applies to us who cannot separate our covenant communities from the faith tradition we have received, a tradition that is itself a culture—an Episcopal culture.

"Now faith is the assurance of things hoped for, the conviction of things not seen." The author of the letter to the Hebrews uses these words to describe faith and in particular the faith of the Israelites.[72] (Hebrews 11:1-19) Faith is something our ancestors had which God blessed. Faith understands that God is creator of all things and that God has spoken the whole of creation into being. It is from things not seen that all things flow. Out of nothingness, from a world that cannot be seen, and from the speaking mouth of God the world is made and fashioned—and it is fashioned for a purpose, God's purpose.

The author of Hebrews then recounts the faith of Abel, Enoch, and others.[73] Abel responds to this faith in a God who creates by making an acceptable sacrifice. He gives thanks to God for all that he has been given. Enoch believes in this God and tries to live a life of faith; he offers his life as a reflection of his belief in the creator God. The great story of Noah is about a man who believes in this creator God and who listens and acts based upon his conversation with God. Abraham listens to the creator God and follows him out of the land of the Chaldeans in the land of Ur. He does this faithfully—following

God, knowing not what his destination. Isaac and Jacob listen to the creator God and understand that their faith calls them to be co-creators with this God and build. Sarah is faithful and is blessed with a whole nation of Israel as children and inheritors of her faith in the creator God.

From a pillar of fire in the night to dry land in the midst of the Red Sea, the creator God has provided a vision and people have followed. It was faith that led a people to understand that when the land became theirs it was because of the creator God. It was Rahab's faith in this God that saved her. There are others too, "[for] time would fail me to tell of Gideon, Barak, Samson, Jephthah, of David and Samuel and the prophets—who through faith conquered kingdoms, administered justice, obtained promises, shut the mouths of lions, quenched raging fire, escaped the edge of the sword, won strength out of weakness... They wandered in deserts and mountains, and in caves and holes in the ground. Yet all these, though they were commended for their faith, did not receive what was promised, since God had provided something better so that they would not, apart from us, be made perfect." (Hebrews 11:32ff)

There is, of course, a dark side to these stories as well. It is not difficult to understand how these stories easily become problematic as they can be used to authorize power and abuse. However, this is not the author's intent; he makes his argument clear. The whole history of the people of Israel is a story of people responding in faith in the creator God. They are, in fact, the faith ancestors of the new growing Christian movement.

These ancestors made their faithful response. They were understood to be God's people by faith. No matter how hard or difficult life was or how long or arduous the journey was, they were commended by God. These people are a "great a cloud of witnesses." (Hebrews 12.1) We are encouraged to see our life of faith to be not unlike their own and to "run with perseverance the race that is set before us, looking to Jesus, the pioneer and perfecter of our faith, who for the sake of the joy that was set before him endured the cross, disregarding its shame, and has taken his seat at the right hand of the throne of God." (Hebrews 12:2-3)

The God of our ancestors was not a God who could be touched. God is present in the images of Scripture, to be sure. These images are of a God who appears in blazing fire; darkness; gloom; in the midst of a tempest; in sounds of trumpets; upon the mountaintop; in thunder and lightning; in the parting of the heavens; in a voice that makes those who hear beg not to hear another word! This is a God who shakes the foundations, who tears down and builds up. (Hebrews 12)

We have in our tradition a beautiful theodicy in which God reminds the faithful Job who this creator God is:

Gird up your loins like a man, I will question you, and you shall declare to me. Where were you when I laid the foundation of the earth? Tell me, if you have understanding. Who determined its measurements—surely you know! Or who stretched the line upon it? On what were its bases sunk, or who laid its cornerstone when the morning stars sang together and all the heavenly beings shouted for joy? Or who shut in the sea with doors when it burst out from the womb? —When I made the clouds its garment, and thick darkness its swaddling band, and prescribed bounds for it, and set bars and doors, and said, 'Thus far shall you come, and no farther, and here shall your proud waves be stopped?'" (Job 38ff)

This is the God of the heavens and a God of the earth. (Hebrews 1.1) It is this God's people and this God's kingdom in which we reside. It is this God whom we follow. This is the God who shakes our foundations and offers us life, and life abundantly is a realm that cannot be shaken. It is this God that we worship and to whom we offer our lives and ministry. It is this God who consumes us through God's love. It is this God who sets our hearts on fire because of God's love. This is indeed a terrifying love.

Twentieth century theologian Paul Tillich wrote a powerful book, *The Shaking of the Foundations.*

He writes:

How could the prophets speak as they did? How could they paint these most terrible pictures of doom and destruction without cynicism or despair? It was because, beyond the sphere of destruction, they saw the sphere of salvation. In the doom of the temporal, they saw the manifestation of the Eternal. It was because they were certain that they belonged within the two spheres, the changeable and the unchangeable. For only he who is also beyond the changeable, not bound within it alone, can face the end. All others are compelled to escape, to turn away . . . For in these days the foundations of the earth do shake. May we not turn our eyes away; rather see, through the crumbling of a world, the rock of eternity and the salvation which has no end![74]

What is present in this text is a vision, an artifact of truth, that somehow the world is one of complex potential, always renewing, growing, dying, birthing, and shaking. It is a creation that at the same time holds within itself the future and the eternal. Each of the ancestors of Christianity was faithful. They did not necessarily see or even experience the results of their faith. This is an important fact in the storytelling, which is often forgotten in a culture of instant gratification. Their faith and the faith of their descendants shape our faith today. In their stories we discover that the life of faith—the creative vibrant life of faith—is always lived in response to God and to Jesus. This is our privilege, this is our calling, and this is what we do as Christians and as Episcopalians. In fact, as faithful people, not unlike the gathering cloud of witnesses, it is our hearts' song in response to this God that beckons us forward into mission.

When reflecting on the disciples and their work, contemporary theologian William Loader wrote, "These few verses offer us snippets of what Christian community meant. It wasn't a holy huddle of worshippers scared for their lives and totally obsessed with religious rituals. It was a community which expressed and shared love and in that context praised God—obviously because God is a God who reaches out in love and compassion."[75]

The author of the letter to the Hebrews invites the reader to consider the work which might result as a response to the faith of Israel and faith in Jesus Christ. The underlying idea is that love from Christ and in Christ will lead to certain actions by the individual follower of Jesus and the community that bears his name. A vision will be born from this interplay of love between God and humankind. The author reminds us of the unchanging nature of God. As believers, we are to return continually to God as revealed in creation and in Jesus Christ. It is from this creator God and his Son that visions are given. It is their Love that overflows the world that helps us to dream dreams. God pours out God's Spirit upon all flesh, and sons and daughters prophesy, and young men see visions, and old men shall dream dreams. (Acts 2:1ff) When our lives are opened up to this God, we discover that our following, our listening, our building, our offerings are all a response to grace.

The whole of Scripture testifies to ordinary men and women whose lives are the narrative of God's life with his people. The narrative of scripture reminds us that we are the ordinary men and women of our day. In our work we are writing the lives of the saints as we respond to God's love. The Church is a grace-filled community; our commons is born out of the grace of forgiveness.

What shall our response be to this God who reaches out to us? How shall we make an offering of gratitude to this God? The author of Hebrews writes: "Through him, then, let us continually offer a sacrifice of praise to God, that is, the fruit of lips that confess his name. Do not neglect to do good and to share what you have, for such sacrifices are pleasing to God." (Hebrews 13) Our response to God and our vision are always offered in the midst of a particular context. Our day and its pluralism are no different from the time of the first disciples. There are many competing gods and many competing truths. What I am aware of is that the Gospel we offer is not about one god among a pantheon of Gods. We are offering something specific and particular in our vision of the living God.

We might remember the Athenians and Paul. The Athenians, we are told, received the gospel from Paul. He was having a particularly tough time of it because the Athenians believed in a lot of gods and what was one more to them. In particular, they seemed to be a bit suspicious of just taking this God from this foreign dude and his culture. They might have said something like, "Who does this Paul think he is? He comes in here offering us this foreign god. I told him we already had plenty. No, thank you. Go somewhere else and peddle your god." They saw a world filled with competing gods and competing religions all vying for their attention. If that was what Paul was doing, then, in point of fact, he probably would have failed. If we are just offering some other god among many gods who is a lot like other gods but different, then we will fail.

Paul seems to have understood this, in part because he understood the faith of the ancestors. He understood the faith of the Old Testament. While he likely did not carry around with him a copy of the Hebrew Scriptures, Paul did carry with him a vision of the creator God. Paul knew well the covenant narrative about a God who reaches out to his people. It is the creator God whom he tells the Athenians about. For Paul there was only one God. He believed in the God who created the whole cosmos. He did not present a henotheistic god. Henotheism (Greek εἷς θεός heis theos) is the belief and worship of a single god while accepting the existence or possible existence of other deities.[76] Paul did not offer them just any old god.

Paul converted the Athenians first to a belief in God, the God of the Hebrews. He began by telling them and helping them to come to an understanding that there was only one God. I can imagine him telling them about how God created the world—and about Abraham, the great deeds of the judges, of God's love for Saul and David, and the great faith community that grew because of their relationship with the creator God. This was faith in the midst of pluralism. Moreover, Paul told them that this God was intent on being with his people—all his people, not only the Israelites. God wanted to walk with his people and talk with them. The God that created all things was constantly reaching out to his creatures in love. Paul offered them the narrative of and belief in a monotheistic God.

We believe in One God. The Episcopal Church is not a henotheistic church. We do not believe in one God among many. If we return to Robert Bellah for a moment, we get some help with this essential missionary notion. He writes: "Converting people to Christianity without Paul's background of Hebrew radical monotheism would be converting them to a sort of henotheism, a belief in Jesus as a kind of 'guardian spirit.'"[77] Truth is, I don't need just another guardian spirit. I have come to understand that Christian conversion and discipleship are not simply about one god among many gods. It is not about a simple "believie" that can be used or not, depending on the context. Instead, Christianity is about belief in the creator God. It is rather about belief in connection with a transformed life that then lives in a particular and unique covenant community—with its own culture of belief. We are at work doing something more than making a choice for a nice "believie."

We are, instead, inviting people into a relationship with a particular God in a particular community, with a particular text, language, liturgy, and social system. Christians who are Episcopalians are called to the work of "discipling" others in this unique tradition.[78] This means not being or making general, superficial or sentimental Christians. At the same time we must recognize the kind of followers we have today are direct recipients of the models of formation over the last 50 or more years.

Without this work of inducting our current community members and our new community members into relationship with God, maker of all things, mover of all things, then we are offering a "henotheistic guardian spirit" as opposed to the biblical God. Again, Robert Bellah makes this striking statement that this, "is true not only for so-called new Christians, but for many of us in our own allegedly Christian society who do not understand what Paul would have required us as Christians to understand."[79] As the missionary-theologian Lesslie Newbigin puts it: "A religion of individual salvation had been taught, along with a wholesale rejection and condemnation of traditional culture. The result has been . . . a superficial Christianity with no deep roots and then -later- a reaction to an uncritical and sentimental attachment to everything in the discarded culture."[80] Bellah then adds this explanation: "...Thus it would seem that a nonsuperficial Christianity must be based on something more than an individual decision for Christ, must be based on induction into the Christian cultural-linguistic system. Without such induction the individual decision may be not for the biblical Christ but for a henotheistic guardian spirit. And that is true not only for so-called new Christians, but for many of us in our own allegedly Christian society who do not understand what Paul would have required us as Christians to understand."[81]

For Christians—and in particular, Episcopalians—the church is a radical place to dwell with a particular nomenclature and unique belief system. We even say that the church is the family of God; it is the temple of the Holy Spirit.[82] Even still, in a humble way, we do well to remember that while this is true the church is also faithless and disloyal to its cause. We are called ever to return to faith in the living God. We are called to have a vision for God's mission. We are called as the church to undertake that mission in every age. And when we recognize our failings, we make a course correction. It is, after all, our prayer: "Gracious Father, we pray for thy holy Catholic Church. Fill it with all truth, in all truth with all peace. Where it is corrupt, purify it; where it is in error, direct it; where in anything it is amiss, reform it. Where it is right, strengthen it; where it is in want, provide for it; where it is divided, reunite it; for the sake of Jesus Christ thy Son our Savior. Amen."[83]

Jaroslav Pelikan said, "Tradition is the living faith of the dead, traditionalism is the dead faith of the living. And, I suppose I should add, it is traditionalism that gives tradition such a bad name."[84] We must be about the work of our own formation as well as the formation of others into a living faith. The "discipling" of ourselves is the first work. The second is "discipling" of others in the way of Jesus as we follow him in this church. Discipleship means coming into a relationship wherein we are using the fabric of our culture as Episcopalians to engage the culture around us and not revising it to make us comfortable. I am not challenging you to come up with your own really cool understanding of our church. We have a theology. We have a language. We have sacramental symbols (signs) and worship (liturgy). We have a teaching. And we have a mission to share the Gospel faith we receive that is particular and unique. I am challenging you to be formed in the Way of the Episcopal Church—to be unabashedly Episcopalian. And, in so doing, to befriend others of every age and of every nation as they discover the Church we love.

CHAPTER SIX
Vision of Who We Are

"We should reward people, not ridicule them,
for thinking the impossible."
— *Nicholas Nassim Taleb, Learning to Expect the Unexpected 2004*

The future Episcopal Church will need clarity about the basics of its faith. It knows that in order to thrive in anew mission era clarity and boundaries are essential.[85] This vision is essential in holding the center as our organization adapts its ministries to the world around us. We have a common life centered in thee of God we have acknowledged in Christ Jesus. You and I were drawn to this church...have chosen to stay...and decided to claim it as our own. Today we are the standard bearers. We are a living sign of the mission of God. We are the ones at whose feet the legacy is laid. It is not given to us but it is given to us in trust for the next generation whom God will call forward to undertake the mission of God in their own time.

The work of the Episcopal Church is well articulated in the words of the former Archbishop of Canterbury William Temple, which were adopted by our General Convention in 1973: "[Our work is] the presentation of Jesus Christ, in the power of the Holy Spirit, in such ways that persons may be led to him as Savior, and follow him as

Lord within the fellowship of his Church." I would add the assumption at the end of this quote that, specifically, we are to do so within the fellowship of the Episcopal Church and Anglican Communion. The church that William Temple understood here was not a general church idea but a real institution. We are the bearers of that mission today. We must not shy away from this work. We must be about discipling Christians as Episcopalians. I would argue that we must evangelize ourselves first. We have congregations with assumed beliefs and common interests and delightful (but not very transformative) guiding spirits. We exist as a group of congregations who have different ideas about our sacraments and discipleship methods. For a while now we have been making general Christians and to be honest—sometimes just clubs of like-minded people.

This is not the faith we inherited. Nor the faith we first fell in love with. I want to encourage you and inspire you to fall in love with the Episcopal Church again! We have a beautiful and particularly unique faith. I want Episcopalians to know who they are and whose they are. Reclaiming what we love and living it out will lead us to the end God desires.

We believe that we were created by God as part of God's creation and are made in the image of God. We are free to make choices: to love, create, reason and live within a sustainable creation—and to do so with God. We believe human beings are made uniquely to give voice to the angels in heaven and to praise God and sing of his blessings. We also know that we do not do this. Because we are human, we do not make good choices. This is simply the way we are. We like to put ourselves in the place of God. This is part of the reason why a henotheistic faith is so comforting and supports our lit "believies" Throughout history we have perpetrated the primary work of self-glorification, self-preservation, and self-manifestation, making us the gods of creation. This is the lie we live and we call it sin. It keeps us from recognizing our vocation—who we are created to be and who God has created others to be. So tragic, so pervasive, so broken is this understanding of creation that we—on our own outside of community only see imperfectly the shape of the world intended by God. As Episcopalians, we affirm that our salvation and our deliverance, in fact our lives in the company of God, are dependent upon God's grace, mercy, love, and forgiveness.

We believe that God comes into the world to reconcile the world, to participate, to undo the powers of this world by reorienting, refocusing, and drawing our eyes to the greater work of God. They asked Jesus, "Why did you come into this world?" He answered clearly, "To glorify God." (John 13) This is his answer and he is our teacher in the life of holiness—in the divine economy.

Jesus' death on the cross redeems us from the bonds of self-service so that we may follow him along the way, imitating our teacher and undertaking the glorification of God. By the cross we are given freedom from sin, which is nothing less than freedom from avarice (the insatiable desire of a god-like self-preservation)—the root of all sinful desires and actions. We are reconciled to God and to one another through the power of Jesus Christ. We are able to see again what God values in us and in others.

God has helped us by revealing God's self through nature, history, saints, and the prophets of Israel. We believe in a God who Jesus called Father. We believe this is the God who creates. God looked on creation and said it was very good. It is so not because of its nature but because of God who creates it, sustains it, and directs it. The creation is God's and it belongs to God. All things are God's and exist for God's purpose. This revelation of who God is has been given to us by the witness of our faithful predecessors—and specifically in the living word of the Old Testament. God desires to be with us. God is faithful to us. God reaches out for us. God commits to us a binding relationship expressed through the Scriptures and in particular to the people of God—the Abrahamic descendants (Israel). God, the Father of his people, invites us to be faithful by virtues of love, justice, mercy, and humility. (1 Corinthians 13)

We believe that God has a mission and that mission is the reconciliation of humans to God. We also know that Jesus' work was to gather up the lost sheep. (Jeremiah 50; Luke 15) God's mission of reconciliation makes all men brothers and all women sisters. (2 Corinthians 5) Humanity is God's family. God's reconciliation is about ensuring that the world God created is a world that is sustainable with food for all, shelter for all, and safety for all. (Psalm 104) God intends that we might be his children and live in a garden where all are welcome and all are heirs of the reign of God. (Genesis 2:15; Matthew 18; John 14; 1 Corinthians 2.6) God's reconciliation offers us life and life abundantly. (John 10) God's reconciliation offers us plenteous forgiveness. (Matthew 18:21ff) Forgiveness and reconciliation, so that we may live a life like Jesus and truly glorify God in our speech, in our embraces, and in our actions of love. (Mark 12: Mark 10; Philippians 1)

God has a mission of reconciliation and that mission must be ours in the Episcopal Church. The mission of the Church is to restore all people to unity with God and each other in Christ. We are always to be about the work this creator God has given us. (Romans 14) So we believe that God calls us and God invites us to co-create with him and to build up the kingdom. We are empowered towards our work and given direction by the Holy Spirit. We are empowered by the Holy Spirit through worship, witness, and ministry. We are given the gifts to return to the work of restoring and recreating with God the world.

God not only enters and claims creation as God's own; but also redeems it, providing a mission map for the work of creation, breathing, on all creation the ever present Holy Spirit, God with us, to strengthen us for the work of glorifying and magnifying God. The lens is polished so that we may see more clearly, with the help of the Holy Spirit, our work and the work of community. (1 Corinthians 13.12)

The Holy Spirit, the empowering agent of Godly life, transforms and binds individual sinners into a divine community of virtuous citizens. The Church is the family of God, a community that is working outwardly, on a daily basis, the inner life of the Holy Trinity. This is the economic nature of God. God's life flows outward through us. The mission of true virtue is co-creating with God a worldly and divine community.

A missionary Church knows the basics of its faith. Following Jesus in the community of the Episcopal Church means that we work on being good disciples. We need to be able to articulate our faith. As a church we need to be forming followers of Jesus who can articulate the essential visionary nature of who we are as Episcopalians.

Episcopalians engage in the work of praying the Ten Commandments. We do it in worship, and we even have a teaching guide in the *Book of Common Prayer* (page 847). When was the last time you picked up the *Book of Common Prayer* and read the Commandments and our Episcopal understanding of their purpose in guiding our pilgrimage through life? The Ten Commandments are some of the first discipleship instructions in the catechism—a guide to faith. The Commandments remind us of God's desire for us in our relationship with God and with others.[86]

Episcopalians understand that we trust God, and we bring others to know him. We put nothing in the place of God. We show God respect in our words and in our actions and in the results of our actions. We are faithful in worship, prayer, and study. To the other we are to be faithful as well—treating our neighbors with love as we love God and love ourselves; to love, honor, and help our parents and family; to honor those in authority, and to meet their just demands. We, as Episcopalians, are to show respect for the life God has given us; to work and pray for peace; to bear no malice, prejudice, or hatred in our hearts; and to be kind to all the creatures of God. We are to use our bodily desires as God intended for the mutual building up of the family of God. We are to be honest and fair in our dealings; to seek justice, freedom, and the necessities of life for all people; and to use our talents and possessions as ones who must answer for them to God. We are to speak the truth and not mislead others by our silence. We are to resist temptations to envy, greed, and jealousy; to rejoice in other people's gifts and graces; and to do our duty for the love of God, who has called us into fellowship with him.[87]

Continuing this faithful work with God and on behalf of God is what it means in part to follow in our apostolic teaching, to continue the work of a covenant community. We, as Episcopalians, hold ourselves accountable to this vision of relationship with God and with one another. We believe we hold up our lives to this image of our being, word, and deed and can see clearly where we fall short of the hope God has in us and so we repent. We return to God.[88]

As Episcopalians, we know that baptism does not make us perfect. We know that we remain sinful and sinning people. That is what we Episcopalians own—that we too often follow our own will and not God's. This really messes up our relationship with God and with other people. We also have managed to make a real mess of God's creation.

We recognize we cannot help but mess up our relationship with God and others, so we understand that we are in need of salvation. We are set free to do the work of creating a community of reconciliation. We know as Episcopalians, we say in our Eucharistic prayers, that God has tried to call us back to God . . . but not yet. It is under this weight of sin that God chooses to enter the world. God comes as the Messiah to set us free from the power of sin, so that with the grace of God, we may live and work as God's people.

We believe the Messiah is Jesus of Nazareth, the only Son of God. He is the Christ. He is not just another prophet, good guy, wise man or great historic figure—no henotheistic guiding spirit. We believe in the Episcopal Church that Jesus is the only perfect image of the Father, and that he reveals to us and illustrates for us the true nature of God. Jesus reveals to us that God is love and that God's creation is meant to glorify God. We believe Jesus was conceived by the Holy Spirit, that by God's own act, his divine Son received our human nature from the Virgin Mary, his mother. We believe that God became human so that we might be adopted as children of God, and be made heirs in the family of Abraham and inherit God's kingdom.

We did what humans do to prophets, and we killed Jesus. (Luke 13.34) God knew this would happen—and yet freely walked to the cross in the person of Jesus; that through his death, resurrection and ascension, we would be given freedom from the power of sin and be reconciled to God. As the ability to glorify God and live in a covenant community with God was given to us, so too was the gift of eternal life. We believe God in the form of the Son descended among the dead and that the dead receive the benefit of the faithful, which is redemption and eternal life. We say and claim that Jesus took our human nature into heaven where he now reigns with the Father. Jesus intercedes for us and we share in this new relationship by means of baptism into this covenant community—wherein we become living members in Christ.[89]

We Episcopalians are lovers of Jesus and have a strong emphasis on God made man in his person. Therefore, we value an "incarnational view of human life."[90] We believe that God intentionally made humankind and that God reaches out to us. Paul Zahl is fond of saying that it is a one-directional reaching out by God to human kind. The incarnation is God's embrace of humanity, even in its un-Godlike qualities. The incarnation says God loves us. Just as God has wanted to walk with us in the garden, so too God raises Jesus from the grave and with him brings humanity into equality with the angels to dwell in light eternal. We believe that "God participates fully in the particularity of human life in Christ."[91] This has impacted our ministry as Episcopalians because we have come to believe that every human being, in every culture, in every context, holds within it God's life. We also understand that humanity can distort that icon into something that lacks the beauty that it was meant to convey. It is this love for our fellow human beings that has caused the Episcopal Church to reach out in evangelism around the world. It is also this love for others that has caused us to stand up for the civil rights of black Americans, women, immigrants, and GLBT people. While at times we distort this longing God has for human beings, the Episcopal Church has a tradition of trying hard to deal with the difficult questions that come with a diversity of people living together.

In our covenant community we have a language of faith that directs our conversations and gives meaning to our words, through which we understand we are invited to believe, trust, and keep God's desire to be in relationship by keeping his commandments. You shall love the Lord your God with all your heart, with all your soul, and with all your mind. This is the first and great commandment. And the second is like it: You shall love your neighbor as yourself. (BCP, 324)

We are to love one another as Christ loved us. We believe that God continues with us, as Jesus promised, in the person of the Holy Spirit. It is the Holy Spirit who gives life to word and language and even to our own Episcopal vision of Christianity. The Holy Spirit leads us into truth, and helps us to grow into mature followers of Jesus, to grow into the likeness of Christ. We believe the Holy Spirit is present when we confess Jesus Christ as Lord and when we live in love and harmony with God, with ourselves, with our neighbors, and with all creation.

We know the Holy Spirit's movement when we see it in accordance with scripture, creed and reason of the church. The creeds affirm this teaching of the Christian Church, and our Episcopal Church; they are basics of everything I have said. The creed is the way Episcopalians remember on any given Sunday the promises of the God in which we believe. As Episcopalians we read the Bible. We do so in worship, in daily prayer, and in our study. We find it a living word and encourage one another to read, mark, and make inward the truth of the living God as revealed within its pages.

Episcopalians are not fundamentalists, while some fundamentalists may indeed be Episcopalian. Our Scriptures consist of books written by the people of the Old Covenant, under the inspiration of the Holy Spirit, to show God at work in nature and history. The Gospels, written by the first followers of Jesus, and the first leaders of our church, set forth the life and teachings of Jesus and proclaim the Good News of the Kingdom for all people.[92] Episcopalians claim that the Holy Scriptures are the living Word of God because God inspired their human authors and because God still speaks to us through the Bible.[93] As part of the Protestant Reformation, we believe all people may seek truth in the Scriptures through the work and power of the Holy Spirit, but we also believe that it is the Holy Spirit guiding the Christian Church and the Episcopal Church in interpretation.

We believe that the Bible should be read with other people; that we should listen to scholars, preachers, and teachers; and that we must work to interpret the Scriptures. It is from the Church, the Episcopal Church in particular, that we as Episcopalians find our meaning and understanding of the Christian faith.

It is one church in the full body of Christ, the community of Jesus, the family of God, the temple of the Holy Spirit, which exists in this world and in the world to come. The Church—triumphant and resplendent, and the bride of Christ—is described as the Body of which Jesus Christ is the Head and of which all baptized persons are members. It is also called the People of God, the New Israel, a holy nation, a royal priesthood, and the pillar and ground of truth. We believe as Episcopalians, and can trace our heritage to, the nature of this church as one, holy, catholic, and apostolic.

Historically, words like "catholic" and "universal" have been used to describe this kind of church. "Breadth" and "expansiveness" have been recent words that help us understand that our history has led us to a place where we honor a variety of expressions of the principles outlined above. This happens within the orders of leadership and orders of liturgy.[94] One can say that we "embrace the classical Anglican ideal of 'comprehension,' the holding together of multiple perspectives (Protestant and [Roman] Catholic, for instance) within one community of faith."[95]

In doing this work as a diverse loving community we are like living stones, part of the kingdom God is building even now, even in this world. We do this work as bishops, priests, and deacons always with the baptized of the church and in relationship with our neighbors.

We believe the ministry of the Episcopalian is to represent Christ Jesus in his or her own life and work. We are to bear witness to the Go in whom we believe. We are to be at work undertaking God's mission, using all our gifts and talents. We are to live into the reality that Christ reconciles us to God. We are to be reconciled with others and thereby become part of the reconciling ministry of Jesus. We also believe that all Episcopalians are to participate fully in the life of the community. We have a place at the table. We may participate in worship. We are to help the church apply the vision of God's work to the missionary structures of the church. This is every Episcopalian's work. It is not a right, but it is a privilege and a responsibility of being a member of God's household.

The Episcopal Church also has specific ministries that share in this work. We have bishops who have the particular charism[96] of representing Christ and his Church through the ministry of apostleship. Apostleship is the work of gathering the faithful, preaching and teaching. The bishop is also the chief priest. This means that the bishop is to be at work ensuring that the community continues in its apostolic tradition of proclaiming the faith, reading the Scriptures, praying, and breaking bread together. The bishop is also one to pastor and care for the diocese to whom they are linked. The bishop is a symbol of Christ as Good Shepherd and as such is to be at work in the caring and feeding of God's people. The bishop also has a special charism to be the chief reconciling agent in the world leading the building up of the church with others who discover their life bound to the love of God. It is also the bishop's work to ordain others to continue Christ's missionary ministry.[97]

The Episcopal Church has a tradition of priesthood. In the absence of the bishop, the priest represents Christ and his Church to the people gathered as a community. The priest pastors the people as well in this role. In his or her life and work the priest is to love those whom God gives them and to care alike for the young and old, the rich and the poor.[98] In his or her life and ministry, the priest is to proclaim the Gospel and to administer the sacraments. And, while the bishop is to model God's reconciling ministry, the priest is to bless and declare God's love and pardon on the people. The priest does all these things as signs of the ministry of the bishop in a particular locale and context.[99] The priest is about the work of making the things of this world "so transparent that in them and through them we know God's presence and activity in our midst and so experience his grace."[100]

The Episcopal Church also has deacons. The deacon represents Christ and the church through the particular work of servanthood.[101] The deacon's ministry represents God's particular love and care for the poor, the widows, the orphans, and the outcasts. The deacon is to proclaim the Gospel in action and by leading the people out into the world. The deacon is to represent the world's needs to the church and call them to action. He or she is to remind the faithful that God comes to them in the naked and hungry of this world.[102]

Episcopalians find meaning by living a life that is in touch with the sacraments. In the Episcopal Church we have two Gospel Sacraments: Baptism and Eucharist. These are the two sacraments given to us by Christ. The other five sacraments are means by which the church reminds people that they are loved by God and were designated by the church as symbols of God's grace.[103]

We are to invite people to Holy Baptism. It is the sacrament by which God adopts us as his children and makes us members of Christ's Body, the Church, and inheritors of the kingdom of God. It is what God does, not what we do. It is an invitation, through the water of baptism, for us to say we are God's. God claims you. You claim God. We make promises for infants so that they can share in God's family and we promise to guide and guard them in the Christian faith. We believe in infant baptism. We believe it is our responsibility (not the child's responsibility) to raise the child within the Church, to know Christ and be able to follow him. For the adult it is an opportunity to stand and say: I renounce evil, I don't want to live in sin, I trust in God and in Jesus as my Lord and Savior. There is nothing that separates us from God. In our tradition baptism is complete, once for all.

This is the way people become members of The Episcopal Church. A missionary church will have people along the edges who may not be baptized or want their children baptized. This is natural for a missionary community. However, if we move away from this core teaching, just like any other, we are moving away from being Episcopalian. There are other churches with other traditions around initiation. Baptism is ours.

The second sacrament is the Holy Eucharist. In the Episcopal tradition this is not a sacrament of initiation. The Eucharist is food for the journey. The Holy Eucharist recalls Jesus' life, death, resurrection, his judgment and his coming again. We make present, through the Holy Eucharist, the sacrifice of Christ and we believe it unites us to God. It is an absolutely essential sacrament needed for the daily living of life following Jesus. It is a sacrament wherein is found forgiveness of sins, the strengthening of our bond with Christ Jesus, and the binding of the individual to the community and vice versa. We believe the celebration of the Eucharist is a key component to community life. It is also called the Lord's Supper, Communion. The purpose in part is so that followers of Jesus experience and may touch the heavenly banquet yet to come.[104] We are bound together as inheritors of the Abrahamic faith of the Hebrews. We are bound together as brothers and sisters. We are reconciled to one another and to God in Christ Jesus.

The Eucharist does not require some kind of right belief or perfect knowledge in order to participate. It does not require righteousness. The grace that is offered does cause the believer to respond with self-examination and to ask for forgiveness for the brokenness we have caused intentionally and unintentionally, and it challenges us to renew our love for God and our brothers and sisters. It is a worship service that challenges us by reflecting on God's grace, mercy, and forgiveness that we, too, are to be characters of grace, mercy, and forgiveness. We are to bless others and live in charity and kindness within the human family. We are reminded that love is the order of the day.

These are the two Gospel and primary sacraments of the Church. In The Episcopal Church we have five other sacraments, created by the Church, revealed through Scripture and built upon tradition. These sacraments benefit of her people as a means of grace and the power of the Holy Spirit. It is the church that has named these symbols of God's grace, and it is the church that has used these sacraments as tools for blessing the lives of its people. These are: confirmation, ordination, holy matrimony, reconciliation of a penitent, and unction.

While these sacraments (with a little *s*) are a means of grace, The Episcopal Church claims, and I believe, they are not necessary for all persons in the same way as Baptism and the Eucharist.

Our understanding of the centrality of the Sacraments of Baptism and Eucharist in the life of Episcopalians means that the Episcopal Church has a quality of worshipfulness. In fellowship, in meetings, in Bible studies, in daily life, many times a day and sometimes only once a day, we are a people of prayer. We have prayers for the death of a pet and for the birth of a child. Meals are made sacred by children's' blessings. We have prayers that can be used for when a child falls from a bicycle or when a person is on their deathbed. Every moment and every hour of this world's clock are covered with Christian prayer, to be sure, and definitely with the prayers of faithful Episcopalians. The *Book of Common Prayer* binds us together on Sunday.

But the prayer book also binds us together as a daughter in Texas says compline with her dying 92-year-old father at the same time as the monks of the Society of Saint John the Evangelist in Boston lift their voices in solemn Psalm 131:

In you, O Lord, have I taken refuge; let me never be put to shame: deliver me in your righteousness. Incline your ear to me; make haste to deliver me. Be my strong rock, a castle to keep me safe, for you are my crag and my stronghold; for the sake of your name, lead me and guide me. Take me out of the net that they have secretly set for me, for you are my tower of strength. Into your hands I commend my spirit, for you have redeemed me, O Lord, O God of truth.[105]

Our sacramental understanding of life means that we see God through the eyes of our prayer and in the things of everyday life. We say, "Episcopalians understand the sacraments of Baptism and Eucharist as touchstones for the church's identity and witness, as they represent God coming to us in the ordinary stuff of the world (water, bread, wine). The Christian life is not an escape from this world, but rather the seeking of abundant life for all within it."[106] As Episcopalians we believe God is out in the world and we are to go out and be in the world with God to bless the world with prayer and to make the common holy.

This sacramental life is filled with liturgy (the creative work of a people worshiping God), art, and mystery.[107] We understand that we are to make an offering to God. In our Episcopal tradition this offering is always in conversation with the arts. We have an aesthetic theology that is rooted in the understanding of God as the first artist and his creatures as his co-creators. Our appreciation of artistic offerings that reveals God and reflect God's glory back to the heavens can, at times, become human-centric and narcissistic in nature. We are not interested in performance so much as we are interested in participation as a people of God making an offering of our creative nature in sacred prayers, hymns and art in the church; and wherever the divine can be seen—dance, fine arts, literature and technology. Such is our worship; such is the sacramental quality of our Episcopal way.

As Episcopalians we are people of hope, who live with confidence and courage, awaiting God's judgment. We believe that we are working with God for the completion of the purposes of creation and unification of all people with their creator through the proclamation of the Good News of Salvation and the unique witness of God in Christ Jesus.[108]

Lastly, we believe Christ will come again and will fulfill his promise to make all things new. We believe in heaven where we are united with God in an eternal Eucharistic celebration of God's love and glory. In death we make our cry of hope as all go down to the grave dust to dust, ashes to ashes, praying God to recognize us as a sheep of his own fold, lambs of his flock, and sinners of his redeeming. We believe that God will raise us from death in the fullness of our being that we may live with Christ in the communion of saints. And that we shall have a new existence, in which we are united with all the people of God, in the joy of fully knowing and loving God and each other eternally. Our assurance as Christians, and as Episcopalians, is that nothing, not even death, shall separate us from the love of God that is in Christ Jesus our Lord. (Romans, 8:38ff) This is who we are. This is what the core of life lived as Episcopalians is to be centered upon. All the rest is part of the diversity of our communal experience. Many Christian churches have some of these beliefs, but it is the unique and particular manner and combination that makes us Episcopalian.

No mission may be undertaken as an Episcopal Church without the embodiment of this faith. If we are going to engage in mission and use the culture around us to help us develop mission tools, we must continue to pass along our long legacy and tradition. While the style and manner in which we engage these core beliefs may change, they should remain our guiding belief system. The fashion changes while the nature of our church does not.

We have not appeared in this place and this time magically but arrive here as part of a great cloud of witnesses who have blessed people through teaching and preaching. There is a great ancestry of Church behind us—good and bad. From its earliest days the Episcopal Church has been responsive to the mission it felt it was given. Often times we think the structures and practices that we inherit as a church have always been there and have never changed. That is not true, though, nor realistic. It is just a coping mechanism so we don't have to do the hard work of remembering the changing times and the changing church that has inhabited those times. The Anglican expression of Christianity in the United States did reprehensible things to the native people; was committed to the monarchy and colonialism; owned and sold human beings into slavery; believed women could not be priests, and all manner of things. Today, though, we are a church trying to re-engage the first or native peoples of this land and the new culture with an eye to repenting from past behaviors. We are a church that believes that oppressive forms of government need to be changed. We understand how our church benefited from slavery in a real way and how some members of our church have safety nets and opportunities others don't have. Today the Episcopal Church is investing in ensuring all people—every race, ethnicity, and gender—are able to find a place in this society, make a living wage, have a roof over their heads, have food security, and are free from violence and oppression.

Our organization, too, has changed over the years in order to meet the changing vision of our work and to navigate the complexities of every age.[109] As the Episcopal Church made its way in a colonial world, negotiating both neighbors of differing Christian backgrounds and the first peoples of the land, it found itself far from the Bishop of London, who was its protector. The idea of church that came with the first Anglicans to America consisted of structures that had existed for hundreds of years back home in a foreign cultural context. Bishops were nowhere to be found and clergy were few and far between, so the church naturally worked out a way of governing that included laity. Lay leaders were not even confirmed... remember, no bishops, just Commissaries.

Following the American Revolution, things changed even more radically. Episcopalians found themselves without a bishop and with no governance at all. I was once told that at this precarious moment in the life of our church we almost became extinct in the new United States. But people got together in common or "general" conventions. There were no dioceses at that time. The first thing we did as a church was to begin to meet in mini representative congresses to develop our rules of life. We then came together as one body and decided on a set of Constitutions and Canons, and decided what version of the *Book of Common Prayer* we would adopt. Then a lot of time was spent arguing over if we should have bishops or not. The "ongoing catholic witness" won out, though, and bishops were secured for the fledgling church.[110] We weren't even "constituent members of the Anglican Communion" at the time because there was no Anglican Communion; that was to enter our constitution later.[111]

Almost 100 years after the first Anglicans made their way to the new colonies, the little church was adapting and growing. As people moved west, they took their church with them. The first Episcopalians in Texas were a handful of lay people and a couple of deacons. Our church, though, decided to become a missionary church in that era, and so formed itself into a missionary society. Bishops and priests were sent out into domestic and foreign fields. Women across the country raised money to fund churches and priests. In fact, we are fond of saying that upon the General Convention's decision to become *The Domestic and Foreign Missionary Society of the Protestant Episcopal Church in the United States of America* Texas was the first foreign mission field.

We did not even have a church center until the 1950s, and our presiding bishop for most of the previous years was simply the senior bishop. What is important to realize is that it was only after the soldiers returned from World War II, and the country went through a baby boom, and we dealt with the racial issues of the day did we see the high water mark of the church. For a while the Episcopal Church was doing so well at navigating the quickly modernizing terrain that our presiding bishop appeared in *Time* magazine as the leader of the Protestant Church in America.[112] Slowly but with great precision, we came to the 1970s as a church that looked a lot like all the other institutions of the day.We had evolved into an attractional church model.

Our ministry was dependent upon people coming finding us and having programs for them to connect into.

It was in the 1980s, though, that things began to change. They began to change for all institutions in this country. There are any number of markers and political events. Truth is the large institution, if it tries to control too much, has a more difficult time navigating quickly changing trends and sociological movements. This was our behavior. The first reductions happened in the 1970s. For almost 100 years the Episcopal Church rode a wave of growth and change in the United States. As the country grew and became prosperous, so did the church. The church was recognized as a missionary leader at home and abroad, and that is important to say.

For the majority of our church's life we have been a church of experimentation and expansion into the community—going where the people were. We had no problem pooling our money to do the mission work we believed was ours to undertake. We had a heart for mission.

It is easy to put words to our history that describe well the quality of our mission endeavors:

Reconciling—When they had differences, they resolved a means of living together and moved on.

Persevering—In difficult times, without clarity about the future, they worked and failure was not a deterrent.

Willing—People in the church put their big boy/girl pants on and got it done.

Creative—They were creative and focused on making church happen. They were undaunted by wilderness, distance, cost, and difficulty.

Generous—They raised money (not for big systems of bureaucracy) to support new church growth and mission—domestic and foreign.

Mission focused—They knew who they were and understood with clarity that they were to take the gospel out into the world.

It has only been in the last thirty years that we have somehow not been able to reach our potential within our mission context at the local level and at the church-wide level.

We have been and are a church with a clear, yet broad, vision. We have a history that tells us that it is well within this institution's ability to grow and thrive as a healthy contributor to the kingdom of God. We must then recommit ourselves to doing the work that has been given to us to do. We are God's people who have the responsibility of leading our church into the future and helping it to become a place where lives are changed, the Gospel heard, people fed, and where the blind receive their sight.

We need to face the fact that we as an Episcopal Church have experienced mission drift. As greater numbers of people became members of our church in the 1950s and '60s, complex programs and ministries multiplied. As social trends and churchgoing attitudes shifted, we were left with programs without people to staff them and shrinking dollars to fund them. In this world, competing for resources became the order of the day. Over the years good intentions and faithfulness have caused the organization to drift as different powers, visions, and individuals pulled this way and that. We have spent a lot of time telling people how to do things and what not to do, rather than getting our hands dirty with the creative work of renewed mission. Old patterns of manipulating organizations through problem-solving techniques have offered few solutions.

CHAPTER SEVEN
Excellence

"Obey the principles without being bound by them."
— *Bruce Lee, actor*

We have been trying to fix things instead of using principled action to guide us. We know who we are and it is important to be clear about what principles guide our mission and how those principles may look if we engage them. The principles are excellence, unity, and connection. These are lived out in the way we undertake our mission. These principles impact service, evangelism, stewardship and formation.

First, let me say a word about excellence. Our tradition speaks to us about the glory of God. We understand and have understood (primarily through worship) that we are to glorify God. Jesus himself comes to glorify God. We are to give to God the best of what we have. We are to give God the first fruits of our work. We do this through the quality of excellence. We know we won't always get it right. We know we can't earn God's love and affection by doing things correctly. Excellence is something we continually strive towards. We must be honest when we fail, never shaming or being shame-filled, and always willing to pick ourselves up and try again. Service, evangelism, stewardship and formation are marked by excellence when a loving, worshiping community engages God's mission.

Evangelism is the work of proclaiming the Good News of Salvation through God in Christ Jesus. It is the presentation of Jesus Christ, in the power of the Holy Spirit, in such ways that persons may be led to him as savior, and follow him as Lord within the fellowship of his Church—specifically for us, The Episcopal Church and Anglican Communion. Service is the work of the Church in mission. We might say that mission is the proclamation of the Good News of Salvation through works of justice, peace, and love. It is the work of loving God through the action of loving our neighbor.

I believe that excellence in evangelism reveals itself in community life that is thriving in biblical study and theological reflection. Such a life will also be changing people's lives by sharing the Good News of God in Christ Jesus. When we do this well we are less concerned with a life that controls outcomes and we are more interested in a life that is shared and ebullient with the Holy Spirit. Those who wish to go deeper will more naturally become interested in learning from Jesus how to live and move and have their being. Excellence in evangelism, though, will not only create followers. Excellence in evangelism will mean developing a community that goes out into the world on the great adventure of apostleship. Jesus never called a disciple (people who follow) that he did not turn into an apostle (people who go) and send him out. He sent out seventy people to the Temple and into towns to preach, heal, and tell people the kingdom of God was at hand.

A community known for its excellence in evangelism will be a community that is busy welcoming people into the church. It will be a community that is intentional about its welcoming. It will be a place that is hospitable and treats every person who enters the house of God as if they were royal guests in God's own house. (Luke 7.45ff) At the same time the future Church will be a church that goes out into the world. The Church must spend more time translating the Gospel message across the boundaries we have erected between the church and the culture. The future Church will spend less time talking about how the culture is evil (which is a straw man argument that is supposed to make those in the church feel better) and more time finding where God is already at work transforming the lives of real people. We must spend more time working on how to engage the culture around us that is multi-ethnic, multi-lingual, and multi-generational. We must spend more time working on crafting the Gospel message that is social, cultural, and regional.

A community that is spending most of its money on itself and its governance will reform if it wishes to be a community that is known for excellence in evangelism. It will spend more time, energy, and money on ministries outside of the church. It will plant all kinds of communities. Most of all, a community that is serious about evangelism will not be one focused on what divides it; on the contrary, it will be focused on God's mission and the proclamation of Christ Jesus as the unique revelation of God and the Good News of Salvation.

This excellence in evangelism will also bring forth qualities of life. Joy and hope are qualities of the community that is at work evangelizing the world. The Gospel is clear: the people who followed Jesus were not interested in an oppressive legalized religious system that expected everyone to come to the synagogue or temple. The people who became part of the Jesus movement were inspired by the hope that Jesus offered, the transformation of life, and the joy that came from realizing that God loves and embraces God's people. The health and strength of the early Christian community was linked to its unity and its diversity. The tremendous growth over the first three centuries happened in a Church with diverse communities and no centralized system of organization. Growth came without a Bible in those first centuries, but instead with the sharing of personal narratives about the healing power of Jesus and the Good News of God's grace. Growth came because of the diversity of community types and the diversity of languages, cultures, and leaders that offered the transformation of the Gospel. This is the witness of Pentecost. Health, strength, and vitality of the Christian community increased because people who loved God believed in the risen Christ, and loved their neighbors and served them.

One of the first things the disciples did following the resurrection of Jesus was to increase their number and to ensure that food and care were given to all those in need. They elected deacons specifically to help the community care for and serve those who had no advocates. (Acts 6:1-6) This, too, is our work. We are to be people who love our neighbor and share what we have. Christian communities living into God's mission will reveal to the world around them excellence in service.

Service is the act of incarnating the Gospel of Good News. God's mission of reconciliation and love is revealed in service to our neighbor that transforms lives and restores dignity. Christian community committed to God's mission can see that the world around them is being changed in concert with Christ's reconciling work. Such communities listen to the needs of the people living in their mission context. They listen and ask what is needed and then invest lives , money, time, and creative energy into the problem as a partner. Excellence in service is not outreach to the poor. It is not some kind of toxic charity that creates dependence.[113] Excellence in service is what happens when a congregation becomes part of the community once again and is one of the many who are concerned and act for the betterment of the whole society.

This listening will bring forth initiatives that are bound to the community and see the neighbor as partner in the work that is needed. Yes, new outreach ministries and schools and clinics will come into being. These will always be needed. Those that are served will have an active role in their own self-care and ministry. Rich people doing something for poor people will not characterize excellence in service. Instead neighbors helping and empowering neighbors is the character of the future Church. If the community around us needs green space, then we will work with them to create green space. If the community around us says they need help because the schools are in trouble, then we must step in and partner to make the schools a better place. If the community around us believes that the neighborhood is not safe, then we must make sure that everyone knows that The Episcopal Church in their community is a safe place for children and for adults. We must be willing to help make our neighborhoods safe—instead of building fences, installing alarms, and creating a barricade against the world outside.

Seeing each person as God's beloved is essential to Gospel service. It understands that the people we partner with to solve community issues are human beings created in the image of God. The care and respect of their bodies, minds, and spirits is a necessary component. Gospel service that has the mark of excellence must see the humanity of others and not dehumanize them with statistics or stereotypes. Our work is to labor with individuals and see that they and we exist within a complete web of relationships. Service to the whole community is important because we recognize that people are more than simply the absence of poverty, the absence of infirmity, the absence of hunger. We recognize that as we engage in service we are engaging in community work that recognizes the community is only as strong as its weakest individuals.

Excellence in service remembers that Christ himself was always ministering in the midst of widows, children, the oppressed, and the poor. Jesus himself offered his message of love to those who in his culture were the weakest and of the least value. It is true for God and it is true for God's Church. We are invested in being a part of ministries that help people move from poverty to living wages; from credit-encumbered lives to the freedom to give; from scarcity of food to food security; and from a deficiency of health resources to access to preventative and participatory health education and care. The wellness of a community is dependent upon how well all of this is achieved. We recognize in order to accomplish excellence in service that we must do this work and that we can't do it alone. We are a church that reaches out and builds partnerships within the community around us. We believe we are called to work with others and share resources. Excellence means that we will decrease the economic footprint of our churches and increase our mission impact. The only way this will happen is by an engagement that includes an honest discussion about money.

Excellence in stewardship is also a goal for the future Church. We believe in a God that has created a fertile garden in which we can live. We believe in a God who has provided enough food to feed the world, enough natural resources and scientific wisdom to shelter the world. We believe in a God who believes there is enough if we will only share. We are the ones who are to be good stewards of the abundance around us. Using it all up, creating a great divide between the haves and the have-nots, and abusing and exploiting workers for the enrichment of individuals is not good stewardship. The church must engage in God's mission and itself be transformed.

Excellence in stewardship will reveal itself in community life that supports the vocation of all people. Such stewardship will recognize and employ the many gifts, the wealth of wisdom, and the generosity of God's people and deploy these resources into evangelism and service. We will work to build sustainable mission and ministry for the new age that is not bound by outdated ideas of communication or buildings. Excellence will use the abundant opportunities around the church to increase dollars for mission. Stewardship will move away from concerns about maintenance and self-perpetuation to investment in mission.

These are the marks of a visionary church at work in the world; excellence is a principle that should guide our efforts. Our church has a history and that history has tried to live out our faith in many different kinds of contexts and many different ages of history. Just as the visionary church leads to an understanding that our ministry will reflect excellence in evangelism, service, and stewardship, so too our history offers us an understanding of the manner in which we are to undertake the work that is before us.

The work before our church is not a problem to be solved. It is not the kind of thing where we put a group of people in the room and we figure out how to fix everything. Problems exist in slow moving systems affected by very little change. Problems are typically well defined and expected. We must engage in making an offering of ministry to God in thanksgiving for his love and his provision. We must walk out of the doors of our church and do the work that God has given us to do, knowing that Jesus Christ's promise to the disciples remains true for us today—he is with us until the end of the ages. We will need visionary leadership for the new age.

If we are going to embrace the challenge before us, we must cling ever tighter to the vision of God in Christ Jesus. We must recognize that God has a mission and God's mission has a church. We must be clear about the kind of God we believe in and the kind of church we are with a sacramental life at its core. Let us renew our commitment and in so doing renew our own vision so that we may be a missionary church. Let us be reconciled beyond our conflicts, be persevering, be a community of the willing, be creative, be generous, and mission focused!

Simon Sinek, a business consultant, writes in his book *Start With Why* that when organizations begin with "why" resolutions are easier and paths forward clearer.[114] Loyalties are stronger while trust is at capacity throughout the organization. Being a visionary organization that remembers its ultimate purpose is not only faithful to the Gospel but also hopeful and will generate innovation and creativity. When we begin with "why" we have the capability of not only transforming our organization but the world around us.[115]

We are an organization built upon faith and we need to return to the basics of our faith so that we may turn outward and realize that we can engage in the mission field. If we keep coming back to our vision as a church and our leaders will allow freedom, we will realize that it is not a disastrous thing to have a variety of new communities and ministries. The future Church is not afraid of people getting out there, pushing the envelope, and doing crazy things. Visionary leadership will enable us to have the ability to celebrate when they grow and mourn when they fail. Doing this will mean we will be less tempted to ride programs into the ground spending costly resources and time when we should shrug it off and move in new directions.[116]

We must let go of the past and stop being enamored *with* structures—*specially* structures that mask control instead of freeing up energy for creativity and mission.[117] We, as an organization, have clarity about who we are and if we will but embrace it and move on we will be stronger. A fig tree doesn't sit around thinking about what if it were a pecan or if it had bark like a pine tree...it is simply a fig tree and its whole natural self-works at being the best fig tree it can be. Our own relationship with the wider community will actually strengthen our identity and our life rather than weaken it. In fact, I believe that the idea of a church separate and outside of the life of its community will actually bring about its demise.[118] Churches do not exist as islands unto themselves. There exists a paradox in living systems: Each organism maintains a clear sense of its individual identity within a larger network of relationships that helps shape its identity. Each organism is noticeable as a separate entity, yet it is simultaneously part of a whole system. In fact living organisms survive only as they learn how to participate in a web of relationships found in the context in which it makes its home. Churches are always inextricably linked to the community, people, and culture around it. Let us be who we are and reclaim our mission heritage and share Jesus Christ, in the power of the Holy Spirit, in creative ways that enable people of every kind to discover him as Savior, and let us join with them and follow him as Lord within the fellowship of his Episcopal Church.

People who call TEC home are people who lead corporate America, who farm the land, who teach in our schools, who work in restaurants and yards, and live on the street. We are people who fix cars and raise cows and alligators; we are people who sell furniture and run banks. Episcopalians are people who bury the dead, help moms birth the living, and sit with the suffering. We are a giant web of life, of jobs, of ministries and missionary outposts. We are an extensive network of delivery points for the unique story of the Good

News of Salvation, in word and deed, the gospel of Jesus Christ. God's mission is fulfilled through The Episcopal Church as its members evangelize and serve.[119] We as individuals are God's ministers. We are the called. There is no one else. The Holy Spirit rests upon us and we are sent out into the world. This is our time and our moment to act as missionaries of a God who is at work transforming the world. Let us have vision, let nothing interrupt it, and let us undertake our work with urgency. Let us see the future that is all around us and let us act.

Written in 1966 and delivered to his first diocesan council in Texas, Bishop Milton Richardson's words could well be spoken today.[120]

Bishop Richardson looked out over a sea of nearly 1,000 people at what could easily have been the high-water mark of the Episcopal Church, and he said:

The World is in ferment today. The Church is in ferment today. Theology is in ferment today. We may mythologize some things surrounding Christ, but we may not mythologize Christ. His Incarnation is a fact. His redemption of us is a fact. The Church as a redeeming body is a fact. And Christ is the great fact—God's fact. And the Trinity is a fact; you cannot say all that you mean by God until you have said Father, Son, and Holy Ghost. The doctrine of the Trinity is as decisively simple and as simply decisive as that.

In an atomic age, the Church with the Holy Scriptures in her hand must proclaim the sovereignty of the power of God as ultimate. In a world of racial prejudice, and national strife, the Church with the historic creeds upon her lips must stand for the unity of the human race in Christ Jesus with no other alternative. In a generation of material wealth, the Church with her sacraments must bear witness to the grace of God as the means of salvation. In a time of great and rapid change and many voices, the Church with her apostolic ministry must speak in no uncertain voice of Him who changeth not and is the Way, the Truth, and the Light. Two things we need to keep in mind. First, the Lord God reigns.

This is His world and He has a purpose for it. Second, we have come into the world at this time to fulfill His purpose.

When the Old Testament Esther hesitated before the danger she faced, Mordecai pointed out her duty, saying, "Who knoweth whether thou art come to the Kingdom for such a time as this?"

I believe that we have been chosen for just such a time as this.

CHAPTER EIGHT
Unity in Mission

"A house divided against itself will not stand."
—Abraham Lincoln, Springfield, Illinois
Statehouse Speech, June 16, 1858

There is a measure of truth in Abraham Lincoln's infamous words. Just as there is truth in Jesus' prayer that we may all be one as he and the Father are one. (John 17.23) "Union with Christ brings union with one another," claims Paul throughout his letter to the Corinthians. (1 Corinthians 15.22; 2 Corinthians 15.17) Unity over uniformity is an Anglican charism. It is rooted deeply in our history dating back to Queen Elizabeth I who unified a divided Church during the reformation. Historical documents like the 39 Articles of faith that were adopted in the sixteenth century by the Church of England and the nineteenth century by the Episcopal Church speak of the creeds as unifying while worship in every place may be different. Yet there is more to be discovered here. Unity is a basic ingredient to undertaking God's mission and the second of our three principles. The mission itself will be unsuccessful without unity. The reason is that at the core of unity is the very heart of the Gospel— reconciliation. If we do not have clarity about the meaning of reconciliation and how it creates unity among believers, we will forever have difficulty being able to understand how we might be in relationship with those who are different from ourselves. It is this ability to be reconciled with the other that is the only effective seed from which evangelism and service may take root. We should not fool ourselves; how we are in relationship with one another reveals how we are in relationship with God and, in point of fact, also reveals how we will treat those who are discovering their own faith.

George Barna in his 2003 book Boiling Point said that the new millennium would be focused more on our differences than what we have in common. Commons building will be one of the most essential ingredients to future social networking. Community building is a piece of what makes us human. And, what makes us human is also what draws us apart into like-minded groups. I believe we will experience polarizing extremes in the new culture. All of us who watch TV, plug into Facebook, or surf the blogosphere know this to be true. We experience a reality where fringe ideas, thoughts, words, and actions come to the front and center of life. In part, this is happening because of the roar being made in order to get noticed within the ever-greater ocean of information. Today, it is easier for people with extreme ideas to gather with others of like mind. Bob Johansen warns that "dark innovation" will thrive in this environment.

At the same time we will also see ideas that would not be viable at any other time in our past take center stage. They will become viable because technology bridges the gap between individuals in such a way that a fringe idea can find followers. Ideas (good and bad) that would have been lost in the sea of time now are gathered into a fringe commons. These ideas now not only make it to the social or real marketplace they can actually compete in it. New forms of cooperation and platforms for creativity will also become prevalent because of this growing commons. There is a mounting randomness and volatility within the culture, and these polarizing extremes buoy it up.

Some of the artifacts for our future are:

- a bigger gap between rich and poor
- more evangelists
- personal religions
- natural resource sharing and lack thereof
- bio distress within individual and community systems
- DIY survival kits—getting off the grid and embracing the grid[121]

As a diaspora community that dwells on the edge of culture, this is good news but challenging news. It is good news because we can connect. We are going to have to be ever more clarifying about the core of who we are so that we can be found among the thousands of things competing for our attention and loyalty. We will be challenged to engage and bridge-build between the widening gap of rich and poor. The new religious age brings with it personalized and amplified religion. Individuals will expect to personalize what they find in our church. We will, on the one hand, need to be clear about who we are and, on the other hand, allow for personalization of the daily spiritual experience.

The realization will come that as we build commons we discover we are all intimately connected in one biological system. Will our commons be polarizing or bridge-building communities? The Church in this coming age will be challenged to help navigate the bio distress felt within the community. This will come from needing to help during extreme natural disasters. Responses to hurricanes, fires, and floods will put the church on the front lines. It will come from helping individuals find healthy food because they live in food deserts. The theme of polarizing extremes will mean just as the society grows, it also becomes more localized and the local congregation/community of Christians will need to be poised to help with the arising issues of a new day with ever greater cost to the individual and the community. The Church is the one who stepped into the gap in 2014 as children left by their parents on the boarder of the U.S. found themselves in a country that does not want them. It is the Church that spoke up and reached out to help what was a human disaster on a massive proportion.

It will be very difficult to be a witness for unity and a bridge builder in the culture if we ourselves are divided. In recent years our own church has fallen victim to these cultural disparities. If we are not attentive, they will continue to dismantle our mission—eating us from the inside out, as the culture devours us from the outside in.

As a bishop I often have the pleasure of hearing the blessed Samuel John Stone's hymn "The Church's One Foundation," which was written in 1868. Many believe that its theme is connected with the Civil War. It was written following the Civil War and the reuniting of The Episcopal Church. It was, in fact, written for a very different reason. In 1866, an influential and liberal Anglican bishop wrote a book that attacked the historic accuracy of the Pentateuch—that is the first five books of the Bible also known as the Torah. Of course, today most Anglicans have come to terms with the idea of a history of the Old Testament that is rooted in the evolution of the people Israel and its collection of ancient narratives for the purpose of kingdom justification. And, at the same time, Anglicans believe that, while this history is true, it is also true that the same books contain the Holy Spirit and revelation of who God is in relationship to his people. As you can imagine, at the time this caused a widespread controversy throughout the Anglican Church. Samuel John Stone, a pastor ministering to the poor of London at the time, was deeply upset by the schism that surrounded him. He wrote a collection of twelve creedal hymns. He understood, above all things, that the foundation of the church must be the Lordship of Christ and not the views of any one group of people. John Stone got it, in my opinion. His hymn "The Church's One Foundation" was based on the Ninth Article of the Apostles' Creed. In his time the words of this section of the creed were different, which read: "The Holy Catholic (or Universal) Church; the Communion of Saints; He is the head of this Body." (Yes Virginia there is a Santa Claus and we have from time to time changed the words of the Creed to better reflect contemporary language.) The words of the hymn today that always move me and remind me of the awesome work we in the Church choose to undertake, and upon whom we depend most of all.

> *The Church's one foundation*
> *is Jesus Christ her Lord;*
> *she is his new creation,*
> *by water and the word:*
> *from heaven he came and sought her*
> *to be his holy bride;*
> *with his own blood he bought her,*
> *and for her life he died.*
>
> *Elect from every nation,*
> *yet one o'er all the earth,*
> *her charter of salvation,*
> *one Lord, one faith, one birth;*
> *one holy Name she blesses,*
> *partakes one holy food,*
> *and to one hope she presses,*
> *with every grace endued.*
>
> *Though with a scornful wonder*
> *men see her sore oppressed,*
> *by schisms rent asunder,*
> *by heresies distressed;*
> *yet saints their watch are keeping,*
> *their cry goes up, "How long?"*
> *and soon the night of weeping*
> *shall be the morn of song.*
>
> *Mid toil and tribulation,*
> *and tumult of her war*

she waits the consummation
of peace for evermore;
till with the vision glorious
her longing eyes are blessed,
and the great Church victorious
shall be the Church at rest.

Yet she on earth hath union
with God, the Three in one,
and mystic sweet communion
with those whose rest is won.
O happy ones and holy!
Lord, give us grace that we
like them, the meek and lowly,
on high may dwell with thee.[122]

Stone understood that the mission of reconciliation led by Christ was the core and that it united us all in ministry, especially as we ministered to the world around us. I believe he understood that without such Godly unity we, our community, and our mission are lost. We seek to live these words today despite our common disagreements, our desire to have our own way, our hope for schism, and our sinful want to fight amongst ourselves.

Our own efforts for unity depend partially on each of us, but only in a limited way. Paul's letter to the Philippians, Chapter 2, offers us these words on unity for the sake of mission:

If then there is any encouragement in Christ, any consolation from love, any sharing in the Spirit, any compassion and sympathy, make my joy complete: be of the same mind, having the same love, being in full accord and of one mind. Do nothing from selfish ambition or conceit, but in humility regard others as better than yourselves. Let each of you look not to your own interests, but to the interests of others. Let the same mind be in you that was in Christ Jesus, who, though he was in the form of God, did not regard equality with God as something to be exploited, but emptied himself, taking the form of a slave, being born in human likeness. And being found in human form, he humbled himself and became obedient to the point of death—even death on a cross.

We are called by God to be "in full accord and one mind" for the sake of the Gospel of Jesus. We cannot begin to offer a strategy on how to best proceed through the conflict that is upon us if we do not proceed in common mission under the headship of Jesus Christ. Effective mission hinges on the unity of the Church. This unity is so essential that in the Garden before his death, Jesus prays for us asking God to make us one. He prays for his disciples and for us saying, "May they become completely one, so that the world may know that you have sent me." (John 17:23)

Throughout his ministry, St. Paul pleaded with the Church to "be in agreement." Let there be "no divisions among you. Be united in the same mind and same purpose," he wrote in his first letter to the Corinthians (1:10). Yet, the first Christians were deeply divided over many different things. They were divided because the mission to the Jews and the mission to the Gentiles were in conflict. The early Christian community inherited religious practices from the Jewish tradition that were icons and sacramental ways of life and were in direct conflict with the Gentile way of life. Much of the Book of Acts and Paul's letters are filled with descriptions of how the early church dealt with what was essentially a conflict created by two colliding cultures. Specifically, we might recall Paul's thoughts on the morality of eating meat offered to idols. In fact, two of Paul's letters addressed this particular pastoral issue because it was so divisive to this growing Christian community. Rather than appealing to the law, Paul reminded believers of the freedom they have in Christ. Christians, Paul insisted, are free to follow their conscience and are free from the burden of judging or changing others. Christians are not only free from but prohibited from indicting and sentencing those who are different because of the freedom we have in Christ Jesus.[123]

"Who are you," Paul asked, "to pass judgment on servants of another? It is before their own lord that they stand or fall. Let all be fully convinced in their own minds. The faith you have, have as your own conviction before God." (Romans 14: 4-5, 22) How can a Church so deeply divided over the morality of this issue still "be in agreement?" The first Christians embraced the Gospel truth that Christ is our unity. What glues the Church together is "the message of the cross," Paul wrote. (1 Corinthians 1:18) Our diverse yet faithfully held positions shall in the end be laid at the altar of God. Until that time, our faith in Jesus Christ unites us and draws us into the mission field.

In this we find a manner of living with one another in a covenant community. If we imitate Christ and his manner, we too will find unity in our faith and in our work. Paul's words challenge us to be unified for mission some two thousand years later.

Paul challenges us: "Do not look to your own interests, but to the interests of others. Let the same mind be in you that was in Christ Jesus, who, though he was in the form of God, did not regard equality with God as something to be exploited." Though we are members of the Abrahamic faith, the family of God, we are not to exploit or use it to our own benefit. We are not to use our partnership with God as a means to judge and condemn others. We are to act with mercy, forgiveness, love, and kindness. This work of mercy is so difficult that, like Jesus, we must empty ourselves in order to be filled with grace. Today, the world tells us to fill ourselves up, to consume, to be served, to attach ourselves to others, to over-identify ourselves with others. Detachment is an ancient Christian practice. Listen to St. Paul's words, "[Be like Jesus who] emptied himself, taking the form of a slave." (Philippians 2.7) This is a radical way of being with one another—we are to serve the other.

In our conflicts we spend so much time attempting the destruction of one another that there is nothing left in the person or in the relationship to be served. From the beginning of Genesis, chapter 1, we are reminded of our long history of blaming others. Adam blames Eve and Eve blames the snake. This prehistoric tale reminds us of our fallen nature and how easy it is to scapegoat others rather than owning our own responsibility. We, by our fallen nature, find it enticing to have an enemy we can consume rather than a brother or sister whom God invites us to make family. The Gospel challenges us through the blessings of a grace received, to empty ourselves (of our desires to judge and condemn) that we may befriend our fellow Christian with the love, mercy, and forgiveness of Jesus: all for the purpose of reconciliation and service.

This is the unifying mind of Christ. It is a unity that understands hospitality and love and is obedient no matter how abusive someone else might get. You and I are challenged by the reconciling love of Jesus Christ to be different than the world around us. Jesus took up his cross and we are to do the same.

After meeting all day, a few bishops gathered late one evening to talk and solve the problems of the world. One bishop got really angry and said the "other side" deserves what they get because they were so hostile to the minority long ago. I challenged him (and myself). I said that the task of the Christian is not to require an eye for an eye, but to be a witness of grace and mercy no matter what is given. In return, the Christian empties the natural desire to harm in order to have the mind of Christ, which is to love.

When ideological opponents in the church can cease judgment of one another and serve one another, only then is the mission of Christ successful. When we have the mind of Christ and act with mercy, grace, love and kindness, then the kingdom of God is revealed before us.

I have lunch with a mentor and friend on a regular basis. He has been caught up in the culture wars that have infected the church, yet he is a man of incredible love and a man of grace. He challenged me to explain how we know what unifies us if we are not unified on our understanding of sexuality and on the issue of marriage or same-gender relationships. He, of course, knew well what the answer was. I believe he also knew that the culture wars have created a great lie within the Church. That lie is that if we are not in agreement on the issues of sexuality, then we must not be unified. This truth has been present with us throughout all the ages, and it is also going to be true in all the future conflicts we are bound to have just as it is true today. Unity is never rooted in our agreement but in God.

God is our unity. This is the truth that Scripture reveals, and Paul and Peter tried to convey to the earliest Church. When someone leaves and chooses to live outside of the community they move away from God. God is building communities of diverse people who don't all agree; that is the way he made us. The rector for whom I first worked once looked me in the eye and said to me, "Andy, God will not bless division and conflict. It is not God's way." I think he is marvelously correct. When we turn inward and fight among ourselves, God does not bless our efforts, and the fruits of our labor rot upon the tree. God does not bless our division because I don't believe that God is present in these battles. When we fight one another we are about as far away from the truth of God's reconciling ministry as one can possibly be.

One might ask if there is a hierarchy to the elements that make up our common life. I believe there is. I believe as Episcopalians and Anglicans some elements of our common life are more important than others. For instance, the Anglican Communion became an idea long before it became a reality. It was birthed out of the conflict between the breakaway colonies in our fledgling nation and a colonial empire. Today it is valued more than at any other time over the last two centuries. I would add that is in large part due to our own work to help bind the global ministry of the Anglican Church together.[124] We have become a unified church in mission. Worship style (meaning high church or low church) has ceased to be the primary unifying principle of our communion while our common worship itself remains unifying.

Theologically, I rank the hierarchy of elements of conformity in this way. I would place sharing the Good News of Salvation and the uniqueness of Christ (Matthew 28:18ff) which we call evangelism, alongside Christ's command to love our neighbor and be an aid and comfort to the poor, those in prison, the young and the old which we call service to others (Matthew 25) as the key unifying elements upon which the missionary church stands. In other words, God has a mission of reconciliation, and the key unifying nature of the church is to be found in our undertaking together the work of that mission. Then come the secondary unifying principles for Anglicans, which help us gather ideas and concepts around these first principles. These are the scriptures, creeds, historic councils, the threefold order of ministry, and prayer book worship as elements of the utmost concern to all in the communion. Entwined and linked to every one of these elements are the two primary Sacraments of the Anglican Church: Baptism and the Eucharist. They impart, "grace unearned and undeserved."[125] They are the two Sacraments of the Gospel given by Christ to his Church. Yet another lower level are the other "sacramental rites evolved in the church under the guidance of the Holy Spirit."[126] The Prayer Book Catechism goes on to say that while they are a means of grace in our tradition, marriage and the other sacramental rites "are not necessary for all persons in the same way that Baptism and Eucharist are."[127]

We are unified but the things we normally spend our time on are the things of less importance in terms of a focus upon our mission imperative. We might then consider the topic of marriage in its appropriate sacramental space within the life of the church locally and the communion globally. Is it important? Yes. Does the conflict on marriage merit the divergence of resources being expended through lawsuits, time, energy, the loss of membership, and the depletion of energy for the proclamation of the Gospel? I think not.

Archbishop of Canterbury Robert Runcie, not unlike our own counterparts today, faced a similarly trying time for the Anglican Communion. In my view the issues that faced Runcie locally were the disaffection between the Conservative Party of British politics and the Church of England, social change and the lack of response by governments including his own, ecumenical challenges and relationships with Roman Catholicism, the ordination of women in England, and global church struggles with theological colonialism.

Into this sea of change and challenge he spoke these words at the 1988 Lambeth Conference.

Are we being called through events and their theological interpretation to move from independence to interdependence? If we answer yes, then we cannot dodge the question of how this is to be given "flesh": how is our interdependence articulated and made effective; how is it to be structured?... We need to have confidence that authority is not dispersed to the point of dissolution and ineffectiveness... Let me put it in starkly simple terms: do we really want unity within the Anglican Communion? Is our worldwide family of Christians worth bonding together? Or is our paramount concern the preservation of promotion of that particular expression of Anglicanism which has developed within the culture of our own province?... I believe we still need the Anglican Communion. But we have reached the stage in the growth of the Communion when we must begin to make radical choices, or growth will imperceptibly turn to decay. I believe the choice between independence and interdependence, already set before us as a Communion in embryo twenty-five years ago, is quite simply the choice between unity or gradual fragmentation.[128]

What I believe Archbishop Runcie was saying is that if we are to live together in communion, as an Anglican Communion (I would even be so bold as to say an Episcopal Church), we must be willing to not only do ministry together but we must listen to one another and make our pilgrim way with one another through issues that threaten to divide us. We cannot run away from the other—for there is no communion in that at all. It is precisely when disaffected people present themselves to God in Jesus Christ that transformation occurs. Therefore, we must in some manner, some way, say "No" to the ever dividing nature of humanity that seeks to boost ego over community.

This is more eloquently stated in the 2004 Windsor Report as the authors reflect on Runcie's statement. They write, "It is by listening to, and interacting with, voices from as many different parts of the family as possible that the church discovers what its unity and communion really mean."[129] In my opinion, finding a way to be unified in mission means not walking away from one another at the exact moment in which we may actually come to know one another in a deeper way. While we differ in many different ways theologically and across different cultural contexts, it is precisely at this moment that we should embrace one another. Unity and interdependence mean that we are self-differentiated, claiming our context and view while at the same time embracing and working together with those who differ. Unity and interdependence are called "both/and" in the business world; we more commonly call it the Anglican way or the *via media*.

Are there fundamental limits to this autonomy? As I have received the teaching of the Church, the limits I seek to preserve encompass the above statements. Our unity finds itself in a mission of proclamation of the Gospel of Salvation and unique presentation of God in Christ Jesus and then in the creeds of the Church, the priority and formational work of scripture, apostolic worship, the threefold ordered ministry in mutual ministry with the laity especially through the sacraments of Baptism and Eucharist.

Yet we must honor the fact that, in reality, we do not all agree. We are not unified and there are emotions and personal investment in our opinions. As one blogger posted: "I am ok as long as I don't have to change my principles." Unity as an effective instrument for mission is more than simply reordering our thinking and living with toleration for our neighbor and our neighbor's ideas.

Many people today are speaking about the work of reconciliation as a Christian value that speaks to this notion of unity. My own diocese has chosen the word reconciliation as a value, stating: "We are reconciled to Christ and to one another." Archbishop of Canterbury Justin Welby has made reconciliation one of his three goals.

As I ponder the idea of reconciliation as the keystone to unity, I think we may be a bit confused. I think when most of us speak about reconciliation, we really are thinking about conciliation. Conciliation is the work of an individual to overcome their distrust or animosity towards others. It is the work of building friendships and goodwill among the members of groups. This is good work indeed! But conciliation is not the same as the Christian value of reconciliation. So what is the difference?

So let's begin with a little bit of scripture. In Matthew 5: 21-14, Jesus speaks about a "new righteousness" that must characterize his followers. To even call a brother "fool" is akin to murder and worthy of hell, Jesus says. We are forbidden to attend worship ("bring your gift to the altar") if we find ourselves not reconciled to our brother or sister. We must first be reconciled before attending worship. And we must not wait for them to come to us. If they are angry with us, Jesus says it is still our responsibility to skip church, find our sister, and be reconciled.

In Matthew 18:15-20, Jesus says, "Let such a one [someone who sins against you] be to you as a Gentile and tax collector." Biblical scholar Richard Hayes notes that "Gentile" is not code for "stop trying to be reconciled," but rather never stop trying to be reconciled.[130] In Matthew, Gentiles and tax collectors are part of the mission field, i.e., the ones to whom the *ekklesia* (church) is sent with the message of reconciliation. And so, if a brother storms off, we "seek out and save the lost," which is the very thing Jesus does for us. This is what it means to treat someone as a "tax collector" —they are part of the mission field. I mention this passage in particular because it is highly misunderstood, and people love quoting it to sanction their refusal to be reconciled with others.

Paul in 1 Corinthians 1:1-25, 3:1-17, and 12:12-26, is dealing with groups who are at war with one another over who "thinks" correctly and who thinks incorrectly. Just like the Corinthians we like to claim that we are in the "this" camp or the "that" camp. I believe that Paul is clear that in God's eyes all camps are illusions. We are one body—God sees us as one.

Paul in Ephesians carries the idea of reconciliation further in 2:11-21. Here Paul gives the image of the "dividing wall of hostility" that God has already torn down. It's worth noting that whatever differences exist between Christians are small potatoes when compared to the historic differences between Jews and Gentiles, formerly mortal enemies, now as Christians joining to form *one* church. Remember Paul himself participated in stoning of Christians before he was converted. Think for a moment about the gulf that we believe has existed between God and man. How often we lose sight of this reality.

In Romans 15:7 and 2 Corinthians 5:17-21, Paul writes: "Welcome one another as Christ has welcomed you." "God has reconciled us and so be reconciled." Here we see that our work of reconciliation flows from God's work of reconciliation—we do not create it. Discipleship is about aligning our lives with the truth of God's reconciliation. Therefore, our unity is always and in everything an icon of our relationship with God. If we are not reconciled with one another, then we are not living in the truth of God's reconciliation with us. Everywhere there is division within the Christian community—a sign of our sinfulness and distance from God's reconciling act. Even then and in that moment God continues to unite us. "Jerusalem, Jerusalem, how long have I longed to gather you under my wing. (Luke 13.34ff)

Paul in 2 Corinthians 5:20 and Galatians 6:10, and Jesus in John's Gospel 13:35 offer still more visions of reconciliation. We wrongly assume that the best way to "reach the world" is to *directly* serve the world. But this is, at best, a half-truth. The biblical teaching is that *only* as we live as a reconciled, loving Body will the outside world be compelled to glorify and worship God. Unity is an essential instrument in mission; it is, in fact, a key sacramental vessel for mission. This is why Christians love all people, but *especially* our church family (Galatians 6:10). Only as we love one another does the world know God (John 13:35). This is what it means to be an ambassador of God's reconciliation. Clean *the inside* of the cup (church), Jesus said, and the outside will get clean, too (world).

I offer this mediation on scripture because the mission of reconciliation is the heart of the Christian Gospel. Reconciliation has both a vertical dimension and a horizontal one. The vertical dimension speaks to God's relationship with humanity. God has been reconciled to humanity through the death and resurrection of Jesus Christ. I believe this applies to all people, not just some. It also applies to the "world" in general. This is the foundation that human beings so often reject but is, in fact, set by God as the cornerstone. (Psalm 118.22ff; Matthew 21.42) This is the Good News meant for all people. This is why Jesus is the friend of sinners. There is plenteous forgiveness and we are all reconciled to God—there is no scarcity in the Gospel.

The horizontal dimension of reconciliation speaks to humanity's relationship with our neighbor. All have been reconciled to each other through the death and resurrection of Jesus Christ (past tense). In God's eyes, our reconciliation with one another is an accomplished fact. "It is finished." (John 19:30)

The vertical dimension of reconciliation precedes the horizontal dimension. In other words, God's reconciliation with humanity and the individual creates and necessitates the individual's reconciliation with his or her neighbor. Both the vertical dimension and the horizontal dimension of reconciliation are fully the work of God. It is ultimately God's faithful reconciliation work that is revealed in us as we are faithful. God has reconciled us to one another. It is God's forgiveness to us that is revealed when we look at one another. We cannot see each other without seeing God's work in us. Thus, the church's work is to "wake up" to the truth that we have been reconciled and to live in accordance with this truth "so that the world might know" God's reconciliation, too. Our eyes are to be wide open. Thus, to borrow Alexander Schmemann's phrase, the Church lives as a reconciled people "for the life of the world."[131] As Paul says, God is making His appeal to the world through us. (2 Corinthians 5:20)

The implication is that when we say things like, *reconciliation is the work of the church*, what we really mean is, *waking up to the theological truth that God has already reconciled us to one another and the world to Himself is the work of the church*. We don't create reconciliation. We wake up to and increasingly embrace reconciliation. Reconciliation with one another is not something we need. What we need is to stop all of our self-righteous, stubborn, and illusion-based behaviors that keep us blind to the truth that already we are One.

To this I add a brief reflection on Acts 15, which I think is informative. Sometimes we forget how very real the issue of circumcision was in the early church. Here was a defining issue of their day. The issue in question is, "in light of the fact that Jews and Gentiles are reconciled with God and one another, what must we require of the Gentiles to remain members in good standing?" Note verse 28. "It has seemed good to the Holy Spirit and to us." . . . It has seemed good to the Holy Spirit? The small list of things the Jews require of Gentiles they still hold lightly. The most they can say of what they require is "This seems about right. I think." Reconciliation means we hold our opinions lightly. "This seems to be best," is our maximum level of confidence. As Paul said, "we know only in part."

The Church is a mystical body of strange, different, sick, beloved and desperate people reconciled to God and each other simply because God thinks it's a swell idea. The Church is not a group of competent God-warriors struggling to unite itself through ideological consensus because one group has it exactly right. Such a cause will mean the death of a living church. "Knowledge (opinions) puffs up;

but love builds up." "Let each be convinced (of his opinions) in his own mind," says Paul in 1 Corinthians 8:1 and Romans 14:5.

In the recognition that God is the reconciling agent in our midst we all come closer to God and to one another. Furthermore, the witness of such a reconciled community draws into itself the beautiful and wonderful diverse people of God. The Church to come will be a church at ease with itself. The future Church will be a church unified and one that works across boundaries of confessional exactitude.

CHAPTER NINE
The Future of Connection

"We cannot live only for ourselves. A thousand fibers connect us with our fellow men; and among those fibers, as sympathetic threads, our actions run as causes, and they come back to us as effects."
— The Rev. Henry Melville, <u>Anglican Preacher</u>, June 12, 1855

Connection is the third of the principles that guides the future Church. The first followers of Jesus were connected intimately with one another. There was first the band of 12 and women who traveled with Jesus. Then there were the pairs that Jesus sent out to do ministry. Then we see early on in the Pauline Epistles that small communities are growing up together as parts of the larger whole. In these early decades the church was an intimate and connected community of committed individuals. This would of course grow over the first centuries of the Christian movement and larger churches would be formed out of a collaborative of smaller networked Christian communities. With the fall of Rome, the Church stepped in as the governing agent and so the churches became places where order and safety were found. By The Middle Ages the church was at the center of the town. Markets blossomed within their walls. People transacted business. It was a focal point for community life. The Church continued to be at the hub of life through the reformation. In the new world the church was one with the state providing order and stability in wilderness settings. The Protestant Church in America was the light on the hill. It was building nothing less than the Kingdom of God. This movement would spread into the high water mark years of the 1950's when the west achieved high attendance and suburbia rapidly expanded the footprint of the Church's mission. As the west participated in global mission work they planted churches at the center of community life in villages and in towns. If you visit Africa you will see that it is the church that is again a large part of the infrastructure of society: schools, clinics, and orphanages. Following the Haiti earthquake and flooding, international organizations turned to the Anglican Church to help disperse much needed resources and supplies because the church in Haiti was the most networked organization on the ground.

The future Church is connected. Technology and the failure of hierarchical structures of government to care for individuals will mean or guarantee that the future living Church will be as networked and an intimate part of people's lives as in the first Christian communities.

I believe that throughout the Gospels it is revealed that Jesus loved his followers as friends and that he intended that they in turn love the world as friends. One time Jesus was teaching his followers about his relationship with God and what that meant about his relationship with his followers. (John 15) Jesus tells them that he is intimately connected with God. He gives them an image of a vine with branches that is bearing fruit. He says, "Being in relationship with God is about being connected. When we are all connected to one another and to God we change the world—we bear fruit. Fruit doesn't just happen—it comes from being connected to God, just like fruit and a vine." Jesus tells them that those who follow him are to be connected and that this connection and their work to love each other will change lives. "Joy comes from being loved and loving others, joy comes from being connected to God, to others, and to me," Jesus says. So Jesus tells them: "This is my commandment, that you love one another as I have loved you."

Then Jesus tells them that they are his friends. He reminds them economies of the world work in a lot of different ways. In the world of Jesus' day there were servants and there were masters. This is true for our day as well. He tells his followers that their worth and their value in the world around them is always and everywhere going to be based upon what they can do, how they can serve, and what they can trade. He then makes it clear that this is not the way God works. God loves. God loves them. Jesus loves them. They are his friends and he needs nothing from them—they are not servants and he is not the master. In John's Gospel, more than any other, Jesus and his followers are bound together by the commandment of loving each other. Their affection will show the world that they are connected to Jesus and through Jesus to God. Affection was the binding tie.

Paul picks this theme of connectedness up in his writing. In his letters to the Romans and the Corinthians he speaks about love and friendship among the followers of Jesus. He tells those communities to whom he is speaking that the quality of their love is "genuine affection." (Romans, I and II Corinthians) The Rev. Dr. Scott Bader-Saye, professor of Ethics and Dean of Faculty at Seminary of the Southwest, in a presentation on *affection* connected Paul's teaching with that of C. S. Lewis. C. S. Lewis talks about the quality of this love and connectedness in his book *The Four Loves*.[132] C. S. Lewis offers that the bonds of affection that we have for one another are essential in connecting us to God. We can have agape love but it is limited because it can be one directional.[133] Love that is connected to God, as in Jesus and Paul's teaching, is mutual—it flows between all those involved. We might have friendship as one of the loves; but most often friendship is something shared between those who are most like us.[134] This has been shown to be true in the most recent Pew Research poll on the politicization of America. It finds that not only are like -minded people likely to live in the same places and like the same things, they are also more likely to hang out with friends who believe similar things.[135] This means that friendship can easily lead to isolating communities. The mission of the Gospel is for everyone and the Christian community is open to everyone. The third love is Eros and this is intimate love and even more exclusive.[136] Affection, Lewis offers, is the broadest kind of love. It is the kind that Paul encourages all followers of Jesus to have. It is the kind of love that is the most natural and is required in all the others. Bader-Saye believes that in affection we have the broadest ability to love.[137] He writes that we have the ability for mutuality and it is not dependent upon friendship, infatuation, or attraction.[138] He says that affection makes possible all the rest.[139] "Affection is connection", wrote American author and economist Wendell Berry.[140] Affection is the quality of relationship that Jesus speaks about and the quality of relationships that people are seeking as they yearn in the midst of a disjointed and disconnected world.

What is true theologically and spiritually is true technologically. Today people place a high value on connecting to their peers, resources, entertainment, and finances; therefore, relationship communities that are Christian will place high importance on the work of connection.

What I have learned from the maker movement is that it takes the same amount of energy and time to customize as it does to mass-produce items. What we are seeing is a rise in personal fabrication that then is marketed and connected to friends and neighbors. We are in the midst of what is called a small batch movement. The small batch bourbon, beer, and bakery movements are good examples of how innovators are connecting to their peers. Scale is no longer the quintessential goal of business. More and more people are baking, distilling, and creating businesses in their homes and selling to their friends. What is coming into view is a society and that is restructuring itself organically. This is our mission field. Bob Johansen writes, "In fields as diverse as education, governance, science, and health, amplified individuals are boldly engaged in de-institutionalizing production, taking value out of traditional ways of organizing, and actively building alternative platforms and tools."[141] Children are writing computer programs, creating art, building their own networks. Adults are crafting things in their garages. Technology and communication tools are shifting monthly. New micro-economy and secondary markets are growing. New currencies and new forms of connecting with investors are changing start-ups with crowd-sourced technology. Science projects and experiments run 24 hours a day using people across the globe—many are volunteers. People are relating and co-creating at a colossal level.

Johansen comments on this saying: "The future lies in micro-contributions by large networks of people creating value on a scale previously unthinkable, bringing sociality and social connectivity back into our economic transactions, in the process redefining notions of rewards, incentives, growth, and currencies."[142] This will affect how our Christian communities work and how they build relationships. This means that Christian communities, thanks to technology and the maker movement, can exist on limited small budgets with few staff and still reach large numbers of people through their ministry.[143] The hallmark of the Christian community of the future is that they will connect people and most of all connect people to God.

The living Church will be a church of affection because connection is what makes all the other pieces work together. The quality of the community discussed above only functions in a networked society. You will see that the important shape of our communities will also depend upon the network of very real relationships.

This network is apparent in one way when we look at the rise in congregations starting new communities. Connections take on a physical nature as congregations create their own web. The younger generations of believers and seekers are interested in very real connection and relationships especially as they navigate their world. Younger clergy have a great interest in this mission field. Nadia Bolz Webber, founder of House for All Sinners and Saints in Denver, does not have an office but has office hours all over the city, shares worship space with another church, and does service ministry in collaboration with other nonprofit organizations. She and her community are plugged into the world around them—networking, sharing, and multiplying. I have been talking about this since I began teaching about generations in the 1990's. Evangelicals and Protestants are reporting surges in this trend of networked communities.[144] These are networks of churches connected and sharing resources. These are churches starting second sites and planting new communities. You might think of these new expressions of church as small batch Christian Communities or missional communities. Non-denominational churches, which are freed from structural concerns, are leading the way in many respects. A few Episcopal Churches in our own diocese are beginning to think this way. Today we have eight second-site communities in the Diocese of Texas. A church networking and connecting into another part of the broader community began each site. I expect that while some will continue to multiply, and others will not be successful, this will be a growing trend across the future Church.

There are many reasons why this is essential beyond the desire for smaller and more intimate community settings. One is the pure cost of building and structures. The other is the lack of availability of large spaces. Still another is that people are less and less likely to travel distances for church. There is a desire for story sharing and building personal narratives. Staff costs—compensation and benefits are a great burden.

What made big news in 2014 were the results of a multi-site report created by the think tank called Leadership Network in 2013.[145] The findings show that multi-site congregations while small, grow as much as 14% per site per year. Because of the size and the personality of these communities, more people participate in leadership. Multi-site communities depend on lay leadership more than clergy. The increase in the movement is strong over the last five years and continues that upward trend. Multi-site communities are found in urban, suburban, and rural settings.

A large number of multi-sites are created when one church combines with another.[146] We see this last characteristic in Houston where St. Luke's Church took on and recreated ministry at the Gethsemane Methodist campus—which was a formerly a free-standing parish. Now St. Luke's shares resources, runs ministry and service projects out of the Gethsemane campus. They have multiplied their connections and networks across the city and into areas St. Luke's never would have reached alone. Large congregations have been the "pioneers," but today congregations as small as 50 are experimenting with the multi-site model. The model is growing in popularity in the U.S. but is also an international movement.[147] The Church's connectivity, though, will not be limited to multi-sites. Small multi-sites are the future now but there is a web of relationships yet to be explored with an infinite number of possibilities and combinations.

The Church will build interconnectivity and networks across the mission field through a variety of electronic media. The church will need to build networks linking to and participating in the digital native's networks. Everyone born in the new millennium will be a *digital native*. This will be true for the rich and the poor alike. I was struck when I visited Southern Malawi in 2009 and saw that everyone had a cell phone. They might not have had running water or indoor plumbing but they had a cell phone. When speaking recently to a doctor at one of the finest medical schools in the country about telemedicine and accessibility he talked to me about visiting the poorest widow in East Africa in a hut who had a stool and little else— but she had a cell phone. We are moving into an era of unparalleled accessibility and connectivity. If you are not a digital native, if you didn't grow up in the digital age, then you are called a *digital migrant*.

Warning: the paragraph that follows is chocked full of statistics. I promise not to do this again. If you are a digital migrant you might not realize what the lay of the land really is. Hold on to your Apple II and Tandy TRS-80's (the first marketed personal computers) because time has flown by. Here are the facts. In 1977, the first home computers made their way off assembly lines. By 1982 "The Computer" was named Machine of the Year by *Time Magazine*. Just as video killed the radio star my 1980 friends, the PC is dead—just a paperweight taking up room on your desk. As of January 2014, Pew Research reports that 91% of Americans have cell phones and 58% of them are smartphones. Even 74% of those over 65 have a cell phone. Even 84% of households with incomes under $30,000 per year have a cell phone. Pew Research also reports that 42% of adults own a tablet.[148] Here is another shocker: 74% of all adults living in the U.S. use social networking sites online. 71% use Facebook alone.[149] Less than forty years ago nobody had a home computer. Twenty years ago, in 1995, only 14% of people used an Internet it wasn't very accessible or user friendly. In January of 2014, 87% of all Americans are on the web.[150] Nearly two-thirds of cell phone owners now use their phone to get access to the Internet. This means that the majority of Americans are untethered from their mice, laptops, and desktop computers.[151] The Internet, our contacts, and the crowd are accessible at all times and in all places because we are plugged into the network.

Over the last decade I have watched the emergence of the Church into this new digital age. Man, it is slow; for example, in 2014 the website is just now marginally something most congregations realize they need to have. Getting congregations to understand how important connections through electronic media are for people has been, as we say in Texas, "like pushing string up a hill." Forget updating that answering machine (which probably now resides on call notes) you better get service times, directions, and beautiful pictures up on Google maps. Leaders and their congregations need to be prepared to be reviewed by a visitor on Yelp. Unfortunately, today the majority of churches and Church leaders do not use social media at all, despite the fact that 74% of the mission field does this as a normal part of everyday life. Most digital natives only go an hour without using a device when they are sleeping. If we are successful in navigating the mission context of our day we will see that in the span of the next 20 years, or by 2035, the majority of the people who are digital migrants will have passed the baton to a church that will be made up largely of digital natives.

Think for a moment about how websites are designed. A decade ago it was complicated to design your own page. Pages themselves were slow and difficult to create and sometimes more difficult to navigate. Then Blogspot, Google, Myspace, and others began to make templates easier to use. People began to create for themselves. The web designers built and designed the first pages on platforms that would be easily navigated by people using their desktop computers. Today designers begin their design with mobile devices in mind. Today, web designers make rich multi-platform html5 websites for your phone and tablet that also work on your desktop/laptop. I'm sure almost every church website does not render to the mobile devices that every amplified human uses. Just about the time we all get websites the culture has moved to new designs and platforms. We are going to have to get quicker on our participation in cultural change and at the same time quicker to discard those things that are obsolete.[152]

I think being connected digitally is the newest member of Maslow's hierarchy of needs. Proposed by Abraham Maslow in 1943 in a paper entitled "A Theory of Human Motivation" published in *Psychological Review*, his hierarchy of needs offered a list of what he considered basics human necessities of sustainable life.[153] His theory included: physiology, safety, belonging, self-esteem and self-actualization needs—in that order. His helpful theory tells us that we need some basic things like food, water, and sleep before we need other things. While the hierarchy's basic physiological needs can be met in the future without world-wide access to the web, it is difficult to move into the second level of motivational needs without adding connectivity and the ability to navigate digital resources as a subset of employment. The cultural move to amplify connections with coworkers, friends, and family into a network of supportive relationships is key in the third level of needs: *Love/Belonging*. After interviewing thousands of people over a ten-year period, Brené Brown, research scholar and speaker writes in her book *Daring Greatly*, "Love and belonging are irreducible needs of all men, women, and children. We're hardwired for connection—it's what gives purpose and meaning to our lives. The absence of love, belonging, and connection always leads to suffering."[154] The fourth level, *Esteem*, will not be measured without gaining respect from peers, and that will be largely dependent on electronic feedback loops that are already making their way into the relational landscape. Maslow's hierarchy is changed forever by the human work of integrating technology into its existence.

This means that the future Church will depend upon the same technology, websites and social media connections of every kind, as essential infrastructure and mission tools. Electronic connectivity is not a side project to be engaged from time to time—it is the future present. What we are doing today will not be enough for tomorrow. The opportunity to make daily connections with individuals and their friends across our cityscapes will be lost if we do not evolve. A living Church sees this as mission necessity.

Over the next 20 years we are going to see the birth of an entirely new Internet that, as it evolves, will connect humans in new ways. We as human beings are adapting and adopting the World Wide Web to fit our demanding lives and our desire for connection in real time and with a global population. In the present past we have had an Internet that was designed to pass information—to push communication.[155] We are reminded that it was not that long ago that we were using computers that filled a whole room and then we were tied to our desktops, today a computer more powerful than those that fueled the flight to the moon are carried in our hip pocket. I can easily remember the Motorola brick phone and then the palm pilot that began to make connection mobile. Today we carry the computing power of corporations in our handheld devices.

The Internet was a place created to store information. Then it became a way of passing information from one source to another. It further developed to a web, where information could be pushed and people could stake out space. In the last 5 years we have completely shifted our focus in the Episcopal Diocese of Texas to push information throughout our networks. However, in the future we will be changing our strategies again as the networking possibilities are multiplied. Yesterday the computer was the center of the experience. I had to learn how to work it and use it. I could in fact only use it on its terms. Today humans are the center of the experience.[156] Computers work more intuitively based upon how we think and how we work. We are mobile and the technology we are using is mobile and responsive to our needs. The environment in which we do ministry is no longer an environment located purely in the physical world, but within an environment of space. Think for a moment about the fact that when I was a child I grew up learning to write and then type. When I typed I had to leave two spaces after a sentence. Now the computer automatically creates the right amount of space between sentences and even corrects my spelling. Today a child knows how to use a touch screen before it knows how to spell his or her own name.[157]

In order to reach the digital natives of the future, communicate with them, and to engage them, the church must migrate into their digital world. We are moving away from the idea that the priests makes house calls and people come to a church building for spiritual direction. In the future a successful priest's ministry will rely upon how well they are able to keep up with their flock electronically—all the time—all week long. They will have to use all the tools at their disposal from text messaging to online engagement on Twitter, Facebook, Instagram or video chatting. While the medical profession is moving to discussions around telemedicine, the church remains firmly rooted in mid-century evangelism and pastoral care models. Ministry in a digitally native world will be one of connectivity on a frequent basis and not a once a week phenomenon.

There is another aspect to this digital network of relationships that will be important: that is micro contributions. Micro contribution is the ability for a group of people to complete small tasks of a much larger piece of work. Communities like Facebook, Twitter, Instagram and Flickr exist because of our micro-contributions.[158] Each person adds a little bit and a much larger community is formed. Today, the slow moving digital migrant is populating these communities. I am so sorry Church. The unfortunate truth is that the digital native has left the majority of these to create new ones. They are now contributing to Snapchat, vines, and the ever-popular Tumblr. Listen, I live with two digital natives and I can tell you in the next twenty years they will have joined, left, and joined several generations of network communities that have not even been created. All of which will exist by the sheer sharing of personal information.

The Institute for the Future has created something called a *foresight engine*. This is a program which allows hundreds of individuals to participate in what amounts to an online game, wherein they actually map out the future goals and work of an organization. Health websites gather and share information using huge webs of micro contributors. Scientists at Galaxy Zoo use contributors to help map the cosmos and classify galaxies.[159] The church is already a network of thousands of individuals across a vast geographical area yet untapped as a network of micro contributors.

The future church will take advantage of the individuals willingness to micro contribute to the health and vitality of its mission. In some small ways they already do this through social networking. Imagine though, instead of a few communications officers across the church running underfunded programs, we have a multitude of communicators sharing information about their church. Imagine the future church where people share with friends their activities and participation in local community activities. These micro contributions will vary from communications about events to sharing exciting news as the events occur. Digital natives are already doing this with their friends as they talk about youth group, mission trips, and service projects. The digital native naturally shares the things they are excited about thereby, becoming a micro contributor to the overall health of the mission. Micro contributions will far outpace the capacity of a communication officer in a community or at a diocese. More importantly, what will begin to happen is that the lines between program ministry and life will blur in such a way that the disciple's life and the life of the church are not separated any longer.

The Church is focused on an old network economy. This is where the Church pays for individuals to be professional ministers and to network the congregation. This era is over. The future Church is a church that thrives on nonmonetary rewards for service and ministry. People today become micro contributors because they gain a feeling of community from participating. They gain in their relationships. They gain by "belonging."[160] They also will do the work on their time, imperfectly, and through their own experience and provide their own witness. This is more authentic. The rest of the culture has become accustomed to homemade video and communications that are real and not staged. The church will have to become accustomed to letting down its guard a bit in order to engage in the micro contributions that are available to it. Yet deep inside of this is a reality that I think we as a Church have forgotten, and that is that Church in the end is not a business but a web of connections. The reward of participation in Church life, in Christian community, has always been a reward far beyond what we receive by attending worship. Micro contributions and their desire for nonmonetary rewards reminds us that if we as Christian communities truly invest in work that is transformative, we will have an army of communicators helping us to get the word out about the good things that God is doing.

The connected Church will be a church that understands that micro contributions and non-monetary rewards work best at the grassroots level. The world economy is shifting. The model that the Church is deeply rooted in is an industrial model of the last century. The big company was king and the Church mimicked the Industrial Revolution with its magnates. Larger than life preachers with larger than life churches have been the goal. The big Church with the large-scale mission and ministry has been a foundation stone of many dioceses. Some believe these will go away. I don't think so. I think they will remain, as long and especially if, they engage in a disbursement model. That being said, if they don't engage in a disbursement model, I believe they will have difficulty navigating the future waters of a VUCA world. (More on that later.) There will be no church, just as there will be no organization that is too big to fail. The micro contributor and the micro economic models are shifting and changing the landscape. Strong networks of many individuals will outperform and out transform larger Churches without the price tag.

In the world of commerce we see companies like EBay and Etsy bringing small batch and small competitors into the marketplace. We see a growing number of small batch Christian communities but one of the complaints has been that because they are not large they are therefore not successful. Old thinking is the church is only successful if it has a lot of people. They *are* successful in meeting individuals where they are, and taking advantage of the micro mission field, where individual transformation and the transformation of the local community are prized over juggernaut type churches.

Industries are re-making themselves locally and the future Church will borrow from this model. There is a new maker generation and technology is catching up, so they can actually turn their home office into a manufacturing center. A good example is the story of Lego Arms.[161] Lego[162] doesn't provide all the pieces that the public wants for their toys—in this case weapons. Lego doesn't make weapons. A father and son decided to make these for their own use. Then as they shared with friends a small company was born to build and provide these for fellow Lego fans. Today it has moved from a small manufacturing mail order company operated in their garage to a successful micro business. This shows that when people are committed to ideas and visions they building new commons for innovation, new platforms for funding products, new production tools, and new delivery methods.

The connected Church of the future will be a church that uses its network of individuals to build new social commons. The connected Church will enable and raise up visionaries to see new mission opportunities for service, for evangelism, and for stewardship. The connected Church will organically raise up digital commons and then plant real life communities. New platforms will be developed to help the connected disciples work together to make people's lives better. While industry will diversify through microeconomics, the connected church will diversify through micro mission.

What we see today in the economic world is that a person is no longer a designer, or an engineer, or a production line worker, or a shopper. Instead one person can be all of these things and be their own company too. With the invention of the smart phone and its new app, called Square, which allows people to zip their credit card and transfer money from one individual to another, commerce is taking place anywhere and at anytime.[163] The future Church will be mobile, can take shape anywhere, at anytime, and with any number of people, without the structures of the present church to inhibit its growth as a necessity of a bygone era. Suffice it to say that the future looks more like the first century church than the high water mark of the Catholic Church in The Middle Ages or the high water mark of the Protestant church with its professionalism of the last century.

For the church the questions will be how do we truly embrace the ministry of all the baptized and the use the various orders of ministry? Instead of a church/community organized around people with "funny" collars, how will we capitalize on the maker culture? People want to be micro contributors and participate in shaping the life of their church. TEC and all other mainline denominations will be challenged to move away from the idea that the "people" are those that get ministered *to* by the "professional sacramentalist." Instead TEC must begin to think critically about capturing the new desire and energy to be involved (not as a volunteer) as a leader and co-creator. No longer is the Church to be led by clergy and supported by people. The future Church will be supported by clergy and led by the people.

The denominational Church still operates predominantly with one building and one priest. We have an opportunity to see that the lightweight structures, networked culture, and new methods of organization offer a whole new model of community and commons making. We used to say in the 1980's that the big churches were getting bigger and the small churches were getting smaller and were going to close. Quite simply put, we were completely uninterested in a church that had 150 people—unless we believed it would grow. Today we need to learn from the small church *and* the big church. We need to imagine cooperative common making for small churches and big churches. The VUCA world is an equal opportunity change agent. We must embrace new models.[164]

The connected Church will be a church that is multi-site and diverse. It will be distributed over the mission landscape. It will be electronically connected and be a church where the digital native can find a home. These small communities will thrive on micro contributors where professional church workers and non-professional disciples participate together in making a full expression of the church's mission. This micro mission will be lightweight with pliable infrastructure. The connected Church will be a church with low overhead for coordination and have "smaller, lighter, and smarter components."[165]

CHAPTER TEN
Autopoietic Communities

"You, sent out beyond your recall,
go to the limits of your longing.
Embody me.
Flare up like a flame
and make big shadows I can move in."
—Rainer Maria Rilke, poet

Niels Bohr and Werner Heisenberg were physicists. They had a problem. They were trying to understand the universe, but every time they would pursue an answer to a question about the universe in an atomic experiment, the universe proposed something that, despite sound reasoning from acceptable premises, consistently led to conclusions that were logically unacceptable and/or self-contradictory.[166] Their discourses were, of course, the beginning of quantum theory. Margaret Wheatley points out in her book *Leadership and the New Science: Discovering Order in a Chaotic World*: "Their problem was not only intellectual but involved an intense emotional and existential experience."[167] The world they knew, the rules of order they functioned under, and the world they were recording at the microscopic level were completely different. Heisenberg spoke of it this way: "I remember discussions with Bohr which went through many hours till very late at night and ended almost in despair; and when at the end of the discussion I went alone for a walk in the neighboring park I repeated to myself again and again the question: Can nature possibly be so absurd as it seemed to us in these atomic experiments?"[168] He also said this, "Every experiment destroys some of the knowledge of the system which was obtained by previous experiments."[169]

What Heisenberg and Bohr's experience has taught me is that the world is filled with explanations for why things are the way they are, and those explanations often contradict one another. Both Daniel Kahneman in his Nobel Prize winning text on economics entitled *Thinking, Fast and Slow* and Nassim Nicholas Taleb in his magnum opus *Antifragile: Things That Gain From Disorder* illustrate that the world is complex beyond our imagination. The world's complexity fools us into seeing linear reactions that are only a small portion of the reality swirling around us. They may not even be linear. Kahneman wrote, "Our comforting conviction that the world makes sense rests on a secure foundation: our almost unlimited ability to ignore our ignorance."[170]

Every system is complex with a large amount of variability and interrelated parts of different scale and magnitude. It takes individuals who lead organizations a long time to step back, accept the paradoxes and contradictions of their findings, and then begin to reframe the questions.

Acceptance is never without some amount of pain. Margaret Wheatley reflects on the process the physicists experienced, "Its effect on physicists' view of reality was truly shattering. The new physics necessitated profound changes in concepts of space, time, matter, object, and cause and effect; and because these concepts are so fundamental to our way of experiencing the world, their transformation came as a great shock."[171] Heisenberg said, "The violent reaction to the recent development of modern physics can only be understood when one realizes that here the foundations of physics have started moving; and that this motion has caused the feeling that the ground would be cut from science."[172] Wheatley adeptly applies this revelation to organizations. It is time that we apply them to the church organization, always recognizing as she points out, "The story speaks with a chilling familiarity. Each of us recognizes the feelings this tale describes, of being mired in the habit of solutions that once worked yet that are now totally inappropriate, of having rug after rug pulled from beneath us."[173]

I grew up in church ministry believing that everything was magically connected to the Average Sunday Attendance (ASA) of my congregation. What had happened is that in the early eighties the idea of congregational development became an important concept for those who deeply wanted to change the downward trend in church. Before this time, diocesan leadership had pretty much treated every priest and every congregation the same. Books and theories began to circulate about congregations and church sizes (which will be addressed later). There was and is a darker side to this theory, and that is that we, as a church, began to make our ASA *the* most important measurement tool for health and vitality. Everything gets focused on raising your attendance. After twenty years of this focus within our church, the ASA number is still the most sacred sign of supposed health for the church. Leaders base our feelings of success and our feelings of failure upon that number.

I first became aware of this when I was reading Bill Bryson's book entitled *At Home: A Short History of Private Life*. The book is about a home that he purchased in England. It was an old vicarage. Bryson describes each room of the house, its purpose, and its history. It is well worth the read. The house had been built for the local Anglican priest sometime around 1851. Among other things, Bryson is interested by a peculiar statistic that he discovers in his research about the home, its resident, and the church. In 1851 the Church of England decided to find out how many of its folks attended church and so they did a survey of all the churches to find out. What they discovered was that only 20% of the people went to church.[174] What an odd thing, I thought to myself. I couldn't figure it out, but I knew something was wrong. What I realized was that I had been *assuming* that somehow before I came along, everyone had just gone to church every Sunday. Now if you stop and think about it for a moment you would realize that, of course, not everyone went to church on Sunday. Didn't everyone go to church, every Sunday, in England of all places? I would have guessed 90% of the people went to church in 1851. In my mind, I had always thought that there were churches full of people. And, it was just my unhappy luck that I was born and called into ministry in a time when very few people went to church.

This little bit of information really blew my mind. I began to ask a lot of questions that seem perfectly natural now but were at the time like waking up after having time traveled from the 1950s. In my struggle to grasp this new reality, I became painfully aware that my basic concepts, language, and whole way of thinking about community life were inadequate to describe the context I now inhabited. That was it. I had inherited a wonderful idea of church. Church was the place where every Sunday Mom and Dad took little Andy, along with all the other neighbors and their children. I began to realize that it was perhaps true that Sunday morning attendance in the 1920s until the 1960s had been the high-water mark of Protestant church attendance in the U.S. But by no means was it normative to the Christian experience. I realized that I had a lot of shame about the ASA numbers in my church as a young priest. I did not feel good enough since my numbers didn't match the magical church ideal of the ever-growing church with its ever-growing ASA. I also realized there was a whole lot more to the reality of Christian community than a church and its ASA number.

While I do believe that the average Sunday attendance numbers of any given congregation can actually predict a particular economic formula for a particular type of church, I have decided that a focus on ASA can be detrimental to the health of the Church at large. In reading Margaret Wheatley's book, I realized that the way we use averages themselves do funny things and can play tricks on our ability to understand real cause and effect. Big numbers are easy to manipulate and get our minds around. However, when we look at the big numbers, we may miss micro information that is essential in understanding community and cultural dynamics. Wheatley believes that in the "small fluctuations" of life and relationships there is a lot of "ambiguity and complexity" that affects the world in which we move and have our being.[175] If you are a large organization, you really don't have time for such detail. Dioceses have to use averages and large frameworks to avoid the complexity of congregational life and context, because such large entities do not have enough staff to deal with the diversity. Wheatley argues that large organizations actually "shield" themselves from the details that are life giving.[176] The problem is that growth, energy, and innovation come out of the micro connections oftentimes hidden within the complexity of the system. In point of fact, the very health of the whole organization rests upon the health and vitality of the smallest relationships. It is out of these micro relationships that creativity and innovation spring, giving life to the whole.

Taleb, in his book *Black Swan*, amplifies theories regarding the reality that randomness and variability are very real participants in making history. He says, "History is opaque. You see what comes out, not the script that produces events. The generator of historical events is different from the events themselves, much as the minds of the gods cannot be read just by witnessing their deeds."[177] He also explains the reality that we have difficulty not categorizing everything. He says, "Because our minds need to reduce information, we are more likely to try to squeeze a phenomenon into the Procrustean bed[178] of a crisp and known category (amputating the unknown), rather than suspend categorization, and make it tangible. Thanks to our detections of false patterns, along with real ones, what is random will appear less random and more certain—our overactive brains are more likely to impose the wrong, simplistic, narrative than no narrative at all."[179] Clear as mud? Did he just use Procrustean bed in a sentence? That is a brobdingnagian concept Taleb! Let us take a moment to read it again.

Kahneman agrees with Taleb, and I am afraid, adds even more suspicion to the way in which we tell our stories about history. He writes, "The confidence that individuals have in their beliefs depends mostly on the quality of the story they can tell about what they see, even if they see little."[180] This is a principle he calls WYSIATI: What

You See Is All There Is.[181] Kahneman says that the systematic part of our brains is lazy and so we typically jump to conclusions based upon intuitive impressions rather than difficult thinking.[182] You can believe this is not true but the Nobel Prize Winning Economist has four hundred pages of in-depth research that says your bias about his opinion is based upon intuition and not reality.

All this reading began to make me think a bit differently about the church history that I inherited. I probably should say it made me rethink how I had ordered my intuition about the Church history I learned. Church history is taught in a linear fashion, and because you can only see what you are taught (and WYSIATI) it is no wonder that we have developed an over-simplified understanding of our church, its origins, and its perfect trajectory to this moment in time. The defense of new prayer books and liturgical movements has amplified the notion of a linear church history. Such a history goes something like this: we have always been heading in this direction so we have naturally arrived here doing exactly what was always predictable. Of course, according to Taleb and Kahneman's suspicions about observation and history, this is crazy thinking. It is actually called a *hindsight bias*. Again Kahneman writes, "The mind that makes up narratives about the past is a sense-making organ... A general limitation of the human mind is its imperfect ability to reconstruct past states of knowledge, or beliefs that have changed."[183] If we are going to ponder what the future may look like, we have to come to terms with the fact that the past probably was not much like what are intuitive biases tell us it was like.

Let us look again, as if for the first time, at the formation of church. The earliest texts seem to reveal that the first followers of Jesus were people who lived in a variety of communities. They lived in urban and rural areas. Many of the first followers of Jesus were Jews and plenty of others were not. There were a lot of different people reacting to the teachings of Jesus and other reform movements. This intermingling of diverse people, on diverse social levels, each living out their faith, created an environment of energized innovation and creativity. This is certainly a vision of the early followers that is recorded and remarked upon in the Gospels, the Book of Acts, and the Epistles. I think we can also say that the Jesus movement was, in its earlier days, a kind of subculture within the culture, and went unnoticed for quite a while. Yet, the Jesus movement grew in every social context with a multiplicity of incarnations. It was not like Jesus was resurrected, the Holy Spirit came down, and boom there were churches.

The letters of Paul to the different communities offer an early and clear record that one way individuals got together was in their own homes. Paul is continually remarking on "so-and-so's house." Paul's letters are often addressed to a church, but it is also true that within each city church, let's say Corinth for instance, there were a number of small house churches. In Paul's letter to Philemon it is clear that his house church was one of many in the city of Colossa.[184] These most likely involved a variety of individuals with different faith experiences and connections to the home where the group met.[185] We must dismiss any theory that says that there were only house churches or there were only urban churches. We see clearly in the literature that both coexisted. In fact, there were other kinds of communal response to Jesus and his resurrection that coexisted also.

Early followers of Jesus were transforming and creating clubs, guilds, and associations. There were colleague groups and burial societies.[186] These were organized a bit differently than the house communities and the larger city clusters. There seems to be a patron client relationship whereby individuals participated in the societies and supported them through their donations and presence. They were more exclusive groups with particular liturgies and criteria for belonging. At the same time, while the Pauline churches appear to have been more unified in terms of social rank, the societies oddly enough, were more open to a cross-section of society because they were based less on the same family of origin or part of the community, and more on the criteria of belonging.[187] These societies coexisted as self-contained and unique organizations. They were particularly located to their context.[188]

There was in fact, still another type of community that was randomly being generated during the same period of time. Many of the first followers of Jesus were Jews and so they founded communities within synagogues. Many of these groups would soon be identified *Christians* and would be kicked out of the synagogues. So the nature and liturgy of synagogue worship was very important to this unique community. In time and throughout the Mediterranean region, unused or abandoned synagogues would be re-inhabited or taken over by Christians. So some of the first buildings we might call churches began their lives as synagogues. The ones we know of from Paul's letters and archeological digs are Duro Europos, Stobi, and Delos.[189]

Schools were still another kind of Christian community. Similar to philosophical schools of the day, this is where followers of Jesus would gather around a particular teacher or noted leader. The disciples met together, learned together and debated one another.[190] These learning groups might include professionals or students. Discourse and guidance given to the disciples were part of the unique nature of these groups. They grew and some would become communities in and of themselves.[191]

While the cities appeared to be swelling with a variety of communities, so too were rural areas. Some of these forms existed in the smaller rural areas. Yet, out of the desert came a more communal expression of early Christianity. Sects, special groups, and movements of God fearers had been part of Middle Eastern life for centuries before the time of Jesus. After Jesus' resurrection, there emerged parallel communities of cave-dwelling desert fathers, small groups of praying women, and communes filled with people who believed in separating themselves out of the society in order to prepare for Jesus' return. These movements can easily be seen as the seeds of the monastic movements to come.

During the fastest growing time of church history we can see that there were multiple groups of Christians of gathering together. I have mentioned the ones we know about. But this cannot possibly be a complete inventory of the Christian communities that existed. Remember, WYSIWTI. These are only the ones we have read about or dug up. There were, in fact, many forms and ways of participating. People believed different things and people worshiped in different ways. People gathered at different times of the week in different places. So what happened?

In this diverse, living, growing, thriving period of our communal life, the focus was upon relationships. It was the relationship with the risen Lord and their relationships with one another that mattered most. Space, liturgy, vessels, roles, theologies, unanimity, and even definitive ways of being community were varied. They were also all secondary or tertiary concerns. The vessels and the spaces were not defining concerns of the community. Archeological evidence reveals that commonplace objects, common places, and common meals were the primary locus of the relational act of gathering. We can imagine full participation in the goings-on of these familial gatherings. There was a give and take and roles were most likely shared. In the few formal societies the roles were more defined.

As the communities (that we know about) grew and organized, more emphasis moved to the defining roles of place and liturgy. By 300 AD we have unified and common liturgies, a developing customary[192], and vessels that are made specifically for liturgical use.[193] The spaces begin to be organized around the gathering of the people as opposed to early space, which just happened to be where people found themselves and where they organized themselves. The importance of space and content would continue to evolve.

By the eighth century, the ordinary has become the special. The ordinary household materials gathered and used for the breaking of common bread in whatever place the faithful gathered are now transformed. The pottery cup and plate taken from the cupboard now are gold and silver formed for the special purpose of the Lord's

Supper. Along with the special vessels comes the standardization of the service itself.[194] Special buildings set apart from the common home now become community centers for the life of the faithful. Abbeys for those who follow the strictest of rules have now formed. Shrines dot the Holy Land. People make pilgrimages to see the sacred sites, reenacting the moments of Christ's life. There seems to be a never-ending evolution of growth in hierarchy, the setting aside of places of worship, and the formalization of worship. Even what were normal street clothes in the first century are now beautiful vestments signifying roles and work in the Eucharistic feast.

By 1517, buildings and liturgy are no longer about the people but about the action. This is the high-water mark of the universal faith that is Christianity. People no longer are participants in the way they were in the early days. The liturgy is no longer for the hearing or the responding. People are distant and what is happening is mysterious and not very earthly. While we can imagine that in some early communities there were hosts, we know for sure that many were simply householders. By the sixteenth century we have a high priesthood that is in charge of the holy items.[195] The holy world is wholly separate from the real world, and the heavenly banquet table is carefully and ritually prepared by the professional.

Now we have arrived at the Reformation. The great divide is also the great moment of reinvention of the church. As the world itself and culture were focused upon the nature of knowing—epistemology—the reinvention was all about understanding. The great movements of the reformation were about the Bible, liturgy, and language. There was a rediscovery of a living theology. All of this was broadcast in the language of the people. Homes and churches were filled with a new vibrancy of faith. This of course cannot be understated. The reform would eventually spread and Christianity would continue to grow. But it grew within the vessel that had become the norm—a church building. The church is the building where the people go for the sacraments (Roman) or to hear the living word preached (reformed). What happens during the succeeding 300 years is a bumpy road but mostly unchanged until the invention of free time.

While some will want to focus on the monastic reformations, or the discoveries of ancient manuscripts, or liturgical revivals, I want to focus on the creation of free time. The Victorians are responsible for this invention. No matter what we look at, the creation of public parks, the decrease of the work week, the increase in what people called pastime, the invention of baseball as the best way to spend that pastime, or the growing understanding of something called "childhood," they all came into fashion during the nineteenth century.[196] During the Industrial Revolution Victorians were the first to begin to think differently about time that was *not* spent working. Think about it for just a moment. Prior to the Victorian age, people worked all the time. It was *survival* that set the hours of the day. From sunup to sundown, people worked every day of the week. They would only from time to time make their way to the local shrine for the holy feast day of their town. But now there is time. What began to happen next will tell the tale for hundred years: the church began to grow in attendance. Not only did the Victorians invent pastime, they decided to spend it going to church. The minister and preaching were some of the best entertainment there was to be had.

The expansion of cities, growth in population in the West, and the unchallenged sacred time of Wednesday nights and Sunday mornings saw the great expansion—explosion—in church attendance. Yay for free time! This was to become a moment in our church history not unlike the very high Middle Ages when we were humming along. We had a great capacity and the church expanded. By the end of this boom in the 1950's, the diocese I serve had planted 5 congregations a year for a decade. It almost doubled what we had had for the previous century. The Diocese of Texas was not alone in this expansion. Resources of the empire-rich Western church began to build monolithic bureaucracies and hierarchies. In our own tradition, our presiding Bishop appeared on the cover of *Time* magazine! Money rich, we sent out missionaries, and our church itself began to expand into new countries, completing the global vision of the nineteenth-century mission movements.

We also turned inward. New scholarship allowed for a reinvention of liturgy in our tradition—though this was true for all the mainline denominations. By the twentieth century the liturgical movement had returned the central action of the Eucharist to weekly worship. The liturgical renewal movement also brought with it a new liturgical fundamentalism; we became overly focused on the words we say, the words the priest says, and the words of the Bible. Fundamentalism sneaked in and Christians began to argue over inherency. Politics crept in and we began to argue about culture issues. Words and their meaning became important and we argued over the gender of God, sexuality, the gender of ministers, divorced people. We argued and we argued. Along with the rest of the Western culture, we divided ourselves into camps at war with one another. We began to break apart our churches, as if playing out C. S. Lewis' *The Screwtape Letters* in which a senior devil instructs the disciple to keep the Christians fighting amongst themselves so that the mission will never happen. Saint Paul's has similar warnings about division. Yet, we become the arbiters of truth, and the great dismantling of Western Christianity begins.

I am not judging this part of our history, though it would have been nice if someone had been paying attention to the dramatic changes taking place. I think you can only see what you can see. The church and her leadership did not see what was coming. Here is the important thing: because we did not do evangelism and discipleship, but waited for people to come through our doors, today, we are in trouble and out of shape.

At the same moment that we were busy, there was a seismic shift in the culture. Philosopher Charles Taylor in his book *A Secular Age*, called it a "mass phenomenon."[197] The culture, Taylor offers, is caught in an immanent frame. The mechanical world jettisoned a "hierarchy of being" and there was an "atrophy of a sense of God."[198] The transcendent world was rejected for a natural world without mystery. Everything could be explained in reference to itself. There was no need for the individual life to be dependent upon or in relationship with God. Instead, the "buffered human being" was self-sufficient.[199] Even society was able to reveal its own "blueprint" for how things are to "hang together" for the "mutual benefit" of the whole.[200] In the end there would be no need for God or religion. The Church was, all in all, unprepared to speak a living word into this culture shift. In fact the Church willingly adapted to it and settled into a diaspora relationship with the culture. Harvey Cox wrote in his musing on the secular city, "The failure of modern theology is that it continues to supply plausible answers to questions that fewer and fewer people are asking."[201] Not unlike the twentieth century, we continue to answer questions and problems from a period that no longer exists.

The shifts in thinking were accompanied by a shift in technology. By the 1960's, all institutions felt the effects of a rapidly evolving smart culture. The world began to evolve in new and amazing ways. Technology introduced itself to people. TV and media began to expand exponentially into the living room. Sacred weeknights were given to sports and after-school activities. Sacred Sundays were taken up by more sports and family activities. Did I mention there was more TV to watch? The 9-to-5 job has evolved to a floating work week. The gap between the haves and the have-nots, along with our desire to shop every day of the week, means that many, if not most of the people in our country, work shifts with schedules that fluctuate. New media and communications mean you can get all the spiritual information you need in the privacy of your own home. The expansion of wealth and travel means you can go on your own pilgrimage. The growth of a maker culture means you can design your own religion, and many do. The end of a great cataclysmic shift has dissolved the church's place at the center of the entertainment, communication, spirituality, family and neighborhood life. So the church shrank, and financial burdens grew, and the culture all helped but put the nails in the coffin in the past model of doing church. We spent a lot of time organizing things. It is like arranging deck chairs on the Titanic. Our Procrustean bed was the categorization of church by size.

What we did next was to try and fix the problem. We thought if we just: were more welcoming, more attractive, bigger, and had more programs we would be okay. We spent time on words, music, and liturgy. We thought that relevance was where we should put our energies so we tried to be relevant which came off a little gimmicky. We thought if we could understand the nature of each generation we could better market the church. What became clear is that we didn't have enough consultants. We knew that if we just had more consultants we would be golden. We bought a lot of books to help us better understand the nature of communities. In the do-better mode we thought we could categorize our churches.

A truly brilliant man, Arlin Rothauge, began a series of books in conjunction with the think tank known as the Alban Institute—to help us understand our life as church according to size. For over two decades we put all our eggs in the basket of the *church size* movement.[202] Rothauge proposed that we place our churches into distinctive size categories believing that congregations of different sizes are organized in predictable and particular ways. Each church is put in a category by size. Rothauge called these categories: family, pastoral, program, and corporate or resource.[203] The idea that everything is measurable by size has shaped the way we discuss congregations. Originally penned on the back of a cocktail napkin as an idea, the size names themselves today are part of our church vernacular. I have bought into this idea of categorizing churches for years. Rothauge had an idea—that there is a set of sizes and each size has a number of ASA and therefore a way of behaving. I think this was a way of quantifying and creating a scientific machine-like order of churches. At the time, it produced some interesting ways of reflecting about our congregations and how we relate. The problem I have learned is that Rothauge, and *I as well as I used his material*, created an observation bias.

Quantum physics and the observation paradox help us understand that no one, neither Rothauge nor I, observes the world without bias and without affecting the congregation by the observation itself.[204] It wasn't that he simply scientifically observed size, he and others actually created categories and influenced behaviors in particular ways—not all positive. Our desire to categorize and measure actually loses or dismisses important information about the congregation. We not only have a bias, we create an observation dilemma. If we think about it for a moment, what we realize is that Christian communities have actually functioned in different models, with different numbers of people, participating for different lengths of time, with different economic models, and different leadership styles for millennia.

You see, Rothauge had indeed made a brilliant discovery. A congregation of 150 was not like a congregation of 500. This is true. Before Rothauge we thought about all congregations in the same way; or at least we had for the past 100 plus years. Rothauge believed that you treat same size congregations in similar ways. I cannot emphasize enough how important and revolutionary this understanding was for us all. However, when Rothauge dismantled one observation bias he created a new one. You see to grow, Rothauge believed, you had to act like the next size up. This statement from Alban Institute illustrates how the observation bias works regarding growth: "In order to break through an attendance plateau, a congregation must deliberately relinquish familiar patterns of behavior and begin to act as larger congregations act."[205]

Rothauge's observation bias was that all congregations of the same size are the same. All congregations of 50 are the same, all congregations of 150 are the same, all congregations of 250 are the same, and congregations of 500 are the same. We have been using this model exactly as Rothauge intended for years because we thought it was the best way of seeing congregations. But after over twenty years of ministry, and ten in a diocesan office, I know that is not true. It doesn't work and it does not help. All congregations are different based upon the people who are in them, the place they inhabit, the cultural context in which they find themselves, how many people attend regularly, how old the congregants are, how much they give, and style of worship. This is one group of factors, and we could add many more, that create a multiplicity of effects that make the congregation uniquely who they are, healthy and unhealthy. Today in the Diocese of Texas we say when you see one congregation you see one congregation.

Margaret Wheatley thinks of this particular problem in this way. She believes that we make a mistake when we discover a concept that works well in an area of the organization and then apply that concept to every area of the organization.[206] The problem is that every context is different and unique. This universal application destroys "local initiative."[207] Wheatley writes, "All living systems change all the time as they search for solutions. But they never act from some master plan. They tinker in their local environments, based on their intimate experience with conditions there, and their tinkering results in effective innovation. But only for them."[208] This does not discount the sharing of ideas and learnings. The past church has too often mandated universal acceptance. This will be different. The future church will share and invite with room for applied and contextual innovation. When we do this the organization is transformed. Again, Wheatley writes, "Information about what others have invented, what has worked elsewhere, can be very helpful to people elsewhere in the organization. These stories spark other's imagination; they help others become more insightful. However, no pre-made model can be imposed on people. The moment they leave home, where they were created, they become inspiration, not solutions."[209]

Something else has been a product of our twentieth century desire to measure everything. Our fanatical focus on size has ground into our denominational thinking the incorrect notion that as Rothauge said, "Sabbath attendance—all ages, all Saturday evening or Sunday worship services combined, over the whole year—is the best single indicator of size for Christian congregations."[210] The second of Rothauge's observation biases is that he based congregational health upon a 1950s model of what church should look like. Complicating the bias is the fact that the models he observed in the 1980's and 90's are forever locked into their time and place. Measuring the success or failure of mission initiatives based upon models that no longer exists in a culture that is over 60 years old makes no sense. Church has not always looked like that. Church does not have to look like that. The future Church will have a diversity of models, not four types. Once you move away from defining Christian community only in the above terms, you quickly realize that effective small communities can crowd source their funding, meet at different times, for different purposes, in public or private spaces, and create their own church economy that is completely outside the model of church size. Small communities can be successful in new and different ways, and are not prisoners to a prescribed way of being church. The healthy thriving Christian communities of the future will not best be measured by 1950s data and goals; but they will be measured by the impact on the transformation of the local culture and how well they are integrated into their community.

San Mateo, Houston, the fifth largest congregation in the Episcopal Church, is full life. It has over 1200 people on Sunday, one priest, very few programs, and a full ministry, which is evangelistic and service-oriented. It does not fit any of Rothauge's concepts of a corporate size congregation. Another example is St. Matthews in the small Texas town of Henderson. It has confirmations and baptisms every year. It has a bi-vocational priest who is known throughout the community as a gifted pastor and teacher. The church is full of life and has an active ministry to families from the whole town every October as it hosts a pumpkin patch. There is food and story time and visiting school children throughout the month. The priest is known as one of the most gifted pastors in town and people of many denominations look to her for leadership and care. Despite the fact that it is small it operates with life and vitality outside of the chaplain model offered in its size description. It is missionary and service oriented, engaging the community outside itself. The Diocese of Texas and the Episcopal Church has congregations that are breaking Rothauge Church size model. What we know is that congregations such as these break all the models and prove that success is not based upon squeezing ministry into a predetermined understanding of church size models. Even though we try and fit churches into the Rothauge boxes, and move them as they grow and shrink, we find that they are living organisms and don't fit. They have a whole complex life outside the box! It isn't about seeing what's in the box alive or dead, it is about seeing that the church is alive and mostly outside the boxes we have created. Churches don't fit into the size models. In fact, I might argue that the more we believe they do fit, the more we are fixated on trying to recreate something that does not exist any longer; and may not have ever existed.

What the present church has inherited as the view of ourselves and how we are to proceed from this point forward is flawed. In the end, we can only see in part and know in part what God is doing. We must let go of a number of things in order to frame our future conversation. We must let go of: our categories, our measurements for success, our narrow leadership job descriptions, and our economic models for doing church. In other words, we must let go of the core belief that: this is the way it has been and this is the way it will be. And, that if we just work harder using the same the model everything will return to normal—the 1950's. I am not the only one challenging the old model. The *emerging* church movement is challenging what church looks like on the surface. They are trying to make church better and accessible to people outside the church. While creative, it is still wrestling within the straightjacket of the current church model. A lot of consultants have even made a career out of telling the boxed church that if they will just mimic what the *emerging* church folks have to say, then they will be okay and reach those millennials out there. As we say in the south, all our efforts are like putting lipstick on a pig. My friend Paul Fromberg says, "The emerging Church is like a new toy, the church will soon break it." Until we break open the box and let the living church out we are stuck. Imagine what would happen if we really freed our leaders who are interested in small batch church to set up shop outside. There are a few who are doing just that: Lydia's in New York (www.stlydias.org) and Thad's in Los Angeles (thads.org), to name a few. Diocesan leadership has to be willing to let these creative leaders be unshackled from their standards of measurement to create new mission criteria.

Margaret Wheatley writes, "Life is about creation. This ability of life to create itself is captured in a strange-sounding new word, autopoiesis (from Greek, meaning self-production or self-making). Autopoiesis is life's fundamental process for creating and renewing itself, for growth and change. A living system is a network of processes in which every process contributes to all the other processes. The entire network is engaged together in producing itself."[211] We must see differently, with new eyes, and work differently, with new ideas, if we are to allow for a living thriving autopoietic church.

One of my favorite books is Simon Winchester's *The Map That Changed the World: William Smith and the Birth of Modern Geology*. It is about the story of William Smith (1769-18369), who was a geologist and surveyor. He is unofficially known as the father of geology in England. What he did was essentially measure England and Wales. He figured out that he could not only map the earth and where things are, he also figured you could map the strata of rocks beneath the surface. His work altered completely how we view the world around us and beneath our feet. This was important because it changed our perspective.

Do you remember when you first looked at Google Earth? It was amazing. Brian McClendon, a Google executive, wrote in a blog post that they were engaging in the "never-ending quest for the perfect map."[212] He wrote: "We've been building a comprehensive base map of the entire globe—based on public and commercial data, imagery from every level (satellite, aerial and street level) and the collective knowledge of our millions of users."[213] Jerry Brotton, professor of Renaissance studies at Queen Mary University, London, commented, "All cultures have always believed that the map they valorize is real and true and objective and transparent."[214] He continued, "All maps are always subjective... Even today's online geospatial applications on all your mobile devices and tablets, be they produced by Google or Apple or whoever, are still to some extent subjective maps."[215]

Uri Friedman reflects in an article in *The Atlantic*, "12 Maps That Changed the World," "There are... no perfect maps—just maps that (more-or-less) perfectly capture our understanding of the world at discrete moments in time."[216] It is thus clear that our perspective also affects our movement out into the world. Our perspective affects the manner in which we navigate our context. The complexity of our mission will require us not only to have the prophetic vision of our core mission but also the means by which to achieve it. Not unlike a cartographer, we will need to use some of what we have learned in the past to help us navigate, interpret, and engage with the new world that is evolving outside our church doors.

For too long, our perspective has been formed as we looked around ourselves from our place in the pew. We are in the business of admiration. Admiration means to express a feeling of wonder, pleasure, or approval; and admiration is the primary mission and ministry of a shrine. The church must be a place with a perspective outside its walls with a developing map that will change our world. We are invited by Christ and the Holy Spirit to leave the building (like Elvis) and go out into the real world with the living risen Lord who is even now in the community already and at work there. The church in the midst of the city of the living God will have to be gentle and meek as it steps out of the shadow of its shrine to a church that does not exist any longer. The church will have to mourn with all sorts and conditions of people. The church will have to proclaim in word the commandments of our God: to love our neighbor as Jesus loved us.

The church will have to show mercy as Jesus shows mercy. And the church will have to seek a non-violent immersion with the world outside its walls no matter how persecuted it may be. We must be fearless in taking our place in the public square, throwing aside the notion that religion and faith are private matters. Through invitation, partnership, and participation we must re-map the streets and public places and spaces as venues for liturgy and life of the church beyond our walls.

It is true that for some the city may always be a symbol of evil, corruption, and decay. But for the living church the city is a symbol of life, human cooperation, human potential, the ever-expanding family of God, and corporate salvation. Our cities are cities of the living God. Only autopoietic missionary Christian communities will survive. Our map will not be perfect but it will give us a new perspective of where we are in the new mission context.

Stepping out, looking around, and figuring out where we really stand, I believe that the most effective missionary and mission organization will be those that are team-led. They will be diverse ethnically, embracing the multiple languages and cultures we find outside our churches. Successful mission will be dependent upon blended leadership talent, blended ages, and blended communication styles. Most importantly, though, is that wherever the individual moves and sets up a tent of meeting for ministry there will have to be investment in the local community. We believe that as Margaret Wheatley says, "Relationships are not just interesting . . . they are all there is to reality."[217] This will mean that just as the world around us is organically connected, so too our organization will have to be organic and rich with networks that connect us throughout the world around us. We are going to have to let go and return to a very rich and diverse understanding of community life and growth.

In order to discover our new context, we need to look at the world around us and imagine how the current living city offers a vision of an autopoietic church. We can see now the artifacts for our future.

CHAPTER ELEVEN
Renewed Mission Field

*"When the old way of seeing was displaced, a hollowness
came into architecture. Our buildings show a constant
effort to fill that void, to recapture that sense of life
which was once to be found in any house or shed. Yet the
sense of place is not to be recovered through any attitude,
device, or style, but through the principles of
pattern, spirit, and context."*
— Jonathan Hale, architect, <u>The Old Way of Seeing,</u> 1994

Let us begin by looking at the urban environment. The church for many years has been focused overwhelmingly on the suburban environment for mission. We will address this in a few pages. We have ignored the signs that reveal that there is an urban mass migration coming. No matter what your observation bias may be, we are in a massive global population shift into the world's cities. Today over half the world's population live in urban areas. Some estimates reveal that in many countries the percentage is a lot higher. We are becoming an urban world. We begin here because this is the place where we have the most opportunity to see the future and move into it.

I believe that when we think about cities we think about downtowns, office buildings, skyscrapers, and the like. We think about the infrastructure. This particular hiccup is what gets us into trouble because as we think about the city we think about the church in the city—and by church we mean the church building. A city is made up of people. A report from the Institute for the Future reads, "For future smart cities to thrive, it must be centered around people, not just infrastructure."[218]

Dan Hill, CEO of Fabrica (a communications research center, www.fabrica.it) says, "We don't make cities in order to make buildings and infrastructure or, indeed, technology—that's a side effect of making cities. We create cities to come together, to create culture or commerce, to live, to work, to play—to create more people."[219] The problem with how we imagine our urban mission is the same problem many in the commercial world face—we forget it is about people and not the structures of church.

The discussion around smart cities might well echo our own. Anthony Townsend, Research Director at IFTF and author of the upcoming book *SMART CITIES: Big Data, Civic Hackers, and the Quest for a New Utopia* writes: "Citizens are not employees or customers, they have to be dealt with on a different basis. So the idea that you can install the smart city like an upgrade and expect people to just live with it—especially when it takes power away from them—means they're not going to accept it. So you have to engage with them and grow it from the bottom up."[220] He continues: "This is an age in which very big things can come from massively coordinated human activity that doesn't necessarily get planned from the top down. We need to stop thinking about building smart cities like a mainframe—which is this industry vision—and think about it more like we built the web, as loosely intercoupling networks."[221]

Dan Hill talks about these 'Smart Citizens.'[222] "Despite the heavy infrastructure-led visions of the systems integrators and IT corporations, the most interesting and productive use of contemporary technology in the city is here, literally in the hands of citizens, via phones and social media," he says. "The dynamics of social media have been adopted and adapted in the last few years to enable engaged and active citizens to organize rapidly and effectively; a network with a cause. Smart citizens' seem to emerge at a far faster rate than we're seeing more formal technology-led smart cities emerging," says Hill. "In the face of institutional collapse, active citizens are knitting together their own smart city, albeit not one envisaged by the systems integrators and technology corporations."[223]

What does this mean for us? We do not build communities to build church buildings. We do not do our diocesan work in order to maintain the infrastructure of church. We are in the business of creating communities so that people may come together, creating a culture of sharing grace, to work and serve others, to play and celebrate life. Just like many city planners and governments, we forget our work is about people.

We have created a system by which people are here to support the church rather than the church support the people in making community. When we do this we take power and energy out of the organization—we take life out of the organism. The only way to build a vital and healthy mission in the future will be to engage with people in real time, where they are, and to listen and work with them to create the new living church.

The largest aspen grove in the world is the Pando Grove in Utah and it is considered by many to be one of the largest living organisms in the world with a massive single underground root system. Likewise, our cities and our churches, if seen as giant organisms, can and will be part of "massively coordinated human activity."[224] The church, if it wishes to be present as a living organism within the life of the city, will have to couple with the vibrant city networks. It will be autopoietic—porous. It will have to build commons (both electronic and human) throughout the city's mainframe. The church will have to participate in organizing and gathering and ministering through the same media relationships that people use in their daily lives. We are looking at a world of "smart citizens" and that will mean we are living in a world of "smart" community members.

When talking about the future of cities, there are lessons to be learned about what is happening now. Some city planners look at Hongdae in South Korea. It used to be a very traditional suburb. Urbanization occurred and masses of people moved into the area.

People built up the city by adding onto already existing structures. Office life, shopping, dining, and small businesses were built onto existing homes and buildings. They were not following the building code. Instead of stopping this massive DIY movement, the leaders of the city worked with the people. They changed some of their regulations and began to steer the life of the growing metropolitan area into a productive and healthy future.[225] What changed? Leaders saw that the city itself was a "platform" interacting in relationship with the people. Most master plans make the people conform. This plan adapted to the people. City planners are asking themselves today: "How can you open up your codes and make a platform that is open and can adapt to bottom-up practices."[226]

We still are in the business of planting churches and hoping people will come into them. We have a church development strategy and that strategy seeks to have the people conform to its existing model. The church has an opportunity to look out and see that we should be interacting with our people in the mission field. Our platform of structure and polity needs to adapt to the world and people around us and not the other way round. We are to be a people-led community with the organization/platform supporting the work. We are not to be an organization/platform that leads and is supported by people. This is a very important and integral cultural change. It is a necessary organizational flip.

How will we begin to be an organization willing to play with our people? How will we engage with them and follow them out into the world? We will have to deliver valuable low cost, lightweight, moveable, transferable, multi-use infrastructure to our people. This is what we can do with our organization's economy of scale. At the same time we will have to allow our people to lead us. The Church organization has to adapt to the people we intend to reach.

Dan Hill writes: "If we're going to figure out what the smart city is about, we need to involve citizens. But citizens themselves won't do enough; you need to engage in the Dark Matter of institutions to resolve it, for it to become systemic. Think about what we want the city to be about, how we want our city to work, how we want people to engage. We have to redesign all kinds of organizations from the bottom up for the 21st century. We'll have to redesign most things and pull them together so we have active, engaged government alongside active, engaged citizens focusing their time on what the city can be in the first place—and with that we may end up with a much smarter city."[227]

If the church is going to be part of the city of the future, we need to be part of the smart city today. We must be involved with the involved citizens. We must direct our attention to relationships and the interconnectedness of lives lived together. We will need to rethink our infrastructure and make sure that it is supportive of the people and their movements and gatherings instead of the other way around. We must pull together people alongside our missionary structures and engage with them "focusing on their time."[228] We must be in their time and in their space, listening and traveling with them as the new urban communities grow and develop.

I recently read an article about the "design tactics" for rethinking the development of communities. It began with this quote: "Historically, America's economic growth has hinged on its ability to create new development patterns, new economic landscapes that simultaneously expand space and intensify our use of it."—Richard Florida, from the foreword to *Retrofitting Suburbia: Urban Design Solutions for Redesigning Suburbs*[229]

As more people are moving to the city, so then a new focus upon making the city inhabitable is taking shape. Designers, architects, and community developers are reimagining the cityscape. They are not necessarily building new infrastructure so much as they are recreating the spaces we inhabit. Anyone in a city center that has watched as an old coffee company building from the 1930s or a 1920 paper factory is refitted for lofts, retail, and office space can testify to this reality. In part, it is because as people return to the urban landscapes those thinking about life in these spaces are asking: "How might . . . existing downtowns be creatively retrofitted—re-inhabited, redeveloped and/or re-greened in ways that are economically productive, environmentally sensitive, socially sustainable, and aesthetically appealing?"[230]

It is one thing to think about doing this for our old church buildings—true enough. But in the thinking of these urban designers, we see patterns of human occupation that give us a clear picture of the mission context for the city. June Williamson worked with others to gather information about what was transpiring across the United States. She wrote in "Urban Design Tactics for Suburban Retrofitting": "We wondered what was being done across North America with vacant big box stores, dead malls, dying commercial strips, traffic choked edge cities, outdated office parks and aging garden apartment complexes."[231] She eventually wrote a book called *Retrofitting Suburbia*. It is worth a look if you are a missionary in the urban landscape that is even now evolving.

After looking at eighty sites, what Williamson saw was nothing less than inspirational. It is hard to believe if you are in a mega city in the South. Nevertheless, as all patterns indicate, it is true. I remember sitting in an urban planning meeting and grumbling about new high-rise multifamily units going into already densely populated areas. I then came to understand that concrete sprawl was ultimately detrimental for the environment. You want to build up no out. It points out the reality that in the end we are going to be (at least in my lifetime) a more urban population. The last 50 years of urban sprawl are over.[232] June Williamson writes: "We spent fifty years building and living in these suburban landscapes, and we must spend the next fifty retrofitting them for the new needs of this century, to help build a resilient future suburbia that is climate-sensitive, compact, pedestrian-and-bike friendly, and responsive to changing demographics and contemporary lifestyles."[233]

Some might say that the answers to resilience must be sought primarily in building up center cities, ignoring that fact that suburbs now comprise the majority—in land area, population and economic activity—of our urbanized areas. This line of thinking overlooks the reality that more potential gain could be achieved by focusing on adapting our least sustainable landscapes, in suburbia, to transform them into more resilient, equitable, adaptable, walkable, transit-oriented, and more public-oriented places. In a stagnant economy it is imperative that the built landscape be as self-sustainable and energy efficient as possible. Retrofitting and planning for retrofitting are more important than ever.[234]

What is true in the urban area is true in the suburban area. Our cities are being remade and we need to be attentive as churches in order to participate whether we are in a suburban church or downtown church. We need to have our eyes open to the reality of values and trends that are shaping life. We also need to see clearly where people are migrating and how they are living. So what is happening and how are people recycling space to build a better community?

People are redeveloping the existing infrastructures from the failed big box stores also called the *safety store*. At our house we called them *safety stores* because as soon as you saw them, we believed people were comforted by their presence. We imagined a person might say, "Ahhhhh, we are okay. There is a Bed Bath & Beyond." Or "I was worried I didn't know where I was. Now I know I will be okay. There is a Starbucks next to a Home Depot. We are safe now." It is safe because you can see it but it is also safe because you can go inside these stores and restaurants and know exactly where everything is—how and what to order. Defunct big box stores and old manufacturing buildings of downtown are being repurposed. Across the country big box stores are being rethought, gutted, and remade into community centers, gyms, and health clinics.[235] In downtown Houston the Episcopal Diocese of Texas Health Foundation now shares space with a spirituality center that used to be a stationary/paper printing building. In the small town where I first served I can think of two places that were once a giant furniture store and one electronics store. Today, they house a community college and a mental health clinic, respectively. These are icons of a culture that is shifting from commercial and commodity centered to people centered.

Reclaiming big box stores, malls, and shopping centers for churches, church-run clinics and service centers is a way in which we can move back into spaces that have long been diminished but even now are being repopulated. Sharing space with new community centers has potential for mission.

Another area of renewal is greening of both the urban and suburban spaces. In downtown Houston there is a huge piece of green space where people gather and play called Discovery Green. There are concerts and movies. One of the largest Easter Sunday services is held there, followed by picnics and other activities. In a neighborhood just outside of downtown Houston, an old train track has been retrofitted for a hike and bike trail. The old concrete bayous are being taken out and new walking and biking trails will connect the outlying suburbs with the heart of downtown. Across the United States there is a movement to restore and reclaim wetlands and creeks long paved over.

Williamson gives a great example from Seattle:

In the Northgate neighborhood in northern Seattle, a little-used overflow parking lot for a busy regional shopping mall was prone to flooding. The headwaters of Thornton Creek were buried in a large culvert beneath the asphalt and local environmentalists lobbied hard for "day lighting." Developers were also interested in the property while planners also hoped to see more density, since the terminus of a light rail line was planned for the adjacent quadrant of overflow mall parking. The win-win solution? A combination of new "soft" storm water infrastructure in the form of a very sophisticated vegetative bioswale [a natural porous stormwater drain]– the Thornton Creek Water Quality Channel— plus mixed-use development with hundreds of attractive new housing units in Thornton Place.[236]

How can existing congregations participate in reclaiming spaces? How can we be present in these green spaces? Also, if we are near a reclaimed space how can congregations put up respite and prayer gardens? Or create a vegetable garden in the midst of a food desert. Christians care about the environment and so we are challenged to connect with those who are doing this work. Whether we are sharing a hike and bike trail through our property or helping a neighborhood create green space, this is an opportunity for community connection.

A third way in which developers are rethinking the urban and suburban living environment is by rezoning spaces. Cityscapes and outlying areas are being re-platted and zoned for new mixed-use development.[237] What happens is that when this is done, new opportunities for community growth occur. People move into housing above retail and restaurants.

The 2013 Kinder Institute Study, the thirty-second study of its type, found that individuals, for the first time, were by and large more interested in living in the midst of these complex and diverse communities.[238] They report that people are shifting away from a desire to live in the suburbs and single-family type developments. They would instead prefer to be in a place where there is a mix of retail, eateries, and homes.[239]

We are challenged as a church to send people out as missionaries into these communities. We need to see them as mission fields. Holding Bible studies in homes or restaurants is only one way to engage. We used to send out chaplains to hospitals. How do we send out the people to build communities within these communities where multi-use is occurring? Can we even put an office or chapel in the building next to the coffee shop? Mini worship centers and sacred spaces for meditation for all to use could pop up in these places.

What we see in general are more beautiful and greener spaces. We see connectivity for pedestrians and bicyclists. We see spaces being re-inhabited and recreated. We see retrofitting and repurposing. We see denser populations focused on play, the outdoors, and coming together for social events.[240] It is the church's work to both help these shifts happen and to participate with our communities in creating healthier environments. It is also the church's work to be evangelists within this new changing community.

People trying to do missionary work in these areas are talking to *nones*—a new category of individuals who claim no particular religious inclination. Journalist Terry Mattingly wrote this about the *nones.* "Pollsters at the Pew Forum on Religion & Public Life and similar think tanks are now using a more neutral term to describe a key trend in various religious traditions, talking about a sharp increase in the percentage of Americans who are 'religiously unaffiliated.'"[241] That's certainly an awkward, non-snappy label that's hard to use in headlines. It's so much easier to call them the *nones.*[242] I once hosted a conversation on Twitter about mission to the unaffiliated *none.* I got in a lot of trouble from those who did not affiliate. They reminded me that they were actually quite spiritual people! Human beings are spiritual people. We have for a long time said that we are spiritual beings inhabiting a physical body and not physical beings alone. There are probably some orthodox theological problems with that statement but I think you get my drift. What has become clear is that they are none and done. They are spiritual people who have no church relationship and are done with church as usual.

We are seekers by trade. Human beings have always been and will continue to be a kind of animal that deeply seeks out the meaning of things. The Most Honorable and Rt. Rev. Rowan Williams, former Archbishop of Canterbury, once remarked that it is, in fact, our charism, given by God, to seek meaning. We are a particular creature that seeks meaning and then tries to give word to it. I remember very well that he was speaking to biologist Richard Dawkins during a debate. It struck me and I think it is important to remember any time we begin to think about people. The people who inhabit our cityscape (and our world, for that matter) are people on a pilgrimage, seekers after meaning.

In a now not-so-recent article, The Barna Group, a research organizations, had to add new categories to their description of the human creature because the old ones (churched and unchurched) just didn't work anymore.[243] Despite the Barna Group's overarching agenda as an evangelical Christian group and their typical "church is dead" message, they actually have some helpful information worth mentioning here, so that we can understand a bit more about the people who are migrating to the center of our cities.

There are a lot of people who do not go to church. That being said, when asked, those who do not go to church (six out of ten) will tell you that they are Christian. A lot of those consider themselves to be people who have recently discovered Christianity. Also, the Barna Group has discovered that a significant number of people who do not claim any particular nondenominational or denominational affiliation still participate in pretty traditional church activities during any given week. I am always suspicious of this, of course, because I think people in general want to be well-regarded and worry that when the Barna Group calls, they are actually a friend of their grandmother or mother checking on their spiritual habits. Still, a goodly number of these unattached people read the Bible and over 60% will say they talk to God once a week.[244] The Institute for Spirituality and Health in partnership with Baylor College of Medicine did a research project within the Texas Medical Center a number of years ago and found that even among doctors, nurses, and patients they generally tracked these numbers.[245]

There are some other interesting facts that the Barna Group offers. A lot of people are more likely to say yes to being invited to attend a small home church. This seems to be an important piece of information if we are to be missionaries in this new context. A lot of folks attend both conventional churches and house churches—not necessarily of the same denomination. Still, there is a fair number of people who attend, but less frequently than did their parents and grandparents.[246] Of course, we knew this already.

The Barna Group also has a helpful list of things these "unattached" believe. I think they probably believe that these "unattached" qualities are not good news for the evangelical church. They are probably better news for a church like the Episcopal Church, which is always interested in a good conversation and not afraid of a wide variety of questions.

The Barna Group says that recent surveys reveal that the "unattached" are:

- More likely to feel stressed out
- Less likely to be concerned about the moral condition of the nation
- Much less likely to believe that they are making a positive difference in the world
- Less optimistic about the future
- Far less likely to believe that the Bible is totally accurate in its principles
- Substantially more likely to believe that Satan and the Holy Spirit are symbolic figures, but are not real
- More likely to believe that Jesus Christ sinned while He was on earth
- Much more likely to believe that the holy literature of the major faiths all teach the same principles even though they use different stories
- Less likely to believe that a person can be under demonic influence
- More likely to describe their sociopolitical views as "mostly liberal" than "mostly conservative"[247]

We have a tremendous opportunity to reach out to people who would find The Episcopal Church a hospitable place. In order to do that, we are going to have to go where they are, actually invite people to attend, and we are going to have to be innovative and think small.

Houston, Texas, where I live, is made up of a global population. We are one of the most diverse cities in the country. Houston has one of the largest rodeos in the world. I always take out-of-town guests so that they can experience the rodeo in all of its beautiful and strange glory. One of my non-Texas friends who went to the rodeo remarked on the ways this was a true cultural experience. If you have never been, like many whom I take, you might be surprised by what you see and whom you see. On a recent trip to the rodeo, at the marketplace (which is an experience unto itself) while a friend was buying a new Stetson *Open Road Silverbelly* (that is the kind of hat that LBJ wore), the two of us stood outside the store in the midst of a sea of passersby. Literally in a few seconds, an Anglo white male, a Hispanic family, an Indian family (woman in a sari), a Muslim family and an African-American family—all of many different shades of color and speaking different languages—passed us. He turned to me and said, "I never thought this would be a multicultural experience." In Houston, at the rodeo, everyone can be a cowboy and cowgirl. It is, in fact, a very odd and yet energizing slice of America.

Every year you can go to the Rice University Kinder Institute website and see the studies they have done and are doing regarding the changing demographics of our city and what it means for the country.[248] The Kinder Institute states: "No other metropolitan region in America has been the focus of a long-term research program of this scope. No city more clearly exemplifies the trends that are rapidly refashioning the social and political landscape across all of urban America."[249] In 1960, which was the last real boom decade for the Episcopal Church (like many denominations), the population of Houston was 1,243,258 people—6% were Hispanics, 19.8% were Black, 73% were Anglos, and the remaining other.[250] There, of course, were other nationalities even then but they were the smallest of numbers compared to these three major segments of our Houston population. Today 33% are Anglo, 18% are Black, 40.8% are Hispanic, and 7.7 % are of Asian or other descent.[251] Over 50% of those Hispanics are between the ages of 18 and 29, while Anglos make up only 23% of that age bracket.[252] We can see the same huge demographic shifts across the U.S. In a 2014 *Forbes* article Dallas, Boston, Riverside, Denver, San Diego, San Francisco, Austin, and Seattle were listed with Houston as having scored a 70% diversity index or higher, and a 20 to 40 age range of 29% or higher. America is literally reshaping itself.[253]

Today, our Episcopal Church has a demographic that is considerably different. As a domestic church we tend to be 86.7% Anglo, 3.4% Asian or other, 3.5% Latino, and 6.4% Black.[254] True, the statistics I mentioned from Kinder are for Houston. But remember that Houston is considered a trending city for the rest of the U.S. So what you see in Houston are the future artifacts of what the rest of the country will experience within its urban environments. The Episcopal Church today is closer to what our world looked like in1960. So you see the problem? Yes?

I believe the future missionary church will reflect the demographics of its culture. To become that missionary church will be to bridge the gap from where we are today to where our culture is tomorrow. This means that the growing majority of our mission field is made up of a diverse population. Our communities will necessarily have to take this into consideration. They will have to be multi-ethnic and multi-lingual. Those who lead will have to be bicultural and able to transfer between cultures. We will have to be "culturally humble." We need to be a missionary Church filled with people who are willing to have others tell them of their culture and show their culture, rather than pretend we know who they are and where they are from.

In our church we possess all the qualities needed to live and thrive in this new mission context. To begin with, we must understand that there is no such thing as a closed system.[255] The Episcopal Church as a community, as a mission society, is not closed. It is always in relationship with the community around it. We are constantly in an interchange of ideas and communication that shapes and forms us. Sometimes it is difficult to see this, but it is nonetheless true. When scientists observe the molecular world of a cell and observe autopoiesis, they have to use very powerful microscopes.[256] Researchers William Hall and Susu Nousala point out in their paper, "Autopoiesis and Knowledge in Self Sustaining Organizational Systems," it is difficult to see how such systems work because we only see what we can see. We have a hard time focusing on the actual participation with the outside world. Every system, whether of social or organic is porous. We are more often than not left only with a hint or idea of the resulting action rather than actually observing the event of autopoiesis as it is happening. Yet, they argue that it does, in fact, happen and is an essential quality of living organizations. The engagement with what is outside is a necessary part of organic life; especially if that life is to thrive. Autopoietic organizations are bounded, complex, mechanistic, self-differentiated, self-producing, autonomous, and porous.[257] Let us take a moment to apply these qualities to the church as a missionary society and understand where our learning edges are.

Boundaries

We are a bounded system. We have ways of understanding our parts and places within the system. We have orders of ministry; we have parts to play and roles to carry out. We are limited, though, because we have so narrowly defined these roles that we are not able to use the roles creatively for ministry and mission in our current context. Here is a great example. We will license an individual (non clergy) to take one piece of communion bread and a sip of wine to one homebound or hospital-bound person. Yet we are unable to wrap our minds around how that same person might be sent out to share the same gift of communion with a small batch community of individuals. We have a way of licensing individuals (non-clergy) to preach and so we do and they preach inside the church. But we do not use them to go outside the church to preach and teach in a small batch community.

Complexity

Human beings are very complex autopoietic creatures and we build very complicated organizations.[258] We have gotten complexity confused with only one form of order. We have a simple order that has been replicated throughout our organization. This order is one that is built upon an antiquated rule of governance, committee, and board structure. While some of this is important and even necessary for the health of the organization, we have so organized ourselves that we are no longer pliable. We will need to be a much more organic system with a variety of ways so we can organize at different levels and for different purposes. The old system was built around the idea of permanence. There are to be organizational structures that are created for the skeleton of the organism called the Episcopal Church. As we move to the outer parts of the organization, though, we will need to attach a variety of skins that live and die. We will have to have the ability to create and to let die. We must organize for a short while and dismantle quickly to make the mission new. We know how to form a church like we have done for over 100 years. We, however, are stuck in the old/current model of church size and must figure out how we might create other forms of communities and how they might belong to the organization. Our definition of what is a *church* is too limited.

Mechanistic

We have a very machinelike set of interactions that manage the church.[259] We have an exchange of financial resources. We have created forms of communication that are clear. We have policies and procedures that help order life. Again, though, these are imprisoned in mid-century modern forms of banking and commerce. We have not updated our business models to keep up with contemporary practices. We are still, for the most part, only using a fraction of the communication potential available to us as we perpetuate a culture tied to newsletters that are our primary form of distributing information. The social and financial mechanism of the new millennia must be engaged and entered into the organization in order for us to continue to thrive, and for the infrastructure to hold up as the organization interacts with the 21st century. We know about pledging and offering plates. People in our mission context, though, function on less and less cash and do most of their giving electronically. People give less cash to organizations, while they still comprehend what it might mean to give to God. They like to give to particular things and have choices. How do we use modern mechanistic structures to enable them to make their gift?

Self-differentiated

Williams and Nousala write, "System boundaries are internally determined by rules of association, employment agreements, oaths of allegiance to organizational rules, deeds, etc., that determine who belongs to the organization and what property it owns." While we have these, we still need to work on this because there are many more qualities of participation and many more forms of belonging. Our limited view of this is part of what is cutting us off from the world around us. In other words, in a world where people used to define themselves primarily as belonging to this and that group our limited understanding of *membership* worked. In today's world where *belonging* has a much broader understanding, our ideas around membership, participation, and belonging actually prevent us from more adeptly engaging people in surroundings. It is as if our understanding of the membership boundary has so shrunk that we are no longer able to engage with many who quite simply think about their participation in organizations in a different way. In order to be a thriving autopoietic community, we will need to broaden the ways in which people can be the church.

Self-producing

We know how to make Episcopalians. We have a variety of classes and we invite people to take them so that they can become members. We prefer indirect recruiting; this means we put an ad in our newsletter or we mention at services that we are having a class—but we rarely invite people personally to attend. We make new members in baptism and confirmation, but we don't really train them in anything other than an old model of church. We also make Episcopalians the good old fashion way—by having babies. We are going to have to do better at this process. One of the reasons why an autopoietic organization lives and thrives is because it makes new members well. It is constantly creating new cells—new members. At the same time those members are changing the organization. If the organization ceases to make new members, it ceases to have new energy, new ideas, and new creativity poured into the system. Just like any living organism, if it does not have new members (cells), it is in the process of dying.

Autonomous

Autonomy is the idea that the organization can stand alone. The organization will outlive any of the individuals that now make up the organization.[260] Let us pause here a moment. The church is a spiritual body and it is the family of God on earth. It encompasses the human being and yet is beyond any one individual. Therefore, the nature of church is to outlive any of the individuals now involved. In theory we as a church do this and will do this. What is important to understand is that we have become so church building-oriented that the structures and infrastructure of the organization are in danger of becoming terminal. In other words the church has become something other than it is meant to be! The individual is the organization in this case. This is why we see that the structures and the polity all need more and more people and their energy to survive. We are an organization that is literally eating our people alive. We are consuming ourselves—autosarcophagy. This is a completely different thing. The people are the ones who are to be the church and autonomously renewing, creating and recreating the living organization of church. If we are to be an autopoietic church, we will need to be one where the local communities are autonomous enough to create and multiply in a variety of ways so that we are a self-reproducing AND a living organism. It will need to do this without the oppressive structure we now are trying to maintain.

We have boundaries but we don't use them to do mission. We are complex but rigidly so. We are mechanistic but not in a helpful way. We are self-differentiated but exclusively so. We are self-producing but unsustainably so. We are autonomous but codependent. We have the DNA for autopoiesis but are misusing it to our detriment. Why? We are stuck in a model that does not work.

In 1962, children were hiding under their desks in America, practicing for what seemed like a sure thing—a nuclear attack from the Soviet Union. By every indication nuclear proliferation was a likely reality.[261] The Cuban missile crisis was hot and the U.S.S.R. and the U.S. were engaged in massive nuclear buildups and ballistic missile systems. Both countries were trying to figure out how they might survive an attack and if they should, in fact, attack first.[262] Hawks on both sides of the world were sure they had the answer. I believe we probably are not fully aware of how close we came to an extinction event.

One of the issues for the U.S. was how would the leaders speak to one another, post-event? Because the military works on a "command control network" they needed one that would survive the disaster.[263] Enter RAND Corporation. RAND was working with the military on a number of projects at the time. They had a man in their office named Paul Baran. He was a researcher and was involved in a lot of a fancy work that probably most people in the day would have believed was stolen from a space ship in area 51. Nevertheless, the hardworking Baran slaved away at trying to figure out this problem. His solution, and therefore RAND's solution, for the U.S. was to build a "more robust communications network using 'redundancy' and 'digital' technology."[264] Of course, nobody really believed that Baran's idea was possible and so they dismissed it, thus prolonging the creation of the World Wide Web by a decade or more,

Basically, Baran's idea was that a centralized communication system relies on only one switch to communicate, store, and send out messages. A decentralized system would do the same but have several kinds of backup or other relays. Essentially both of these would easily fall victim to an attack as in one particular area might completely cut off a region where communication was needed or worse, in the case of the destruction of the centralized system where the effect would completely shut down communication altogether. Baran imagined a different kind of system.

Basically, Baran created a *distributed* system of communications. Through the system, information is carried from one node to another on its own. Each node, while still part of the unit, acts autonomously and independently. It receives the piece of information, stores it, and sends it along to the next node. If there were a problem with one of the nodes, then the information could take another route to its destination.[265] Here is what Baran actually offered in his paper:

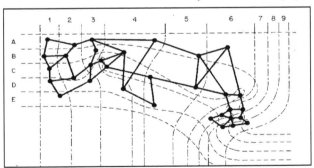

Figure 1: Baran's Example of network nodes.
(Paul Baran, August 1964)

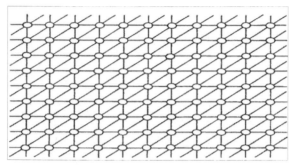

*Figure 2: Baran applied his design to a real world geometry
and landscape. (Baran, August 1964)*

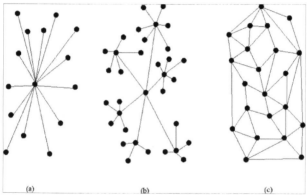

*Figure 3: Illustration of Centralized, Decentralized,
and Distributed Network (Baran, August 1964)*

Wired magazine interviewed Baran in 2003, and he talked about the system he had created: "Around December 1966, I presented a paper at the American Marketing Association called 'Marketing in the Year 2000.'[266] I described push-and-pull communications and how we're going to do our shopping via a television set and a virtual department store. If you want to buy a drill, you click on Hardware and that shows Tools and you click on that and go deeper."[267] When, in 1969, the RAND group founded ARPANET (Advanced Research

Projects Agency Network) for scientists to share information, they could hardly have imagined the vast expanse of social and commerce that is today networked globally by the click of a button.

So what kinds of churches will we see living and moving in the Western world in the future? What kinds of communities will reach the multi-ethnic, multi-lingual people who inhabit our mission context? How will these congregations inhabit the suburban and urban environments of tomorrow?

Let's apply Paul Baran's concept to the church for a moment. The church that we inherit is primarily a centralized model. It is hierarchical in nature, true enough, but it is basically organized in this centralized manner. People come to a central point—the church. There they are ministered to and there they receive programs, sacraments and pastoral care. Sometime the priest or ministers will travel out to the parishioner's home or to their workplace or hospital. It is, by and large, a centralized model of community which itself may have several levels of similarly working parts.

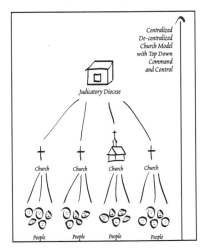

Figure 4: Current Church model—centralized.

We have made large strides towards a more decentralized model. We have done this primarily at the higher levels of the organization.

Yet even in the parish there has been some substantial movement through the growth of programming ministries in the 1990s that created decentralized systems. Yet it is not a farfetched thing to walk into a small parish in a small town and see a centralized system at work. In many ways, both the centralized and decentralized ideas of organization might be found in Rothauge's work around pastoral, program and corporate congregations. (In later years a "transitional" stage was included and "corporate" was changed to "resource".)

The form the missionary church will take in the future can be found in the artifact of the Internet and distributive system thinking. We are a weak organization today because we still believe that everyone must come to the same center. When that center is disrupted (for whatever reason—and there are many), the system is weakened and can even die. There are models where the decentralized system is working well. I believe, though, in order to engage with the culture, we are going to need a distributive system of mission.

A distributive system of mission creates multiple communities connected together. These communities are of different kinds and they do different things. They share information that they collect from the organization. They then multiply it through their own webs of connections. A distributive mission doesn't store everything in one place. In other words, a distributive system is not a bunch of centralized systems connected. It uses what it needs within the particular context of ministry. It then shares with others what it learns and receives from others what it needs to be successful.

I remember when I graduated from seminary in 1995, we used to say that big churches were getting bigger and small churches were dying. That is not quite true today. Every church, regardless of size, needs to move to a more distributive model of ministry wherein church finds itself part of a web of relationships throughout its interdependent context. In the future we will still have churches like we have them today. They will be of every size. However, they will be connected to parts of their communities. They will be one network node within the larger church-wide system. They will also be one network node within the worldwide network.

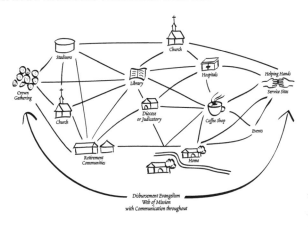

Figure 5: A disbursement model of a networked future Church.

Large churches will have moved into a mix of ministries that are decentralized and distributive all across the city. They will be running multi-site communities in people's homes, in retirement communities, in other church spaces, in rented spaces and office buildings. If these large congregations are to survive in the coming decades, they will have to figure out ways in which to connect to their massive membership out in the world where they are.

While the Episcopal Church has largely abandoned college campus ministry over the last two decades, it is time to reengage. This is one of the prime mission contexts for the future Church. However, mission on college campuses will not look like blown up youth ministry for college kids. Instead the future of campus missions will look like a disbursement model mission. No longer will undergrad and graduate co-eds find their way to a campus center where the one campus missioner works. Instead the campus mission, like the networked church, will have nodes of connection throughout the campus. A college campus mission at a tier one school might actually start college missions on local community college campuses as well. The future church no longer sees campus mission as a secondary isolated ministry for kids but as a primary mission site where the gospel is shared throughout the campus community.

At the Episcopal campus ministries that remain peer ministry was and still is largely used as the dominant model. An insular model with one clergy leader running program limits the distribution of the ministry because it centers itself on the place and person of a campus missioner. The distributed college campus mission will be aided by a move away from this insular and centralized ministry, to a student leadership team aimed outward. The Rev. Joe Chambers at Rockwell House at Washington University in St. Louis changed over to this new model several years ago. The Rev. Mike Angell from The Episcopal Church Office supports campus and young adult ministries, and he believes the outward facing team-led campus mission is beginning to catch on and spread. Young adults on college campuses are interested in creating real communities, bound together by relationships, and with dispersed mission across the campus.

We will also see the proliferation of small communities in this new distributive model. We will see house churches in urban, suburban and even in rural areas. Some of these will be connected to the larger church community as mentioned above. However, many more will be stand-alone. You may have one missioner priest with a team of lay leaders overseeing 20 or more of these small communities.[268] The Barna Group has been predicting this since the 1990s and I have been teaching and talking about this for over two decades. Yet, the Episcopal Church has had difficulty engaging this model because we have been primarily stuck in a centralized churchy model.

In the future in the Episcopal Church there will be many kinds of churches. We will have cyber churches.[269] Some people have taken cyber church to mean a Sim-City[270] type environment where people go to church online. (www.simcity.com) People have created online gaming-type congregations similar to the Sims. The cyber church of tomorrow will be a church community that gathers online, shares information and news, but does not have a permanent place. The cyber church of the future will use the distributive model of ministry to connect nodes of ministry in space and time throughout the community. It will be a church that uses different public spaces for worship, teaching, and Bible study. It will adopt other service ministry sites for its outreach. The primary connection point for members will be the smartphone, and they will be connected through the Internet to their brothers and sisters, sharing prayers, thoughts and experiences. They will find out the community schedule and go to the coffee shop for a Bible study, meet in a park for prayer and meditation, and work at a local clinic serving the poor and those in need.

Another kind of community in the future Church is described by the Barna Group as an event church: "Frustrated with politics and structures in the standard church, many will participate infrequently in worship events in public places."[271] I think we are going to have communities pop up for limited times around special events or other gatherings. I think we might see communities pop up during the Daytona 500 or in the parking lots on Sunday mornings during tailgate season at the local NFL game or Saturdays on college game day. We already see this on Easter in parks and on other special days. But I think congregations engaged in a disbursement model will be looking for ways to send missionaries, pastors, and priests out to be present where people are. Flash mob Eucharist[272] and the presence of the church in the midst of the modern day public square are mission opportunities of the future.

Service communities will be another kind of church that emerges strongly in the next ten years.[273] These will be communities that rise up around particular ministries. We see this already occurring where there is an outreach to the poor or those in need following a disaster. Communities spring up. People chose to worship with those they are serving. A great example is the outreach of Trinity parish in Houston, which grew up around ministry to the homeless. They started serving Eucharist following Sunday morning breakfast. What first started as something that was done *for* the homeless is now something that is done *with* the homeless and working poor in Houston. People chose to make this early morning service the service they attend. The community does its own Bible study, is creating a pastoral care ministry, and is becoming a mix of people of every ethnicity and every social stratum who choose to work together. I know of similar communities in Atlanta and Los Angeles.

The monastic type community will spring up as a revitalized part of the church's mission.[274] In the Episcopal Church we already have a service corps whose chief hallmark is living in community together. (episcopalservicecorps.org) Focused on a ministry of service, they live in community with daily prayer and Bible study. They have a chaplain who mentors and watches over the community life.[275] Still, others are simply communities that share a common rule of life. The Missional Wisdom Foundation operates a network of distributed but connected new monastic communities in North Texas. (missionalwisdom.com) Small groups of individuals choose to live together under one roof and one rule of life. They participate in the community. We are even now talking about how these same models might be adapted for people in their senior years who would like to live with others.

Many individuals will find community life by participating in what Barna calls "dialogue forums."[276] These will be where people gather in small groups to talk about spirituality or discipleship, or read the Bible. This will take place in people's homes, in coffee shops, in condominium community spaces, and in pubs. Many Episcopal Churches have dipped their toe into this well over the last two decades beginning with "Theology on Tap." Diocese of Texas churches joined churches across the country in 2003 in offering conversation over beer and food at a local pub. These were extensions of existing congregations. Every church will need to be doing this kind of disbursed mission in the future. Individuals are going to look for spiritual opportunities closer to home or closer to their workplaces, and such communities will be an important way in which community life is lived out outside of the parish. It literally creates new doors into the community. Many people who are not attached to a community will find it much easier to be invited and to connect to communities like this. This is going to grow and become an essential ingredient of regular community life.

The compassion cluster is a short-term community located around a particular effort.[277] These will grow up in the midst of tent cities that are doing work around a particular crisis. Along the Gulf Coast we see these pop up after hurricanes. People come from all over and participate in a community of faith that springs up like the temporary towns, which house food, volunteer support, shelter and showers for those being served and those serving. We also saw this happen in the midst of those who went to help clean up and rebuild after devastating wildfires in Bastrop, Texas. During the Occupy Wall Street movement in New York, clergy went in and preached and celebrated the Eucharist amongst the protesters. As we become more aware of events such as these, people engaged in them will bring both their desire for community and worship with them. The Episcopal Churches in any given area of the U.S. need to be aware that such compassion clusters are opportunities to reach out, to serve, and get to know others.

Small groups and prayer shelters will continue to multiply.[278] Some of these are around reading books together. Others were kaffee klatsches that now have developed a life of praying together. The individuals in these small communities may belong to other organizations or they may not be affiliated with any. They are primarily based upon friendship models. Throughout the 1970s and '80s, Episcopal Cursillo Reunion groups served as a way to organize a growing popularity of this kind of mission. They were essential in the growth that was seen during those years for many communities. They began to fizzle out for the same reason as do many ministries. They became institutionalized. Such groups, like the discussion groups, have an important potential of undergirding a distributive missionary system.

Another community that will be part of the distributed autopoietic mission strategy is the "marketplace ministry."[279] I remember that we actually stopped this from happening in our diocese. We had several clergy who had begun to provide pastoral care for workers at a local chicken-processing center. At the time, I don't think we could wrap our minds around why this had value. There are still a number of companies who have chaplains on staff to help take care of their workers. I actually believe that these corporate chaplains are not long for the world. The economic situation has caused the funds for such excesses to dry up, and as an ancillary part of the corporation, such services are being dropped. Hospital chaplains are also going by the wayside as the cost of health care and the margin for financial success are growing slim. We must engage in this ministry. These places are still places for ministry. We need to send lay and ordained people out to be with people in the places where they live and work. The church must recognize that we still have a mission into these marketplaces, hospitals, and retirement communities, even if we do not own them or if we are paid to do them. These are the many and varied places where the people are and where God is. Therefore, it is imperative for us to make this an important part of our distributive mission focus.

This is of course, not meant to be a complete list of the future Church's communities. There will be more kinds of Christian communities created by future missionaries that we cannot even imagine today but will be intimately tied to future cultural contexts.

Just recently, Warren Bird, Director of Research at Leadnet, wrote an interesting article pointing out the impact that multisite communities were having on church participation. The numbers highlight the fact that the models mentioned above are even now taking root in our communities.

Bird reports the following in 2014:

- 5 million—the number of people who worshipped at a multisite church in one weekend in the United States alone, according to the National Congregations Study sponsored by Duke University
- 8,000—the number of multisite churches currently found in the United States, according to the same study. (The wording of that survey allowed churches to call themselves multisite if they had multiple venues–such as services in the sanctuary, chapel and gym, but all on one campus. This is not what I am describing.)
- 9%—the percent of all Protestant churchgoers who attend a multisite church
- 3%—the percent of all Protestant churches that are multisite
- 80%—the percentage of U.S. states that have known multisite churches[280]

These many and diverse kinds of communities will be essential in the large congregation as it steps out into a distributive system of organization. While still other churches may leave their buildings behind and engage in one of these new forms of community, others may transform their community into a monastery or service community in place. Regardless of how these forms are adapted and take shape, they are the face of the new Episcopal Church.

This is a vision of a distributed network of communities across a geographic and mission context. These will include all ages and all ethnicities. They will be monocultural and multicultural. They will be mixed classes and rooted deep within suburban and urban environments. They are visions of a living autopoietic organization that is bounded in multiple forms with *belonging* being shaped by the type of community. The diversity and multiplication of these forms will build a strong, healthy, and complex system. Each of them will be self-differentiated, not unlike individuals within a wide web of social relationships, but they will all be connected to the church. The churches' current mechanisms will need to be retooled to provide for these new visions of church life. New forms of leadership and new freedoms will allow these congregations to be self-producing, self-replicating, and autonomous. They will adapt and change as they engage in their mission context and in relationship to real people and real spiritual pilgrims.

There are many prophets heralding the death of the church. They proclaim the death of the church at large and they proclaim the death of the denominational church. Some even get specific, making sure that everyone knows which denominational church is next! It is yours, I am pretty sure. You certainly can believe them if you wish, but I am unconvinced. We are a living and ministering in a "e" moment.

Ilya Prigogine, a Nobel Laureate in Chemistry, helps me with this idea. He won recognition for his understanding of a new concept he called "dissipative structures."[281] In nature there is a contradictory reality, and that is that disorder can be the source for new order. Margaret Wheatley say this, "Prigogine discovered that the dissipative activity of loss was necessary to create new order. Dissipation didn't lead to the death of a system. It was part of the process by which the system let go of its present form so that it could reorganize a form better suited to the demands of its changed environment."[282] Our problem is that we in the church are formed by a different perspective rooted in Western science. We believe that entropy is the rule.[283] So, if we do not constantly work harder and harder to keep pumping energy and resources into the system, then the system suffers from entropy—loses steam and dies. Yet even now life is flourishing and new life is being born. Of course, you immediately can see that this is a biblical understanding, but as Episcopalians, sometimes it is easier to see it through the eyes of science.

Prigogine offers that in a dissipative organization those things that interrupt and interfere are essential to the health of the system itself. The system receives the communication and decides if it is to respond, change, or ignore it. Change happens either way. If the disruption grows so that the organization can't ignore it, then transformation and rebirth are possible.[284] Wheatley says, "Disorder can be a source of new order, and that growth appears from disequilibrium, not balance. The things we fear most in organizations—disruptions, confusion, and chaos—need not be interpreted as signs that we are about to be destroyed. Instead, these conditions are necessary to awaken creativity... This is order through fluctuation."[285]

We are in a "dissipative" moment. We cannot ignore the flotsam and jetsam of the future that is even now washing upon the shores of the Episcopal Church. We can see partly what will only become clearer in time. But we have a vision, nonetheless. As Bob Johansen says, "Leaders make the future." It is time that we participate in the world around us. We are to be about the business of making and remaking. We have for too long suffered the sin of trying to get it right, and the shame of coming up short. But in a "dissipative" era we must have a greater sense of process and participation and experimentation.[286] If we are to move outside of our centralized structures and old exoskeletons, we must shed our skins and put on new ones. Jesus says, "No one puts new wine into old wineskins; otherwise the new wine will burst the skins and will be spilled, and the skins will be destroyed." (Luke 5:33ff)

A new urban and suburban world is emerging. We will continue to see people move towards the cities of the future. What we are experiencing across The Episcopal Church is globally true. People are entering city life by the millions and will continue to do so for a long time to come. The shape of our cities and the multiple possibilities for Christian community are before us. We have an opportunity. The question for us as we stand in this "dissipative" moment is: will we shrink from the challenge or face it? It reminds me of a story I know about a man named Joseph Needham.

We are largely indebted to Needham, a quirky Englishman, for the information that changed our understanding of China. Much of what has become common knowledge is due to his work. He was a man who author Simon Winchester said, "loved China."[287] Needham recorded the science and discoveries of an ancient people who, in the 1930s, were believed to be living in the dark ages. He discovered that much of what the modern Western culture took for granted had come from China.

Needham told us that the Chinese invented technologies such as papermaking, the compass, gunpowder and printing (both woodblock and movable type) long before anyone else. They also invented: the blast furnace and cupola furnace, finery forge, paper money, fire lance, land mine, naval mine, hand cannon, exploding cannonballs, multistage rocket and rocket bombs with aerodynamic wings and explosive payloads, the sternpost rudder, chain drives, large mechanical puppet theaters driven by waterwheels and carriage wheels and wine-serving automatons driven by paddle wheel boats, semilunar and rectangular stone knives, stone hoes and spades, the cultivation of millet, rice and the soybean, the refinement of sericulture, the building of rammed earth structures with lime-plastered house floors, the creation of the potter's wheel, the creation of pottery with cord-mat-basket designs, the creation of pottery tripods and pottery steamers, the domestication of the ox and buffalo, irrigation of high-yield crops, the multiple-tube seed drill and heavy moldboard iron plough, to name just a few. In fact, Needham points out in his 18 volume magnum opus, Science and Civilization in China, they did all of this before the end of the first century, before Christ, and in many cases a thousand years before the West.[288]

During one of his many trips to China, Needham was invited to meet with Mao Zedong. It was not his first visit with the leader but it would be his last. Needham was unaware of why the Communist leader wanted to meet with him. When he arrived, he sat across from Mao and listened as the leader asked him a question. Mao remembered that Needham loved automobiles and had invited him to help with a very urgent question. It was 1972, four years before Mao's death, and one can imagine the West was pressing in on him.

At this time, modern conveniences were still out of reach for the Chinese population, including cars. Mao said that he had to make a decision as to whether he should maintain his policy of allowing his people to have only bicycles or allow his people to own and drive automobiles. This was a huge moment. Here Mao sat at a visionary crossroads. He asked Needham what he thought. Needham sat at the same crossroads. He paused and in his mind's eye he could see the mass of men on bicycles making their way to work every day down China's streets. He then began his argument by saying that he had a bicycle that he liked very much and served him well in Cambridge. He took a breath before proceeding to say that he believed it was time to allow people to have cars. However, in that moment Mao put up his hands, showing that Needham need not continue. Mao had heard his expert and chose to continue his bicycle-only policy. It would be four more years before Mao's successor allowed people to commute in cars. Hua Guofeng became party chairman following Mao's death. Hua vowed to bring China into the future and so allowed automobiles, leading in time to a country that is now a leading manufacturer of automobiles and the leading consumer of automobiles.[289]

Leaders see the changes that are all about them and act in a manner that guides their community into the new reality, which is yet still before us. In this case both decisions were essential to how life would be lived out in China. Both created and caused a reality for the people of China. Both had good consequences and bad consequences unforeseen by the leaders. Both men saw the changes around them, and they made different choices about how to react to those changes. It is important for us to see clearly the changes that are already affecting our congregations and communities in order for us to see the future that is before us. We are to see clearly the changes that are needed, and we are to have a strong central vision with allowance for its application in new cultural contexts that emerge in time. It is time we step into the future and begin to plant these new communities. What will they look like and how will they make their way into the new missionary age? The Christian in the new millennium will bring new challenges and opportunities. For us to be successful, we will need leaders who are digital natives and who can act within the new VUCA world. We need different kinds of leaders, and we need to rethink ways of forming and training leaders. This particular task will require that we revisit how we raise different vocations within the community. How will the digital native relate to the institutions of seminary and diocese? It has been given to this generation to undertake the "dissipative" moment and to answer these questions. We are a living church with a vital and necessary mission into the world.

CHAPTER TWELVE
Into the Cloud of Unknowing

"You do not need to know precisely what is happening, or exactly where it is all going. What you need is to recognize the possibilities and challenges offered by the present moment, and to embrace them with courage, faith and hope."
— Thomas Merton, <u>Conjectures of a Guilty Bystander</u>

Sometimes I wonder if Richard Phillips Feynman[290] was looking up at the sky when he connected Bohr and Heisenberg's atomic model with the heavenly white fluffy mascarpone shapes we call clouds. Feynman was an American theoretical physicist specializing in quantum mechanics. He received the Nobel Prize in Physics, sharing it with Julian Schwinger and Sin-Itiro Tomonaga, in 1965 for his work in electrodynamics. He was a member of the Manhattan Project team and later an investigator on the Space Shuttle Challenger disaster. For our purposes he is the man noted for coining the phrase the "electron cloud".[291]

In science class in the 1980's I learned about the atom with brightly colored pictures that showed atoms clearly defined with an electron orbiting around the nucleus. Feynman describes the location of the electrons in terms of probable regions with fuzzy boundaries— like the puffy outlines of a cumulous cloud. The exact place of an electron just cannot be determined.[292]

The largest objects subject to Newtonian physics have a more predictable pattern. Not so in quantum physics. All the quantum physicist can say is, "It is kinda over there...it is probably in this area over here." When you take the flat model and turn it into a 3D model it looks even more like a cloud. These areas are called orbital regions. It is like a little cotton ball—the puffy kind we used to glue to Popsicle sticks and turn them into sheep in Sunday school. The truth is that the electron cloud is unknown.

When I was in undergraduate school, an American Orthodox priest taught me meditation and the art of contemplative prayer. We prayed together and we read a book entitled *The Cloud of Unknowing*, written by a Christian in the Middle Ages who is unknown. Like an early quantum physicist, the author offers that the only way to meet God is to abandon all that you think you know about God and enter the cloud. The true disciple must have courage to enter the unknown without all the propped up ideas and certainties of definition. One enters the cloud of unknowing and the heart is brought into union with God.

The author writes:

For He can well be loved, but he cannot be thought. By love he can be grasped and held, but by thought, neither grasped nor held. And therefore, though it may be good at times to think specifically of the kindness and excellence of God, and though this may be a light and a part of contemplation, all the same, in the work of contemplation itself, it must be cast down and covered with a cloud of forgetting. And you must step above it stoutly but deftly, with a devout and delightful stirring of love, and struggle to pierce that darkness above you; and beat on that thick cloud of unknowing with a sharp dart of longing love, and do not give up, whatever happens.[293]

The work of the contemplative is to leave the world of certainty behind and venture into a cloud of uncertainty. I was once on a mountain in Colorado and a cloud engulfed the mountaintop. Moist, invisible visible droplets, my whole skin tingled, cold and mysterious. The disciple of God ventures into the cloud with its mix of observable reality and its mysterious invisibility.

Jesus was engulfed in a cloud—the story goes that he ascended into a cloud. Byzantine Christians built a church in the year 390 on the Mount of Olives called the Chapel of the Ascension. I went there— the clouds were low and hung above the treetops. The whole area is a sacred place where pilgrims pour in to see the place where Jesus, forty days after the resurrection, ascended into heaven. He did this as the clouds descended, making their way across the Jerusalem valley, and engulfing him. Jesus is unified with God in the cloud of unknowing.

If we wish to follow this Jesus, to be disciples, we must abandon the security of the certain current structures of our church and walk bravely, courageously, into the future—into the cloud of unknowing. It is in this cloud that we will meet God. To cling tightly to our certainty will keep us rooted in the swiftly fading past.

The future of the church will not be about a church, or a church building, but about creating Christian communities. The distributive model of church will mean smaller communities. We will be robust and stronger in this cloud model of mission. Today we are fragile because we have a model that says go big or go home. I like big, for if we become a church of a few large churches, we will have actually succeeded in becoming a more fragile organization. Everything breaks, and when the large community breaks, great is its fall. By engaging a missionary model that simulates the cloud, we will create a system of small batch communities that generate, regenerate, live and die, riding random events and the unpredictable economic and societal shocks that shake larger more fragile communities.

We will need a church filled with people who, like quantum engineers and tinkerers, are willing to build smaller, diverse communities. As leaders we will need to reject what Nassim Taleb calls a "fragilista" lifestyle—one that is afraid of fragility. [294] Our observation bias is that a larger congregation is less fragile. Our model is to build bigger and bigger congregations thinking that will protect us from fragility. This is the fragilista mindset. In fact Taleb is saying when you put all your eggs in one basket you have actually created a more fragile organization. Taleb warned the financial sector that the 2008 economic crisis was coming in his 2007 book *Black Swan*. Applied to the future Church, what I am telling you, is that a diversity of Christian communities will make our mission more antifragile.

Everything we are told by seminary professors to diocesan leadership regarding the Church today engrains in us an avoidance gene that ensures we will not venture into that which we do not understand. Christianity is rooted in the mystery—the *mysterium tremendum*—the tremendous mystery—that is God. The unknown God speaks to us from in the midst of wild places. We believe in and worship a Trinitarian God who is community Father, Son and Holy Spirit, and is also incarnate in the man Jesus. We are a people whose story is told at fiery bushes, mountaintop encounters, and desert voices of fire and storm. God speaks from a cloud and says of Jesus, "This is my Son with whom I am well pleased." (Matthew 3:13ff, Luke 9.28) Today we have become a people who avoid things we don't understand and cling to certitude, and it is killing us.[295] The Church is in need of mystery, the cloud, and a willingness to be fragile—a willingness to step outside the box—no, even destroy the box itself—and allow some parts of it to die and some to be reborn.

Our current church is a complex system that believes that we will be resilient if we have the right complex policies and procedures. We have all become fundamentalists—we are fragilistas. We are clinging to liberal and conservative casuistry,[296] attempting to govern our organization one way or the other. We continue to create a more and more fragile system. It is no coincidence that as our canons and our canonical structures have grown our church has become more broken and fragile to the VUCA world around us. Our longing for predictability and order is a rejection of a God who sends Abraham from the Land of Ur of the Chaldeans, who sends Moses into the wilderness, who calls prophets and sages to speak from the mountain caves to the people in their cities, who destroys temples and governments, who brings down Babel, and who brings about Pentecost.

If we are to have a thriving missionary church we will need to spend time cultivating people and communities that live in the midst of the cloud of unknowing. There is a "cluster" of qualities that are needed by our church if we intend to be successful and antifragile in our mission. Christian communities will vary and deal with internal variability—we will no longer be a church of programs that all have a curriculum and work in the same ways. Our organization will need to be able to work with imperfect, incomplete knowledge, and be constantly willing to shift and change as we have glimpses of understanding—recognizing always a humble stance that we do not see nor comprehend the vastness of the possibilities before us. We will relish chaos and enjoy the thrill of riding the energy created. Our Christian communities will seek opportunities that appear in the midst of changing cultural norms and attitudes, and use these for conversation and communication about who we are. As a church we will be more disorderly, and able to adapt to the people and gifts that make up our communities.

We will be a future church that understands that areas of entropy are areas where we have opportunities. Rather than rejecting ideas that do not fit into our mechanical way of structuring our community, we will reward innovation. The unknown and the random will be ingredients that are embraced in order to learn. When there is turmoil or stress, we will use these as opportunities to discover and be challenged rather than as opportunities for anxiety. Failures will be seen as learning moments and time will be taken to ponder the reasons. Adaptability and pliability will become intrinsic values in the system.

Finally, Christian communities will be disbursed but they will also be cells with an interconnected network of communications, sharing learnings and outcomes. In this way the whole system benefits from the dispersal of creativity, experimentation, and engagement. This is the living Church of the future. The Church that does these things will become an antifragile Church and benefit in growth and viability, regardless of the cultural context.[297] The Church that exemplifies these characteristics will be a Church living its mission within the cloud of unknowing.

We have already illustrated how the Church's history is one where such characteristics were descriptive more of our past than our present. This is also true when it comes to the nature of the life within Christian Community. Today we have a fixed understanding of what church life is supposed to look like. Church life is nothing if it is not predictable. People come on Sunday morning to a service. Every church has a liturgy—a routine that is normative. In the Episcopal Church and other mainline denominations, we have a written Book of Common Prayer—that I love by the way—but it is predictable. Even non-denominational congregations have a routine. People go to their Bible study or to their Sunday school. There are seasons and there are things that happen routinely throughout the year- Christmas pageants, stewardship drives, potluck dinners, and youth groups. There is very little randomness in our systems and programs. Consequently, we have been unable to adapt and change as people's lives have changed. The Church continues to believe that what we need is for people to change their behavior and go back to church attendance and a regularity of life that existed in the 1950's. This is not going to happen.

The problem is that the Church today is a large system. Large systems do not do small well, because small cannot support all the organizational requirements of predictability. People become numbers and as long as they are not disruptive to the system they are welcome in it. The church can get out the volunteer brigade for a death in the family, but is little equipped to deal with mental illness for example. We don't have time for the small or anything that challenges normal. Baptism, funerals, a hospital visit, Sunday school, youth group and service attendance are about all we can handle.

As leaders in a large system we have had to look at abstract and theoretical ideas about what is happening. We are looking at large numbers, and averages; and, personal experience turned into macro trends to make decisions. We do this because this is manageable. The impersonal is all we can handle in a large corporate structure. What happens is that we fool ourselves into believing that when we make decisions based upon these views, we are making rational decisions based upon facts. In reality, we are making decisions without the benefit of stopping and thinking about what might actually be taking place on the ground. Remember, the chain of cause and effect is opaque.

There is a great deal shifting within the lives of our parishioners and the lives of people in our culture. We must work to see, and ask questions about, the smallest possible unit of relationships within the system. We will need to lean into the local and the tangible. In order for us truly to navigate the future, we will need to realize that the future is about Christian communities rather than churches. We will have to face the fact that the future is about relationships. Without relationships there is no reconciliation, and without reconciliation we are not fulfilling our mission. This is the defining nature of our church's work.

When we invest in one person–to build a reconciled relationship with them–that in turn opens up the opportunity to invest in that person's neighbors, family members, and community. This is called optionality.[298] This is how the first Christian communities grew. This labor-intensive ministry places the individual over the corporate desire for security and strength. Why? Because what we know is that the organization that seeks security and strength by using the rule of averages, the rule of canon, and the rule of repetitive systemic order, will actually erode the relationship with the individual and create a fragile system.

The church system and church focus we have today haves created a world of religious tourists. They come into church in order to do churchy things. Then they leave for the other six days of the week not thinking much about their experience or how their faith might impact the rest of their working week. In the words of Taleb, we need to detouristify ourselves. What is true for organizations in Taleb's writing is also true for the church. As long as we are a church of religious tourists, we will lack the depth of relationships to transform the world. To understand this is also to recognize the difficulty of it and the reality that we do not have time for this "relationship" nonsense. Here is the beginning of wisdom. This means we will need to investigate how people in this new missionary age shape themselves into Episcopalians and connect with others and to God.

There are many types of clouds. The cumulonimbus cloud is that fair weather cloud that heaps up and towers above a pretty day. The cirrus is the curly hair wisps that feather a sunny day. The cumulonimbus in Montana is that thunderhead which engulfs the big-sky country in the summer. The electron cloud has shape and form. We know there are electrons in there. The author of *The Cloud of Unknowing* believes God is in the cloud. The ascension story tells us that Jesus is consumed in the cloud. The cloud has qualities and types. We have explored some of the general qualities of Christian communities above. We have talked about the nature of Christian communities as smaller relationship-oriented organizations. There is more to the shape of the future Church, and that is what this second half of the book is about. I believe that if we look at the trends in the wider culture we can see some of the shape of the Christian communities to come. These communities will redefine stewardship, service, and evangelism. The Christian communities that will exist in the future will do each of these well. They will maintain the qualities of relationship, dispersal, randomness and creativity.

CHAPTER THIRTEEN
The Future of Stewardship

"Theologians talk about a prevenient grace that precedes grace itself and
allows us to accept it. I think there must also be a prevenient courage that
allows us to be brave—that is, to acknowledge that there is more beauty than
our eyes can bear, that precious things have been put into our hands and to do
nothing to honor them is to do great harm. And therefore, this courage allows
us, as the old men said, to make ourselves useful. It allows us to be generous,
which is another way of saying exactly the same thing."
— Marilynne Robinson, Gilead: A Novel

When we glance over the history of the Christian Church, what can we see when we look for telling signs of stewardship? We know that some of the early Christian communities shared everything they had. They lived in commune like settings—everything was held in common. We know that they took up collections for the poor. Special attention was given to widows and orphans. In part because they thought the Lord was returning soon, they did not consider the business of the church—such a notion is a modern concept. As the Church grew and became associated with the state, it received money and support from taxes and benefactors. We know from architecture and history that by the fifth century, the Church was built with a diaconal area where the deacons could collect and distribute alms and food for the poor. By the 17th century poor boxes enter the church narthex.[299] This was a way that the Church could take up a collection as people entered and then disperse the monies to the poor.

It would be another two hundred years before American congregations made the weekly collection of money part of worship. That's right—we have not always had a collection. (We have always had an offering—of bread and wine). The reason is because congregations did not depend upon voluntary giving by its membership. Most American churches were still established by governmental authorities like their counterparts in Europe.[300] The congregational churches and the Anglican churches alike were dependent on funds from home and then from the state. The Church was seen as more than just a societal norm; it was seen as necessary if you want good citizens. Church was a public good, so taxes and fees were collected from the people to support its work. Even after the American Revolution, and the writing of the Establishment Clause of the First Amendment, churches were still by and large supported by the state. This would last until 1833 when Massachusetts revoked the religious tax and every other state soon followed. This changed everything.

Christian communities, for the first time in centuries, had to figure out how they were going to survive without government assistance. This is the time period when pews became rented and paid for by local families. You can see George Washington's family pew at Christ Church in Philadelphia. He also had one at St. Paul's Chapel in New York City, and one at Christ Church in Alexandria, Virginia. You can still see some of these in historic churches in New England. The leadership of the church sold, taxed, and rented the pews in order to secure funds for the building and for ministry.

Eventually, the pew rentals went away as congregational leadership found it better to set a budget and invite the parishioners to pledge the funds needed for the year. They would literally pass a book around to the heads of the families and have them write their pledge in the book. By the 19th century, many churches had a few churchmen meeting and setting the budget with the priest. This was common in some congregations in Texas into the middle of the last century. Then a plan emerged by which people would give each Sunday for a different need within the community. So, on the first Sunday they would collect for the priest's salary; second Sunday might be outreach or the priest's discretionary fund; third might be for the building; and fourth might be for the diocese. At the same time, still other congregations had moved to a once a year ingathering of pledges (typically around Christmas), when parishioners could tell the church how much they intended to give. Eventually, in the second half of the last century, pledge campaigns or stewardship drives were the *modus operandi* of churches in the United States. Until recently, stewardship was how the Church funded church's ministry.

The theological shifts and changes have been about as diverse as this brief history might lead you to imagine. Theologically, stewardship has been moved from a call to possess land and give thanks to God, to the Church's right to oversee the governments of the world, to the divine right of kings, to *noblesse oblige*, and finally in the last century, resting in the pulpit teaching of the biblical tithe as the norm of Christian giving. Nevertheless, modern Protestants have made the biblical tithe the tried and true theme of every stewardship campaign. It is worth remembering that the actual passage wherein the biblical tithe is mentioned is not what most people think. The tithe is actually more like 22% when you add up the total God requires in Leviticus and Numbers (Lev. 27:30-33, Num. 18:20-21; Deut. 12:17-18; Deut. 14:28-29).[301] Moreover, the tithe is the minimum gift that is to be offered, not the norm or maximum. The requirements of percentage giving and animal sacrifices during the age of the first and second Temple, in the Old Testament, far outnumbered a tithe.

Jesus teaches about stewardship as well. He is clear that the economy which the religious leaders have created is flawed and in need of reform. He says that when the poor give, they give more out of the little that they have than the rich do when they make a large gift. The poor make a proportionally larger gift.

Jesus offers a particular theology. He tells those who follow him that everything is God's. God is the creator of all things, the maker of all things, and the one who oversees all things. Jesus offers a radical vision of people who are directly in relationship with God because of

God's love. He teaches that their care for one another and the community in which they live is essential to the health of their relationship with God. He tells those who will listen that they are to make use of the wealth they have, to multiply it, and to be generous and honest with it. Jesus teaches us that the stewardship question we are supposed to ask is *not* about what to do with all the stuff that God has given us. It isn't my stuff. It isn't your stuff. Instead, Jesus tells us to question ourselves about what we are going to do with all of *God's* stuff, with God's world, and with God's resources. This was a much more important concept and the theme of giving throughout the New Testament epistles and the early church. The early Church fathers do not mention the biblical tithe. Remember Jesus says when questioned, "Give to Caesar those things that are Caesar's, give back? To God the things that are God's." (Matthew 22:15-22) He is actually saying everything is God's—not Caesar's.

This intimate connection between God and creation is highlighted in the work of Radical Orthodox theologians like John Milbank and Catherine Pickstock. The creation is neither something that is given to humanity, nor does it exist wholly separate from God.[302] Creation is always in an analogical relationship with God—there is always a connection. God makes creation a gift of God's own being and so it is sustained. This is a finite participation in God's own substantiality. This means simply that creation does not have any existence by virtue of itself. God did not create, and then, there is creation separate and independent from God. The authors of *A Radical Orthodox Reader* write: "Creation has no autonomous existence. Creation does not stand alongside God as another focus of being or existence, neither does it lie 'outside' God. When God creates the universe, there is not one 'thing' (God) and then, suddenly, two 'things' (God + creation).[303] Milbank and Pickstock's argument is that modern theology and philosophy has incorrectly separated creation from God and in so doing has created a false disconnect. When applied to stewardship we can easily see how it has undermined our understanding of the world and our work in it. How do we go about the stewardship of creation which is intimately tied to God? We are called as part of the creation to restore it—to reconcile it. Radical Orthodox theologian William T. Cavanaugh writes that we are to relocate "true citizenship beyond the confines of the earthly empire." And, "It is the Church, uniting earth and heaven, which is the true 'politics.'"[304]

Convincing people to make a tithe pledge in order to support a church will no longer be sufficient to help Christians navigate the world in which they find themselves. Today the world is in an ecological crisis. There is a failure of governments to provide for the wellbeing of all its citizens. There is a gulf growing between the rich and the poor. These forces, and the anxiety people carry with them about their financial future, have shifted the contemporary stewardship conversation to focus upon the individual, their place within the context of their community, their relationship with others, and most of all their relationship with the world around them. Mix these social trends together with electronic funding and new platforms for connecting and giving, and the future of Church stewardship begins to emerge. Stewardship will be for the future Church a discussion dependent upon the health of connection, and its focus will be much broader than support of a building and a priest—stewardship will be about nothing less than transforming the world.

Connection is an essential ingredient to any discussion the future Church will have about stewardship. Bader-Saye believes that affection is the key to this discussion because people no longer want simply to give money.[305] People long for affection and this desire to be connected across the social boundaries of rich and poor leads them to want to be a meaningful part of the lives of others. No longer will there be anonymous philanthropy[306]—the point is not the money but the connection of real people one to another, bound together in bonds of affection, working for the betterment of lives an communities.

The future Church, living Christian communities, will thrive only if they are intimately connected to the community which surrounds them. As God and Creation are not separate, so Church and Community are not separate but one. The non-profits, non-governmental organizations, and churches that survive in the next twenty to forty years will be entities which are committed to improving the intrinsic value of their community and those who live therein. To do this, Christian communities will have to have considerable connections with people and their civic context.[307] Christians and their communities will have an accountable and conscientious bond with the world around them. They will have to have affection for the people and communities in which they find themselves. Discipleship and citizenship will go hand-in-hand.

Christian communities must understand that they do not inhabit a world apart from the world around them. They are not separate, nor are the Christians themselves somehow separate, from the world. Stewardship conversations of the future will understand that we exist in a particular place, that we belong to it, that we are called to care for the things that God has made. Future stewardship will speak about our unique place within the kingdom and our responsibility to be answerable to God about what we did with it. The future Church will have affection for the society and be inextricably connected to it. This will be an ecological, economic and a social understanding. As we find our community and are rooted within it we will also find our neighbors, friends, loved ones, and strangers "with whom we share our place."[308]

Wendell Berry writes:

The word "affection" and the terms of value that cluster around it—love, care, sympathy, mercy, forbearance, respect, reverence—have histories and meanings that raise the issue of worth. We should, as our culture has warned us over and over again, give our affection to things that are true, just, and beautiful.[309]

Whereas in the present we see stewardship conversations that have themes of ecology, economy, social activism, and church finances, in the future we will have conversations about stewardship that help form individuals who understand that everything is connected. The microcosmic conversation about electricity for a building will be understood as being one of global importance. Christian communities who wish to be part of the lives of new generations of individuals, formed in the midst of a global economy and ecological crisis, will treat these themes reverently and with much consideration. The future Church cannot ignore these shifts.

In a lecture given to the Institute for the Future, Jerry Michalski, founder of REX—the Relationship Economy, offered a vision of how organizations can thrive in a "relationship economy."[310] As a young country we have moved through an agrarian economy into an industrial economy. Michalski began his lecture by telling the group gathered that we had moved most recently to an economy based upon information and knowledge, both of which (like agriculture and industry) have now been commercialized.[311] We are growth-addicted and focused upon our national wealth—our gross ability to produce.

In our current economy Michalski argues:

Scarcity = Value
Time = Money
Content is King
Knowledge = Power
Monopoly is best
IP [Internet Protocol] is your principal asset

Protect that asset at all cost
Externalities don't matter[312]

Michalski like Nassim recognizes the fragility within this system and the vulnerability that it brings. We recognize that this economic model is not one built on connection or upon a stewardship theology of affection. The new relationship economy that is developing is one that rejects scarcity and understands abundance and that this abundance is rooted in relationships. Social networking and platforms that enable this to happen are everywhere. The next step is to develop technologies to support the Christian community that creates and shares: "meaning, purpose, and greater good."[313]

Michalski believes that organizations that will thrive in the future will be those that are not fake but genuine—rooted in the real and in real people. These organizations will be open and open to participation by all. They will be free to the user, social in nature, and embody a sense of trust.[314] Here is the biggest takeaway from Michalski's presentation: relationships are not economic and they are not between an organization and a human being.[315]

The future Church and its Christian communities must grasp the essential stewardship ingredient of the future—stewardship is not about church economy, it is about relationships. And, stewardship will grow when it is a relationship between human beings and God; it is not about the relationship of the individual to the church. Like the rest of the culture we have gotten into a mindset that offers stewardship as a means of supporting a church while making a response to God out of our beneficence *and* it is about the health of the relationship between the church and the individual. Christian community has one purpose and one purpose only (and it is not an economic one) and that is to connect people to God and to connect people with people—reconciliation. Stewardship will be about the health and vitality of the relationships Christians have.

All organizations are trying to figure the new relational economy out—primarily in order to capitalize upon it! This is not our purpose. Our purpose is to have a conversation about stewardship which helps people connect their giving with their values, and their belief in a God who cares and who helps people connect to one another. Michalski offers organizations some ideas about how to begin this conversation and his points are worth reflecting here as we think about the future Church. We must begin by rebuilding trust—relational trust.[316]

The price we must pay is that this kind of trust building does not bring financial benefits. Trust is rebuilt when the community is the beneficiary and not the church. Leaders will have to choose to make trust and community impact the measurements of health and vitality and not the old economic measurements of pledges and average Sunday attendance. Christian communities of the future will have to be visible to the world around them embracing new partners. Language like "pledging units," will all need to evolve.[317] We cannot treat people like an interchangeable unit and then expect them to behave like a human being.

What is taking shape globally is a gift economy; this is one of the future artifacts that is present today and is important for our conversation around stewardship. Our goal as a transformative Christian community is to reach huge numbers of people, motivate them for the common good, and at the same time decrease overhead cost and any negative drain/drag on our mission initiatives. We are trying to create platforms where our "technology tools are highly participatory and social. They take advantage of intrinsic human motivations to contribute in order to be noticed, to share opinions, to be a part of something greater than ourselves."[318] People receive rewards and compensation that are social in nature. Relationships are our currency and our mission of service is to increase the intrinsic value of individuals in the community. Enter the reality of the "gift society." This is a radical change in economic theory and it is underway as the power within the economy shifts from corporation to individual.[319]

In the industrial revolution, the individual had to work for the machine; today, the technology is being adapted to human need. A gift economy, like the economic values that Michalski speaks about, is part of the "decomodification" movement. Gift economies are an ancient economic form. "Whether within rural communities or open-source programmers, the focus is on acts and experiences instead of relying on alternative commodity structures such as game points or social currency. Interactions in such circles are based implicitly on intrinsic rewards—giving, creating, being—rather than openly utilitarian trade in commodities," writes Marina Gorbis in her book *The Nature of the Future.*[320]

Engaging in stewardship for a new millennium will mean losing some predictability and creating more work around connecting individuals with one another and their causes, using new technologies and new methods as giving platforms. Those wishing to give might be moved by a news event or life event, maybe even in the middle of the night; so opening doors to accessible giving will be essential for future stewardship.

Stewardship conversation in the future will not tell the members what we are doing and invite them to give to a budget. New conversations will look for giving partners who understand the mutuality involved in stewardship. God is looking for partners, and as partners we are to work together for the mutual building up of God's creation and God's community. Future stewardship may include sweat equity and hands on work. No longer will stewardship be the work of check writing. The difference will be that the service and hands-on work will be outside of the church building, instead of in service *to* the church. Just as there will be no more anonymous philanthropy, there will also be no *toxic charity*. Instead people will look to improve the lives of their neighbor in cooperation with them.

Healthy stewardship in the future will be transparent about where the funds go and how they are used. It will be evident that the use of the funds is responsible and responsive to the world. Future Church stewardship will not demean or undermine the individuals it seeks to serve, but will treat both the donor and the recipient with respect and dignity. I believe that connection is essential in the conversation about stewardship. The church's currency is relationships and as such it is primed to participate in a world economy shifting from shallow consumerism to transformative-shared lives.

As we look for artifacts in our present time we can see this change occurring even now. The ability to pledge and set up a bank electronic monthly disbursement have leveled out giving and created more predictable budgeting. It means that there is no summer lull for many givers who are on vacation. Electronic banking is slowly doing away with cash and inventions such as the *Square* mean that even small businesses are mobile. This trend will bring about the end of carrying cash, and we will have to rethink how we deal with the offering plate or collection on Sunday morning. Remember the offering plate is a relatively new invention. It is okay if it goes away or morphs into something else. I believe that electronic banking will move this process along. Many parishes see electronic banking as an important ingredient in maneuvering into the future stewardship. We now have more and more Churches with giving kiosks. The temptation will be to see this as the future. Electronic banking is only the first step of technology affecting stewardship.

A kind of disconnect between individual and community comes with electronic banking. Once the giving is set up on a monthly basis, it is unlikely that the individual will go in and change it—either to make it lower or higher. This works in the community's favor when a decrease is likely. Conversely the opposite is true as well—without continued storytelling and involving the individual and family in the community narrative, it is unlikely to increase. This disconnect can lead a community into a false sense of security. The old envelope system and annual campaign are unlikely to work on digital natives. The goal for Christian communities will be to build a constant narrative of involvement with real stories of transformation and multiple opportunities to participate and give throughout the year.

Constant and competing communication will mean that Christian communities will have to be attentive, and adjust to what works in order to keep people's attention, and communicate how giving changes lives. The annual campaign will in the future be transformed into yearlong stewardship conversations—real people making real connections with real opportunities to make a difference through their giving. We already see this transition taking place in the church with yearlong stewardship calendars being created and posted for sharing. The Diocese of West Texas is one of the leaders in this effort.[321] Year round stewardship fits with our theology that we are stewards of God's creation every day and have constant opportunities for giving. However, we need to take the model and run with it. We need to translate the idea that we don't just tell people to give once a month for twelve months, but we connect them to ministries and giving opportunities all year round. Yes, it is good to talk about stewardship. It is better to connect parishioner Bob into a mentoring relationship with a young person from the community and then have them share their story of transformation. Bob might say, "It all started when I went online to give to St. Timothy's mentoring project. Then I got a call from St. Timothy's liaison with the program and she invited me to come along and meet some of the participants in the program." Stewardship will follow, and grow, out of relationship building. Year round stewardship connections will be made when *theology* and *personal narrative* are amplified by electronic giving tools.

Christian communities must have a goal of leading individuals through their communication and connection tools to opportunities where they can make a financial or time transaction—giving to those things that they believe in, understand, and feel to be important. We have a difficult time currently undertaking annual campaigns. The future Church will spend time in conversation with those who make financial gifts to ministry. They will spend time working with people on projects that they are interested in supporting. By making the intimate connection, the future Church will increase its stewardship impact on the community. The future Church will be one that finds new ways to create small giving economies. In the past, big box churches have had the most impact. I believe that in the future Church we will see a diversification of communities making even bigger impacts. Not unlike micro-industries, small congregations can have a big impact on their local community. In the new stewardship economy the most important technology is the "technology of social relations," regardless of size.

The Christian community engaged in stewardship forty years from now will be a community that is creating social opportunities such as meet-ups. Meet-ups are settings, with individuals (normally a mix of parishioners and non- parishioners), enlisting support and time for a particular topic or project that impacts the wider community. This is not part of our current stewardship model but it will be essential to the future of Christian community life. People have to be involved in the organization they are helping to fund and the demand will be availability of information on a weekly, if not daily basis. This will be about relationships and not efficiency.[322] Remember, it takes the same amount of time to specialize as it does to generalize—it is relative. The future Church will understand that specializing in unique opportunities helps to resonate with the charisms of the individual community members and ultimately drive opportunities to give.

There are several new ways of using technology to build economies and illustrate further ways in which stewardship will be shaped in the church of the future. David Eggers, a forward-looking author, created ScholarMatch. (scholarmatch.org/) Since 2010, donors interested in creating scholarship opportunities for graduating high school seniors can go online and help to pay tuition. The students in need of funding tells their story online. Together, real students in need meet real donors and together make their way through college. As of 2012 ScholarMatch had raised $130,000 for students, many of whom are the first to attend college in their families.[323] Imagine linking graduating seniors in a church with this type of a tool. Or imagine a collective site called SeminarianMatch where future scholars, priests, and teachers for the church can navigate training, thanks to the help of donors committed to Christian Education and the formation of ministers for the Gospel.

LendFriend, Lend4Health, and Grow VC are microventure sites. (lendfriend.com, lend4health.blogspot.com, and group.growvc.com)[324]

Venture capital and loans used to be the purview of banks. Today donors and investors are able to meet up online with projects, individuals, and start-ups. Some investment plans require as little interest as $20. Helping individuals pay for costly health care with secure lending has stemmed medical bankruptcies for many. Peer-to-peer relationships are allowing boundaried and safe investments as well as low interest ways of building an economy.[325] In 2005, a startup called Kiva began to help entrepreneurs and small business owners in third world countries get low interest loans. Their first project in Uganda is today a huge piece of their economy in one of Africa's most populous countries. In 2009 Kiva began domestic loans in a similar fashion.[326] They are built on personal relationships that begin as simple investments and a desire to help many who currently have no other means of receiving a hand up.

The future Church will be involved in creating similar structures. We will see congregations, parishioners, and members of the community in which the church makes its home all working to create micro financing and other ventures possible. Connecting ministry opportunities with those who are interested will take the forms of Kiva-style sites. Still others may develop projects linking the Christian community and a community project, enabling a broader denominational participation in a local innovation that can change the community. These may be focused on service opportunities like health, clean water, wellness, or micro loans to help families in need. Imagine a future Church that is interested in helping improve the financial security and overall wellbeing of the community. Archbishop of Canterbury Justin Welby's desire to have Church credit unions that out-perform payday lending businesses by offering lower interest rates is a good example of one way micro ventures can shape stewardship. Imagine if this micro lending was available online for congregations connecting those who wish to lend and those who need to borrow in the community.

One of the most popular the new funding tools for the maker movement is Kickstarter (www.kickstarter.com). Kickstarter is an entrepreneurial tool that enables investors to connect with individual inventors looking for marketing support and funds. The *Veronica Mars* film is an example of how this new economic tool has made a startling difference. *Veronica Mars* was a novel made into a TV series and written by Rob Thomas. It aired for three seasons and then was canceled. There was a huge fandom though, and they and Rob Thomas were determined; using Kickstarter, they raised enough money to make a feature length film that aired in 2013. As far as the fandom was concerned it was a huge success: 91,000 individual backers raised over $5 million for the film.[327] Today more than 5 different films have made their way through Kickstarter to the Sundance Film Festival. Adrianne Jeffries, an editor of the *New York Observer* and founder of BetaBeat (a tech commentary blog) wrote, "Taken to the extreme, you can imagine a future in which the nation's movie houses are running hundreds of Kickstarter-funded films instead of the same eight Hollywood movies. Which would be fantastic. Small films would be made once they hit a certain threshold and would only open up at locations where the showings have already sold out. What if Steven Spielberg put his next script on Kickstarter and made the movie entirely under his own discretion, without the pressure of Hollywood suits."[328]

Episcopal Relief and Development (ERD) has one of the most brilliant communication strategies in a denominational church. Their leadership has harnessed the power of social networking to build a broad community. They have navigated the switch between paper and electronic media with a balanced approach. All of their material leads donors to their website www.episcopalrelief.org.[329] ERD's Twitter and Facebook posts include regular updates and links to direct giving opportunities. They update donors on projects regularly. They visit actual ministry sites and create real time relationship building between donors and recipients. They are focused on a particular suite of projects and offer clarity to those interested in making a difference in a global way while focused on local economic change. Their disaster relief partnerships, and their work with mosquito netting have galvanized a strong and broad-based donor population. They are doing much of what we have spoken about in this section. The future Church must have this same high quality of social networking stewardship at the local level with a focus in the local community, and with ties to the global work of organizations like ERD. We will see a steady advance of this electronic stewardship community build across denominations, creating a mammoth networked community of stewards, focusing their giving on real people and making a real difference they can speak about to family and friends.

Service is not the only way that the future church will use crowd funding. In 2012 the Episcopal Church planted 3 new churches across its 110 dioceses.[330] I believe that a successful Church planting strategy in the future will not be unlike a crowdsourced funding tool like Kickstarter. I believe the growing mistrust of sending money to a large central institution like a provincial or regional office will require new and innovative forms of funding new Christian communities. Both non-denominational churches anddenominational churches will use crowd-funded dollars to start new communities. Some of these will be stand-alone congregations where a church planter will use crowd funding for their ministry. Some existing congregations will use a Kickstarter-model for planting satellite congregations. Diocesan leadership might use crowd funding to start congregations for new immigrant populations—increasing participation in building venture capital for new churches. I also imagine that some of the congregations birthed in the decades to come will use shared and public space to meet, participate in non-governmental not for profit service ministry, and use coffee shops for their office hours and Bible studies. These new Internet based Christian communities will use a form of crowd funding for their stewardship and the support of their mission. Such a funding apparatus will be helpful as both a tool for raising capital and also raising interest and participation in a new adventure in mission.

What is happening in this new maker movement will be a catalyst for an energized living future church—innovative economies and innovative stewardship. The new makers are not selling out their ideas to big corporations and so they remain small batch and focused. The future Church will dabble at the local level with innovation and creativity in the same way. Because of the network they will share their ideas. For the future Church we can see that localized and adapted community mission is possible when it moves away from having to look like all the other big box churches in a denomination. There is little in overhead funding required for these new entrepreneurs and their ideas.

Freeing new Christian communities (especially in the denominational world) from the need to have overhead dollars going away from the mission project to the institution is a financial necessity in the expensive world of church planting. Money is available for the new idea as it is needed and not before—decreasing overhead interest that is carried and can shrink financial pliability at a time when it is most necessary. This also decreases the work to get upfront capital. Denominational church planting is always focused upon building a big church building and filling it with people. Only in the last five years have we seen a concerted effort to start smaller communities. What happens for the maker product is essential—customers and clients are part of the community backing the project. To have a healthy and whole Christian community in the maker model means having parishioners and community members backing ministry. In the maker world of crowd funding, those funding the project are part of the creation and idea, generating the work of getting something ready for market. They are invested. They then become the chief evangelists for the new idea and product. Likewise parishioners and community members will become the chief evangelists for the new Christian community or service ministry. And, if it doesn't fund, then it is either the wrong time or the wrong place.

We are not in the business of growing financial returns so that the diocese can maintain its budget. We are in the business of God's mission, and vocation in response to that mission. Stewardship is about participating in God's economy—in God's provision for the world where there is enough. It is about using what we have to enlarge God's community. Stewardship is not simply about giving but it is about being involved in creating a new world—a transformed world. Stewardship with all of its networking and crowd sourcing potential ultimately is about connecting individuals with God and with their neighbor.

What we are learning is that how we participate in the variety of economies around us is integral to how we are linked to the society in which we live. Futurist Marina Gorbis writes, "The transactions facilitated by social platforms are creating a different kind of value and a different kind of wealth, which is not necessarily measurable in monetary terms. This wealth is in part a matter of how we feel when we engage in these transactions. Socially embedded transactions increase our levels of connectedness and engagement with others."[331] Jonathan Haidt, professor of psychology at the University of Virginia writes, "We are, in a way, like bees: our lives only make full sense as members of a larger hive, or as cells in a larger body. Yet in our modern way of living we've busted out of the hive and flown out on our own, each one of us free to live as we please. Most of us need to be part of a hive in some way, ideally a hive that has a clearly noble purpose."[332] It turns out that our very happiness may actually be rooted in how well we are connected and how much we spend and give to others.[333]

In 2010, I read an important book by Clay Shirky entitled *Cognitive Surplus*. In it he says that since 1940 there has been an exponential increase in free time. (This is not unlike what I argued in terms of Average Sunday Attendance.) There are many more opportunities for us to use our free time today—perhaps more than ever. He would argue that we have more opportunity to be creative and collaborative. The time we have to contribute is growing and we as individuals are participating across many new portals and in many new projects.

Shirky, like myself, grew up consuming large amounts of television; in fact we watched a lot of the same shows. Today my daughter has several creative sites that she runs with literally hundreds of participants sharing ideas with her and she with them. We are, according to Shirky, creating a new era of human expression. Marina Gorbis in her work on the nature of the future says that digital natives are now sharing themselves across a multitude of platforms, giving and sharing ideas and money in a new more socially connected universe. We are doing a lot of this work, this using of our cognitive surplus, without receiving what is essential in modern economies—monetary rewards.[334] The question for the church is what kind of surplus do we have that might be networked with this wider global movement. The answer is: the stewardship of our relationships. The living and thriving future Church will participate in this global evolution by using its surplus of connected individuals and communities across the globe, and supporting a new stewardship of ideas, money, and support. Future Church stewardship will be the means by which we live out our connection to God and to our neighbor.

CHAPTER FOURTEEN
Communities of Service Built by Neighbors

*"If this is going to be a Christian nation that doesn't help
the poor, either we've got to pretend that Jesus was just as selfish
as we are, or we've got to acknowledge that he commanded us
to love the poor and serve the needy without condition and then
admit that we just don't want to do it."*
— Stephen Colbert, 'The Colbert Report'

John the Baptist believed that the essence of the Gospel could be summed up in this way: "Anyone who has two shirts should share with the one who has none" (Luke 3:11). A connected future Church of stewards is not meant to serve itself. In fact if it does, it will not work. One of the ways that the Church does its mission of reconciliation is through service. We are called to do the work of caring on God's behalf in the world. We are to respond to God's love and provision of grace by in turn loving and providing grace through service in our communities. Jesus says a lot about the poor and he is intent that those who follow him are to engage in service within and as part of their community. Jesus told this story to explain the importance of our actions:

There was a rich man who was dressed in purple and fine linen and who feasted sumptuously every day. At his gate lay a poor man named Lazarus, covered with sores, who longed to satisfy his hunger with what fell from the rich man's table; even the dogs would come and lick his sores. It was really gross.

The poor man died and was carried away by the angels to be with Abraham. The rich man also died and was buried. In Hades, where he was being tormented, he looked up and saw Abraham far away with Lazarus by his side. He called out, "Father Abraham, have mercy on me, and send Lazarus to dip the tip of his finger in water and cool my tongue; for I am in agony in these flames." But Abraham said, "Child, remember that during your lifetime you received your good things, and Lazarus, in like manner evil things; but now he is comforted here, and you are in agony. Besides all this, between you and us a great chasm has been fixed, so that those who might want to pass from here to you cannot do so, and no one can cross from there to us."

He said, "Then, father, I beg you to send him to my father's house—for I have five brothers–that he may warn them, so that they will not also come into this place of torment." Abraham replied, "They have Moses and the prophets; they should listen to them." He said, "No, father Abraham; but if someone goes to them from the dead, they will repent." He said to him, "If they do not listen to Moses and the prophets, neither will they be convinced even if someone rises from the dead." (Luke 16:19-31)

There is a man at the gate and it matters how we treat him—says Jesus. It matters to the man, it matters to Jesus, and most of all it matters to God. It matters how the wealthy man treats Lazarus specifically and how the rich treat the poor generally. Day after day, as he passed through the gates, the rich man paid no attention to Lazarus. God, on the other hand, has a special concern for the man at the gate.

In Matthew's Gospel, chapter 25, Jesus explains the way to participate in the Kingdom of God. He says that those who wish to be part of the new Kingdom of God must be ready like bridesmaids waiting on the bridegroom. They must stay awake and be ready to meet the kingdom when it comes. Jesus says that those who follow him and want to be a part of the kingdom must invest their gifts and talents in the kingdom. They must not bury and hide and hoard.

Instead, those who follow Jesus must invest in the world around them. They must be a part of it and they must use their money and their own abilities to help God build up the kingdom. God does not do this alone and needs our help.

Then Jesus tells a story about how a crowd will gather when the Kingdom of God comes. The King will look to those who participated in the kingdom building and he will say to them, "Come, you are part of the kingdom. The kingdom has been growing since the beginnings of the universe. You are now to be part of it." The crowd did not understand. So, the king said, "I was hungry and you gave me food, I was thirsty and you gave me something to drink, I was a stranger and you welcomed me, I was naked and you gave me clothing, I was sick and you took care of me, I was in prison and you visited me."(Matthew 25.31ff.) The ones whom he is talking to are still puzzled and they do not understand. So they say together, "Lord, when was it that we saw you hungry and gave you food, or thirsty and gave you something to drink? And when was it that we saw you a stranger and welcomed you, or naked and gave you clothing? And when was it that we saw you sick or in prison and visited you?" The king looked at them and said that whenever they did these things, whenever they ministered to their neighbor, whenever they offered a bit of kindness and love and charity they did so to the king himself. Jesus tells this story and emphasizes it by making it clear that those individuals who do not give food to the hungry, who do not give drink to the thirsty, who do not take the stranger in, clothe the naked, and visit the sick and those in prison are not followers of his. Those who do not do these things are not part of the kingdom builders Jesus is looking to as partners.

In the Gospel of Luke, Jesus returns to the region of Galilee—the place where he was raised. Jesus had been away learning and teaching and he had returned to his hometown. He enters a synagogue there. He sits in their midst. (Luke 14.4ff) It is a day of gathering and friends and family are there. The people sit around the edges of the small building—the synagogue—to hear God's word read. They offer Jesus an opportunity to read the scriptures. And, so he does. He opens up the scroll, and he reads from the prophet Isaiah. He reads: "The Spirit of the Lord is upon me, because he has anointed me to bring good news to the poor. He has sent me to proclaim release to the captives and recovery of sight to the blind, to let the oppressed go free, to proclaim the year of the Lord's favor." Jesus then tells them that this is his ministry. He is going to bring glory to God and show his love for God by bringing this good news to the people. He will do this in word and in action.

We can read the story of the miraculous healings that Jesus does because he cared for the sick. We can read about how he fed people with bread, fish, and wine. He fed thousands of people. We can read about how he washed the feet of his disciples and served them at table. The gospels tell us of a few certain things and one of those is that the kingdom of God depends upon God's friends serving one another in a united community of affection.

The Gospels are clear and speak with one voice on the subject of service—Jesus believed that we are to serve our neighbor. Jesus makes it clear that, if we love him, he expects us to care for those who have been abandoned, marginalized—for the sheep who have no shepherd. Remember the questions the resurrected Christ asked Simon Peter: "Simon, son of John, do you love me more than these?" Peter felt hurt because he said to him the third time, "Do you love me?" And he said to him, "Lord, you know everything; you know that I love you." Jesus said to him, "Feed my sheep." (John 21:15, 17)

True, we are responsible for ourselves. But what the Gospels and the passages about healing, feeding, and helping teach, which is radical, is that we are responsible for the people in our lives and in the world around us. This work is more than just the rich tending the poor, though that is certainly part of it. Caring is often seen as something the "haves" do for the "have nots." But Jesus' challenge to us all is one that goes far beyond *noblesse oblige*, the obligation of the nobility on behalf of the poor. Jesus' message goes beyond anonymous giving. It goes beyond charity for the sake of charity—

which often does more harm than good. The radical message here is that we care for each other, I for you and you for me. This moves us beyond the notion of a Samaritan helping out a beaten and abandoned neighbor or a rich man helping out a poor man. On the contrary, Jesus' message is that we are now part of a radically reconfigured family wherein each one is a brother and sister for whom we are responsible. This reverses Cain's answer to God's question: "Where is your brother Abel?" Cain having killed his brother then replied, "Am I my brother's keeper?" The answer from Jesus is, "Yes."

Through the cross, Jesus has taken on responsibility for us, for the whole world. Now he needs us to do the same, to take up our cross and follow, and care for the world. That makes us responsible for our communities, our cities, our states, our nation, other nations, and even our enemies. All the sheep are our responsibility.

Not just the ones who are like us.

Not just the ones who go to our church.

Not just the other Episcopalians.

Not just the Christians.

The hard lesson here, one we are all too eager as sinful broken human beings to ignore, is that it matters to God how each one of us lives. It matters to God the manner in which we care for and stand with others. There is someone standing at the gate of our lives. And that person, that community, is waiting for us to stand with them as extensions of God's mercy, grace, and abundant love. This is not something that can be done on our behalf so we do not have to be bothered. A key and essential ingredient to the discipline of Christian life is that we are inconvenienced by the work of helping other human beings.

The first Christians believed this was important and they continued the work of service. It is clear in Paul's letters that collections for the poor are taken up and shared among the churches. The biblical Book of Acts tells of how money is shared and how individuals are given specific work of caring for widows and orphans.

In his letter to the Galatians, Paul writes that it is the main mission of the church to provide for those in need and those outside their community (Galatians 2:10). The first official church action after electing apostles was to feed the poor (Acts 6:1-6). The Christian community that lifted up the letter of James as revelation understood that the primary focus of Jesus' ministry, the primary recipients of the Gospel, were the poor. (James 2:5). It is also written in the book of James: "Pure religion is this: to visit the orphan and widow in their affliction" (James 1:21).

Early Christians were known as those who cared for and served the poor. The early church saw that the work of the Gospel as relationships built between the faithful for the benefit of caring for the poor, housing the oppressed, and feeding the hungry.

Long after the Gospels were written, early Christian communities continued to care for the elderly, widows, orphans, prisoners, and the shipwrecked. [335] They also supported families who lost loved ones because of their faith during the great persecutions. Even the pagan emperor Julian confessed, "the godless Galileans feed not only their poor but ours as well."

The great bishop and early church leader Tertullian (AD 155–220) wrote:

> Each of us puts in a trifle on the monthly day, or when he pleases; but only if he pleases, and only if he is able, for no man is obliged, but contributes of his own free will. These are, as it were, deposits of piety; for it is not paid out thence for feasts and drinking and thankless eating houses, but for feeding and burying the needy, for boys and girls deprived of means and parents, for old folk now confined to the house: also for them that are shipwrecked, for any who are in the mines, and for any who, in the islands, or in the prisons, if only it be for the cause of God's people.[336]

Almsgiving was simply understood to be a keystone of Christian discipleship. In a letter from Saint Clement written in the second century, he wrote that almsgiving "lightens sin." He writes: "Almsgiving is good even as penitence for sin: fasting is better than prayer, but the giving of alms is better than both."[337]

By the fifth century, things changed and service became something the Church did as part of its operations. The rise of formal monasticism and mission meant that the institution itself housed the work of caring for the poor. This rested on the monks, priests, and bishops shoulders. They did this on behalf of the whole society. The deacons who had been so involved in the first part of the Church's life now fade into the background.[338] Giving became largely one of gaining distinction and virtue from the saints and from God. People were beginning to distance themselves in some ways from the poor as levels of society began to be created by the developing worker classes. The real purpose of almsgiving was to free the person of wealth from the sin of private property.[339]

The early Middle Ages, with its chaos, would transform service and almsgiving again. During the time of Constantine it was the local congregation or the monastery's responsibility and duty to care for the poor, needy and infirmed. In the eighth century the tithe became a compulsory tax—a new invention for the Christian Church. In England a third of the tithe was to be taken from the rich and given specifically to the relief of the poor.[340] What shifted is that the care of the poor during this time period moved from the sole responsibility of the priest and bishop to a shared responsibility of institutions—hospitals, guilds and individuals.[341] Monasteries continued to play a part. In part the reason was because these institutions now existed in new forms as never before. By the end of this period in Christian history almost all the offerings went to support the structure while hardly any of it made its way to the poor. Sometimes ingatherings on special days were used for relief. The priest and bishop are still the social workers of the day though this is fading as they take on new responsibilities.

Service ministries come to a new era as society moved into humanism and modernity. The reformation brought with it a renewed connection of piety and care for the poor. Despite the efforts of Middle Age saints like St. Francis, the church understood well that good theology does not bring with it increased social services. Protestantism gave back to the church the notion that Christ indeed had a special connection to the poor.[342]

By 1903 the United Nations reported that the Church was undertaking one-third of benevolent work through her institutions—hospitals, orphanages, homes for poor, mentally unstable, and the elderly.[343] During this march to the post -modern age, the Church would continue its involvement in service, transforming most of its energy in increasing its voice to advocate for slaves, women, factory workers, and finally in civil rights. That being said, as we move into the present what is real is that much of the work for the poor has migrated to the government and non-governmental agencies.

Today the church is far better known for telling people what to think and how to be right, than it is truly known for transforming the world through the work of service. The challenge that Edmund H. Oliver, professor at St. Andrews College, Saskatchewan, Canada, leveled to his Presbyterian students and the Church in 1930 remains unanswered. The Church will have to re-engage a "prophetic vision" of Christ as conscience to the society. The Church of the future will have to educate people about the society around them and "inspire" them to action. While caring for the poor, the Church will have to be a "pioneer" in new efforts to meet the changing nature of social need. The Church will have to deal with "causes" and not only "symptoms." Finally, the Church will need to be at work to transform the "helped into helpers."[344]

Oliver's words speak poignantly as we shift our focus to the future Church:

The Christian spirit is continually adapting, and is continuously adaptable. It will use every particle of human capacity and energy for the ever-changing tasks of the Kingdom. The process is not complete for the Church until the objects of its compassion have had kindled in them hearts of pity and love to seek and to save others who may be in need. The Church must believe that all of human kind are not only redeemable but, also, usable for, and in the Kingdom. The spirit of ministry will impoverish unless it begets in those who are ministered unto, the passion and the power themselves to serve in their turn. The impulse to social service must be transmitted to all members of the social organism before the work is complete.[345]

Today and in the future if the individual followers of Jesus intend to have any integrity at all we must we must help one another make the sacred journey with God come alive in service to the poor and our neighbor.

The twin to our proclamation by word is proclamation by deed. Christians believe that serving our neighbor is the way in which we incarnate God's love for all people. Episcopalians are the only ones who, when renewing their baptismal vows to God, promise publically to act on God's behalf in service to those in need. We respond to human need that stretches from our work together to help neighbors recover from natural disasters to helping our neighbors survive the human disaster of greed. We believe we are to work to transform unjust structures in society. We are invested in the work of sustainability and safeguarding resources because we live in God's creation. We are to renew the face of the earth and life upon this fragile planet.[346]

The future church will not be invested in service ministries as we are invested today. We must repent from doing *toxic charity* and return to a church entwined with the health and well- being of its community. God has a mission that engages the world through our feet that take us to places that are forgotten. God's mission engages the world through backs that do the heavy lifting of rebuilding homes. God's mission engages the world with hands that are invested in lives, and that help people to stand; rather than handouts that so often leave people stuck in the same circumstances.

Dambisa Moyo wrote in *Dead Aid*, a World Bank report, that 85 percent of aid to Africa does not reach its intended destination. She wrote in the introduction, "Has more than US $1 trillion in development assistance over the last several decades made African people better off? No. In fact across the globe the recipients of this aid are worse off. Aid has helped make the poor poorer, and growth slower. Yet aid remains a centerpiece of today's development policy and one of the biggest ideas of our time."[347] The future Church understands that the idea that aid can alleviate systemic poverty, and has done so, is a myth. Moyo continued, "Millions in Africa are poorer today because of aid; misery and poverty have not ended but have increased. Aid has been, and continues to be, an unmitigated political, economic, and humanitarian disaster for most parts of the developing world."[348] What is true in Africa is also true across the United States and the Western hemisphere. Here is a great example from Robert Lupton's *Toxic Charity*. He writes, "Expenditures for a week of service by church and college groups are grossly out of proportion with what is actually accomplished. U.S. mission teams who rushed to Honduras to help rebuild homes destroyed by hurricane Mitch spent an average of $30,000 per home—homes locals could have built for $3,000 each. The money spent by one campus ministry to cover the costs of their Central American mission trip to repaint an orphanage would have been sufficient to hire two local painters and two new full-time teachers and purchase new uniforms for every student in the school."[349] This challenges our understanding. It is about the relationships but if we cared about the work we might be able to create a different model of service.

Some statistics report that over 90% of all Americans are involved financially in the charity industry in the U.S. *The Orlando Parade* in March of 2010 reported that 90 percent of Americans say that it is "important to be personally involved in supporting a cause we believe in."[350] This is evident in our conversation about stewardship above and how the future church will see its connection to the community. Service is no longer a Christian value but a value that has been embraced by our culture. It is present in corporate offices, fraternities and sororities, and schools. This is a wonderful thing except that when we give to people in need who could provide for themselves we "destroy people."[351] Lupton introduced me to these words by French philosopher and author of *Money and Power*, Jacque Ellul: It is important that giving be truly free. It must never degenerate into charity, in the pejorative sense. Almsgiving is Mammon's perversion of giving. It affirms the superiority of the giver, who thus gains a point on the recipient, binds him, demands gratitude, humiliates him and reduces him to a lower state than he had before. [352] The Future Church will redefine the meaning of neighbor, as they become partners in ministry with those who live in their community.

Lupton offers an "Oath for Compassionate Service" that the future Church takes seriously.[353] (1) Never do for the poor what they can do for themselves; (2) Limit one-way giving to emergencies; (3) Empower the poor through employment, lending, and investing, using grants sparingly to reinforce achievements; (4) Subordinate self-interest to the needs of those being served; (5) Listen closely to those you seek to help; (6) Above all, do no harm. Within the oath is a deep and abiding understanding that what true neighbors are involved in is "asset-based community development" (ABCD).

The future Church will be a church whose individuals walk out of its doors and into the community and seek to know their neighbors. The living Church will be involved in and be a part of the community's strengths more than its needs. The individuals involved in this future service mission will be those who believe that the poor and those in need are indeed individuals with gifts and talents, with dignity of purpose, and equals. The future Church will be a church that is focused on its community context in its efforts to serve.[354] It understands that each community is different—each congregation is different. The Church of the nineteenth and twentieth centuries became global; the Church of the new millennium will be a church that is local. It will intrinsically understand that a neighborhood is both a geographical location and a network of relationships.[355] Service ministry in the future will be asset oriented. It will build upon contextual strengths and resources rather than try to meet the need gap. It will see opportunities and be invested in creativity, imagination, and inventiveness. It will risk new things and encourage new partnerships and the creation of new networks.[356]

Often times Churches today focus on issues they think are important. They decide, based upon their limited knowledge of the situation, and limited conversation with the poor, that they know what is needed and so set off to fix it. I have been in more than my share of these kinds of meetings. The future living Church will be directed by the front burner issues that the community itself raises.[357] By building real-time partnerships with individuals in the community who are neighbors and in need those invested in service will listen and hear the issues that most affect their new friends. The future Church will always be focused on the first issues first and then work towards the deeper and more in-depth issues as time and trust builds. A living Church understands it is there as a partner in the community for the long haul. If people in our community care about safe public spaces, transportation, economic development, crime, or education—then God cares about these things and so the Church of the future in a living partnership with the community will care, and join hands to create a well community.

The future Church will be an investor in the community.[358] It invests therefore in economic development and partnerships. Loans, payment plans, and incentives are all used to empower those who are in need of creating a better living for themselves—they are never handouts.[359] Along with the financial investment and time investment, service communities of the future will understand that they must be focused on increasing the leadership within their community.[360] This does not mean being the leader but *raising up* leaders. "Indigenous leadership" is essential. Service organizations that are successful in the future will be those who empower, organize, and support local neighbors to have their voices and do the things they did not think were possible. It isn't that we as a Church will help and be nice, but we will support them in doing the things we know they can do and achieve.

Lastly, the service community of the future will have a quality of patience.[361] It will do its work with a long timetable. It will allow the service work to move at a pace comfortable for the whole community and not one based upon the needs of the Church. Progress will be measured based upon how the whole context and the people in the community take charge and begin to invest in one another's work and achieve the goals they have set out to achieve. It will not be based upon a budget requirement, or vestry desire to see results.

Today what the church calls *outreach* has a few façades. If the church is large enough they may have person or two who help organize where the money goes and how it is spent on local outreach projects. They may even organize groups to work in the community or go on mission trips. If the church is small, outreach is typically the project of a parishioner who has a particular passion or interest. So, the congregation in this setting takes on the work of the parishioner as their own: crop walk, a local shelter, or perhaps a feeding ministry. These individuals, in the large and the small congregation, operate as a kind of program manager. These managers are responsible for motivating and organizing people within a larger system for the best performance. They are part of a hierarchy or power structure that is focused on fulfilling a charitable mission. I don't think this will end. The service ministry of the future Church will look more like community organizing than management.[362]

Individuals who are pioneers of networked communities and non-toxic service ministries are individuals who are today playing outside the church's *outreach* categories. They are individuals who have left the structure of typical non-governmental, non-profits, and churches behind and are now setting out to implement service strategies that are DNA for the future church. They are uniting people in a room who share a common values and a shared desire to improve their community. They are connecting and networking in person and via social media. They are gathering people together— members and non-members. They understand that it is imperative to grow their group and build a movement. They invite individuals to participate and help build the service ministry.

The leaders understand they do not have all the answers or vision and must depend upon the group to help form and define their goals and aspirations. The leaders of the new service communities are advocates and supporters of the individuals involved. They are crossing the threshold of service organizations like churches and inviting leadership from all quadrants. In each scenario they recognize that because they are all working together to solve a common and shared issue that it is the social structure of the work that is important. So time and goals can be met and missed as long as the community is learning and building strength as a neighborhood family. A healthy community is their cause and it is a cause worth working for, and worth doing without pay, or other economic incentives. This is non-monetary reciprocity. Centered in this entrepreneurial service is the fact that they celebrate being together (have built a commons) and shared a common experience. The work is hard and the drive is internal but it is joyful and worth doing. The living Church of the future will be a community filled with individuals who are empowered to do this work inside and outside the church.

Alex Carmichael is a social organizer and a health service leader. She was motivated to contribute because of her own personal interest and cause, and so built a social organization call CureTogether (curetogether.com).[363] She was suffering a pain-filled life and doctors could not help her or diagnose the cause.[364] She believed, correctly, that she was not the only one with this pain issue or problem with diagnosis, and that people like her would be interested in understanding their malady and share common treatments. So she created CureTogether, an online community, where people can seek treatment, support, and find better health and health care together. It is the winner of the *Amen Patients Award*, nominated for the *Nokia Health Award*, and received the *Mayo Clinic iSpot* award for ideas transforming healthcare. Imagine Christian communities of the future networking online and in person with individuals in their community for the purpose of improving the state of their community. People like Carmichael are trying to change the world by gathering people together around shared concerns. They are creating their own service projects. The local church will put the power of its community network behind the creation of new service ministries in partnership with its neighbors.

The preamble of the constitution for the World Health Organization defines *health* in this way: "Health is a state of complete physical, mental and social well-being and not merely the absence of disease or infirmity."[365] We are currently in a culture locally and globally that is unhealthy. In the United States health care cost is skyrocketing. A new governmental health policy brings with it major changes. The fact that the U.S. parallels most countries in health care spending until the final two decades of life and then costs go through the roof is an important indicator of where our attention is—the end of life rather than a whole healthy life.

Beyond the local economy of health are the presenting issues of global travel and the real scare of pandemics. Globally and locally there is a gap between the healthy and the unhealthy that parallels the gap between the rich and the poor. Rural health in the U.S. has been decimated by the loss of doctors, clinics, and small hospitals. Bob Johansen and IFTF, among others, document clearly the growing anxiety about "health, hunger, and longevity."[366]

This insecurity is clearly visible within the culture as we consider these future trends:

- Location based health access
- Online tools and access to medical records

- Healthy shopping vs. lack of healthy of food in the community
- Determinants of health—quality, access, genetics, environment and behavior
- Extreme environmental deterioration[367]

The future Church will be involved in shaping service as it integrates health and spirituality. The Church is interested in the whole person: body, mind, and spirit and so wellness is a perennial part of our ministry. We are a church interested in the way in which the person lives within the broader community. In the past we have done this through hospital ministry (which the church owned) with resident chaplains. We have done this through philanthropy and outreach. The new era and issues of health insecurity and the wellness of communities will challenge us to think in different ways. The church will be challenged to think about how it provides pastoral care and services to hospitals and the aging, living within communities (independent/assisted/nursing) without owning the facility. We must answer the call to missionary presence in these institutions. We have not done this and in most dioceses across the continental U.S. we have abdicated our place in this particular part of our service ministry because of the health economy. The need is nevertheless present.

We will be challenged to understand that our communities may be access points for primary care and for mental health resources. As the culture investigates new ways to deal with health issues within the community, future congregations have an opportunity to be involved in both providing online connection tools, real space for clinics, and aid in navigating new health opportunities, working to organize communities to provide for its own health and wellness.

Desiring to be part of healthy communities will also call the church into reflection on its own contribution to the toxicity of its relationship with the surrounding community. Where is the church wasteful? What is the carbon footprint of our church? Are we building out of recycled and recyclable materials? How do followers of Jesus and believers in a creator God respond to the disintegrating health of the environment, neighborhoods, and communities? We understand today something that will shape our service tomorrow— everything in God's creation is connected. Humans are intimately connected to the context in which they live.

Churches of the future will be invested in their community because they understand their own health is dependent upon it. In 2011, the *New England Journal of Medicine* reported on a study of health for individuals who lived in low-income housing. What they discovered is that if we worked together on improving local neighborhoods, people who live there would be healthier.[368] There is a direct correlation between the community in which people live and their individual health. Jens Ludwig, the University of Chicago Law Professor who conducted the study, found that health outcomes changed based upon the kind of neighborhood in which h people live. He summarized the discovery this way: "The results suggest that over the long term, investments in improving neighborhood environments might be an important complement to medical care when it comes to preventing obesity and diabetes."[369] When individuals work together to improve social structures, green spaces, access to health care, access to jobs, and a strong economy, the individuals who live in these places will actually be healthier and decrease the drain on the wider public system. Everyone's health and wellbeing are tied together. The study shows, "Beyond simply pinpointing scales of action—our social structures and environments—their study, at least by implication, opens up a much broader set of opportunities for local communities to act collaboratively to improve their health, such as improving access to parks, grocery stores, and otherwise acting through local communities to improve health that have the potential to be a lot cheaper, and a lot more effective, than a lot of traditional biomedical interventions."[370] The future Church will be an active participant in building well communities, physically and spiritually

The Episcopal Health Foundation of Texas (EHF) is a leader in redefining the future of service between the local church and their community context. We believe that in response to the future of service and community needs, the Church will be focused on building capacity in individuals, families, and institutions to enable them to create and sustain these well communities. Therefore EHF will invest in community development projects that incorporate health and wellness. It will support programs that build tenacity and resilience between the local church and the wider neighborhood in which it finds itself. The future Church will be interested in building capacity by partnering with local nonprofits already working in the neighborhood. It will focus on the real needs of neighbors with a special eye towards enhancing childhood development because of the long-term societal impact such investments will have.

A second strategic goal will be to improve the health care delivery system by increasing access to high quality community-based preventive, primary and mental health care. This will mean that the local church will partner with schools to help provide health care on site. It will use technology to expand access to care in churches, schools, and throughout the neighborhood in which it finds itself. It will help to integrate spiritual care with primary and mental health care. The future Church will invest in ways it can be part of delivering more providers to underserved populations. This can be done either through shared space or collaborative funding. All in all it will endeavor to increase access to health opportunities.

The third set of goals for the future Church will be to engage. The diocese, local Church, and local NGO's will work together to develop new and sustain continuing service ministries in health and wellness that work. The local church of the future will be invested in community-based research and development insuring that it is working on real need based ministries. The future Church will marshal its numbers of parishioners to volunteer and serve in a variety of health care settings. In order for the local parish to do this work it will have to train and organize its people and their neighbors.[371]

The future Church must be focused on long-term transformation. "Most charities take care of immediate needs. They are interested in finding the gaps in the social safety net and then filling them," says Elena Marks who is a nonresident fellow in health policy at the Baker Institute as well as the president and CEO of the Episcopal Health Foundation (EHF). The work at EHF is to focus our congregations on making lasting sustainable change in their communities. Our service goal is to change the lives of our neighbors by adding intrinsic value. In this way we are able to not only help them fall into fewer gaps, but also by changing the world where there are fewer gaps to fall into. We envision nothing less than a transformation of the relationship between the church, our parishes and

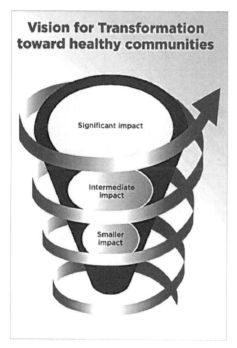

Figure 6: A vision of creating transformational communities. Created by EHF in 2014.

institutions and the wider community. The future Church must reinvent how our worshippers serve the communities in which they find themselves.[372] .

This will mean that Church leadership at the diocesan level, and the church wide level, must support capacity building for the local congregation. Only by doing this can the Church hope to create strong human connections across communities, so that parishes, Diocesan institutions, health systems, individuals, and communities are enabled and equipped to see opportunities and to solve problems together. At EHF we believe that capacity building is a critical part of creating sustainability, self-sufficiency and empowerment within communities, whether at the institutional, family, or individual level: it is about "teaching to fish." Capacity building will play a critical role in how the future Church supports improvement in current efforts, as well as the development of new skills, new ways of working together, and new visions of ways we can be instruments of God.[373] In a transformed community, all groups are valued and participate in problem solving, including "the least of these." The future Church will understand that transformation also means that health disparities are reduced in the short term, and root causes are addressed in the long-term. The future Church will take on a completely new value system around service. It will place health at the very core of its life, with well-designed communities an objective, and new interconnected economic and faith-based structures supporting it. The future Church that is engaged in service will build transformed communities where institutions and systems are aligned, integrated, effective, and sufficient for meeting the community's health and wellness needs.[374]

Stewardship of the diocese and wider Church will have to be focused strategically on transformative community work, if we are to be successful at changing how we serve. When we aim at a transformed community as our objective, we must move away from the "charity based model" to a transformative model. In my opinion, this intentional shift will only occur when we change the way we fund service ministries. The future Church must think carefully and fund judiciously those projects that support the characteristics of a transformed community over the long-term. This means that a high value will be placed on "evidence and impact evaluation."[375] Continuous reflection and evaluation will enable the future Church to make mid-course corrections and strengthen impact whenever possible. We know that there are many factors that influence wellness, and that often times they fall outside of our purview. This means that the future Church will have to work collaboratively with other funders to create sustainable networked systems to ensure the best stewardship of God's resources. The future Church will invest over the long term, building capacities, programs, and relationships with key actors in the community to pursue common purpose. Christian communities invested in transforming the places in which they find themselves will work alongside the populations they serve rather than simply "doing things for them," and will engage the talents, resources, and commitments of the church in the service of the Kingdom of God.

After a local congregation chooses to do transformative service with their neighbors, sets their goals of interaction, and writes their oath for compassionate service they must be strategic in stepping up their work intentionally. At EHF we believe that there are three levels of interaction needed to building the transformed community. (See figure 6). The first is the investment in capacity building to strengthen partners and their impact. This means the first step is always to create better connections between the local congregation and their partners. The local congregation will work with other community members to build a common vision with clarity around where the gaps are and what essential services are needed. The second stage will be to figure out, with the community members, new ways for partnering and accomplishing mutual goals. The local congregation will work with other organizations and neighbors to figure out how to integrate their ministry. Service leaders, like deacons, will help to be proactive in building conversation and leading initiatives that have a direct impact on the first stage goals. The local congregation will continue to train and raise up partners to do hands on work with the neighbors; constantly fine tuning its interaction. The third stage comes after time has passed and proven sustainable structures and processes have been put into place. This means that there is a level of self-sufficiency for the service ministry as it matures. It organizes on its own. The next set of deep impact goals comes naturally as regular conversation and relationships are established. The local congregation exports what they have learned and shares widely new models so that the wider church at all levels is impacted and benefits from the local work.[376]

In order to help, diocesan and wider Church organizations will need to understand that their work is specifically to assist in the development process through coaching and funding. Sometimes the work is to secure the preconditions to transformative change, other times it is to deepen transformative work already taking place. The enlarging funnel represents the increasing resources to be rolled out incrementally, particularly during the early years of any given project's lifespan, always scaling up to full funding and then down. The developmental process along the pathway to a transformed community occurs over time as we move from small toward significant impact. This involves a shift from shorter toward longer-term investments; moving from downstream to upstream interventions; and supporting capacity building initiatives leading to self-organized, sustainable communities.

I believe in order for this to work, congregations and wider Church leadership in the future will have to commit to becoming a continuous learning organization. This means continued evaluation, measurement of impact and work, assessment of internal/external organizational effectiveness, attention to new research and best practices, recognition of new opportunities for capacity building and training opportunities for all involved, and research on the changing context in which the community is working. This means that service is an iterative process—we are constantly reflecting on our work.[377]

Ultimately, this work will be an investment in the empowerment of the local Church citizens to work with the community citizens to transform the cities where they live.

Recently, my wife and I made a trip to San Francisco. We are garden lovers and a friend recommended that we go to see the gardens just below Coit Tower by way of the Filbert Steps. The steps are steep stairways on the East side of Telegraph hill. They are the only access to the homes there and the individuals who live there have covered the whole area with gardens. There is even a feral flock of parrots that reside there. The residents themselves are responsible for the tending and caring for their community. This is an example of an urban movement that is intimately tied to the creation of healthy communities. People are taking city planning and the creation of pedestrian friendly blocks in a movement some are calling "pop-up urbanism."[378] Future Christian communities will be actively involved in tactical urbanism and movements like it.

Part of what has happened is that city governments no longer have the ability to care for and support the transformation of public space. In the Houston area we see many individual philanthropists, entrepreneurs, and foundations filling the breach. Churches can do similar work. However, as Churches become more integrated into their communities and seek to build healthy communities more and more, combined efforts will help transform the current neighborhoods into well communities. Part of the reason is that socially engaged/organized communities can undertake urban design without the high public cost. Sometimes this work even changes the way in which the local municipality does their own work.[379]

The Better Block project (www.betterblock.org) was founded in 2010 in the neighborhood my parents grew up in—Oak Cliff in Dallas. Organizers raised $1,000 and used found objects and materials to change the community. Their goal was a "complete street."[380] Wiki defines a complete street as "one designed, operated, and maintained to enable safe, convenient and comfortable travel and access for users of all ages and abilities regardless of their mode of transportation."[381] Together members of the community organized and they painted a bike lane and greened up the space with the help of a local landscape company. They used free space for a café, flower market, and art studio for children with a space for musicians to hang out.[382] Today Better Block is all over the country and is an urban movement.

These grass roots community improvement projects are called: "tactical urbanism, pop-up urbanism, urban acupuncture — or in one blogger's ornate locution, 'Provisional, Opportunistic, Ubiquitous, and Odd Tactics in Guerrilla and DIY Practice and Urbanism.'"[383] A New York design firm Macro Sea (www.macro-sea.org) has even created swimming pools that can be moved into the area where no public recreation exists.[384] The goal is to integrate individual participation with community improvement for a lifestyle that is collaborative, creative, and participatory. They use social media, small house gatherings, social funding, and a host of other connection tools to organize people into actually making their community a better place to live. Responding to a Better Block initiative in Fort Worth, deputy-planning director Dana Burghdoff said, "It was inexpensive and fast. It mobilized public support for the city's ultimately successful effort to convince the state to reroute the highway. Two traffic lanes have been given over to on-street parking and bicycles, and plans are in the works for wider sidewalks, street trees, new lighting, and benches. South Main is once again just a city street."[385] These tactical urban strategies will in the future be intimately linked the whole wellness initiative.

Remember the example of the networked Church St. Luke's Methodist in Houston that adopted the Gethsemane campus as a satellite? Here is the rest of the story. St. Luke's began the process of adopting the site. They then tried to figure out what ministries might be done through the new acquired campus. They sent a layperson, Gene Graham, and one of their clergy, The Rev. Justin Coleman, out to survey local neighbors, business owners, and community leaders to discover what the needs were in the Sharpstown area. It became clear that the issue was urban gangs. Graham and Coleman then brought in Charles Rotramel who is the founder of Youth Advocates in Houston. Youth Advocates is a nonprofit that works with kids to help them stay out of jail, in school, and making progress towards their goals. Break dancing, soccer, skate boarding, and def jam poetry are some of the ways in which the kid's natural interests are connected with mentors. Rotramel's work has changed the lives of thousands of Houston youth. Rotramel brings in Eric Moen who has a specialty of bridging YA with church communities. Moen works at St. Martins Episcopal Church. Together the new foursome developed a funding apparatus, built relationships with the County (judges, parole officers, police, and social workers), and launched reVision. (houstonrevision.org). Today ReVision is an ecumenical service ministry that was built from the ground up and pools charitable and government dollars to recreate the local community around the Gethsemane campus. Their mission statement reads: "reVision leverages the power of community by connecting kids on the edge with mentors, positive peers and life-changing resources." Parishioners, young adults, and kids all work together to support one another. The collective theme of their stories is the transformation of life. This is a glimpse of the future of service ministry by engaged churches.

Stewardship and service is not the business of redistributing wealth; it is the business of building relationships. The reciprocity is not a financial exchange but one of story. We do this in church, yes. But we do this through our partnership and mission with our peers, the poor, and the undocumented worker. We do not forget the laborer or the lost. We help people in our community by being their friends and by living into our real connection with them. The church is called to go out and proclaim a gospel that is more than just words. We have a foreign mission field in our own backyard. The neighborhoods and communities that exist outside the doors of our congregations are farther away than the foreign cultures we send hundreds of missionaries to every year. We have a mandate from God to tend the fields at home too; to walk out of our congregation and find the needs of our neighbor, to introduce ourselves, to say we are here to help you, and to ask what does this community need. Then we must undertake the sweat labor it takes to help.

On our watch there exists a care vacuum that must be addressed across every region of the denominational Church. This vacuum includes: access to health care, prevention, community and environmental health, poverty, education and health disparities. Millions have no health insurance. Forty percent of all emergency department visits are for conditions that could have been treated in a primary care setting. African American women's rates of breast cancer mortality are higher than white women. Why? These women are less likely to get mammography screening and more likely to be diagnosed at a later stage of cancer. Mental illnesses begin by age 14, 75% by age 24. Nationally, one in five children suffers from mental, emotional or behavioral disorders but only one in eight of these are currently receiving treatment. "Food deserts" are creeping like the sands of the Sahara across the communities within the 17 countries of The Episcopal Church as a great migration moves to the cities where there is not enough access to healthy food. These food deserts along with the high stress of poverty result in higher rates of diabetes, obesity and heart disease—and higher medical/insurance cost for us all. As the disparity between the rich and the poor grows, we are seeing more children in the U.S. grow up in "food insecure" households. Extreme poverty and the homelessness that often accompanies it, decrease the life span of an individual by an average of 25 years.

God has a mission. God's mission has provided over the years missionary outposts. In these outposts are people who stand at the ready to make the neighborhood better, healthier, and safer. These are the things that matter to our communities. The church of the future, invested in the lives of the people in their communities, will be holding and convening neighborhood conversations. The living church that cares and serves will be a partner with those in the neighborhoods and towns across our various missionary contexts.

We are the church that says we are invested in the dignity of every human being—the future Church will be invested *in* every human being. We must dream. Dream with me about an Episcopal Church health mission which understands that health is a state of complete physical, mental and social well-being, not merely the absence of disease or infirmity. Dream with me about lowering breast cancer deaths for the poor and helping children find the care they need. Dream with me about unleashing the resources of people across our Episcopal Church to bring health care to the poorest of the poor, health education to our neighborhoods, and public gardens that bring forth a bounteous harvest in what today are food deserts. We have the opportunity to be our neighbor's best partners because as a church we know their problems and struggles are our own.

CHAPTER FIFTEEN
Generous Evangelism

*"Jesus himself did not try to convert the two thieves on the
cross; he waited until one of them turned to him."*
— *Dietrich Bonhoeffer, Letters and Papers from Prison*

Service is the Good News of Salvation put into action. Evangelism
is the sharing of the Good News of Salvation and the uniqueness of
Jesus Christ with others. Mainline denominations have an easier time
with charity, than with service or evangelism. Evangelism is normally
disregarded and dismissed because people think it is about recruiting
people with personal salvation as the bait. Jesus did not spread the
Good News of the Reign of God that way and neither should we. Yet in
a future of competing narratives and an abundance of
communication, the Gospel can get lost—but not for the future
Church. The future Church must be alive and well and proclaiming a
clear message of Jesus Christ and God's mission in the world. The
Church must do so with clarity, because in a VUCA world, clarity is a
necessary commodity. Bob Johansen writes, "The best leaders will
understand why people crave easy answers, but they won't fall into
the easy answer trap. Leaders must develop clarity while tempering
certainty. Clear-eyed leaders will experience hopelessness on
occasion, but they won't accept it; they will see through it and be
determined to make it otherwise. Leaders will immerse themselves

in the VUCA World and—even if they become disoriented for a while—make a way to clarity as they make the future."[386]

We are a Christian enterprise. We have already been clear about our vision and understanding of God's mission. Evangelism is about sharing that vision specifically. Evangelism, the sharing of the Good News of Salvation and the uniqueness of Jesus Christ has forever been part of the essential work of the Church. Based upon Jesus' teaching, his incarnation, resurrection and ascension, his first followers recorded his life through stories and wrote down their beliefs in letters. Generation proceeded to generation and the first three hundred years after Jesus' earthly ministry saw much division regarding the theology of the person of Jesus, while they were in the end, unified about the notion that art, literature, and philosophy revealed God. God was present in the workings of the world and it was the Christian's work to interpret God's presence, and work for the world in God's stead. They sustained a belief in the uniqueness of Jesus and their particular vocation in imparting this message to others.

When Christianity entered the life of a village there were already a number of competing religions in the public square. If we were to look at the small town surrounding the Roman garrison in Dura Europos, present day Syria, in 240 A.D., we would find a multitude of conversations about gods and how to live eternally. As you entered the town you would pass a temple to Mithras, one to the Palmyrene gods, a Jewish synagogue, a temple for Adonis, a sanctuary for Tyche, a Christian house church and a shrine to Zeus Kyrios; and that is only on the main thoroughfare.[387] Around town you would find temples to Gadde (another Palmyrene god), Zeus, Theos, Zeus Megistos, Atargatis (a Syrian goddess), Artemis, and Jupiter Dolichenus (a Syrian Baal), as well as the temple near the garrison for easy access.[388] At the time of Christianity's' greatest expansion through word of mouth, it was in the midst of a pluralistic world with many shrines, gods, goddesses, and competing belief systems. People were not sitting around looking for a new religion and god to worship.[389]

There is not a lot of evidence about how people shared the faith with one another, but we can be sure they did. Rodney Stark in his book *The Rise of Christianity* notes these statistics:

Year 100:   7,500 Christians, .01% of population
Year 150:   41,000 Christians, .07% of population
Year 200:   220,000 Christians, .36% of population
Year 250:   1,170,000 Christians, 1.9% of population
Year 300:   6,300,000 Christians, 10.5% of population
Year 350: 34,000,000 Christians, 56.5% of population[390]

One can imagine that most of this happened much as the New Testament Book of Acts describes it—people shared with one another who Jesus was and how his resurrection and grace made a difference in their lives. Stark's text goes into the complex sociological reasons why this new movement might have had a foothold; nevertheless, it did, and it took off, and pretty soon it was everywhere, beginning in households and then growing throughout the city. Historians in general believe that it was as simple as that. Ordinary Christians talked about Jesus as humanity's certain hope. They "gossiped about the Gospel."[391] The pagan Celsus, a second century Greek philosopher mentioned by the early Church father Origen, complained that "wool workers, cobblers, laundry workers and the most illiterate and bucolic yokels" were sharing the story of Jesus and how God loves everyone.[392] Origen mentioned that there were people traveling to different towns and cities—taking the idea of the great commission seriously—and sharing the old story with whomever would listen.[393] By the middle of the fourth century Christianity began to supplant all the other religions and temples, and by 381 became an official religion—thanks to Constantine's mother. Catechism, which had been a time of teaching for new Christians, was replaced by instruction in "ritual and custom".[394] In fact, evangelism began to fall away across the Roman Empire as Christianity was simply adopted upon conquest. This was especially true in Armenia, Germania, and with the Celts and Slavic tribes.[395] The people became Christian because their leaders became Christian.

In The Middle Ages, it was the sword and imperial victory by Charlemagne, the Teutonic Knights, and the Crusades which spread Christianity.[396] Meanwhile, Saint Cyril translated the Bible into Slavonic. The idea that people should be able to hear the word of God in their own language was born. What took place in The Middle Ages was a shift in who did the evangelizing. It was most definitely not the layman. It was the monk, the priest, and the bishop—the missionary—who was working to share the Gospel in foreign lands. This would last well into the twelfth and thirteenth centuries when lay movements began to do what the others were no longer doing. By this time in church history, monks and the like were either hermits or focused on building the buildings and politics of the medieval church.[397] This leads us to the reformation.

Lutheran professor Richard D. Balge wrote:

When some monks in the West returned to hermitism and others concentrated on the aggrandizement of the institutional church, a number of lay movements sought to do what the ordained churchman were neglecting to do. In the 12th and 13th centuries the Humiliati, Beguines, and Beghards were voluntary (but disciplined) lay people who cared for the bodies and souls of society's castoffs. Peter Waldo's followers went out two -by -two in the 12th century. They preached repentance, they distributed Bibles, they heard confessions and spoke the word of forgiveness. In England, in the 14th century, John Wycliff trained itinerant lay preachers. Hussites and a remnant of German Waldensians combined in the mid -15th century as the Unitas Fratrum to evangelize in Europe and to take the Gospel to Turkey, Syria, Palestine, and Egypt. Formally, none of these groups preached an unconditioned Gospel.[398]

Each in their own way shared a Gospel across the reachable world: that God acted through Jesus and that God's love was sufficient; and, then they called upon all those who would follow Jesus to respond to this grace

The *next* era in evangelism is characterized both by the growth in the monastic movement which sought to evangelize the growing colonies of the great countries. Then came the reformers themselves. Martin Luther (1483-1546) said, "Every Christian is also an evangelist, who should teach another and publish the glory and praise of God."[399] The confession of Jesus would be the hallmark of the Protestant movement. "The most aggressive of the 15th century 'left-wing' Protestants were the Hutterites. Stressing that every baptized believer has received the Great Commission, they evangelized where they were and sent missionaries to distant points in Europe, where some of them were put to death as heretics," Balge wrote. During this great reform, the gossip of the Gospel would be the primary medium—the poor, the household workers, the tailor, the weavers, the farmer and the nobles would all be whispering about the power of God in Christ Jesus.[400]

The Wesleys, Whitefield, and the Moravians all would join the colonists in a new world, expanding with the idea of spreading the Kingdom of God. The Great Awakening (1730) and the spiritualization of the Gospel would take root in the American colonies. While revolution and war would come to Europe and the new world, evangelism was also taking on a new form. Individuals were again firmly in charge of the offering of Good News. The poor and the worker were of concern and the mix of service and the Gospel is found in missionary societies. These societies were funded and supported by their respective denominations and communities.

The YMCA (1844) and the YWCA (1858) ministered to Civil War vets and urban youth. The Salvation Army (1865) went to the poorest of the poor. John Mott's World Student Christian Federation and Dwight Moody's Student Volunteer Movement recruited world missionaries and home evangelists. This would lead to a new spiritual awakening and a new global missionary zeal.[401] By the 1950's, evangelism was firmly rooted in evangelical movements and for the most part had left the mainline denominations. Urban flight into the suburbs would bring about great prosperity for the denominational Christian church in the U.S. Like the middle of the first millennium, evangelism seemed unnecessary because everyone went to church. This was the height of the Episcopal Church. This is thirty years away from the boom in the technological revolution.

By the 1990's, the denominational churches would were trying to reverse the decline in Sunday attendance by reclaiming evangelism for a decade—called the "Decade of Evangelism." During this decade the mainline denominations would shrink even more than in the previous ten years. In fact, I would say that more often than not, people today within denominations are not interested in evangelism, and are less likely to share the good news of Jesus Christ with their neighbors.

It is probably a good thing at this moment to say that as Christians we must own the reality that the Gospel has not always been an invitation or a benefit to those who heard it. For with the Gospel has come a sinful broken Church. It has been an organization that sometimes has persecuted the people that were supposedly in their care. The crimes and misdemeanors of the past, committed by those who abused the Gospel, are, however, no reason for us to discharge our duty as followers of Jesus to share the grace and love of God. It is important, I believe, to recognize that when Christianity and evangelism were at their best, it was not typically the organized Church at work but rather people, simply people, sharing hope, grace, and a sense of transformation with their friends and neighbors.

The future Church must be a church that uses innovation and creativity to share the age-old Gospel message. Generous and innovative evangelism is the manner in which the denominational Church will proclaim the Good News of the Kingdom of God. It is the bedrock ministry of teaching, baptizing, and nurturing those who chose to make their pilgrimage with Christ. Evangelism itself is one of the primary characteristics of a church that responds to the human need for the divine and the sacred. The future Church will be a church wherein evangelism is a lay-led sharing of the good news of God.

Today, for-profit companies are investing in evangelism, transformation, and disciple making. The chief apostle in the "church of the customer" is a man by the name of Guy Kawasaki. He is literally the one who invented the position at Apple Computer referred to as the "chief evangelist." The for-profit sector has been using these terms and making disciples since the early 1990's. What happened in the decade of Evangelism is that our terms were co-opted to sell stuff. Guy Kawasaki's two books *Selling the Dream: How to Promote Your Product, Company, or Ideas*, and *Make a Difference—Using Everyday Evangelism* in addition to his latest book *Enchantment* are important resources if you are interested in learning what the "E" word is all about. Instead of debunking evangelism or rejecting the culture's appropriation, the future Church must reclaim it and use it as a point of introduction to the Christian faith.

Not unlike Paul and the "unknown God" of Athens, the Church must re-engage and explain that the God we believe in doesn't want you to buy something. (Acts 17.23ff) The God we believe in is a God of grace and is invested in our lives. Unlike the gods of the market place that demand product-loyalty, tribute in order to be saved—and specially branded clothes, our God gives free grace, mercy, and kindness. Our God forgives debt and debtors.[402]

The gospel of Jesus Christ revealed in the life of a living Church can spread, and it will happen steadily, organically, and exponentially through generous evangelism. Generous evangelism is when our church, out of the sense of abundant grace, overflows its boundaries into the world. Generous evangelism listens to others as they tell their pilgrim tales of seeking God in the midst of a wilderness culture. Generous evangelism takes place when people are willing to walk with other persons as they make their journey. It waits to hear about, and then names, Jesus Christ in the lives of the others, revealing the icons and images of God acting in each person's life. It invites people into community. It welcomes them. It helps them to find a language (and particularly in our case an Episcopal language) for entering the faith conversation. Generous evangelism is concerned with welcoming people into the family and bringing others into a sacramental life with God through the Episcopal Church.

This renewed evangelism will take many forms, as diverse communities are inspired to be creative in God's vineyards. In existing traditional church contexts, generous evangelism will take the form of invitation and newcomer hospitality. These first steps will lead to discipleship where people are formed through the sharing of our particular Episcopal way. They will be formed as they belong, and come to belief, charting their own pilgrimage and journey with Christ. It will take place through our liturgy, Bible studies, and discipleship classes. In turn, they will help others find their way into relationship with God. Jesus did not call disciples in order that they stay disciples. Jesus called people so that they might inherit the Holy Spirit and become apostles—those who are sent.

New Christian communities that sprout up around cultural commonalities or diaspora groups will also be important innovative centers of evangelism. Music, art, and shared expressions will bind these communities. I am calling these small batch churches. Small batch churches are communities formed in context and will have many diverse expressions in the years to come. Evangelism will take place in these regardless of what form they take. Even service ministries will have an evangelism component.

The living Church of the future will have to take a catholic, or universal, approach to innovative evangelism. We will have to launch many different kinds of Christian communities and be willing to use different styles of engagement with the culture. As we do this, our core teaching will have to be strengthened. We will need to rely upon clear basic principles like the catechism. Not as the end-all-be-all of belief, but as a means to engage believing people as they make their journey into our church community. If we are to engage different people, with different life experiences, we will need to be prepared, by having a touch-point with our own faith. This communal discourse will have to begin with listening and be led by laity and clergy alike, in the church and more importantly out in the world.

The living Church must again embrace a missionary spirit that sows seeds with wild abandon. It will have to sow seeds in places where there are birds and be willing to shoo them away. It will have to be willing to pick up the stones so that the seeds may grow on the soil beneath. It will have to sow seeds fearlessly and gently protect them from the weeds that will want to choke the tender shoots. (Matthew 13) Resources (both human and financial) need to be diverted to this work. Stewardship and development will be core strategies that complement the communal work of individual, one on one, loving conversations and generous expressions of evangelism.

The evangelists of the future church will burn with a clear and compelling message that brings good news to the world. The Episcopal Church has such a message. We believe that Jesus loves all people, and that the Holy Spirit empowers us to spread God's love with the world. The Episcopal Church makes people's lives better. It battles poverty and works against injustice.[403] The future Episcopal Church will have many evangelists because the living Church will be filled with people who love their community. The spiritual interconnections that are made as the Christian community of the future interweaves itself into the fabric of life in the surrounding community, will mean that being an Episcopalian, being a Christian for that matter, will easily be an integral way of life. It will be the way in which the evangelist of the future navigates the world around them. If evangelists do not love their Church and its proclamation of Jesus , they will not make a very good evangelist.[404] Let me see... how can I say this? If you think your church stinks, evangelism will not come easy to you. The future Church will have many evangelists who love the cause of Jesus and the Episcopal Church throughout its ranks.

Here are some basics criteria for good evangelism in our current context. Good evangelists will focus their efforts on those who are

looking for God, who are exploring Christian communities, and who
are genuinely interested in a new spiritual experience. Guy Kawasaki
says, and I agree, that a good evangelist knows within five minutes if
they have a chance of success with an individual.[405] This has been
true in my experience in both retail sales and as an evangelist. It is far
better to focus on interested seeking parties who are curious than it
is to attempt to convert people who are happy with their current
Christian community or other faith. The future Church works
intentionally with those who choose to visit, choose to look around
their website, choose to participate in their social media, and ask
inquiring questions. The evangelist will look for all of these
opportunities and may in some cases create them. The evangelist
remembers that those who used to be Episcopalians or who were
part of the denominational church at one time or another are more
likely to find something of interest in our Church. Regardless of who
the evangelist is speaking to, they remember always that being kind
and a good friend first are essential. The Episcopal Church that is
thriving in the future will be one that is known for its hospitality,
kindness, and helpfulness as people are trying to make their pilgrim
journey. We hope most people will say, "We found the Episcopal
Church and we loved it!" But when they discern we are not for them,
we hope they will say, "It was not quite right for me but the people
there were incredibly kind and supportive of my spiritual journey."
Evangelists are kind.

The evangelist must get beyond insider church-speak. The
evangelists of the Episcopal Church and its Gospel know that people
may be interested in mystery but they are not interested in
vocabulary they cannot understand. Those are different things.
People are not going to choose the Episcopal Church because we have
great hymnody, fantastic liturgy, high church or low church liturgy.
They will choose it because at the end of the day what the evangelist
tells them is true—being an Episcopalian who loves Jesus makes a
difference in your life—for all the reasons we have talked about in
previous chapters. Guy Kawasaki says, "Macintosh wasn't positioned

as the third paradigm in personal computing; instead, it increased the productivity and creativity of one person with one computer. People don't buy 'revolutions.' They buy 'aspirin' to fix the pain or 'vitamins' to supplement their lives."[406]

The Episcopal Church that is thriving in the future will be one that understands that while it has boundaries for community membership, it also has plenty of room for people to come and go and to test drive the community. The Episcopal Church is meant for everyone even though it may not fit everyone. For some visitors it will be a stop on the way to another faith community. The evangelizing community that flourishes in the future will be one that understands this, and instead of belittling those who do not choose it, will be the kind of community that trusts the individual's discernment. The masterful evangelist trusts the product and trusts the discernment of the individual to figure out if the church is right for them. The living Church of the future will be one that does not bludgeon visitors, but rather does what it does best—invites, welcomes, and connects them to others in and around the community.

The innovative evangelist serving the Church tomorrow will be a person who can easily talk about their community and why they love it so much. They have to be able to give a "great demo."[407] They cannot use sentences like, "I like the liturgy." Or, "The priest is nice." Those are good qualities, but they really are meaningless to people on the outside. They might simply ask, "What is liturgy? And, you have priests? Do you have priestesses?" The evangelist knows that while they have the prospective person's attention, they have to help them experience the best of the Christian community. First the generous evangelist invites people to come to church! "What? That is crazy?" you say! This is *key*. The generous person actually shares their community with others by inviting them into community. This *can* mean having them join you for church. But in the future Church there will provide many other opportunities for the individual to come and meet members of the community, and to experience what

God is doing there. At the end of the day, no matter how it happens, the generous evangelist will invite people in person and through a variety of media to *demo* their Christian community experience. The evangelist of the future invites a newcomer to a great event, hooks him up with the people that are the best, and brings him to a gathering when the topic is something the visitor might be interested in. The evangelist shows them around the really cool parts of the church or helps them navigate the worship service. The evangelist, by giving a demo, helps new people have a good experience and interpret their experience. Not everyone can give a good demo but that is not the only part of evangelism.

The next piece is essential for the generous evangelist of the future—listening. I have been in retail sales and have over 100 hours in mediation training and thousands of hours of experience. Regardless of what the work is, it is always about listening. Sometimes leaders can forget to listen. The future Church and its generous evangelists must be good listeners.

Generous evangelism is chiefly about transformation. Transformation comes as the individual seeker feels empowered to make a choice through the understanding of, and recognition that, the Episcopal Church can be a good addition to their lives because of its particular and unique presentation of God in Christ Jesus. The generous evangelist is not simply making a presentation of material but is inviting the other person to have a personal and strengthened understanding of themselves and God, the church and others. This is not going to happen by simply being an evangelist who sells the Gospel—if you will pardon my crassness. The generous evangelist listens.

The generous evangelist listens by asking questions and being quiet while the person answers or tells their story. But it is not just about a question. Sometimes a pause in the conversation, a nod, and an invitation to continue, will allow the individual to share their story. The evangelist knows and understands that what we are doing is weaving a common story, and that this common story only happens as the one searching is given a chance to do some of the weaving. They must have the opportunity to see if their weaving will fit within the long woven cloth of the Episcopal Church.

As Richard Buff, a sales consultant, reminds people—it is not enough to listen, the person you are listening to must to know you listened.[408] After all, listening is not an inactive occupation. While listening, an evangelist needs to test what they hear—make sure you have it right; and, give the speaker some time to correct or add to what they have already said. You might summarize or reflect back to them what they are saying. Do not share your story unless they ask! Sharing too soon can tell the person you are evangelizing that this is all really about *you*. Listen to how they are speaking about their experience. The qualifiers they use in their storytelling will give the evangelist an idea about what the individual thinks is important. Non-verbals are also an indicator, so pay attention if they are animated or not, as they tell the story. You have to do all of this because as an evangelist you are presenting to them the Church. You are also a sign of God's work reaching out to them where they are. If you do not listen, and focus too much on your church, and on what you have to offer, then as an evangelist you will fail to make the transformative connection. What interests you about the church may not interest the person you are visiting with—so do not over-share.

Make sure, by listening, you are connecting them to the things that they think are important. Buff says this, "A classic trap is doing a really good job in talking about the wrong thing. This means periodically asking and really listening to the response as to whether the topic under discussion is a priority for the customer. If the answer is no—it's time to change topics."[409] The same goes for prospective members. We are not just listening because we want new customers; we are listening because we care about the individual. A generous evangelist is a great listener and knows when to speak and when to be quiet. The future church will be known as a church that cares about people and that will mean having the hallmark of listening and companionship.

The Future Church will have many opportunities for an individual to take their first step. There are multiple ways in which a seeker might engage in the Christian community. Generous evangelism knows that the first step for a person considering the Christian faith and the Episcopal Church is not the crucifixion. "Welcome. Glad you are here! Here is a cross now you and your sins have to die on it." These are not comforting words. This is certainly an important part of understanding the breadth of Christian discipleship. As Richard Dreyfus says to Bill Murray in the movie *What about Bob?*..."Just take baby steps." We are not doing "death therapy."[410] Adopting the Episcopal Church as your community and its Gospel of God in Christ Jesus, as your gospel, will be life changing. It need not have barriers so high that no one can feel that they are worthy to be part of it. That is not a grace filled way of going about being Christian community. The Future Church and its evangelists will understand that God's mercy, forgiveness, and love are truly free and there is nothing anyone can do to earn God's mercy, forgiveness, and love—not even joining the Episcopal Church.

Likewise, becoming a participant in this life of grace is not that hard. Kawasaki writes, "For example, the safe first step to recruit an evangelist for the environment is not requiring that she chain herself to a tree; it's to ask her to start recycling and taking shorter showers."[411]

Evangelists are individuals who are humble, not proud or belittling to other churches or religious experiences.[412] Evangelists love their Church and Jesus, but they are not putting down others. Good evangelists also do not focus only on the people with whom they want to spend time . They will spend time with anybody who is truly interested. They are eager to help someone try on the Episcopal Church, renewed, or new faith in God. Because the evangelist is humble about their work and their community, there is no reason to lie. Evangelism is not lying or selling a product you don't believe in.[413] Evangelists are honest about their community and how it works. It takes a lot of energy to lie. If you are an evangelist and you have to lie for your community, then you either need to go find a cause and community which better suits you or you need to stop and help your community sort itself out. Do not be passing along bad stuff to others. I believe we all know what is good and what is not. Passing along a dead church to a new generation who will resent and hate it—that is not our work.

CHAPTER SIXTEEN
Generous Community

*"One of the marvelous things about community is that it enables us
to welcome and help people in a way we couldn't as individuals. When
we pool our strength and share the work and responsibility, we can
welcome many people, even those in deep distress, and perhaps help
them find self-confidence and inner healing."*
— Jean Vanier, <u>Community and Growth</u>

In my role as bishop, I travel to each of the congregations under
my care. In my first year, I noticed something interesting about our
Episcopal Church. In every place, in every sized town, and in every
kind of congregation there were visitors. This meant that on any
given Sunday in my Diocese literally hundreds of new people were
choosing to attend our Church. In fact in a month's time over several
thousand people were putting on their big boy pants, wrangling
children, setting their morning paper aside until later and making
their way into the Episcopal Church. I began to wonder about this
and pose this question to anyone who would listen, "What would
happen to our Church if we kept 50%, or 25% or even 10% of those
who actually chose to worship with us each Sunday?" What would
happen is that we would grow. We could share God's love with more
people. We could be stronger, healthier members of our
communities. We could make the world a better place through a
growing community.

In 2009, I was invited to be the speaker at the annual Blandy
Lectures at Seminary of the Southwest, Austin. I wanted to talk about
how we might do the work of discipleship. By the time I finished the

lecture outline I was convinced that we all had to begin with welcoming people.

We, as a community, had to do what I call *front door evangelism* well. I asked for help from my friend and coworker Mary MacGregor, who was then the director of Leadership and Congregational Development, and she pointed me towards The Leadership Training Network resources on *The Equipping Church* published by Zondervan. Here I saw a clear sweeping process of discipleship that invited people, welcomed, helped individuals become members, shared a Biblical understanding of ministry, and invited them to take their place in the community. I adapted it to the Episcopal Church theology and practice. My presentation was received well and I was convinced that there was more to this for the Episcopal Church.

The Leadership Network process lacked the theology, liturgy, and language of our Church. It just did not quite fit. So I went back to MacGregor and we made it a priority for our diocese to create an Invite/Welcome/Connect process for our diocese and for the Episcopal Church. She in turn went to the one individual who has had the greatest success in creating a welcoming process for an Episcopal church in our diocese—Mary Parmer, a consultant. She, along with our staff, is the one who helped put together the best resource on what it means to be a generous evangelism community. You can find these resources at www.epicenter.org/newcomer.

Front-door evangelism is about meeting the stranger who comes into our community as Jesus. The Book of Revelation 3:20 reads: "Listen! I am standing at the door knocking; hear my voice and open the door!" God in Christ Jesus is at the front door of our churches.[414] Jesus is incarnate in the stranger and the visitor.[415] This is in fact connected to our ministry of service mentioned in our Biblical understanding of Matthew 25:40, from above. How we welcome the stranger at our door is in direct correlation to how we welcome Jesus himself. The Rev. John Newton, on our diocesan staff as Canon for Lifelong Formation, helped frame the theology for Invite/ Welcome/ Connect.

He wrote:

The theology for our front-door evangelism is about providing such a home for Jesus in how we invite, welcome and connect our newcomers and visitors.[416]

The future Church will engage the work of front-door evangelism and more as part of being a generous community. The living, thriving Episcopal Church of the future believes that God is the one sending us newcomers. The future Church understands that how we welcome and connect with them is a primary way in which we make our witness to the grace and love we have received from God. Newton continues, "Front-door evangelism is rooted in an understanding that God sends us newcomers and that as a community we begin bearing witness to our hope in the Gospel—or don't—the second these newcomers set foot on our property. Front-door evangelism sees all visitors as part of the mission field. When a front-door evangelist sees a new family or a lonely student or a scared senior entering the sanctuary (or parish hall) for the first time she immediately thinks 'the harvest is plentiful.' Front-door evangelists approach visitors so as to encounter them."[417] The generous community of the future is filled with people engaging in front-door evangelism.

The generous community recognizes that individuals come to us with their own narrative. They are people who have been hurt by other churches. They are people who are busy. They are burdened and sometimes feel lost. They are people who are searching. They are individuals who have courageously decided to step out in faith (literally) and enter the doors of our congregation. Generous communities do more than welcome people—they loudly proclaim that we want you to be part of our community.[418] Generous communities in the Episcopal Church embrace the stranger and help them to find a place. They believe that when we fail to make a home for those without, we are being unfaithful to the God we believe in.

In the Diocese of Texas we say: "As followers of Jesus Christ... All are sought and embraced in worship, mission and ministry in a spirit of mutual love and respect."[419] This is our vision statement. I believe that the future of, not just our diocese, but the Episcopal Church as a whole, will be known as a generous community where *all* are sought and embraced in a spirit of mutual love and respect. The future Church understands that the life of the community is enriched as new members are incorporated.[420]

The future Church will discard the belief that people want to be left alone.[421] How can that be true? Well, the newcomer actually got up early on a day off and intentionally entered a church. People who want to be left alone would not go through all that it takes to get to church. That does not make sense. This is simply a lie we tell ourselves, so we are removed from the responsibility of meeting Jesus in the stranger. The future Church will cultivate new practices of invitation, welcome, and connection that are rooted and grounded in the Gospel of Jesus Christ, building and growing generous communities.

Big or small, the thriving Episcopal community of the future will engage in front-door evangelism in an innovative, generous and accountable manner. Many churches fail at their work of evangelism because they only work one part of the generous evangelism equation. They work on invitation and are unprepared to connect people or they work on the welcome piece but never invite; or any combination of the essential ingredients. Generous communities must be prepared with an intentional process of linking newcomers into the community. The Church will take this seriously enough to have designated people who will connect and keep track of newcomers. They will be generous listeners and be trained in this ministry. They will help the newcomers understand how God is moving in their lives and aid them in using their particular life journey, gifts, and talents to enrich the community.

The future Church will have clarity about the needs of the community and how individuals can enter deeper community life.

These communities have clear boundaries and can articulate and explain the rites of initiation (baptism, confirmation, and reception). The communities will have clear entry points/doorways for deeper spiritual engagement. Past generations who were raised in institutions knew how to navigate church life, which was at that time less complicated. Individuals today, in a culture where everything can be personalized, have less experience navigating complex community life. Church life tomorrow will both have to deal with the translation of community ideals and the individual desire to personalize their experience. This will put pressure on the best of organized communities with clear boundaries; it will cause disruption and conflict in Christian communities that do not take seriously the importance of being a self-aware community.

A generous community knows that intentionality is essential in empowering people for ministry. Ways of learning (classes, small groups, and one-on-ones) help individuals discover their spiritual gifts and passions. Leaders in the community know that their work is to disciple people. Out of a generous self-giving, they engage newcomers. Ministries are shared and communicated throughout the Christian community so that people know what work the community undertakes. In larger communities, connection is essential through the various ministries, so that individuals find smaller groups in which to be known and give back. At every level, in every kind of congregation, a generous community evaluates honestly how well it connects the members of the community.

Once a community understands how to do connection it can work on the tools needed for welcoming. Generous communities know that front-door evangelism will always come easier when first impressions are at their best. The whole experience has to be good. Everything the newcomer experiences will impart a message of generosity and care, or it will not. Today, churches are used to communicating only with people they see on Sunday morning. The future Church must communicate beyond Sunday morning; be consistent in messaging with facilities which are clean and signage which is visible and understandable. Generous communities will have teams of people to greet, help people make their way through the service, and create a hospitable environment. Each of these individuals will be warm, friendly, and informed about the service or community event of the day. Generous communities use diverse leaders of different ages, ethnicities, and languages to welcome people because they know that God will come to us in many different incarnations. Regardless of size, these communities have clergy who are involved in this work. The clergy and the welcome team are intentional about following up after the newcomer visits for the first time. Then they hold their hand as the newcomer explores the community. They will help the visitor learn more about the community, its purpose, and its ministry, how it makes a difference in the world and in the lives of its members. Generous communities share copious amounts of time with the visitor in making them feel welcomed and in helping them to find their way into the community.

Generous evangelism will shape the future of community life chiefly in being both prepared *and* inviting. They invite people to investigate and experience their community. Simply put—the future Church invites people to meet Jesus and experience the living God in community. The generous community gives business cards, postcards and electronic flyers to its members so they can easily share the invitation with others. They make part of their work to educate and form people who will be big hearted with their invitations.

Generous communities know and are known by their neighbors. These communities are good neighbors to the people who live next door. I have discovered that most congregational leadership do not know the names of the people who live in the houses or apartments across the street from them. The future Church is part of its neighborhood and knows its neighbors. These service communities participate in neighborhood activities. They participate in civic groups and work together to create well communities. Members of the generous community are known within the wider neighborhood as essential and helpful citizens. They understand that evangelism is dependent upon knowing people and being in relationship.

Generous communities communicate. Clergy and laity alike will be constantly involved in communicating the good news. Generous evangelism takes place between individuals and through social media to be sure. The future Church, though, will have cultivated relationships with the local media as well. As civic leaders and good neighbors, they will share the voice of their local context and therefore be engaged in communicating to and with their neighbors about the particular life within the Christian community, as well as the life in the wider neighborhood. The generous community will have an up-to-date, relevant newcomer friendly website. It will have a front facing site for the seeker—minus all the insider language and acronyms. It will also have an insider website either buried below the front facing one or a separate one for members. The future church will engage with newcomers who visit the site. It will invite them to participate in events or share important news pieces, or help them find spiritual resources. Newsletters will in the future be only electronic and social media like Facebook, blogs, Twitter, and other apps will be helpful. The future Church is aware of the technological trajectory that is even now moving towards live video streaming. The future Church will take feedback from Yelp and Google reviews seriously; and, it will encourage members and visitors to use these as a means of receiving feedback. They will be fully engaged in evangelism that is connected and entwined with the newest technologies.

Some Episcopal churches are already engaging in generous community evangelism. We can see the artifacts of the future in these parishes. While many Episcopal Churches are dealing only with what is presented to them, still others are engaging the first curve of innovation. The generous Episcopal Church of the future will be engaged in technologies that today are hovering on the next curve. These second-curve technologies are already changing business and how they engage their clients. You and I are already participating in and using many of them as we buy music, go to dinner, or choose a local cleaner.

The technological age began as a means of manipulating information—massive room sized computers doing complicated equations. Humans still had to do a lot of the work in order to get the machine to do what they wanted. Then the Internet became a way that humans could share information. Only a decade ago the Internet was a way you put information out there for people to find. As information became mobile technology, it also enmeshed itself in our lives and became more attune to our desires, more available and helpful. These technologies are tangled in our lives and are engrained in our context like never before. The future Church will, like its citizens, be enmeshed in these systems, and so as our context changes, we as a Church must enter the new world of persuasion, for here lies a new mission field—as real and as vital as the great missionary movements of the past. The Institute for the Future reports: "Networked sensor data, semantic analysis, vibrant virtual and augmented realities, compelling data visualization tools, video everywhere, and mobile supercomputing: these systems create new avenues for self and collective expression, they also open us up to new avenues of persuasion."[422] The report continues, "Our understanding of persuasion, attitude formation, and behavior change is evolving, not only through traditional disciplines like psychology and economics, but increasingly through neuroscience, game design, and the development of new persuasive technologies."[423] There will have to be moral and ethical debates about the use of this technology to be sure. Yet our work here is to think seriously about how the Church will participate.

Part of what is happening is called the creation of our *digital mirrors*. Perhaps you have taken a quiz recently on Facebook, posted something to your blog, tweeted a particular quote you liked, filled out your likes and dislikes, or even forwarded a news article to your friends—this is your digital mirror. Complex programs (algorithms) are able to capture and reflect our digital activity. Opinions we have, how we act, where we go, who we are connected to and who we are digitally may be collected and seen as a kind of online profile.[424] This might be news to you. Remember all those user agreements you have signed over the years—and not read? Well, guess what? That has given permission to your social networks to mine your information.

If I choose to, I could share my fitness routine (in real time), my list of contacts, my schedule, pictures of my confirmations and parish visits in a public way. I am after all a public figure. So, while you might not care how many miles I walked today, the rest of it might be of interest, and as a public figure it might be expected of me to provide this public profile. All of us are creating these digital mirrors of ourselves. It might be fun to figure out what character in the Disney movie *Frozen* I am (I did this and I am Sven The Reindeer) but the greater challenge as with all technology and innovation is to figure out how these algorithms and information can be used to make my life easier—our lives easier. How can my digital information help me to navigate the complex world I live in, lose weight, or make my calendar work smoothly? These are more important questions. Self-improvement is one of the fastest growing areas where digital mirrors help individuals improve their lifestyle.[425]

One of these new technologies is the Personal Performance Coach created by a group called Accenture Technology Labs.[426] Designed for business and sales, the technology, will enable an analysis of a phone conversation, aiding the individuals to share more equally in the conversation. Remember that listening is important in evangelism. In sales it is essential, and this software will give real time coaching to the individual on the line and offer accolades for change. What is happening is that technology is being programmed to watch us, record us, and give us feedback on how we can better perform at those things we want to improve.[427] Accenture labs are focused on self-comparison. One can easily imagine using tools like this to train generous evangelists or assist clergy in preaching performance.

For the competitive among us, many more systems will give feedback based upon other people's performance. TweetPsych is exactly this kind of second-curve technology.[428] TweetPsych creates a "psychological profile" for the individual based upon their Twitter postings.[429] TweetPsych then compares one profile to another. Whether the tweet is positive, negative, and what the topic is are all parts of the measurement being taken. Then this, is given back to the individual creating a crowd feedback loop. What we know is that humans are likely to deviate or alter performance and conduct, based upon what the crowd is doing or thinks about us.[430] Human beings are susceptible to conditioning by their peers. Many people want to believe humans are beyond such influence and purely self-motivated—that just is not reality. As social creatures, we are inclined to a pack-mentality. This technology gives us the opportunity for greater transparency regarding such influences.

These digital mirrors will give us greater opportunity to be self-reflective and it will enable our technology to be more adapted to our individual lifestyles. These mirrors can allow us to be more thoughtful about our behaviors with others and in the wider community.[431] There will be plenty of opportunity for abuse as well. As I write this, Facebook is in the midst of a huge PR issue over testing their clients. Advertising groups use these tech fingerprints and mirrors to sell items. RapLeaf and Facebook use digital mirrors such as TweetPsych to sort and monetize their massive "friendship data."[432] The online community, and its environment, is changed as we react in relationship to different initiatives. That is how all those ads that we actually might be interested in arrive on our Facebook page. I was just recently shopping for some shoes on Google for my wife and later checked my Facebook newsfeed and up in the right hand corner was an ad for the same shoes! That is how it works. Google, Facebook, AOL, and all the rest feed us news stories we like and keep stories we might not like from us. All of this is based upon the digital image we create.[433]

Future Church leadership must acknowledge that they and their churches will have digital mirrors. They understand their reality, their importance and their power. The age of persuasion will create digital mirrors for institutions and Christian communities will have them—good and bad, wanted or unwanted. These technologies are important because people will use them to connect to the church. It is all about the crowd and how we network with others. Moreover, churches and communities that do not take this seriously will be less discoverable within the world where the digital native dwells. I believe that some churches will in fact use digital mirrors to help them connect with interested seekers, leading to new members. The purpose of understanding this is to comprehend how individuals will use these mirrors to participate in the world around them.

The digital native exists in the world with the whole network at their fingertips. Others surround us constantly. Like the game show Who Wants to be A Millionaire we can call a friend at any time. We also can be surrounded and influenced by the mind of the crowd.[434] In the span of time since 2004 (the birth of Facebook) we have moved from very little contact with other individuals to complete access. This is of course changing everything from business to parenting. Instant messaging (IM) has completely reshaped the art of the conversation. I recently sent a text message to my daughter on a mountain in Tennessee, from a mountain in Rocky Mountain National Park with a funny video of her sister. I also sent her money from the same phone from the same location. My car carries an interactive database with my friend-lists, and can even check my social media and take verbal direction and reply if needed. Like many new cars it also has Wi-Fi. As a person who offices out of my car, this can be helpful and distracting. These are new norms that are shaping our behavior in positive and negative ways. These networks are becoming more and more interactive. They are proactive. Recently while traveling through London's Heathrow Airport, one app told me that there were friends nearby and invited me to contact them so we could connect. IFTF believes that, "As devices sense behaviors and environments, they will begin reporting not only to their owners but also directly to online networks."[435]

While traveling through Amarillo, Texas we compared breakfast restaurants and people's opinions. We did not go and make up our minds for ourselves. We only tried the restaurant that sounded the best based upon the weight of peer reviews. Thanks to the app Urbanspoon we had a lovely breakfast that matched exactly what we all wanted. Currently most of these programs and applications are opt-in programs.

There are some types that can follow behaviors and environmental change in the workplace. Daydar is new software being beta tested at MIT Media Lab.[436] The program is connected to your desktop and tracks real time job performance. Reports are available to the users and managers. This creates a new normal. There are other software programs that aim to help individuals track their own lives: how happy are they, how is their productivity, their health and wellness, even sexual intercourse.[437]

The future Church must be involved in creating a space within the crowd. A place where people can perhaps track their life of meditation, pilgrimage, keep their spiritual journals, or participate with others in group reflection. If a person wants to make sure they get in 20 minutes of silent time each day, imagine a program that can track the data. Just like the Fitbit strapped on my wrist right now currently tracks my sleep patterns, it could just as easily track meditation. The Nike+ app helps you measure your activity by GPS. Imagine if you wanted to track your Church participation. Both apps also enable crowd creation so that friends can cheer you on. The future Church will use the "crowd on our shoulder" technology as a means by which we might grow in relationship with one another. Individuals will be using these technologies to improve their lives. They will make a natural jump to include their spirituality and time off in these crowd technologies. This will be an important part of the future Church's mission efforts.

I loved *The Benny Hill Show*—a British comedy program that aired in Houston during the late 70's on PBS. One of my favorite skits as a junior high kid was the one in which Benny Hill and his friend were escaping from jail. They come upon a city map that has an arrow that reads, "You are here." They immediately throw their hands up and surrender and say, "We better give up. They know where we are!" Everyone knows where everyone else is. Recently my daughter, a new driver, got lost and so, using her cell phone and my Apple "find my phone" technology on my iPad at home, we could help her get to her destination via Google maps. I was a parental air traffic controller for your lost kid. There are, in our phones, on our computers, in our cars, and in our work environments many different sensors that are tracking our location. American Express knows where I am based on my spending patterns and so is able to better protect me from fraud. This is helpful to me but it is also a way in which they are able to intervene in my life through their network. Stanford University innovator and psychologist B. J. Fogg believes that, "timing is often the missing element in behavior change."[438] He calls this *timing* "triggers."[439] Being able to connect these triggers is essential in helping individuals to change behavior. IFTF offers this perspective, "There have been many visions over the years of the persuasive potential of technologies if only they knew something about our immediate context, such as our mood, schedule, location, or health. Sensors that track such factors could know just the right time and right place to persuade or intervene."[440]

These sensors will be everywhere and further connect us to the network of individuals and within our environment. My friends have a similar tool which controls the temperature of their house based upon their movements inside and outside of the house. It sets the temperature of the room based upon movement in the room. There are many more smart objects on the market. My car senses things around it and highlights what it finds for me. iPhone has applied for a patent that will enable their mobile device to sense your heartbeat.[441] They have just released a new apple watch that will chart and keep your biorhythms along with your exercise progress. Soon these devices will know where we are and how we are feeling physically. These are called telepathic technologies. They are programs or applications that sense who we are and how we are doing and then respond to us.

One of these new programs enables what is called the instant discount. I already get these coupons and incentives to purchase or stop by a favorite coffee shop or restaurant when I am nearby. . They do this by using the sensors combined with a geo-fence.[442] The geo-fence senses telepathically my location and invites me in. Starbucks tells me when I am nearby a coffee break.

The future church will tap into these networks. Today we talk about the importance of a website. Today we rely on people finding our church by passing by, invitation, or a Google search. I predict that as we enhance our Church's geo-fence this will create triggers for people who pass by. Based upon their chosen likes/dislikes they will be told what is happening at a church near their location. Google glasses, your smart phone, or your car computer will use the church's geo-fence to share relevant church information. Imagine a person who is committed to being socially responsible, or interested in helping the homeless, discovering (as they pass by a church) that the church has the same interests. Perhaps the person even receives an invitation to join a Saturday food service project.

Just think what happens when you combine the power of geo-location or geo-fences with chosen likes and the ability to know how you feel. Imagine that your phone reads your bio state, you are hungry, then recommends a good Thai restaurant because you like Thai food and you have not eaten Thai in while. Microsoft and others are designing software that will "automatically detect frustration or stress in the user" and then "offer and provide assistance accordingly."[443] We will drive cars that know when we are fatigued. We will sit in office chairs that know when we need to move.[444] All of this telepathic programming aims to help us manage the world around us.

Imagine then the same users creating spiritual interfaces. In a world of constant stimulation and communication, spiritual seekers may choose to have their technology find for them places of peace and quiet, places of retreat, places of groups interested in religion or spiritual practices. The Church of the future will be plugged into these networks so that individuals who are seeking such respite, self-improvement, pilgrimage, and spiritual enlightenment can easily access communities like the Episcopal Church where we specialize in just such a ministry. Imagine a phone app telling you that you are overly stressed and that St. Swithins in the Swamp has a yoga class at 6:30 followed by a healthy meal. It is around the corner. No charge. Then it includes a list of other neighbors attending—perhaps even a few you know. Imagine an app that notices you have had a busy day of errands and that St. Julius has a meditation class this afternoon or a speaker on a better organized life on Saturday. You are free both of these time slots. Then it asks, "Would you like for me to schedule Saturday for you? Your schedule is open." Users are going to be looking for telepathic technology to help them, and the future Church understands that this technology is a way in which it can spread the news of mission. Using digital mirrors, geo-fences, and other technology, the Christian community engaged in generous evangelism will see these opportunities as way to connect with people in real time and offer a bit of grace and peace in an over-scheduled world.

The digital natives are swamped with choices. We all are! Barry Schwartz, in his 2004 Book entitled *The Paradox of Choice*, introduced modern civilization to the idea that too much choice is not a good thing.[445] In fact he makes the case that so much choice actually brings with it "anxiety, disappointment, and ultimately unhappiness."[446] So he offers that as human beings, we are actually happier when decisions are made for us. Not long ago my wife and I were talking about Schwartz' paradox when we had a difficult time picking out a movie—there are literally thousands at our fingertips. Yet we seemed paralyzed and unable to make a decision.

Think about it for a minute:

85 different varieties and brands of crackers
285 varieties of cookies
165 varieties of "juice drinks"
75 iced teas
95 varieties of snacks (chips, pretzels, etc.)
61 varieties of sun tan oil and sunblock
80 different pain relievers
40 options for toothpaste
360 types of shampoo, conditioner, gel, and mousse
90 different cold remedies and decongestants
230 soups, including 29 different chicken soups
120 different pasta sauces
175 different salad dressings and if none of them suited, 15
extra-virgin olive oils and 42 vinegars and make one's own.
275 varieties of cereal

And more than 20,000 new products hit the shelves every year.
In a consumer electronics store:

45 different car stereo systems, with 50 different speaker sets to
go with them
42 different computers, most of which can be customized in
various ways
110 different televisions, offering high definition, flat screen,
varying screen sizes and features, and various levels of sound
quality
50 different DVD players[447]

All of this choice makes us unhappy people, and unhappy people
will try to figure out a way to fix that reality. So, as we move into the

next few decades there will remain an abundance of choice and there will be a desire for a technology to simplify things.

We as a culture have a great desire for no-click technologies. Individuals will begin seeking programs and apps that do the interface *for* them. These tools will help make choices for us. Think for a moment about Urbanspoon; that program that helped us out in Amarillo with a restaurant. What Urbanspoon is most used for, it turns out, is not the recommendations but its shakeability. When you shake your phone, it will pick a restaurant for you. As of March 2010, Urbanspoon had been collectively shaken half a billion times.[448] IFTF reports that the goal of apps like Urbanspoon will be to "reduce barriers" to action because of choice. In their report on persuasion they wrote: "One of the most important powers of augmented reality will be to make nearby opportunities more visible and more actionable."[449] What is important here is not the fact that an app will pick your restaurant for you, but that more people want an app that will help them with choice. Let us look at what Yelp developed with its app called Monocle.

Monocle is an "augmented reality (AR) overlay" that reveals nearby business listings over a real time video feed of the street in front of the phone.[450] In layman's terms, what it does is it shows the businesses that have listed with Monocle and that are nearby, then gives the distance to them, and invites them to visit. The program is about urban curiosity helping users to discover places they might not know about. Ultimately such interfaces combined with technologies we have already talked about will create an environment wherein the digital native can choose to navigate or avoid their surroundings. There is a lot of information being shared here, but the interface with the user is minimal. Like the Ford Focus Hybrid that has a digital plant that grows healthier the more r the driver conforms to fuel efficiency or the Fitbit digital flower that grows as the user reaches their target—these apps are not only about simplicity but behavioral change in a non-obtrusive way.[451] Imagine then that the future Church, interested in reaching these digital natives, not having just geo-fences but actually being part of the health of the environment. A person sees that a Christian community meets here for coffee on Thursdays. Another shows that St. Julian's has a recycling program closer to their home. Christian communities will use these technologies to participate in the virtual world that is growing around the digital native.

The future Church, must participate because if it is not involved in these technologies, making life simpler and better, then it will not be part of the digital native's world.

The future Episcopal Church will be engaged in generous evangelism. It engages intentionally in being a generous community using all, tools at its disposal for its work. The future Church is interested and engaged with the digital native because it understands this is its context. Most of all, the generous community of Christ is engaged because it desires to be a transformational part of the world culture that will be enmeshed with the digital world. The future Church believes and shares the Gospel of God in Christ Jesus as an essential building block to well communities and does this through a network found in the digital universe, and on the shoulder, of the digital native. Generous evangelism empowers people to act, and builds the individual's capacity for deeper spiritual connection with God and others by becoming a full participating member of the cloud and crowd. I recognize that not everyone in the Church or Christian community is called to be an evangelist. However, the future Church that is thriving will have many evangelists—each in their own way sharing the good news of the Episcopal Church and God in Jesus Christ, through their participation as digital natives in the crowd. They will do this in many different contexts and in many different ways. The future Church will do a good job in its work of formation, helping people to find their way into community, after they walk in the door. To do that, we must pause to understand the kind of individual that is likely to be part of the future Church—The Amplified Human.

CHAPTER SEVENTEEN
Amplio Hominis—The Amplified Human

*"Don't let us forget that the causes of human actions are
usually immeasurably more complex and varied than
our subsequent explanations of them."*
— Fyodor Dostoyevsky, <u>The Idiot</u>

Who are these digital natives, these amplified humans that we are aiming to evangelize? What is the character of the human within this culture? How do they live and move within their world? Kalle Lasn, activist, and creator of "Buy Nothing Day," and "TV turn Off Week" has a sobering view of our current life. He wrote this short meditation in the 1990's and it is worth pondering.

You decide, as a tonic, to go on a camping trip—a pit-latrine-and-flame-cooked-wieners experience uncorrupted by phones, faxes or Baywatch. In the absence of electronic distractions, you will get to know each other again.

After only a few hours in the wilderness...Your kids experience actual physical withdrawal from television...If you have read Elisabeth Kübler-Ross, you will recognize that the stages your kids are going through—denial, anger, depression, bargaining—closely mimic the stages of grief, as if they are adjusting to a loss. Which in a real way they are: the loss of their selves. Or rather, the loss of the selves that feel most authentic to them. Their mediated selves those selves that, when disconnected from the urban data stream, cease to function.[452]

Perhaps for the first time in human history we are becoming amplified human beings. Our ancient texts from Genesis tell us that we are created to live in community—that we are to be connected. Technology has empowered us to be connected in new and various ways. The individual is becoming part of a world wide web quite literally. When we disconnect from those devices and tools, we feel a measure of loss. How have we reached this point in our human development? What does it mean to be an amplified human and how are we dealing with this new reality?

Of course we have not always been dependent upon devices. To think that our technological connection is the end of the *self* or even the end of real *community* is perhaps a little Luddite[453] of us. Yet, we must take seriously our evolution because without an understanding of this time and place in which we find ourselves, it will be difficult for us to take the next step in our conversation about the future Church—that is the formation of amplified Christians.

Regardless of what history or sociological text you choose to read, it is clear that humanity has lived in community for its whole existence. Whether humanity was reflective enough to understand that it was in community or that it was in a network of relationships is not of our concern in this book. I simply want to acknowledge that we are, amplified or not, people who are creatures of a crowd, a pack, or a family. These communities have navigated the world from the time of nomadic life to what we call civilization. In the midst of all of that change, their focus and their interests have changed, along with their communal religion. In the beginning, we know that our distant ancestors spent their time searching for food and shelter—a repeated process on a daily basis. This was the routine—survival. The priests and shaman were to do the work of intercession with the gods on behalf of the community. Our own faith reveals these same truths. When we read the ancient texts and hear of our faith fathers and mothers, who intercede and speak with God, we understand that the whole family or tribe just did not go around mixing with the divine.

Wandering tribes eventually gave way to the Mesopotamian agricultural life. Even though those who plowed the land and those who shepherded animals have always been in conflict with one another, we see a great settling of humanity into agrarian communities. Until recently, most individuals in the whole world lived as peasants working fields they owned or rented. They would sow and reap and store up for themselves. Faith and religion were pastimes at most. The work was, for the most part, the routine of subsistence living. This is true for many parts of the world today. Some live this way because of their birth context, while there is also a whole movement to live a subsistence lifestyle in the west, and there exist multiple articles about how to go about doing it online.

Eventually societies in many parts of the world reached a kind of complexity and human beings began to specialize. Certainly the complexity and hierarchies lent themselves to these new ideas of jobs and the training required to do them—this then is the rise of the master and apprentice class. Blacksmiths, carpenters, bakers, tailors, doctors, and even the religious worker—the priest, begin to trade their services for the services of the farmer and field worker. The great food baskets of the world began to provide an abundance that allowed for such specialization and continues to do so today.

This abundance and the industrial revolution has enabled the workweek for many people to gradually shrink, leaving more and more time for activities like religion. The Australian Readers' Digest version of the History of Work offers this perspective: "Over the course of the past 150 years, the working week of an average European or American has grown shorter and shorter. In 1849, when Britain's industrial might was at its peak, an English factory worker would be at his station for 12 hours and 15 minutes a day, six days a week; the working week for an unskilled person was 73 hours and 30 minutes. Shop assistants worked even longer, often 18 hours a day, six days a week—or 108 hours."[454] Robert Whaples of Wake Forest University published a paper corroborating these statistics.[455] In

Whaples' paper he suggests that the workweek will continue to shrink over the next 3 decades.

Estimated Trend in the Lifetime Distribution of Discretionary Time, 1880-2040

Activity	1880	1995	2040
Lifetime Discretionary Hours	225,900	298,500	321,900
Lifetime Work Hours	182,100	122,400	75,900
Lifetime Leisure Hours	43,800	176,100	246,000

Notes: Discretionary hours exclude hours used for sleep, meals and hygiene. Work hours include paid work, travel to and from work, and household chores.[456]

This shift in work and discretionary hours is all part of a growing surplus of time. As we have discussed the human in the midst of community has migrated from spending a great deal of time at work and little in religious activities, to less time working and a lot of time spent in religious activities, to less time working and less time used for religious activities and more discretionary time for other activities including spiritual ones but not necessarily religious ones. We have in the great sweep of modernism become more of an individual. We have been able to journey farther from the land, and away from home. We have left our families and we have journeyed across great expanses of the world. As we entered the new millennia we had never been more alone or more on our own. As our wealth and free time has increased, so has our unhappiness.

Regardless of where humanity has been in our journey over the centuries, regardless of our place or work within community, regardless of how much time we have had or not had, we have repeatedly sought out community and intimacy with God and with one another. This is especially true within the Christian tradition and it is true today in our Episcopal faith. Over the great sweep of our tradition, it has been the normal people, the working people, the field laborers and the shop owners who have found some connection through God in Christ Jesus. They have been sinners and saints, and most of them have been just like you and I. They have worked and toiled, they have celebrated and mourned, and they have lived and died just like you and I.[457] Like most of us, they left barely a footnote in Christian history, yet their lives were ones of faith and service. Each believed and prayed and offered sacrifices. They have prayed in the fields at the toll of a bell, and made their way to the church on their name day to light a candle while the mass was being said. Regardless of their task or place in life, they have for centuries attempted to find a bit of transformation, a bit of something beyond themselves, and bit of peace in the midst of chaos.

Dom Gregory Dix in his book *The Shape of* Liturgy describes well the power of this eternal return to the table of Christ that so many Christians have participated in.

He wrote:

Was ever another command so obeyed? For century after century, spreading slowly to every continent and country and among every race on earth, this action has been done, in every conceivable human circumstance, for every conceivable human need from infancy and before it to extreme old age and after it, from the pinnacle of earthly greatness to the refuge of fugitives in the caves and dens of the earth. Men have found no better thing than this to do for kings at their crowning and for criminals going to the scaffold; for armies in triumph or for a bride and bridegroom in a little country church; for the proclamation of a dogma or for a good crop of wheat; for the wisdom of the Parliament of a mighty nation or for a sick old woman afraid to die; for a schoolboy sitting an examination or for Columbus setting out to discover America; for the famine of whole provinces or for the soul of a dead lover; in thankfulness because my father did not die of pneumonia; for a village headman much tempted to return to fetish because the yams had failed; because the Turk was at the gates of Vienna; for the repentance of Margaret; for the settlement of a strike; for a son for a barren woman; for Captain so-and-so wounded and prisoner of war; while the lions roared in the nearby amphitheater; on the beach at Dunkirk; while the hiss of scythes in the thick June grass came faintly through the windows of the church; tremulously, by an old monk on the fiftieth anniversary of his vows; furtively, by an exiled bishop who had hewn timber all day in a prison camp near Murmansk; gorgeously, for the canonization of S. Joan of Arc—one could fill many pages with the reasons why men have done this, and not tell a hundredth part of them. And best of all, week by week and month by month, on a hundred thousand successive Sundays, faithfully, unfailingly, across all the parishes of Christendom, the pastors have done this just to make the plebs sancta Dei—the holy common people of God.[458]

Today we can look back and see that different kinds of people have tried to be faithful followers of God in Christ Jesus. Some of these followers were raised within Christian communities and still others choose it for themselves. Who are we today? And, will the amplified human, naturally see the Eucharist and prayer as a way to transcend the profane into the holy? Today with our new ability to amplify our connections we might wonder what kind of humanity are we becoming? What characteristics shall shape our communities in the future? In all of this time we, as humans, have become more and more connected through technology but less and less connected in traditional ways.

Humanity today might be characterized as spirited and mischievous. The postmodern creature could be called a work of irony with a tendency towards schizophrenia. We are humans who consume and are tourists. This newly evolved human condition is something of the past, and can often be seen as without spirituality, and with a lack of true engagement with the metaphysical. We are willing to revel in shock value and "brutal aesthetics."[459] At least this is literary critic Terry Eagleton's idea of what defines the character of the postmodern man. As a child of the postmodern age, I like the idea that we are in a time that deconstructs the "monotony" of the universal idea that modernism (and the generations before me) had of the world.[460] I was trained as an artist in the postmodern tradition. These forces of change have crafted a new people living within a new context. Some of the side effects of this cultural hyper- amplification are serious.

This nascent culture and its amplified humans have also had other effects. There is a new globalism and new global creative conversation. Overall, the postmodern movement has had an exciting and considerable effect on everything from literature to science. This book is a product of those discussions and this culture. R. Rorty reintroduced philosophical pragmatism in his book *Philosophy and the Mirror of Nature* (1979). There has been a shift in the philosophy of science. T. Kuhn in his book *The Structure of Scientific Revolutions* (1962), and P. Feyerabend in his work *Against Method* (1975), began an upheaval that continues today. Philosopher M. Foucault's *Power/Knowledge* emphasis upon discontinuity and difference in history, and his privileging of "polymorphous correlations in place of simple or complex causality" has impacted everything from philosophy to human resource management. There continue to be new developments in mathematics emphasizing indeterminacy (catastrophe and chaos theory, and fractal geometry). There has been a re-emergence of concern in ethics, politics, and anthropology for the validity and dignity of "the other," all indicative of widespread and profound shift in the "structure of feeling."[461] What all of this has done is to give the deathblow to most metanarratives. It has deconstructed the notion that there is one universal story. This means that culturally we are awash in many narratives, none of which are concerned with legitimacy. Science, literature, philosophy, and religion have all had to step back from the grandiose, and step into the quantum—the micro narrative of life.[462] While we are on the one hand free from modernity's grasp and the notion that we all must be the same, we are now imprisoned in a culture where meaning is longed for but difficult to find.

With postmodernism has also come a sweep of new ailments for society and for the individual. If we look at just the psychological ailments from which our society suffers, we have a disturbing picture. In the U.S. ten million people suffer from Seasonal Affective Disorder (SAD). Fourteen million are alcoholics. Fifteen million are pathologically socially anxious. Fifteen million are depressed. Three million suffer panic attacks. Ten million have Borderline Personality Disorder. Twelve million have restless legs. Five million are obsessive/compulsive. Two million are manic-depressive. Ten million are addicted to sex. Factoring in wild-card afflictions like Chronic Fatigue Syndrome and multiple chemical sensitivity, and allowing for overlap (folks suffering from more than one problem) [we] might conclude that over 70% percent of the adult population is in trouble.[463] The amazing thing is that in the same time period of growth in psychic illness, we have also grown in pharmaceutical treatments. These treatments have created an explosion in the pharmaceutical industry. Moreover, we have watched the systematic shrinking of services to the mentally ill over the past two decades. While everything is coming apart into a creative stew in the postmodern world, we may be coming apart ourselves. All in all, this has radically shifted the focus of parents and children. The meta narrative battles over sex, money, and war are a distraction in this culture from what is truly ailing us.

Our families have changed dramatically during this time period. The Victorians created the idea of childhood. The growth of free time and a society where children could play instead of work has slowly lengthened childhood. We have become a childhood society in some way. [464] The absence of the parents from the life of the children has created a gap in formation and education. Its presence is noticed especially as the family narrative and history are lost to the children. These narratives are in large part now passed on through the media. Being hooked up and connected the very real ways these children are actually connected. They participate in gaming and epic movie fandoms and look to one another to help them understand. In the absence of wisdom people (parents and grandparents), the maturation points in the lifecycle of humans are being missed. We as families are not nurturing our children as communities for thousands of years have done prior to the modern and postmodern age. [465] Instead, I fear we have left them largely at the mercy of a manufactured world of products that are so focused on children that they actually keep the children in adolescence. Some believe there is an actual neo cortex connection between what we see socially, and what we see individually with children and the whole human race. We are quite literally being rewired. [466]

We do not mentor our children to become adults. With the intergenerational connection lost, there is no natural way of forming them into adulthood. They are becoming individuals without the amenity of community. We have been dependent upon other organizations to do this. Without real adventure and family connections, they are isolated. We have not helped them have a healthy connection with their bodies or with nature. They are led by desire alone because we have not taught them the icons or told them the narratives. [467]

As adults we have not valued the narratives and so we have all forgotten the importance of allegory and wisdom—we have simply deconstructed everything looking for facts. Not long ago I sat up late with a middle school teacher friend and we discussed this fact. Somehow we have not only forgotten to pass along the narratives allowing our children to wonder and imagine what might be of value, we have also created a whole generation without milestones and markers that help them interpret the world.

What is truly miraculous and gives me hope is that somehow we are wired to look for allegory, metaphor, and markers, even though as families we have failed to pass along our stories. I believe that future generations of adults and their children are interested in changing this by discovering who they are and where their family comes from. As former Archbishop Rowan Williams says, "We are the only sense-making creatures."[468] Children have grown into parents and have had children of their own. Without answers for their children's difficult questions they have longed for the missing narratives and so this new generation is re-engaging in adventure and story. There is a natural desire for spirituality, just because the post-modernists sought to deconstruct it has not changed this fact. There is a natural desire to make sense of things and the world around us. We are at the edge of a new era we might call the era of narrative aspiration. Quantum narratives, and macro narratives, will be turned to by this new culture over the next decades. They want stories that reconnect them with one another. They want stories that connect them to the sacred, holy, and the ancient. There is in us a natural desire to grow old spiritually—to become wise.

This new generation is looking for physical connection and ritual that connects us to God. I believe the church has an opportunity in the midst of these families and younger generations. However, offering what worked over 50 years ago or even 20 years ago—dressed up in new clothing, will not fool them. They know that there is transcendence, wisdom, transformation, and story available to them; but they are not willing to be told to memorize or take it as truth. The amplified human who is connected to all their peers, and more facts than any human has ever had at their fingertips, will not be fooled for long by cheap grace, easy answers, or a "Bible tells you so" kind of formation.

The amplified human is cynical of such trite attempts as pseudo religion. In part because the amplified human experiences community, real community, that is complex and mixed between family members, friends, peers, and those in their digital neighborhoods. The human walks between the real and the digital world community of values and often turns our friends into substitute families. If we are in a church, it is one that has a cohesive way of life, not one that seems to be EZ God-Lite for casual consumers. They are skeptical about claims to "have the truth," not only because we have been educated to consider such claims to be a mask for the will to power, but also because we know instinctively that truth is not a dead propositional object you can "have." The big question isn't "What is the meaning of life?" It's something more like "Who can I really count on?"

These digital natives can be cynical and ultra-pragmatic, but that doesn't stop them from wanting to make a concrete difference on a local level (as distinct from 60's- era "save the world" ambitions.) The amplified humans with all of their connections have little problem allowing for contradictory ideas. They just figure they make sense in different contexts or different communities. This new digital human is connected and so is formed by pop culture. If you are a native of the older modern era, using pop culture to make meaning seems odd. Here are some of the new narratives. Pop culture is where they debate their religious worldview.... Did you see [insert movie reference here]. Violent or not, sexually explicit or not, these are the place of major theological reflection.

The amplified human is not just suspicious of institutions, but inclined simply to ignore them and get on with the journey—the pilgrimage. In part, they might say, "we need to grow up and institutions need to get a life." These cultural natives grew up in the age of mass communication, advertising, and consumerism as the law of the land, and are so at home in this world that they can smell manipulation a mile away. So do not even try. These individuals have set out on their journey, many are wounded people from institutions (especially religious ones) which took advantage of them or did not take them seriously. They long for the parenting they did not receive and actually do not have a problem with religious references that are familial in nature. They are longing for deep and meaningful stories and are eager to share them with their children. These are the amplified humans who are stepping into leadership at this moment.

In 20 years there will be yet another shift as the digital natives' children enter a new stage in life causing a cultural shift. Today this generation (sometimes referred to as Generation Z) makes up one quarter of the population—and growing.[469] Even though this generation is young they influence their parents and peers about technology and have a purchasing power of $44 billion dollars a year. They are worker bees and are hopeful they can turn their hobbies into jobs.[470]

The future Church must be in tune with the new quantum and macro narratives that are shaping this new generation. Knowing pop culture references will not be enough. New languages connected to the amplified human's digital reality will be essential. The amplified human will actually be more civic and community minded than any other group since the Builder Generation (born after 1901, also called the GI Generation). These amplified individuals have seen the state of things left to them and they are not happy about it. They will roll up their sleeves to fix it and restore the connections lost in the last half century.

The future digital native will not have a lot of use for the word "I" because in reality they are never alone and never experiencing life alone. They are always "we." They are hooked in and connected to massive amounts of friends and peers. The digital natives live in an even more complex world and so their tolerance for other viewpoints is high. They will engage in the shocking and the wild as part of the adventure of life but at the core they are also reacting to the past generation's carelessness with their bodies and with nature. These digital natives (thanks to all of the self-esteem building activities in grade school and their ability to navigate the digital frontier) are brash.

The digital migrant today is overscheduled because they have over-spent their free time –because in part it was all so new. The digital native 20 years from now will have technology and apps and be accustomed to greater free time and will use it more wisely on those things that bring adventure, meaning, and require courage and faith. The coming decades will bring a culture of shared spiritual (not religious) longing and a willingness to go on a quest to find it. The future Church must be willing to move away from trite answers and join the new amplified humans in their multi -dimensional world and on their pilgrimage. The future Church knows it cannot mandate the terms of engagement.

The digital natives of the new culture are adept at shape shifting. They experience the world in a variety of contexts and are able to blend seamlessly into each of these worlds. They are accustomed to the complex nature of cultures and societies. They enjoy the discovery and the art of it all. Amplified humans, with multiple crowds on their shoulders at all times, are able to enter into complicated worlds and shift themselves into the new context by taking on a new identity. [471] This shifting allows the digital native to experience these worlds on their own terms. They are willing to be part of many different narratives as they seek wisdom and understanding. This will enable them to manipulate their new worldview. This experiential learning is who they are; it comes naturally to them and they are energized by it. They are self-learners. Gaming, texting, selfies, and instant vines uploaded and shared are the new maps that chart their spiritual journey. The future Church will understand that the person they are dealing with inside the Christian community is of greater depth and has other personalities than appear visible in the religious context. The future Church understands that the person appearing before it is a complex shape shifter.

Future digital natives are masters at manipulating and traveling along the hidden infrastructures of their world. They do not know any different way of being. Remember, these are the kids who used iPads before they could speak in full sentences. They are already connected to the things that are necessary for their pilgrimage. They are part of the network—they come wired. For you Gen Xers, you might think of the image of Neo (who is the chosen one in the1999 movie entitled the *Matrix*) seeing all of the matrix code in the air and being able to touch it, move it, and bend it. Contemporary moviegoers, I ask you to think of the image of Scarlett Johansson in the 2014 movie entitled *Lucy*, where she is able to use all of her brain and can actually see all digital data, the movement of time itself, and manipulate it all. These are images of the digital native. The digital native of the future is at home, effortlessly moving between the real world and the digital world—they don't see a separation. They are able to have access to money, clothes, tickets, everyday products, movies, music, apps to help them, and transportation all within the palm of their hand. The amplified human of the future will be so native to this new world that they do not see these discussions as novel but rather as assumed.[472] The future Church must think carefully about the infrastructure needed, what is visible and what is invisible, so that it can increase the doorways by which the digital native enters and investigates with God and other seekers.

Amplified humans of the future will continue to long for family; so, they will make family. They will have many kinds of "familial-type clusters of relationships in their networks."[473] Just as digitals natives are comfortable shape shifting between contexts, they will also be comfortable moving seamlessly between families. To them the network of relationships is a larger than life family. In both the digital and real world they will build communities and relationships in different ways. They will redefine what family is, and they will be looking for narratives to add meaning to these new multi-connected relationships.[474] When I was growing up, we learned a lot about peer pressure. Peer pressure was something that was outside of the familial system. For the digital native of the future, all peers are family. All have value in helping the natives navigate their spiritual journey as they come of age. They are not only willing to have them as family they are willing to seek them out, and build the family they need for their particular life walk. It is not unlike building a team. In this new landscape the family of origin itself will be in search for new meaning and new understandings about how it connects and is connected throughout the network of relationships. The future Church will move beyond seeing the individuals before them as family units and begin to see them as a group of interconnected individuals. The Church will work to become part of the wider and larger family systems the digital natives are creating and rely upon.

Evolution and change are normal. Technology has a built in obsolescence and so there is a built in need for change. The amplified human lives in an ecosphere that is constantly shifting and moving with fads, increasing technological innovation, and creativity.[475] Groups and networks change and they change their connective nodes. Not unlike the dispersal system above, when one network node does not fit anymore the connectivity quickly shifts to one that does. The digital native is always on the move and is attracted by strong connections. Healthy and vital connections that improve their quality of life are important. Connections that increase wellness, and connections that increase the intrinsic value of their lives are of interest. Those connections and network nodes that do not do this are quickly dropped. In part this is true because at the core of the digital native is an assumed truth that the social network defines who you are. You might remember a parent saying to you, "Tell me who your friends are and I will tell you who you are." In a world of super connectivity this is also true. The native knows that the social networks that they belong to define who they are.[476] Therefore, they choose them carefully. The groups pick and choose clear lines and boundaries of belonging. This clarity is important for the digital shape shifter so he or she knows who they are to be in this particular context. Meanwhile the digital native is collecting these connections as a kind of "suite of personalities" that makes up their character. The natives are "complex" and "participate in multiple networks and have various roles and identities."[477]

The church has a hard time keeping up. The church does have creative people who can participate at the same rate of change. Now we are a little off in our timing. We lag in our execution. Remember in

2012 the Olympic swim team put out the "Call Me Maybe" video (www.youtube.com/watch?v=YPIA7mpm1wU).   It went viral instantly. What also went viral were people spoofing and making their own "Call Me Maybe" videos. For a couple months these were fun and funny. Six months later a very talented group of acolytes and a bishop put together a very well done "Call me Maybe" video. It was hilarious! (www.youtube.com/watch?v=BB5eVhOXPIA). Today it has 82,000 views, which is fantastic, but if it were put out when the "call me maybe" videos were going viral it would have reached over a million. It isn't that we cannot do it, it is as if we are always a beat off the culture. We did a little better with the ALS Bucket Challenge. Nevertheless, we were weeks off the original challenge. This kind of lag happens all over. While some technologies/internet fads are here for the long haul, others are not , so we better jump on board quickly and then let it go when the rest of the world does.[478]

The thriving Church plays well within the constantly evolving ecosphere of the amplified human, and is creative in making new contexts. It no longer sees the digital world as a separate context but is immersed as an amplified community within it. The future Church will be an amplified Church. Therefore, like the other network clusters the Episcopal Church in its various forms of church (liberal, conservative, traditional, emerging, contemporary, small and large) is clear about its boundaries and belonging so that the digital native may understand and see the pathways into community. The future Church must understand that the amplified human looks to the Church to help amplify a portion of his/her life; and so, the Church is eager to discover roles and identities that can be held within the Christian community.

The amplified human is an incarnation of Neo and/or Lucy. They are individuals who are not only interested in connecting to networks of various kinds, but also are interested in full engagement with everything. All network clusters are different and have a variety of qualities. Some digital natives are interested in "colonizing" the organization and taking it over—changing its makeup and DNA.[479]

Still others will want to create their own networks and their own communities.[480] For instance, they will want to make new expressions of Christian community. Irrespective of which style the digital native engages, they will see the other members of the community as essential to life and health.[481] They value the roles their friends and co-workers have and expect them to work together within the network cluster towards the common goal of either colonizing or creating anew. The future Church will partner with the amplified humans to rethink and remake old structures, morphing them into renewed living communities. The living Church accepts this challenge and while working to impart the meta narrative and its universal trajectory, it also makes room for the new natives to create and move the narrative into quantum relevance. The future Episcopal Church will also be willing to engage and underwrite the amplified human desire to create new community. There will be a tolerance for this kind of tinkering and creativity. The future Church sees this as tenacity, and enjoys the pilgrimage with the amplified individuals and their ability to play with the visible and invisible structures of the community.

The amplified human exists within a global and local environment. It is not that the world is flat; the digital native lives in a multidimensional universe that is real, natural, cyber, local and globally networked. The digital native defines "global" in a different way. Yes, he or she may understand that global means that in their local context exists a global representation of ethnicities and cultural contexts.[482] Houston, New York, and Los Angeles are global cities. For others global will mean having actually made a pilgrimage to experience another part of the world.[483] Both of these are of tremendous value to the amplified individual, who desires to incarnate the virtual reality of an interconnected cosmos. They want to make networks and connections real. They are not satisfied living within a virtual world. The virtual world only has value if it is able to become a real experience. Global and local connections are always moving in the direction of real life experiences. The future Church will engage in making these real connections happen. The church will value the global networks and the real diversity available to it in its local context. It will also make real connections and create new partnerships with global individuals and other communities. In part the future church will do this because it values what the amplified human values, and so it will help its members build real face-to-face relationships.

Into this world will step technology as the ever-present key to amplification and connectivity. The world of power is changing quickly and so everything is getting powered up and mobile. Amplification and connectivity will be everywhere.[484] The Church will figure out how to integrate spaces for charging and supporting the digital natives need for power supply. The tools that the digital native carries with them are getting smarter.[485] IFTF reports the following: "Over the past century, we have learned how to create specialized materials that meet our specific needs for strength, durability, weight, flexibility, and cost. Now materials may be able to modify themselves in each of these dimensions on their own—that is to adapt intelligently to their environments."[486] The future Church will integrate into these systems. Not only members will be connected but also the sacred spaces themselves will integrate into the digital environment so that the native may travel seamlessly into and out of the space; and, find it with ease.

The Rev. Brandon Peete in Houston has created a formation experience called Kadosh—which means holy. The class generates topics during the week via social networking. Then there is class participation that includes the ability for those in the classroom to text thoughts onto a running banner at the bottom of an interactive screen. Images, music, poetry, prose and news are all used in a multi-media interaction led predominately by those engaged in the class. One can also imagine a liturgy that uses sound, images, and technology for a fully digital, interactive, interpersonal experience of worship. These kinds of experiences in church will require that the community is interactive technologically with media across its space.

At the same time turning off, disconnecting, and quiet may be the goal of the service. In these environments the church will be tasked with figuring out how you help the digital native disconnect. Restaurants offer phone charging cubbies where people can store their smart phone and charge it while enjoying a meal of personal interaction with other guests. We are challenged to remember that the Church will not eject one model but that the future Church must engage many models. It will be the pliability of community and its space to connect in a variety of different ways that will be a requirement for the future Church. Today most congregations do not have functioning Wi-Fi for their parishioners to use while on campus. This is a requirement for all spaces where business takes place today? Why? Because information sharing is essential and such former luxuries are now the basics of good business. The future Church will be amplified and/or have the ability to turn off and disconnect intentionally.

Anything will be able to be transformed into a display.[487] This means that the old "make room for a screen" will go away as any wall will be expected to be display worthy. The future church will engage this technology in both its worship space and formation space in order to bring the digital and virtual world into sacred space. Any space can be a classroom. There will be growing interactivity between the real and the display of images and icons as the Church interprets and reinterprets the digital native's own world of video, music, and images. Along with voice technology, such displays will engage the digital native virtually, allowing them to navigate the Christian community from street side. Harry Potter fans remember "The Fat Lady" who stands watch at the Gryffindor common room that students must tell the secret password to in order to enter. Imagine a reality where an individual walks up to the front of a historic Church building, speaks to the display on the outside wall and asks questions about the community within. The screen shares the information about the goings on at this particular Episcopal Church with the digital pilgrim.

More than likely the pilgrim got there because the church and its members were tagged in a network they participate within. Tagging is going to be a key link between the physical and virtual world. It will be the key way in which the digital native finds the different connections within their universe of travel.[488] The future Church must be willing to be tagged, make its own tags, participate in tagging other people/events, because it understands that this is how search engines find and interpret both the physical and digital world. The future Church knows this is how it gets on "the map." I recently looked up a friend's address online using Google Maps. I found the house using "street view." Google immediately asked if I wanted to see tweets near this location. Imagine the individual looking for a church and think how important those tags buried in posts will be in terms of investigating new Christian communities.

Let me give you an example of the kind of the kind of interactivity I am talking about. Normally, a visit to your local art museum, or any museum for that matter is an experience of meandering through the halls observing an exhibit with a little descriptive card positioned to the left that identifies the work and artist. I recently visited the Toronto and the Art Gallery of Ontario (AGO). We went to see the renovation by Frank Gehry. There was an intriguing exhibit entitled "Art as Therapy." The project was a collaboration between the AGO and the British philosopher Alain de Botton and the philosopher and art theorist John Armstrong which brought to life their book *Art as Therapy*. Their interest was in experimenting with how art can do the work of engaging the patron. Specifically, the AGO and philosophers were interested in how art might engage a conversation of universal significance like love, politics, sex, power, and money, with the viewers. The exhibit was interactive. It included a catalog of art displayed in several rooms. The floor was marked with arrows to help self-guided participants. There were video installations that talked about the topics and the art chosen. Beside each piece of art was a narrative. The narrative described the work, the artist, offered a viewpoint on one of the themes, and then asked a question. There were iPads in each themed room so that participants could write reflections or draw pictures. These in turn were shared on the video screen for the participants to see. The exhibit was tagged throughout so those viewing the exhibit could interact with others online. There was a children's section with interactive projects. The exhibit also had an Instagram site so that uploaded photos could be shared with others. Can you imagine a church that is this interactive with its newcomers and visitors? Can you imagine how a church could be opened up to tell the Gospel story and create a wider experience of interaction with God? This is the kind of interactivity that the future missionary Church must be about creating.

The 1996 British movie entitled *Trainspotting* starring a young Ewan Macgregor as Rinton is one of my favorites. In it, Rinton says, "Choose a life. Choose a job. Choose a career. Choose a family. Choose a ... big television. Choose washing machines, cars, compact disc players and electrical tin openers... Choose DSY and wondering who ...you are on a Sunday morning. Choose sitting on that couch watching mind numbing, spirit crushing game shows, sticking junk food into your mouth. Choose rotting away in the end of it all, [spending] your last in a miserable home, nothing more than an embarrassment to the selfish, fucked up brats you spawned to replace yourself, choose your future. Choose life... But why would I want to do a thing like that?"[489] The comedy/crime film is and about escaping the world around us through addiction. In a scene called "All the fresh air won't make a difference,"[490] Begbie, Spud, Sick boy, and Rinton are dry, they are off heroine, and have gone for a hike in the countryside. They are at a hill. For the average viewer they are simply out for a walk, trying to keep their minds off their addiction and on their beer.

The setting is important and it is essential if you are to understand the dialogue. The setting is Glen Coe, where in 1688 the last battle of the Scottish fight for nationalism took place. Coe of the McDonalds, who inhabited this hill, took an oath to William of

Orange, but it arrived too late. So, a regiment under Robert Campbell set off to make an example of Coe and massacred 33 men, 2 women, 2 children plus others who died during the ensuing winter. The battle became a symbol of the horrendous abuse of hospitality by the English. Campbell had stayed in these people's homes for some days. He also took advantage of William of Orange's dissatisfaction with the clan to settle a feud between the Campbells and the McDonalds. The massacre has become a symbol of economic oppression of the working class Scots by the English. It is not happenstance that this movie and these lads inhabit this particular space. They belong to this landscape by way of their Scottish birth, class, and addiction. They belong to the landscape of domination by one country of another, and it will, in the rest of the movie, play out as an ironic and sad self-destructive return to heroin.

The narrative story, the environment, and the people are all intimately connected. We too belong to the history and cultural landscape that surrounds us. Oftentimes our lives of ministry within the present/past church are blind to the broader landscape outside our doors—to the future church that is out there. The amplified humans are many and connected. Some digital migrants are as well. We have the potential for amplification and the potential to enter the world of the digital native. They may see us as nodes in the network—nodes that do not function terribly well. We are connected; we are tied together. We are part of the same narrative—quantum and macro.

A few words from Alexander Pope's *Essay on Man* come to mind:

Look round our World; behold the chain of Love
Combining all below and all above.
See plastic Nature working to this end,
The single atoms each to other tend....

Nothing is foreign: Parts relate to whole;

One all-extending all-preserving Soul
Connects each being, greatest with the least;
Made Beast in aid of Man, and Man of Beast;
All serv'd, all serving! Nothing stands alone;
The chain holds on, and where it ends, unknown.

The future Church knows that we are all connected with huge potential for interaction. We have the possibility even now to becoming an interactive working node of a great network. The future Church can read the context in which it is living. It can interpret the hillside, the path, the location and the people who are making their livelihoods in this eco-scape. The future Church knows that to engage the amplified human it must rethink how it does formation as a missionary church. The future Church must intentionally reconsider how it engages the sacred conversation with the amplified human—it has a living model of formation.

CHAPTER EIGHTEEN
Self-Forming Creative Christians

"If you want to build a ship, don't gather people together to collect wood and don't assign them tasks and work, but rather, teach them to long for the endless immensity of the sea."
— *Attributed to Antoine de Saint-Exupery*

I wonder how you became a Christian? And, what kind of Christian are you? Regardless of the answer, your story and pilgrimage to this point are unique. I was visiting with a friend of mine the other day, and she described a conversation with her 15 year old. Her daughter was telling her about her discovery of Christianity and was asking her mother about why she did this or did not do that. As I listened, it reminded me of the Socratic method where one asks questions of another to stimulate debate. Her mom had her own set of questions. In the end she imparted a bit of wisdom that seems most relevant here. She said, "I have made my journey, this is your journey, kid." Our journey, finding our way, is uniquely ours. It is our journey to make and to direct. The very fact of you and your story speaks to the great diverse creative power that is at work in the cosmos around us. Yet somehow we in the Church have gotten things a little mixed up. We have, along the way, begun to think a dangerous thought. That thought is: the Church makes the Christian. And, in order for the organization of the Church to make such a thing, it must manufacture it like any other great industrial machine.

The age of the machine and cookie cutter Christians is over, except the Church has not figured that out yet. It was not much of a reality anyway. In order to be the future Church we must awake to the reality of a world filled with self-learners, storytellers, and people making their self-directed way. Today we are moving into a new creative era where we remember an ancient truth—God is weaving a beautiful tapestry of stories in and amongst us. We are the strands, the stories that God has made. It is the living of that story and the sharing of that story that is vital to a living future Church.

Sir Ken Robinson is an internationally recognized leader in education. He is a speaker and author. In a TED (Technology, Entertainment, Design) talk he gave, he shared the following story. Robinson, it seems, had visited with Dame Gillian Barbara Lynne. Gillian Lynne is the choreographer that worked with Andrew Lloyd Weber on *Cats* and *Phantom of the Opera*. Robinson was visiting with her for a book on finding talents and passions. He asked her: how did she find her way to becoming a dancer? Lynne said that she was a miserable student. Then the school wrote her parents and said, 1"We think Gillian has a learning disorder." Lynne described her classroom reality was that she was fidgety and could not concentrate. It was the 1930's and people didn't know about ADHD or things like that. So her parents, who were concerned, took her to see a specialist. They sat her in a corner, where she sat on her hands for twenty minutes. Her mother described her trouble in school: how she bothered other people, how she always turned things in late, etc. The doctor listened carefully then came to her and said, "Gillian I've listened to all these things that your mother's told me, and I need to speak to her privately." He said, "Wait here, we'll be back, we won't be very long," and they left her. As they left her sitting there he turned and switched on the radio before leaving the room. As soon as they were out of sight Lynne was on her feet, dancing to the music on the radio. After watching privately from another room for few minutes the doctor turned to her mother and said, "Gillian isn't sick; she's a dancer. Take her to a dance school."

Robinson asked what happened next. Lynne said, "She did. I can't tell you how wonderful it was. We walked in this room and it was full of people like me, people who couldn't sit still. People who had to move to think." They did ballet, they did tap, they did jazz, they did modern, they did contemporary dance. It was from there that Lynne interviewed and tried out for the Royal Ballet School and was accepted. She rose to become a soloist and have an exceptional career with the Royal Ballet. She would graduate and establish her own dance academy and sometime later meet Andrew Lloyd Weber.[491] Today Lynne is recognized as one of the most influential individuals in musical theater, having a history of contribution to the art second to none. The alternative of course could have been medication and forced compliance and a different outcome, different journey, a different contribution to art and society, and an altogether different story.

Our story is a story of creativity. We are human beings. We are about being in the world and specifically (according to our ancient scriptures) about being collaborators with God in the great cosmic experiment of creation. We are co-creators with God. As the great Episcopal educator Verna Dozier once said: we are made to be partners with God. It is about story, and our response to story, and our writing of the never-ending story. Dozier wrote, "The biblical story is always to be prefaced by, 'This is how the faith community that produced the record saw it.' It is never to be absolutized as 'This is the way it was.' The story always points the way to an understanding of God that is greater than the facts themselves. I think any understanding of the biblical story that fails to see it as a human response only pointing to the dream of God is itself idolatry."[492] Canon for Lifelong Formation, The Rev. John Newton writes in his book *New* Clothes, "Scripture is the only narrative that we can immerse ourselves in where, after a while, we hear God say, 'You take the pen for a while.' Although creation and redemption are both finished in God's mind, in a mystical way, as we enter the story, we soon discover that we are characters and have been assigned a leading role! We come to know ourselves as co-laborers with God."[493]

All of us have a part. We have a chapter to write. We have a strand to weave with God. Rooted deep in every story is God's reconciling love. That is what we believe together. As Episcopalians, we have a unique way of telling that story as a community woven together.

This is our meme (/ˈmiːm/) if you will. A meme is a unit of social information. Richard Dawkins' evolutionary theory has developed the word, but it is a good one to use here. A meme is a story—particularly told and passed along.[494] The word meme is itself a relatively newly coined term and identifies ideas or beliefs transmitted from one person or group of people to another. The concept comes from an analogy: as genes transmit biological information, memes can be said to transmit idea and belief information. Dawkins is famously agnostic. But I like his idea.

A meme acts as a unit for carrying cultural ideas, symbols, or practices, which can be transmitted from one mind to another through writing, speech, gestures, rituals, or other imitable phenomena. People who use the concept regard memes as cultural analogues to genes, in that they self-replicate, mutate, and respond to selective pressures[2]. In a debate with Dawkins, Archbishop Williams offered the idea that we as human beings are the only creatures who have the ability to create these memes—these stories. We are the only creature that is capable of looking out into the vast cosmos and reflecting about what we experience and see.[495]

For Episcopalians, and brother and sister Anglicans, our tradition holds that language is more than a social construct and is itself sacramental and adds both meaning and substance. Being is rooted in the language we speak. We believe that God spoke and created. God spoke and called us into community. God spoke and created great diversity. God spoke and sent us out on a journey. The story, our language of journey, is itself the vessel in which we do our work as followers of the God who created us, and Jesus his son, and all the mystery that lies therein.

The total number of contemporary languages in the world is not known despite human efforts to catalogue the number. Estimates vary depending on the extent and means of the research intended to discover them, the definition of a distinct language and the current state of knowledge concerning the identities and vital statistics of the various peoples of the earth. Even the number of languages that are known varies as some of them become extinct or are newly discovered within the lifetimes of the active investigators. I stumbled upon a frightening reality some time ago. In a September 2007 *New York Times* article it was claimed, based upon research at the time, some 7,000 languages are endangered.[496] So I investigated a bit more. Normally the transition from a dead to an extinct language occurs when a language undergoes language death while being directly replaced by a different one. For example English, French, Portuguese, or Spanish replaced Native American languages as a result of colonization.

American linguist, Michael E. Krauss defines languages as safe, if children will be speaking them in 100 years; endangered if children will not be speaking them in 100 years; and "moribund" if children are not speaking them now. He estimates 15-30% of languages (900-1800) are moribund.[497] Why all the fuss over languages and their potential extinction? Well, one language that appears to be passing away is the language of storytelling. With each language that dies so also dies their sacred story. The future Church needs to recognize that the story of the Episcopal faith, with its focus on creativity and creation, is a valuable story. It is a story worth telling. It is in fact, at this time and in this era, a story that is essential to the wellness of culture and society. How we pass along that story, how we invite others to tell their story, and how our stories are intertwined is the work of a self-forming community of Christians.

We might begin with the teaching of Jesus. We know that Jesus went around visiting with people. He was a wandering teacher. The Bible holds him up as a prophet—he said challenging things to the religious leadership of the day. In Luke, Jesus was a wisdom teacher.

He used materials from this ancient tradition when he spoke with ordinary people. They called him rabbi, in part perhaps because he was their teacher and they were students of his way. (John 1.29) When we read the gospels we see that he spent time with all kinds of people and engaged parables in teaching. It was almost a Socratic method of teaching, with his followers using allegories, and dialogue. He did this on the road to Caesarea Philippi. (Mark 8.27)

What seems important as I read the Bible is that Jesus engaged with each person on an individual basis. They came to him as they were, the rich man, the woman at the well, Nicodemus, the Pharisees, the Sadducees, his family, and his friends, and they brought with them their own bag of stuff. Jesus also spoke to crowds of people and in public settings. (Matt 5ff) Here he addressed them in a much more direct way with stories and sayings. Jesus also seemed to have a tradition of opening the scriptures to them and helping them understand, as he did on the road to Emmaus after his resurrection. This was one of the reasons why they later recognized him. (24.13)

I should pause here to remind people that Jesus and his followers did not teach with a Bible in their hands. They simply remembered or retold the stories of their tradition. After listening or being attentive to the context in which he found himself, Jesus engaged each person. Jesus also was attentive to physical needs as well as spiritual ones. He often taught or began his teaching by acting—by doing something. Jesus had a healing ministry and this healing ministry was oftentimes an opportunity for teaching. He healed people on the Sabbath (John 9), which gave opportunity for engagement with authorities and reminded people that God made the Sabbath. The Jesus movement therefore began in a simple way with its first followers being formed in conversation with Jesus himself.

We know that Jesus sent his followers out to people's homes where they might be received. (Luke 10) We can imagine that this was the primary way in which the first followers began to spread the word and invite others into the movement. Jesus engaged every strata of society. He had followers who were poor and followers who had money, like Joseph of Arimathea. The movement has always been, as Dix said a movement of the "plebs sancta Dei, the holy common people of God."[498] The movement was literally from one person to another—remember the "gossip" about Jesus. I suppose if we leave out being born into Christendom or being conquered by Christians, one could argue this is the way people have forever been formed in the Christian faith.

Nevertheless, we might ask, how were the first Christians formed? I am not sure if they thought of formation so much as they thought in this early period about sharing Jesus and his teachings. If we look at the New Testament we can see that his followers did mostly what he did. They told stories of Jesus' life, death, and resurrection. (Acts 2.1ff) They told and retold the stories of their faith as Jesus had done for them. We can see this between Philip and the Ethiopian Eunuch. (Acts 8.26) The apostles addressed crowds, religious leaders, taught in synagogues and in homes. They went to people in their homes and taught them and were taught by them as in the story of Peter and Cornelius. (Acts 10) They appear simply to have continued the formation practice of their teacher. They engaged people in many forms and talked plainly with them about Jesus and about how his presence and resurrection reinterpreted the stories that they already knew from the Old Testament.

We know that writing was precious and that very few scraps remain from this earliest period of Christian formation. We may overstress the importance of writing materials because we come from an age of the written word. Yet if we look at the earliest writings from this period, we see that they were Jesus sayings, and stories about Jesus. We see these in the texts that offer stories about Jesus like the Gospels themselves.[499] We also have of the Gospel of Thomas and the Gospel of Peter that are not included in our Bible. These are part of the Nag Hammadi find. They are writings that were found in the desert by a shepherd in 1945. Some of the earliest texts include stories about Jesus, stories about the apostles, creation stories or stories of origin, and collections of Jesus sayings. They reflect only one group of Christians and their thoughts, but we might suppose that many communities, not unlike synagogues at the time, might have had collections of writings. We could look at the letters of Paul and others that were simply instruction-based regarding individual problems that were coming up in the midst of the early Christian community. What seems important here for us in trying to understand how formation took place in this apostolic age is that people gathered. They gathered as families or in synagogue groups. They gathered in societies. When they gathered, they did not have books for everyone, but rather, maybe one scroll for the whole group if it was an urban synagogue. Just as this was not an age of books it was not an age filled with readers. Across the Hellenist population, about 10 to 15% of the people were able to read and write, while within the Jewish population it might have been a bit higher but only for those closely associated with the rabbinical schools.[500] For instance, we know that Jesus read, so he probably received training of some kind in a school. (Luke 4) As in the many years before, people likely gathered and they shared stories, sayings, and reinterpreted older stories. This was their primary mode of teaching the faith.

I believe that we can characterize this first period of formation to be one that was much more individualized. It was a time of great growth and one-on-one conversation wherein the individual himself directed the learning. Take for example Philip and the Ethiopian Eunuch. "The eunuch asked Philip, 'About whom, may I ask you, does the prophet say this, about himself or about someone else?' Then Philip began to speak, and starting with this scripture, he proclaimed to him the good news about Jesus. As they were going along the road, they came to some water; and the eunuch said, 'Look, here is water! What is to prevent me from being baptized?' He commanded the chariot to stop, and both of them, Philip and the eunuch, went down into the water, and Philip baptized him." (Acts 8:26ff) Here we have a clear example of individual inquiry preceding instruction. What we see is that we have people inquiring, and also apostles teaching and offering a witness to the person and character of the Messiah Jesus.

Not unlike the method of Jesus' own teaching, we see individualized conversations and dialogue.

The secondary mode for teaching faith to ordinary people was through the liturgy itself. Baptism and the sharing of the Lord's Supper or Eucharist were to become regularized within these communities at this time. Certainly there were many varieties of liturgy and practice. Within any given community, the regular way in which they gathered, spoke to them about who God was and what God was doing.[501] Early writings tell us that baptism happened sometimes after a formation conversation and sometimes before. Either way, the conversation of formation was connected to baptism and the symbolism of the act was itself a teaching tool. Being submerged was entering into the death of Christ, and being brought up out of the water was a rising with Christ. Furthermore, when you sat at table you were doing what Jesus did with his first followers. When this was reenacted, Christ was present with them. Sharing holy food and drink pointed them back to Jesus' own actions of breaking bread with his followers. Regardless of the form during this apostolic age (for there were many kinds of table celebrations) the basic goal of liturgy or the sharing of stories was to help the community members grow in their understanding of the events of Jesus' life and sayings. It was to connect them to that life and to reinterpret their own lives as being part of the continuing story.

Quickly people were gathering in communities and the Christian movement was growing. In the postapostolic time there is some regularizing of the movement. Scholars think that texts and liturgies become a bit more normalized during this period and there was sharing between communities of materials. Naturally people in this time wanted to understand how to live a life worthy of following Jesus. During the next phase of Christian formation, historical evidence reveals that the leaders and followers were engaging in a conversation about living a holy life.

The *Didache* is a good example of just such writing. It was probably used in the second century, 100 years or so after Jesus' resurrection. The *Didache* was a document written as a tool for instruction after baptism. This is important. The tradition seems to be a generalized witnessing to individuals about who Jesus was and then a relatively low bar of knowledge for the common man before baptism. Then, after baptism, some concern for how one might then go about living one's life as a follower of Jesus. Now, again, we have to understand it was not that there was a *Didache* in the hands of every disciple. This was a scroll that probably was kept in the community meeting house, just as the Torah scrolls were kept in an ark or room of some kind in a synagogue. The leaders of the community might read from it from time to time; maybe even in liturgy to members of the community. It is unlikely that every Christian house church or synagogue church even had one, though scholars believe it was widely circulated. After all, the Didache appears in Greek, Syriac, Latin, Coptic and Arabic.[502]

What we see in it is important to us if we want to understand the kind of formation of Christians that was taking place in the second century and beyond. It is argued that this is a training manual for baptism. This is true for about a third of the text. Two thirds of the *Didache* is devoted to instruction for those who are in charge of the community life and those who are new and already baptized. "[Saint] Athanasius describes it as 'appointed by the Fathers to be read by those who newly join us.'"[503] It includes teachings on how to fast and pray. It has lessons on baptism and the Lord's Supper. It also talks about leadership, church officers, and who is to be trusted. It has some discussion on the life of the community. What seems important to our discussion from this time of development within the Christian community is that instruction was something done *after* baptism. Formation was seen as part of the growing into the stature of Christ post baptism. (Ephesians 4)

The *Didache* assumes some basic instruction prior to baptism. Reading the seventh chapter, we see instruction to the leader of the community: "This is how to baptize. Give public instruction on all these points, and then baptize in running water, in the name of the

Father and of the Son and of the Holy Spirit.. If you do not have running water, baptize in some other. If you cannot in cold, then in warm. If you have neither, then pour water on the head three times in the name of the Father, Son, and Holy Spirit. Before the baptism, moreover, the one who baptizes and the one being baptized must fast, and any others who can. And you must tell the one being baptized to fast for one or two days beforehand."[504] So we know that according to the *Didache*, before baptism a neophyte was to learn that they are to share what they have with others. The person is to seek to be guileless, humble and good. They are to refrain from adultery, lying, theft, blasphemies, idolatry, lust, pedophilia, sex, and evil deeds—a kind of basic set of commandments. The individual is also to be a servant to all and obedient to authority.[505]

During the period of the persecutions and martyrdoms in the fourth century, the next period of evolution, scholars on Christian formation spend a lot of time on the philosophical schools. I want to wait to discuss this more formal development in the chapter on seminaries keeping here to the formation of the everyday Christian. We do know that there was some focus upon preparing individuals for martyrdom; there were even martyrdom schools.[506] We also know that people gathered around the ascetics living in the desert to learn from them how to be faithful Christians. This of course is the beginning of the monastic movement.

It appears that the *Didache* would be the standard form for several hundred years. The basics of the faith from the second period of postapostolic formation would be affirmed in a later document called *The Apostolic Constitutions*. This writing dates from the middle of the fourth century—perhaps 325.[507] Several hundred years after the *Didache*, they added a bit more to the formation principles. They were taught about God as Trinity. The new convert was to learn about creation and then about the prophets of the Old Testament. They were to understand about basic pious living as in the *Didache*.[508] We add into this time period, the instruction of the church father Hippolytus, who advised an instruction period of three years. During which time the candidates are to dedicate themselves to God and be exorcised from doing evil.[509] Within three hundred years formation for the person entering into community expands from a requirement of desire and conversation to a three-year time of strict preparation, instruction, fasting, exorcism, and prayer. This development parallels the movement of Christianity from a self-organizing movement to an established institution. We might also note that this movement is in parallel from a time of disbursed communities and a diversity of teachings, through a time of persecution, the great internal quarrels over heresies, and into a time of control what was taught for doctrinal reasons. The more Christianity was established the more it was controlled.

As Christianity continued through this time period it grew. Christianity became a publicly accepted religion, and then by the fifth century was in fact *the* faith of the dominion. Baptisms increased as Christianity become the faith of the whole culture. Parents wanted children baptized which was in conflict with the kind of labor-intensive preparation imagined. So the grand catechumenal development hit its high water mark in the fourth and fifth centuries and began to be relaxed after that. This meant that formation itself was less stringent. Participation in the liturgy becomes the act of piety in and of itself. By the early middle ages the person to be baptized did not have to repent, go through instructional classes, exorcisms, and shows of piety. Instead, baptism itself had become the Sacrament wherein the cure for original sin was received. This was in part due to the philosophical movement called Scholasticism. Modernism would bring with it the reformation and a new focus in the formation of the follower of Jesus.

The Reformers thought the above approach too lackadaisical. They believed in the individual's ability to learn and understand, to teach and to question. After all, the reformation was a product of humanistic inquiry. The reformers trusted parents and pastors/priests to communicate formation to their children and those in their care. They believed formation primarily took place through study of the Bible and prayer. It was the reformers that returned us to catechisms and their use. They established schools to teach people how to read and write, for in doing so, they could better understand the Bible. Baptisms moved to adulthood when people could once again have some measure of understanding about what they were doing. In this manner everyone received instruction and continuing education on the basics of the Christian faith. The printing press added to the availability of such pamphlets and literature that spread the work of formation into the home, where reading and books had been a scarcity. Even in our own Anglican tradition we see that the person to be baptized was instructed in the principle elements of faith and then would recite them prior to baptism. The 1979 Book of Common Prayer includes a much longer Catechism— introducing elements of creation and the work of humanity.[510]

The Reformation concept of teaching people to read and write while teaching them about Christianity would continue to make its mark on formation practices far into the eighteenth century in England, when it gave birth to the Sunday School movement. The need for these schools arose during the industrial revolution. Working children were not getting any education at all. So, Robert Raikes introduced a school for children on their day off.[511] They would learn to read, write, add and subtract along with learning the Bible. By 1785, these Sunday Schools were educating over a quarter of a million English children.[512] During the first years of the movement everyone in the family attended; adults with their children. Eventually each denomination began to set up their own schools. The Anglicans set up the system that eventually became the national school system in England with the Education Act in 1870.[513] Episcopal priest, The Rev. William A. Muhlenberg, who was ordained in 1817, promoted the Sunday School movement in America.[514] He was known as a good speaker, and after one such talk, Anne Ayres was convicted to begin a religious order for women called the "Sisters of the Holy Communion."[515] Together they worked on educating inner city children throughout the second half of the nineteenth century. They even created a rural community for poor inner city people to live in.[516]

In the Roman Catholic, Episcopal/Anglican, Lutheran and Methodist traditions, catechetical formation was moved primarily to the period of time after baptism. Sunday Schools were for education. The whole system slowly evolved into our current practice. Today there is little pre-baptismal formation at all. Almost all instruction is left to either a time prior to adult baptism or confirmation. This time of preparation/formation can take as little as a few meetings with a clergy person, or weeks and years, depending on the faith tradition. Today Episcopal formation is done for adults through a variety of formats.

As a bishop, I have the opportunity to visit many different kinds and sizes of congregations. Fewer and fewer are doing some kind of formation. What I see is primarily a Sunday oriented formation program—except in a few cases. The primary place and time where conversations about Christianity are occurring is in Church on Sunday morning. The typical offering is a Sunday School type program left over from a bygone era. In some innovative places, they are doing a Catechesis of the Good Shepherd or Godly Play ministry. This is a Montessori style children's ministry. Children's programming is focused on sharing Bible stories, making crafts, and doing a play from time to time. In many places there are no vestiges of adult formation hours or Sunday Schools left. The adult programming, where it does exist, is modeled on a mini seminary prototype. There may be Bible studies that pepper the week. Men and women's Bible studies typically have a convener who acts as a teacher. Many large churches have an adult forum, but the smaller the church the less likely it is to have regular adult programming on Sunday morning. The ones that have adult forums tend towards a pedagogically styled classroom model: a professor/expert teaching class. One imparts knowledge and the others intake with opportunity for discussion. In larger congregations you may find more than one option and groups that meet throughout the week.

In the Episcopal Church there are a few, in ever declining numbers, courses called Education for Ministry (EFM). This is a course that is designed and produced by the School of Theology of the University of the South in Sewanee, Tennessee and intends to impart, through a group model, the first year of seminary to its participants in a four year period of time. In some churches there will be a seasonal speaker program—for Lent or Advent. Formation or discipleship classes for the new member are rare across the church. Where they have newcomer classes, they are usually modeled on classroom style pedagogy as well. The prevailing belief is that if we give you information you can make a choice and be an Episcopalian. Even our own Discovery Program that was designed in the 1990's in the Diocese of Texas is now out of date. It depends on a classroom setting, video/DVD watching and a course curriculum. All this is to say, we are at the end of something, though I am not quite sure what it is. Theologian John Westerhoff says that he is "convinced that the very foundations upon which we engage in Christian education are shaking."[517] This has not always been true with respect to the formation of Christian disciples. We have many and varied models that pre-date our current circumstances though we have largely forgotten them. We repeat, poorly, the model we inherited from the last half of the twentieth century.

Instead of helping individuals find their story, we only get serious about formation when a person declares they want to go to seminary. Think of the difference between the ancient pattern of baptismal preparation in the fourth century and the contemporary pattern of ordination preparation. It used to be that people would declare to a mentor their desire to follow Jesus and enter a time of apprenticeship. Today the process of serious Christianity begins when you tell your priest that you believe you are called to ordained ministry. It used to be that you would then be introduced to the community as a neophyte. Now, you are introduced to the Commission on Ministry and then sent to seminary. It used to be that you would undertake a three-year time of learning and discovery in the community, now you spend three years in seminary. Today you go deep in your relationships with others in your formative seminary years. It used to be that small personal community was essential in the early church. Today you get a new vocation after seminary. It was once the reality that you got a new vocation upon entrance into the community. In the last weeks of seminary formation, you are tested and selected for ordination. It used to be that there was an intensive in the last weeks of Lent as you approached your baptismal day—the day when you and the community became one. In the year 350 your baptismal liturgy would have been at the Easter Vigil, a long solemn service that clearly marks new family relationships along with a new identity and name. Today, it is the liturgy of ordination that recreates the individual. You get new clothes, where it used to be that when you were baptized you got new clothes.[518] Any new priest can tell you their well-rehearsed spiritual autobiography by the time they do their first Eucharist—while many individuals within the church today are disempowered or think their story is relevant. Some will say that this shift in process is about a growing focus on the clergy that dates to the scholastic movement. "Maybe," I say. More than likely, it is just that we are ill prepared for the new culture around us and that we continue to use a model of formation that no longer works in our context.

We see great sweeps of practice back and forth across the millennia of Christian formation. What stands out in the brief survey above is that we have a tradition of engaging individuals. We have been story-centered. We tell the story of Jesus and tell people how Jesus and God are part of their story. We have a tradition of helping people as part of our teaching. We believe that stewardship, evangelism, how to live well, and how to resist evil, are essential to helping people follow Jesus and live in faithful community. Questions and answers are vital to help people learn the story of God and the story of those who believe in him. This Q&A format has been part of our tradition in a variety of ways. For example we have seen it used by Philip and the Eunuch in a self -directed style. We see in the early formation tradition, a model of master and apprentice, or mentor and student, where inquiry and instruction go together. And, while this was the model for the most part in the reformation period, we also know that the Reformers felt as though with prayer, Bible, and a catechism, a person could begin a journey of self-discovery. It will take all of these methods to navigate the nature of formation in our present context.

Figuring out how we are going to approach formation in the future is essential for us and for our society. Margaret Wheatley believes that in this modern age we have organized our society like the machines of the industrial age. We have done this with our institutions and we have treated our families and bodies as if they were a machine to figure out, and manipulate with the correct mechanism and code. Wheatley says, "There is a simpler way to organize human endeavor."[519] Somehow the solution, she believes, is rooted in the spirit of our story.[520] Recently we have attempted to impose control and compliance upon life by trying to organize it so it fits with machine-like organizing principles.[521] When things have not gone our way, modern leaders have tried to force control using "fear, scarcity, and self-interest to do their work rather than the more noble human traits of cooperation, caring, and generosity."[522] Remember, Nassim Taleb believes this simply makes for more fragile systems. The more we attempt to control, the more fragile the system becomes. The more we experiment and try different approaches, the stronger the individual and organization becomes. Life teaches us the importance and strength of self-organization.[523] Wheatley writes that in order to lead into this future we need more storytellers, she says, "because people are forgetting there is any alternative to the deadening leadership that daily increases in vehemence. It's a dark time because people are losing faith in themselves and each other and forgetting how wonderful humans can be, how much hope we feel when we work well together on things we care about."[524]

What is true in our own living institutional organisms is true in biology. Diversity and self-organization are how biologists like

Francisco Varela and Humberto Maturana believe life itself flourishes and adapts to changing environments. It is not so much that life has the code "survival of the fittest," but instead, life is "survival of the fit."[525] Life takes on countless strategies. Life takes on voluminous variations. Life's very character is one of countless attempts at living.[526] Organisms throughout creation participate in variety far more wildly than we do, because we are always trying to get it right.[527] I am not saying that we need to let everyone do whatever they want without structure. I am saying that in order for the future Church to flourish it must have many varieties of living out its ministry—countless strategies. The future Church will enjoy freedom to experiment because it understands that our mission of formation is *stronger* through diversity, many adaptations, and variety. The future Episcopal Church will be known as a network of Christian communities that innovates, and has a diversity of ways in which people may discover God and their life with God. It will be a Church known as one that engages in storytelling and its members are invested in new discoveries about one another and those who choose to follow Jesus with them. The future Church will understand that each Christian community, and each participant within that community, is engaging in the work of formation by self-directing their journey through a variety of forms. The future Church will make room for those entering community, and those on the outside, to observe within their own lives creation at work.

Formation practices in the future will chiefly be about enabling individuals to see that the miracle of life, present in their being, is the same miraculous force that is at work throughout all creation. The power of God which formed the cosmos, shaped galaxies, made heavens and earth, has given breath to every creature under the heavens, and life to the creeping things and the leviathan is the same force that is at work in their own body, mind, and spirit. Formation in the future Church will be about connecting through a diverse network of experiences and conversations. Reconciliation will be the theme of the future Church, as it works to enable humanity to chart a course of discovery to understand, and then speak out the reality of our connection with God in Christ Jesus, who has formed all things, and so our health and wellness is tied to all things.

Perhaps you will say that this is the work of all Christians and God fearers, and perhaps you are correct. While we should always we aware that we have, at times, treated formation as a psychological way of colonizing the mind, we also need to recognize that our particular story is an important one in the life of society. God does indeed have a mission of reconciliation and as part of that mission we have real work to do. The Church was never been meant to be a machine focused on productivity, though that is what we are left with in many places today. Instead it is intended to be a vessel of God's love and mercy to the world. Abandoning the field of forming individuals with a capacity to serve and work for peace, in many places, has meant our people have been left adrift.

Anglican theologian John Milbank has said that the growing atheist movement is not good for society. Outside of our communities there is a serious argument, because people are beginning to see that all kinds of things are connected. Milbank said, "There is a connection in our discussions between politics, pushing civil society and the role of religion or there is a connection between atheism, extreme market liberalism, or else extreme stateism. Vaclav Havel [poet, philosopher, and democratically elected president of Czechoslovakia] who is not particularly a religious believer only the other day raised the issue that probably that an atheist world is very very dangerous world."[528] I bring this up because the future Church understands that within the wider global organism, it has a voice and a story to tell. It both learns from listening to other stories, and it offers opportunity for our story to be told. In doing so, we ,as the future Church, participate not only in forming followers of Jesus, but we are also forming a healthy civil society. How we form and who we are forming makes a real-world difference; the future Church must understand this as part of its mission.

The future Episcopal Church will engage in creative formation through a diversity of practices. The work of formation will take us into a future that we cannot grasp today. Its creativity and conversation will reveal for the individual and the Christian community the path(s) forward.[529] Imagine for a moment: the babies we are baptizing in our churches the year I am writing this (2014), will retire in the year 2079. They will enter the workplace in the year 2035 give or take a couple of years. That is the world we are preparing these Christians to enter. The work of Christian formation has never been only about introducing people to God through Jesus Christ. It has forever and always been about helping people find their way to baptism and then to help them figure out how to live life. It is about helping live a life as a believer in the creative God, the reconciling Son, and the loving Holy Spirit. Everyone, children and adults, have a remarkable capacity for life. Living the creative life is an essential part of formation for the future Church. In order to do this we must engage in a variety of formation activities. We have to be willing to try things, be ok with getting some things wrong, and if they do not work out, try something else.

Ken Robinson tells this story about a play that his son was in. When his son was 4 he was in a nativity play. He had the part of Joseph. Three boys with towels around their heads walked in as the three kings. They presented their gifts to Joseph and the first boy said, "I bring you gold." The second boy said, "I bring you myrrh." And the third boy said, "Frank sent this." Everyone howled, of course. But the kids just moved right along. After Robinson went up to the little boy and said, "You OK with that?" and he said, "Yeah, why, was that wrong?"[530] Robinson's point is that children, when they start out, are not afraid of getting things wrong. They grow into it.[531]

We have been running our churches with the fear and anxiety that we might get it wrong. Our formation practices have in fact echoed this reality. At our worst we have been trying to convince people of a story about a creative, reconciling, and loving God, through a process of formation that saps the creativity out of the seeker. We dampen the spark of questioning, inspiration, and longing for the divine. We have essentially educated people out of their creative capacity and in the process undermined the story we are trying to tell.[532] They are looking for mystery and we are in many cases offering facts. Picasso believed that all children are born artists. He said, "All children are artists. The problem is how to remain an artist once he grows up."[533] Robinson says, "We don't grow into creativity, we grow out of it."[534] He continues, "If you were to visit education as an alien and say what's it for, public education, I think you'd have to conclude the whole purpose of public education throughout the world is to produce university professors."[535] I think in some way our aim is to form people into monks and priests. Well-meaning as we are, we actually make formation so inaccessible that most people tell themselves they just are not smart enough to understand.

Our formation practices came out of the industrial age. They are intimately tied to education practices that have had similar and parallel development over the past two hundred years or so. The goal, like public education, was to produce good members of the industrialized age. Learn what you need to learn in order to get a job is education's goal, according to Robinson.[536] For the Church it has been the notion that you learned what you needed to know—which is not much—unless you are going to be a monk, priest or professional religious worker. We are a faith that is dependent upon the sharing of the story with one another. We have failed to pass along our story to our own.

The future Church must adopt a new way of thinking about formation. It will engage in diverse opportunities for individuals of every age to play and experiment with Christianity, and their story, as it relates to the Episcopal way of life. It reclaims the virtuosity of sharing story visually in art, icons and images. It reclaims the art of storytelling through sound: continuing our tradition of hymnody, but with all kinds of music and music traditions. Sound includes speaking and poetry as well. The thriving church of the future will engage movement, pilgrimage, work, play and dance in all of their myriad forms, because it knows that people learn kinesthetically.[537] It will reinvigorate the art of formation as a multisensory active and participatory experience where the individual is a self-learner and self-director of their own exploration. This will mean that Christian communities, of every shape and size, will actually recreate the way in which they think about, integrate, and share story through formative experiences.

The future Episcopal Church will be a network of communities that has essentially created a new human ecosystem whereby individuals are growing in their creative capacities to build well communities that exhibit traits of reconciliation, sustainability, service, and love. Robinson says of education, "Our education system has mined our minds in the way that we strip-mine the earth, for a particular commodity, and for the future, it won't serve us."[538] The same is true for the present-past Church. We have neglected to help individuals find formation as followers of Jesus.

I believe that some of our difficulty in doing the ministry of formation is that we have, like the educational systems around us, not believed that people can self-learn.

Instead we have, as our forefathers and mothers did in the fourth century onward, played out systematically, a notion that the work of the Church is to educate people. We are the authority, we are the power managers, and therefore as the intermediaries between God and man, we are the ones responsible for imparting knowledge to others. We have done this blind to the fact that our story from creation forward is about a God who wants to walk in the garden of creation with his creatures. We have a God who requires no middleman. We have a story that tells us that God is interested in communicating with humanity directly—Abraham, Sarah, Moses, David, Samuel, and prophets like Jeremiah. We forget our story that says—God comes into the world in the person of Jesus and speaks directly to us, and invites us to participate in the recreation of a peaceable kingdom. We have a story that says that God is invested in us learning for ourselves. This God says, "Come and follow me." We have a God who is experiential and interested in us making our journey and pilgrimage with God, and that at the end of days we might sit at table with God and share our stories. Nevertheless, the church has insisted upon a pedagogical model of transaction and direct instruction that has been dominant for over a thousand years. That transaction model is: person enters church + classroom introduction + Baptism/Confirmation + adult classes (maybe) for Christian continuing education = Christian. This is a model that worked from the time of Constantine and Hippolytus in 350, when the world was Christian. The models we need to look at are varied and many, and should be the ones used in the time when Christianity was the minority. The future Church reclaims for itself the story of a God who wishes to be in communion directly with his creatures.

Human beings are naturally, created by God to be, self-learners. It is our nature. It is the part of us most deeply connected to our instinct. We are created to be curious co-creators and to try new things with a tenacious spirit until we figure it out. Dr. Sugata Mitra is an educational researcher who has shown through a vast number of experiments that supervision or formal teaching is not necessary for individuals to learn.[539] In the absence of a transaction model of formal education, children can and will teach themselves and each other, motivated out of pure natural curiosity and peer interest.[540]

In 1999, Mitra worked in an office that was next to an Indian urban slum. He and his office mates cut a hole in the wall and put a powerful PC outside—embedded in the wall. Outside was a touchpad and monitor. It had a high speed Internet connection. They said nothing and did nothing. They just turned it on. Eight or so hours later an eight-year-old boy was teaching a six-year-old girl how to surf the web. There was no instruction, no language education, no interaction with these two kids at all. So, Mitra decides to create a more controlled experiment and to this he goes to Delhi. He went to Shiypuri, a place where, Mitra said, "nobody had ever taught anybody anything."[541] The hooked up a computer next to an old building and replicated the experiment. A 13 year old came and began to manipulate the touchpad and computer. It took him two minutes to figure it out. Then he accidently made a click by touching the pad. With that, Internet Explorer changed the page. In eight minutes he was browsing and in a bit more time he had called the neighborhood kids and pretty soon 70 children were browsing the web.

Then, Mitra went to a village called Madantusi where the children had not learned English. Ran the same experiment. There was no Internet, so he created a program with CDs. When he came back three months later he found two kids where playing a game on the computer in English. They came up to Mitra and said in English, "We need a faster processor and a better mouse." Mitra asked, "How on earth did you know all this?" And they said, "Well, we've picked it up from the CDs." So I said, "But how did you understand what's going on over there?" So they said, "Well, you've left this machine which talks only in English, so we had to learn English."[542] Mitra said, "So then I measured, and they were using 200 English words with each other—mispronounced, but correct usage—words like exit, stop, find, save, that kind of thing, not only to do with the computer but in their day-to-day conversations."[543] Mitra ran the experiment for five years all across India with the poorest of the poor. These were children who had no school and many had not seen a computer, let alone used one. The first thing in each circumstance the children did was teach each other English so they could then use the computer for games or to search the internet—without any adult intervention. He found that in a little over a year some 500 children taught themselves and each other basic English, Windows functions, browsing, painting, chatting, email, games, educational material, music downloads, and how to play video.[544]

How much can self-learners learn? How much can self-learners teach others? Are there limits? Will it really work for something as complicated as theology or values or stories and storytelling. Perhaps Mitra's next experiment will offer some insight. Tamil is a south Indian language, and Mitra wondered if Tamil-speaking children in a south Indian village could learn and teach each other the biotechnology of DNA replication in English from a street computer.[545] He actually believed the children could not do this. He set up a computer in Kallikuppam in south India. He put on it everything a person needed to know about DNA replication—most of it he could not even understand.[546] As he was installing the computer the children came up to him and asked in Tamil what he was doing. He simply said, "It's very topical, very important. But it's all in English." They said, "How can we understand such big English words and diagrams and chemistry?" So, using a self-learning pedagogical model, he said, "I haven't the foggiest idea. And, anyway, I am going away." He left them for a couple of months and came back. They said to him in English, "We've understood nothing." So Mitra asked, "Okay, but how long did it take you before you decided that you couldn't understand anything?" They said, "We haven't given up. We look at it every single day." So Mitra said, "What? You don't understand these screens and you keep staring at it for two months? What for?" One of the little girls raised her hand and said in broken Tamil and English, "Well, apart from the fact that improper replication of the DNA molecule causes disease, we haven't understood anything else." He tested them and they scored 30% out of 100. "How could he get them to passing?" he wondered.[547] Not wanting to break the model a teacher wasn't quite what he wanted. So he found a 22 year-old girl. Mitra asked if she could help them learn DNA replication in English. She said no and she had no idea what they were doing under that tree with that computer all day. Mitra said just use the "grandmother method." She wanted to know what that was. He told her, "Stand behind them. Whenever they do anything, you just say, 'Well, wow, I mean, how did you do that? What's the next page? Gosh, when I was your age, I could have never done that.' You know what grannies do." She did that for two months more and the scores jumped to 50%. The Kallikuppam kids had caught up to the control school in New Delhi—a wealthy private school with a trained biotechnology teacher.

The process is that one child is operating the computer with several others around watching. They are telling him what to do. Around the four is another group of 16 who are also talking and trying to get a word in. The conclusion after six years of work, scientific evaluation and testing is: "education can happen on its own it does not have to be imposed from the top downwards."[548] Mitra says, "learning is most likely a self-organizing system. An educational technology and pedagogy that is digital, automatic, fault-tolerant, minimally invasive, connected, and self-organized."[549] Mitra concludes his discussion about developing a school in the cloud with this challenge. "We need a curriculum of big questions." The future Church must be engaged in discovering, with a community of self-learners, stories about the big questions.

We may think that church is different. Church is only about educating people in real time and space. Today, as I write this we know that most people are choosing to visit an Episcopal church because they look at the website. If you know nothing about a school, business, or a restaurant, you look on the Internet. More than once I have gone to a restaurant website to see what people are wearing so I know what is appropriate to wear. The same is true for people looking at churches.

Here are just a few sites that are listed if a person types, "What does the Episcopal Church believe" into the search engine. First you get our EpiscopalChurch.org site on beliefs. Second you get an article on Wikipedia. Then third, you get a site that says that the Episcopal Church is like the people Ezekiel was sent as a missionary to convert, "My people come to you, as they usually do, and sit before you to listen to your words, but they do not put them into practice. With their mouths they express devotion, but their hearts are greedy for unjust gain. Indeed, to them you are nothing more than one who sings love songs with a beautiful voice and plays an instrument well, for they hear your words but do not put them into practice." (Ezekiel 33:31-32). Next comes The Diocese of Texas website. Then one that says the Episcopal Church is straight out of the pit of hell. Searching the web is a primary way in which self-learners are looking for what the Episcopal Church believes, and this is their first formative contact with our belief system and people's opinions of it. These results are based upon my previous searches but show the diversity of information available to the seeker.

The Church has moved into a knowledge economy where exchange and conversation that build capacities for formation and spiritual transformation are valued over data, logistics, and organizational practices.[550] Becoming a better machine, churning out general Christians will not be the way of the future Church. That Church will differentiate itself around mission and service evangelism, be fully invested in forming creative Christians. It is no longer focused on building efficiencies, systems, programs, and methodologies—instead it is focused upon innovative processes and how they connect people. It is focused on any and every tool that will create a user interface that is simple and easy to manipulate, thereby putting the power of connection and discovery directly into the hands of the self-learner. Our Church will tap the social aspect of knowledge, creativity, and wisdom. It engages in symbiotic relationships with technological tools to do its work of formation, thereby making itself accessible to the amplified human through their world. The future Church uses everything at its disposal to "enable cooperation, collaboration, and organization on a massive scale."[551] The Institute for the Future states that "traditional knowledge chains controlled by gatekeeper institutions and organizations, such as publishers or universities, will give way to knowledge ecologies controlled by no one in particular but with access for all."[552] In the past the Church has functioned more like a gatekeeper trying to control access to its life and community, instead of being characterized as an organization with a story of sharing wisdom within an ecosystem of accessibility for the self-learner.

The future Church will be prepared for the self-learner and understands the kind of community that they wish to engage. It knows the seeker is even now at the door and looking to see who we are and what we are about. It is invested in its story of creativity and is adept at sharing it. The Future Church must out-communicate the narrative of meaningless consumerism by building collectives of storytellers who themselves are exploring and learning as they live. It recognizes that it has a multitude of ways in which it can help self-learners find formation and transformation, and it uses them all to build a creative faithful body of Christians who are living together in a socially-networked community. So what are the characteristics of the new self-learner and what is their community habitat like?

CHAPTER NINETEEN
Extreme Techno Learners and Their Habitat

"The secret of education lies in respecting the pupil. It is not for you
to choose what he shall know, what he shall do. It is chosen and
foreordained and he only holds the key to his own secret."
— Ralph Waldo Emerson, Education, The Complete Works, Vol 10

In 1945, Vannevar Bush was President Roosevelt's science advisor. He was the mastermind behind the Manhattan Project among other things. He wrote an article that year for *The Atlantic* magazine entitled "As We May Think."[553] In the article, he outlined the idea of a device in which "an individual stores all his books, records, and communications, and which is mechanized so that it may be consulted with exceeding speed and flexibility. It is an enlarged intimate supplement to his memory."[554] He called it the "memex." I call it my iPhone. Bush's notion would influence the creation of the Internet, the PC, and much of the way in which we navigate our global stores of knowledge today.[555] Today Bush's idea of knowledge access, storage, and sharing is a reality. When I told a friend that I was working on this book he handed me John Naisbitt's bestselling book *Megatrends* published in 1982. Naisbitt pronounced: "we are moving from the specialist who is soon obsolete to the generalist who can adapt." He continued, "in the computer age we are dealing with conceptual space connected by electronic, rather than physical space connected by the motorcar."[556] Remember that is the year the desktop computer appeared on the cover of Time. Today we know that this new ecosystem is where self-learners live.

In a self-learning world the Church will be integrated with knowledge tools that help it to do its work of formation. The user and the tools are co-evolving.[557] Traditional computing was used primarily for database management—the manipulation of large amounts of information. The future Church will exist in a world where innovation in computing will remake technology, thus shaping an environment where creative knowledge is more of a verb and not a noun.[558] George Mason University professor of public policy Christopher Hill believes we are on the edge of a new kind of creative revolution he calls "The Post Scientific Society"[559] Hill defines a post-scientific society as "a society in which cutting edge success depends not on specialization, but on integration—on synthesis, design, creativity, and imagination."[560] The Church will be integrated into creative knowledge sharing that will be the same as the fabric of this post-scientific society in which it dwells. In order to make this shift into the new era in self-learning formation, the Church will draw on many perspectives and expertise in order to provide flexible tools. As mobile devices get more powerful, and interface technologies get more sophisticated, interaction with Christian communities will become "always communicating, always forming."

Ross Mayfield, CEO of Socialtext Incorporated, an enterprise social software company based in Palo Alto, CA, and leader in information-sharing, says it this way, "NetGens (Net Generation) think of the computer as a door, not a box."[561] The future Church will not be limited to access only on Wednesday nights and Sunday mornings—it will be forming people throughout its network whenever and wherever the self-learner taps into the community. It will exist in a world where sharing in this manner is more "intimate, more oblique, and more immediate."[562] Formation will tap into the lives of individuals, crowds, and groups. It will do this on the one hand, to create conversations and mentoring, while on the other hand to connect and convene. It will use tools like Google, Flickr, blogs, contributions to Wikipedia, Socialtext, meetups, posts, subscriptions, and feeds in real time to share who it is, what it is about, where it is, and what it is doing. These are no longer tools but space where formation is happening. [563]

The future Episcopal Church will be filled with amplified humans who are extreme self-learners.[564] They are accustomed to trailblazing new learning landscapes and applying creativity to sorting out their terrain.[565] Whereas their predecessors were interested in getting it correct, making a good exam score, and having the right degree, these extreme self-learners find that the creative process is the product. It is in the learning and the sharing that life happens. God is not a thing to be grasped. Humans are not to become gods. The extreme learner understands their place in a large web of relationships and so is consistently probing, learning, discovering, and creating new nodes and forms of faith. The extreme learner is powered by technology and has mixed their faith into their life and lifestyle. [566] Knowing that formation is constantly about being aware means that they are creating new places for their faith to go, new conversations for it to enter, and new venues in which they can tell their story.

The importance of knowing "who we are as Episcopalians," and then sharing that through a variety of settings now becomes clear. Extreme learners direct their own education, formation and learning.[567] They automatically share what they are learning and experiencing. For them there is no one classroom with one teacher and a group of students. Everything is a classroom experience and everywhere is the teacher. If you want to learn about the history of education go find it. How about the story of how the church has been involved in social change...here it is, learn it, and share it. The extreme learner redefines libraries, classrooms, labs, and the teacher student relationship. Therefore, the extreme learner within the Christian faith setting will in the future have redefined the role of apostle, catechist, youth director, priest, deacon, parent, and Sunday School teacher. Just as they are designing their own curricula and online courses in universities today, the extreme learner will rethink and recreate the process by which they become a Christian. The future Church, knowing this, makes part of the process of becoming a Christian and preparing for baptism, the creation of their own introductory class on Christianity and its practices. The future Church does this because the extreme learner is active in the learning exchange—they are in fact helping others to learn as they share and make their pilgrimage. They are hacking what is today a closed formation process and sharing it freely into their own networks. They are a node and teacher themselves as they plow along through the information.[568]

The self-learner is on a pilgrimage with God and with any Church that will help them network and gain access to the Holy. They are interested in being like Abram and Sarai—journeying out from their own land of Ur into the wilderness and there to receive a new name. (Genesis 17) They want to discover their own path with God and the extreme learner must know the future Church is there to help. They also want to connect within and without the community. Not unlike Jesus and the disciples, they are ready, willing, and able to share what they are discovering about God. With a little guidance and direction (like the "grandmother method") they, with the aid of the future Church community, will spread the Good News—always sharing what they are in the process of learning.

The extreme learner knows that journey and sharing stories is of the greatest value. [569] The digital native's learning-life is like being part of the story of The Acts of the Apostles. It is the traveling, uploading their discoveries, and who they meet along the way that is of interest to them. They are constantly in the mode of being formed by discovery. These real touches with real humans are the whole point of the wider network and learning process.

The extreme learner is plugged-in so that they can connect with other extreme learners. They meet, make, and choose their own community of mentors. Mentors used to be chosen for you. Tomorrow's church will be engaged in making a network of potential mentors and allowing individuals to choose multiple mentors for the varied tasks and learning challenges they have before them.[570] Just as the extreme learner is dictating their own formation path, so too, they dictate who will be their mentors for any leg of the journey.

The extreme learner asks a lot of questions. They do this to challenge and to understand. They also do this for the benefit of others, so that others may understand. They listen carefully and are constantly processing. They are eager and they will make mistakes and say odd things, as they are putting the formation puzzle together. This will drive present day Christians crazy and test the community's tolerance. The Church understands that this is part of the formation pilgrimage. Learning fast and failing fast helps the pupil to learn.[571] This is how apprenticeships work and the future Church must be willing and able to tolerate the extreme learner's eagerness.

One of the many specific areas of modern day frustration will be the kind of connections and webs the extreme learner builds. He/she connects people, science, business, technology, art, and music in new and different ways. Faith and formation in the future Church is no longer a private or diaspora experience. Faith is another piece of the puzzle; it is part of the web of life for the self-learner. The extreme learner is eager to have a variety of subjects connected to faith. They want and need to connect God and Jesus with everything, and mix it all together in order to see how it works, and process the information it might hold for their own journey. Formation is a multi-disciplinary experience in the future Church.

The future Church is ready for this learning revolution. It is accustomed to the redefining of relationships and the ease at which the extreme learner plays within the community of faith. Not unlike every present-day institution, the future Church has to figure out how to resolve the issues created by the extreme self-learners and an old system of hierarchical knowledge transactions. The future Church makes the leap because its story is one of creativity and innovation; its God is a God of creation. It believes in a God who is constantly muddling around in chaos and inviting transformation out of the whirlwind. It makes the transition because it invests everything in the individual's pilgrimage and desire to co-create with God a new community and world. The future Church understands that it is its responsibility to take a step into this new culture of creativity and be part of building the "collective future."[572]

It is part of the newly formed civic sphere. It participates in its local context and the lives of the "educitizens."[573] It is a creator of networks of self-learners, artisans, writers/poets, businessmen and women, scientists, and priests building a collaborative of discovery and innovation for the health of the community. This will be a new commons. It has applied social justice to its own formation practices, and has reshaped learning so that it is not oppressive or a colonizing of the mind. Instead it has recreated itself as a living communal faith lab that has tensile strength and resilience in the midst of extreme self-learning that is constantly and dependably in flux.[574] It leverages vital resources, is flexible, accessible, and adaptive. The reality is that the Christian community dwells within a whole ecosystem of learning and is an active and contributing positive influence within the wider network/community of self-learners.[575]

The value for the future Church will be in the process of learning exchanges where peer-to-peer Christian communities expand their boundaries and connections. The great educator John Dewey (1859-1952) invented not only an idea about how people interacted with the learning process, he imagined an integrated relationship between the pupil and the mentor. He did not think the teacher should stand at the front of the room spewing out knowledge to be swallowed whole by the inert student. Dewey believed that the role of those invested in the formation of the apprentice, the disciple, the pupil, the student should be the role of guide and mentor.[576] Above all else the future Church is a potential guide and mentor to the cultural context around it.

The future Church must, itself, be a learning hub. It is invested in the democratization of material and content, and invests itself in the production of meaningful materials for the self-learner to access.[577] It creates multi-media online hubs with accessibility for all people and all ages. Spirituality, formation, even vocational discovery are resourced and made available through a variety of platforms. Theologians, professors, spiritual leaders, monks, catechists and mentors are essential ingredients in the networks. They are accessible to seekers. No longer is formation limited to the one priest /one church model. Its liturgy, preaching, and sacramental life will be shared and available anytime and anywhere. Church Publishing will work to create for the future Church accessible resources of music, art, poetry and the written word. It was not long ago we laughed at the idea that people might have iPad/tablets with the liturgy on it. Today I do not go to a Bible study or worship service where someone is not accessing the Bible or other texts via their smart device. The future Church will open-source everything. It will invest in creating a flourishing formation ecosystem of two millennia of spiritual teaching, sacred texts and wisdom writing for the theologically interested. This rich accessible information will be a companion to an environment filled with real life mentoring and discipling.

Learning, even for the digital native/extreme learner with the wealth of Christendom's wisdom on their shoulder, is always a social reality.[578]

Learning is relationship based and always personal. It is the relationship that is the driver in the education process. It is the crowd on the shoulder, the crowd surrounding the terminal in the small village in India, it is the peer-to-peer relationship that propels the self-learner forward into discovery. Marina Gorbis in *The Nature of the Future*, writes, "Many proponents of distance learning miss the importance of relationships and social connections in education. I believe online learning and resources alone will not provide a solution to our educational needs. One needs mentors, someone to look up to and to guide the learning process, to help filter what one needs to know and to provide feedback."[579] It is within the community where ideas are shed, shared, and created. It is in the communal atmosphere that the "desire to learn" is inflamed.[580] With the aid of your friends and chosen mentors, the self-learner is able to access and benefit from of the "rich ecology of content" we have been talking about.[581] Into this rich ecosystem we must add formation leaders for the future Church.

Leaders in formation will be of varying types given the complexity of the learning environment: there will be *learning partners*.[582] Learning partners are self-learners themselves who in turn help others to navigate the terrain. These are individuals who themselves are relatively new but within the world of shifting peer relationships, know the key individuals within the community that can help the newcomer in the community.

There will be *personal advisors*.[583] These are individuals who are trained within the Christian community and selected to help individuals and their families or friendship circles to create their own formation environment.

There will be *wellness guides*.[584] Due to the involvement by the future Church with health and wellness in the community, and the integration of the body, mind, and spirit, communities will have an individual or group of individuals who will help people make these connections and move to a healthier lifestyle as part of Christian formation.

There will be *edu-vators*.[585] Edu-vators will help build the technological "platforms", explore innovations and keep formation accessible across the community. They are the ones who will keep the Christian community from becoming an isolated, inwardly focused diaspora. The edu-vator is one of the cutting edge individuals who will convene commons groups and share with others throughout organization how they can continue to manifest creativity and innovation across their networks.

There will be *formation cartographers*. They will be essential in mapping the external community context.[586]The cartographers, like their counterparts in other organizations, will help the Church have access into the collective networks and nodes outside the church's geo-fence. They will be able to help leverage social networking, push and share communication and news, plant smart-mobs (formation oriented flash mobs) so that there are continually new learning opportunities. The cartographer will help connect community members inside and outside of the Christian community so that there is resource sharing and mutual learning.[587]

There will be *social capital designers and developers* who will plan and create strategies for people to make their learning pilgrimages.[588] They will help the seeker and self-learner to discover, share, and create resources through collaborative process that multiply formation opportunities. These individuals will by hyper-focused on the social network itself—testing, accessing, and designing it.[589]

There will be *learning journey mentors* will be the ones who work with all the groups to help create unique formation experiences for the self-learners.[590] Remember, none of this works or will be of value to the self-learner if they are not personally connecting with other people. *Learning journey mentors* will help ensure this happens.

There will be *formation curators who* will communicate outward the personal stories and personal experiences of those involved in making their pilgrimage through the community.[591] They people are like art curators. They will broaden the circle of formation out beyond any one individual's experience so that one experience has the networked impact of connecting with the many. They will do this through technology we know about today: blog posts, pictures, podcasts, and videos.[592] They will also work with the other members of the team to ensure they are using the most accessible media to keep the stories in front of the community for purposes of service, evangelism, and stewardship.

These are the names of the future education team members. Regardless of what you call the team members in any given Christian community, or how many of them are full time employees (which I do not imagine will be many), the future Episcopal Church will need these people. Some Churches will have all of these people. More than likely they will be shared regionally. Today in the Diocese of Texas there are three churches of different sizes sharing a social networking person who does some of this work across the city of Austin.

Eri Gentry is the founder of a community called BioCurious— Experiment With Friends (www.biocurious.org). She is not a biologist, but got involved because she knew people in her circle of friends who were involved in interesting scientific studies.[593] She had a desire to be part of the community and participate. She wanted biology to be available and user-friendly for herself and others.[594] She created the space online so that biology, experiments and classes could be available in an inexpensive and usable manner. She says of the community, "I am realizing that I have to provide these classes though BioCurious in order to make them affordable, do it around my schedule, make it fun, and be around people who I like."[595] The mission statement that Gentry and her cohort Tito Jankowski came up with for BioCurious states: "We're building a community biology lab for amateurs, inventors, entrepreneurs, and anyone who wants to experiment with friends."[596] What is amazing is that the community is made up of individuals anywhere from people at universities who are doing super-advanced biology research, and teenagers trying out interesting and sometimes odd experiments, and everyone in between.[597] The future Church will create TheoCurious communities where everyone from the systematic theologian to the neophyte self-learner Christian can participate in making meaning through conversation and discourse.

The future Church, if it is to thrive, must be untethered from a Sunday-only formation process. It is so much more than learning Old Testament Bible stories and stories about Jesus. It is not about sitting at the feet of professionals. Formation in the future church is about individuals joining together globally and locally to enjoy the pilgrimage of faith discovery. The future Church is not about making knowledge transactions for your stewardship in return for mini university attendance at your local parish. It is about including the self-learner in a creative journey of discovering the story of God an how God's story is intertwined with their own story. Every member of the Christian community of the future is a learner regardless of age or time in the community. Everyone is learning from everyone else in a mutuality of sharing stories through innovative means. The future Church will be engaging all the technological tools at its disposal to network and build new hubs where formation can happen without direct supervision and yet as part of a seeking community. It will move far beyond discipleship. Jesus called disciples—that is true. But no disciple stayed a disciple forever, they all became apostles and were sent out.

The gap is closed between apprentice and master in the future Church because the identity of the teacher and student is merged into the self-learning pilgrim. I believe that the potential for socially structured formation brings us back to the vision that Jesus had for the community of God. He envisioned a community of self-learners who were engaged in the work of formation for themselves and others. He envisioned a community making its journey with God and in so doing being remade as a new community of transformation.[598]

CHAPTER TWENTY
Vocations

"Before I can tell my life what I want to do with it,
I must listen to my life telling me who I am."
— *Parker J. Palmer, Let My Life Speak*

When we look at the historical tradition of the three-fold ministry of deacon, priest, and bishop, we see that most of the development took place 160 years after the death of the last apostle. Certainly Jesus chose his disciples. He trained them. He sent them out. He did not send them to a commission on ministry and he did not make them go to seminary. The church in this informal and less structured time grew and thrived. It was perhaps at its most anti-fragile organizational stage. It was a Church that was completely disbursed with traveling evangelists and an emphasis upon the charisms of the Spirit. During this time, the diverse community spread out across the Roman Empire and found itself under the threat of persecutions by the state. It also encompassed diversity in teaching and practice. I can only imagine that this was problematic to the growing number of reasonable Roman Citizens who were even then becoming Christian. The response that appears to be chosen collectively was to continue to place authority in the hands of the leadership.

Even in Acts we see a continued deferral to the Apostles in Rome. In time a hierarchy was ascribed to those with the closest connection to the first followers of Jesus. Certainly we see this at the Synod of Whitby some six centuries later, when the major decision on the date of Easter was made purely on the idea that the date Peter followed should be chosen because he was closest to Jesus. By the post-apostolic age we see that both in St. Clement's writings and in the Didache there is a clear move to the threefold order of ministry.[599]

The idea of ordination itself is rooted (literally and figuratively) in the Roman class system. The rite of ordination was itself reserved for imperial offices.[600] The term was also used in pagan Roman society. All of this is to say that ordination was understood by the early Christians as a way of setting someone apart, into a new order, and with an increase in their social rank.[601] This ordination is present in the life of the Church by the time the great theologian and Church unifier Ignatius of Antioch writes in the early part of the second century. He believed that one bishop was to govern each church in collaboration with priests and deacons. He wrote, "Let the bishop preside in the place of God." He continued," and his clergy in place of the Apostolic conclave, and let my special friends the deacons be entrusted with the service of Jesus Christ."[602]

St. Irenaeus, in the second half of the second century recorded the Apostolic Succession of church leaders from the Apostles. This placed bishops and all that they ordained in a direct lineage with the first Apostles and to Jesus. St. Jerome by the middle of the fourth century, wrote, "There can be no Christian community without its ministers." [603] By the time we reach the Council of Chalcedon (451) we see that the laying on of hands by a bishop was the normative practice.[604] This overall movement of order strengthened the Church by giving a class of leadership to whom the Church might turn. It provided a common voice for its apologetics[605] thus unifying its teaching. It gave strength to its unity by means of joining what were previously disparate groups of Christians into an interconnected family. This is how the Church organized itself; and for many historians it is why the Church moved from a sect of Judaism into a thriving religion.

The three-fold ministry of the ordained is today a charism of the Episcopal Church. It is the way we are organized and continue to be organized. We can plainly see that there was indeed an evolution to this trajectory. It is our way of life as an Episcopal Church. To change the threefold ministry or to laicize (to do without the ordained) our sacramental understanding, is in effect to become a different church. Just as to create a stronger hierarchy without the laity does the same. This is not who we are. We also see, in our overall history of raising up leaders, an important truth. We see that in every age the Christian Church has raised up ministers to help undertake its mission. Jesus chose the first disciples, from diverse occupations, and sent them out to share the good news of the Gospel. The apostolic Church in turn chose ministers to be apologists to the philosophical world of their day, and to build up the growing, unruly, and disorganized Church. The building a Christendom state brought with it leadership that required politics in the fifth century. Meanwhile local churches employed leaders of many kinds to help with everything from formation of new Christians to sacramental rites.

The postapostolic age brought with it leaders who were monks, and they in turn brought reform. The Church of The Middle Ages would choose for itself a variety of leaders who could organize and oversee the vast Church that seemed to be on edge of truly becoming universal. Reformers would be the leaders of the next age and then the counter reformers. The colonial age brought with it missionaries, along with both their positive and negative impact. Industrialization and war brought leaders with prophetic socialist voices and pacifists, with those who supported the hierarchies of the modern era and were chaplains to the new families of wealth. American Church leaders have spoken against slavery, against war, and for women's rights and for the rights of the freedmen. The last fifty years leaders in social activism sought to lead in new ways while church hierarchies searched for leaders to help return the ailing denominations to their rightful state of domination within the American culture. The Church has raised up prophets, preachers, sacramentalists, priests, deacons, monks, laity and bishops for the mission and purpose of the kingdom of God.

The death of the last apostle and that of St Cyprian in 258 AD are separated by approximately 160 years. It took only about 160 years for the church to depart from its New Testament roots and thoroughly embrace sacramental ecclesiology, where the sacraments of the Church officiated by the ordained ministry (a sacrament itself), rather than individual faith, became accepted as the means of salvation.

In every age God has called and the church has listened. Sometimes the Church has ignored God's call and sometimes despite itself it has fulfilled God's invitation. The future Church is no different, for even now we are searching for the leaders of tomorrow. What are the kinds of leaders and vocations the future Episcopal Church needs? Who will help to give a clear and positive vision? Who will invite unity? Who will be the voice for the poor and innovate the service ministries? Who will create the new missionary tools for evangelism? Who has the courage to rethink stewardship? Who will help form the next generation of digital natives and self-learners?

The Rev. Dr. David Gortner, Professor of Evangelism at Virginia Theological Seminary, says that there are extraordinary markers for leaders that appear across categories of denomination, age, gender, and race. [606] He breaks the clergy up into three groups. We can see that these three groups, all of which are ministering today, are a good example of clergy of the future Church who are here now, clergy of the present-past Church, and clergy of the present Church. Gortner's categories reinforce what I am trying to say about the future Church leaders. His research notes that markers for what we call future Church leadership tend to have a "positive regard and expectation of people and groups."[607] They have a "moderate degree of assertiveness and decisiveness."[608] These leaders put this together with an expectation of "collaboration" and "interest" in others. They have the ability to work in a context of conflict.[609] They also have the ability to foresee conflict and deal effectively before it happens.[610] Leaders who are being successful in this current stew of ideas are "creative, well-managed," and spiritually "grounded."[611]

Clergy working for the present-past Church have other tendencies. Gortner describes these as "placeholder" clergy.[612] These are the clergy that are ministering out of and to a Church that no longer exists. They have basic skills in preaching, pastoral care, and sacramental ministry.[613] They do not exhibit the same capabilities as the future Church leadership. Then there are the clergy who are members of the present Church leadership. These clergy Gortner describes as "talented but tenuous."[614] They are lacking in "self-confidence and decisiveness."[615] They have good ideas but they do not have the "will" to help "communities bring ideas to fruition."[616] They are "kind, thoughtful, dedicated, considerate of others' thoughts and feelings, and full of ideal visions of what the Church could be; but they are also conflict-averse, anxious about and watchful for opposition."[617]

As I have pointed out, the problem is and can be that the present-past or even a present Diocese is picking leaders for an age that no longer exists. They may stumble upon future leaders but this tends to be by accident. Only bishops and commissions on ministry that have a vision twenty or more years out are picking future leaders and setting that vision as their standard. Amplifying our own opinion of the fix, Gortner says that, "denominations as systems seek out people with, and shapes people into these patterns. The Church as a system and culture is wired to select, train, and deploy for what it values most."[618] If you value the past then that is the kind of leader you choose.

Let us say that a person who begins to think about becoming a priest of the church today takes one year to think about it before they mention it to their local rector. That rector then embarks on a one-year discernment process with the person. Then that person is recommended to their local commission on ministry. If they are lucky the process with the diocesan commission only takes a year. They are approved and go off to seminary for three years. After r seminary, they do a kind of curacy / apprenticeship with a rector for two more years. They spend the next year looking for a church of their own. This is really a transition year. The next two years are spent getting their feet firmly planted in a congregation in order to effect change. That means that the future priest sitting in their living room considering church leadership today will not effect change in the church for over ten years. The Church that they see and believe they are called to serve is a church that is past. It is ten years old. If the person is young today, that person is going to work for thirty years. The span of their career is forty years from today. Therefore, the leadership of the present Church today has to have a vision that looks out over the horizon, and discerns what the future Church looks like ten, twenty, fifty years from now, and begin to set the standards for *that* leadership. What we are doing today, and what we have been doing for the last fifty years or more, is choose leaders for a Church that no longer exists by the time they are ordained.

I have a friend who drives fast cars. He holds a land speed record. He once told me that when the car (which is more like a rocket on wheels) is going in excess of 250 miles an hour you have to see miles ahead of where you actually are. If you look at the road in front of you and react to it you are already miles past that reality by the time your actions have any consequences. Looking where you *were* has dangerous consequences when you are moving so fast. Why? As a rule you go where you look. Your actions follow where you are looking. This is true in racing and it is true in leadership. It is especially true for future Church leaders. We have to be looking far down the road because the horizon is coming faster than you think.

The leaders of the future Church are going to be second-curve leaders. The first curve is in front of us. The second curve is that horizon out beyond the present—it is the future. Second-curve leadership understands that the Church has a traditional business base.[619] What the local church does today is what its members think is indelible. People are accustomed to this church—the one they see. This is the church they give their time and money to support. For those who are first-curve leaders today they are invested in this leadership model, this hierarchy, and this traditional way of doing things. They are devoted even if "traditional" only means what we have done in the last two decades or even fifty years. Ian Morrison says in his seminal book entitled *Second-curve Leadership*, "Almost every successful first-curve business was a second-curve business in its day."[620] Most leaders in the church today are first-curve leaders. They are reacting to what people like or dislike about the church today. The first-curve leader can manage the current trajectory fairly well in any business or church. But they are always only reacting to a past model of church. These are Gortner's *placeholder* and *talented but tenuous* clergy. They are going to miss the second-curve. More importantly they will not have prepared the next generation or the church for what is coming.

The living Church, the positive Church or the future Church, is a church that has adapted and changed in every age. The second-curve leaders know this is its nature, and is prepared to help make that shift happen. They know what is driving the change, and how it is affecting the organization. They see and imagine what the next Church looks like, and can begin to chart a course towards it. They actually begin to make the future by making changes that help the organization get to the second curve. The second-curve leaders understand that people are changing, their culture is changing, and the tools they use to navigate the world around them are changing. Everything is constantly changing.

Second-curve leaders know that anything can happen. Without the false luxury of security that the first-curve leaders has, the second-curve leader in the future Church knows that what it sees is not a stable, stagnant reality simply twenty years from now. Morrison says, "The biggest mistake that one can make is to assume that the second-curve phenomenon is just like the first-curve only in a different place."[621] Second-curve leaders are not about making predictions, but learning about the facts of the changing environment around them and acting upon those facts. They know there will be mistakes but the same leader also knows if they are looking at the carefully laid out artifacts of the future, they are going to be on target more than not.

Most first-curve leaders: either over -estimate the changes that are coming and their impact today, and make overcorrections causing huge fluctuations in ministry that disturb and cause problems; or, they underestimate how changes will affect the long term and so they do not make the needed changes. Second-curve leaders keep the heat on, driving change for the second-curve without blowing off the top. The future Church must always have second-curve leaders. They will stand in the distant future, some twenty and forty years from now, and be imagining and leading towards an even farther horizon fifty years in the future.

Future leaders also have some key characteristics that are their strengths as they aim for the second-curve. They are individuals who enjoy the gifts of others.[622] The future leaders do not have to be alike and can thrive together by celebrating their diversity. They neither need to have all the gifts or define their communities so tightly that others cannot come in and bring new gifts with them. The future Church leaders know that such diversity in talents is necessary for health and communal vitality. They know that their "uniqueness adds to the collective ability of the whole."[623]

Future leaders know that they need one another. Margaret Wheatley writes, "I believe we adults have inadvertently helped you here. We have ignored you, denied you, and seen you as a problem. You learned to stay together because older generations couldn't or wouldn't invite you to join them."[624] These leaders will use their experiences around exclusion to transform connection, building huge crowds of chosen support groups and mentors. These leaders are reinventing, reinvigorating, and reimagining the nature of community and the relationships that hold them together.

Future leaders of the church will be creative.[625] These leaders will have grown-up in a world where they can manipulate almost everything and they can make it their own. These leaders do not tolerate boundaries that try to contain this creative urge they have to remake things. An important and essential thing to understand is that these three particular characteristics (giftedness, inclusion, and creativity) will work best together. Together a synchronicity can thrive and build capacity and energy for change. Together these qualities will shape a particular kind of organization: one that will be always on the move, quick to recreate, and open to all kinds and conditions of people. These leaders, for the first time in a long time perhaps, will be leaders like those that Jesus called away from their normal day to day jobs and invited into an extraordinary adventure. In so doing, he changed the course of history and the future of community. His actions then are today calling forward a new set of leaders who imagine a church future that is alive and thriving in a new global era. They see it and they are eager to move into the second-curve with the church on their hip.

As we look for these leaders, we will be challenged because in some ways they are not like us. Yet we know that the future Episcopal Church is beckoning and calling them into service. It is our work, our vocation, to help call them forward. To say out loud that we need individuals who have the characteristics of the second-curve leader. We must look at the church we have described, and believe lives in our positive future, and we must raise up leaders who are also representative of the great ethnic and social diversity that makes up our context. We need people who come from every kind of background with every kind of skill set. We are looking for mission-focused, entrepreneurial, collaborative, and adaptive leaders. We are looking for people who can see the church that we are seeing. These new leaders believe in and will do anything they can to work towards our positive future of a diverse people of God.

This means that we need leaders who are not only representatives of diverse populations but who are "cross-culturally competent."[626] Leaders need to be adaptable to shifting ethnic population movement, customs, and social complexity. The younger generations are globally aware and global travelers—even just electronically. This will help them be leaders in the future church. It is important to speak another language, but even that is not as important as being able to be sensitive to the complex social customs of a particular ethnic group. Scott E. Page, director at the Center of Study of Complex Systems at the University of Michigan writes, "Progress depends as much on our collective differences as it does on our individual IQ scores."[627] He believes that crowds/commons that show a "range of perspectives and skill levels outperform like-minded experts."[628] Therefore the people we raise up for leadership will need to be able to illustrate in their lives some ability to achieve cross-cultural competency.

The future Church is looking for people who love God in Christ Jesus. They have a deep reverence for the sacraments at the heart of their own lives. They have a sacramental worldview and are able to tell the story of God by using many images and tools. They will be digital natives who are not afraid of the multiplicity of contexts and are able to move in and out of them seamlessly. These future leaders will already be connected and networked through a wide web of social media outlets. They will have an ability to "critically assess and develop content that uses new media forms, and to leverage these media for persuasive communication."[629] In other words, they will have the ability not only to navigate but also utilize constantly evolving media. They need to be "new media literate."[630]

This will mean that we are looking for people who are "novel and adaptive thinkers."[631] New situations, new tools, and new cultural shifts in an uncertain world mean that the Church needs to have individuals leading it who can think and develop / create / innovate solutions.[632] Rule-based solution makers are less effective in the VUCA world. Just as industry will need these kinds of people, so too, the church will depend upon them. In fact, no new church starter should be sent out if they are not novel and adaptive thinkers.

The future leaders will be people who are "socially intelligent."[633] Machines, even artificial intelligence (AI), will not be able to assess the emotions of groups.[634] Teams and collaborations will be essential (even electronic team work now has video that enhances communication). People read people's faces and situations in a way that today is unmatched by machines. The more we return to an age of living and working in groups/pods the more this social intelligence will become essential. [635]Leaders of the future must be literally able to read the room and use that information for leadership.

These leaders (lay and ordained) will share their story easily and be of interest to their peers and those they engage. People will want to listen and connect naturally—in part because of the three characteristics above. The future Church leaders are trustworthy and accessible. They communicate and collaborate across cultural and ideological boundaries as agents of God's reconciling love in the face of cultural forces that polarize and divide. They are transparent, but manage to shape shift easily, as they hold to their convictions with clarity of faith, and show a capacity to stay in relationship with many different kinds of people.

The future Episcopal Church leaders are pilgrims. They are themselves making their way through life as seekers. They are authentically on a journey and are interested in their own growth spiritually. These leaders are self-aware of how they are perceived. They tolerate failure in others, they expect to fail themselves, and they are able to talk about failure because they know intrinsically that this is where growth occurs.

These leaders are conveners. They naturally are people who gather others for formation, learning, pilgrimages, studies, conversations, and storytelling. They are able to hand off leadership easily—they share leadership. They build their mini -communities with such diversity that they are always strengthening and gathering for the purpose of the overall health and vitality of the community. They are willing to share leadership but also willing to help do/experience all parts of community life. They do this in person and virtually. They are adept at figuring out the kind of collaboration that is needed, and then the means for making those connections happen. They have grown up in a world of virtual gaming, which mixes real-world parallel play with virtual peer groups. The digital native is accustomed to "immediate feedback, clear objectives, and staged series of challenges."[636] The new group of leaders is less limited by time, travel, and the economy, in accomplishing the task. The will naturally work better in groups and they will desire to connect with others for the sake of building stronger teams. They do not see a difference between doing this in person or online. Moreover, and importantly for all supervisors, they are not going to waste their time doing something in person if it can be done just as well digitally. They value their in-person and personal time, and want to use that for themselves.

The leaders of the future will be wise counselors, preachers and teachers. They are able to articulate the deep meaning of things. They do this for religious stories and sacraments. They also do this for secular movies, stories, and for city events. The future will need "sense-makers."[637] They are able themselves (*before they ever go to seminary*) to communicate the Gospel in ways that people and communities find engaging and relevant to their lives: in the pulpit and in personal conversation. Machines and technology will never tell a good story or be able to navigate complex sense-making. Thinking, contemplating, metaphor making, and the sacramental interpretation of life will depend upon the future leaders being gifted sense-makers.

Along with this sense-making skill they will also need "computational thinking."[638] This does not mean that they need to be computers. The amount of information that is traded in a knowledge economy is huge. The complexity of the social structured world is illustrated by the variety and number of networked communities. The future leaders, as digital natives, will not see this as strange. They will also be able to "manage their cognitive load."[639] They are able to "discriminate and filter information for importance."[640] While the digital immigrants are awash in a sea of competing information bytes, the digital native is able to assess importance quickly, take what is needed, and leave the rest. Those who are able to translate what they see, read, experience, and learn, into abstract concepts and new ideas are the ones who will rise above their generation in leadership.

This means they will also need to be "transdisciplinary."[641] In every axial age, the key people have been those who were not specialists in any one thing, but able to navigate across specialties, piecing seemingly divergent ideas into holistic life strategies, new sciences, and new philosophies. Howard Rheingold, and author, writes, "transdisciplinarity goes beyond bringing together researchers from different disciplines to work in multidisciplinary teams. It means educating researchers who can speak languages of multiple disciplines—biologists who have understanding of mathematics, mathematicians who understand biology."[642] This means we need people who understand church, sociology, culture, history, business, and accounting. It is not that we are looking for people who are experts in everything. We do not need that. Remember these leaders work in commons, networked relationships, and groups. They will build teams of depth. It does mean that we are looking for leaders who are "T-shaped."[643] The people we want to engage will bring a deep understanding of one field but have the ability to speak the language and culture of a "broader range of disciplines."[644] It will not be enough to know a lot and be able to put it together in a novel way. In order to truly engage sense-making, the future transdisciplinarian will be able to put the pieces together in the right way so as to make them work. Computational thinkers and transdisciplinarians are the kinds of people the Church will need to help navigate the future mission context.

The future leaders will be people who have a "design mindset."[645] The future leader will need to be a person who can look at the task and create a strategy, plan, or ministry to reach the desired outcomes of the mission. It is not just about planting a Christian community. It is about creating a mission in a particular context with a unique combination of people, language, and culture, then after assessing and making sense of it, putting together the pieces to accomplish the goal of a new service ministry or Bible study. They will do this as a secondary act of designing, based upon what they experience and see as needed. The present church simply does what it does. The future Church will depend upon individuals surveying their mission context and then designing the mission to fit it, rather than believing they have the answer to questions that are not being asked or a healthy church for people who do not know they need one. A design mindset looks first and then designs.

Leaders of the future will be humble. They have to be humble in order to tolerate the failure necessary for learning. This will also breed in them a tenacious spirit. Tenacity is not doing the same things over and over again until you accomplish the goal. Tenacity is the willingness to *try everything* until you are successful. This group of leaders is willing to work hard and spend their own capital in order to achieve their goal. They will use their cognitive surplus to bridge the gaps between where they are and where they believe they (or their community) are heading. This will be seen by many as a deep and abiding sense that they are entitled to very little, but will work hard to experience the creative process. This adventurous, almost frontier spirit, will mean they are vocationally flexible. They enjoy new things and participating in different exchanges and experiences. The future Church leaders, and their families, are willing to move to and go where their interests lie. Meaning, if they are devoted to a missionary opportunity, and there is no full time position, they are more likely to get a secular job so they can make the vision happen, than they are to take a job of less interest because it pays.

These leaders will reshape the nature of the ordained ministry. What seems essential to say is that, as a bishop, I know that looking for all these qualities in any one person, is like looking for the messiah. And, if the leaders of today can raise up such a person, the future Church needs her! Here is the big news though, for Commissions on Ministry, and those who are going to participate in this raising up of future leaders: we are not looking for a person—we are looking for a group. Remember the digital native is a creature of the pack. What we have to do is raise up T-shaped individuals with those Ts fitting together to form a group that will bring all of these skills to the new church. T-shaped leaders are people who have a broad variety of skills with one or two skill expertise. When you put T-shaped leaders together in a group you multiply expertise and cross over skills. The present past Church looks for leaders who are specialists or who can become specialists, and will be solitary leaders. The future Church looks for team members who help build a team that will have a depth of these skills and the ability to scale their other talents with their fellow missionary leaders. This is how the future Church will build its cadre of leaders.

The bishop in the future Church will continue to guard the faith of the church, but will be more of a hub, than a person who polices the boundaries of the Christian community.[646] They will be a unifying figure; at ease with their own beliefs and willing to listen and bring others along. The bishop will be a person who redefines the continuing discipline of the Church. They are wise enough to hold quickly to tradition, but transparently and honestly know that things have not always been any one way. The bishop of the future Church will be present in their communities—churches and wider culture. They will be known more by their geographical area than where their office is located. They will have a *see* and *cathedra*[647] but they will sit in the midst of their Christian communities and sit within the wider cultural context. They will no longer be associated only within their own church but as a community member who desires the best for the people who live within their diocese—and I don't mean only the Episcopalians. The people of any given area and of any given denomination will know the Episcopal bishop of the future Church. The bishop will be a celebrant of sacraments in the world and within the community. The bishops of the future will be bishops of the people, and go about with and among their people. They will not be one to stay in an ivory tower or diocesan center. No matter what the administrative call might be, the bishop of the future Church remembers that he or she is to be out and going (as an apostle) to God's people where they are.

Bishops will see the different kinds of ministers that are needed and will raise up people from every walk of life, and of every profession, to take on the mission of the church. This future bishop will ensure that there are many paths to ministry. They will send people to all kinds of programs and courses. The bishop of the future will place the highest priority on the mission—the criteria being the growth of the kingdom of God and the transformation of the world through the reconciling power of God in Christ Jesus. Therefore they will make the measure of success not one of degrees but on how well the life of the future Church leader accomplishes the work we have discussed throughout this book.

The bishop of the future church is a bishop who is himself or herself a second-curve leader with all of the criteria and characteristics we have already discussed. They are people who work with other bishops of the same kind to move the future Church and its vision forward. The future bishop represents well the best of leadership throughout the ages and is always willing to be a prophetic voice. Yet the bishop of the future is not one to shake his fist at the wider world. No. The future bishop is willing to offer leadership to change those institutions that must be changed. This kind of a bishop is willing to work hard to make change happen in those areas of the culture where change is needed. Words without deeds will be a foreign concept to the bishop of the future Church. This bishop is a bishop of hope.

The future bishop believes in the positive future of the Church they serve. They believe that life and vitality are present and they offer a *living* vision of a *living* Church to their people. The bishop is willing to work towards that vision, making hard decisions along the way. The bishop believes. The bishop joins God on God's pilgrimage to reconcile the world. The bishop is always willing to serve and figures out ways in which the most good can come from the church's presence in any community. The bishops find joy in upholding and supporting the many ministries of their diocese. These bishops of the future love their work and would do nothing else. They thrive in a sea of challenge and are excited (which shows) by the prospect of making a difference.

The future bishop lives a particular and disciplined life. He or she is faithful, and continues the practice of studying. The bishop knows the scriptures and the life of Christ and the saints well. The bishop is also willing to seek revelation and vision from other sources because the bishop knows that God in Christ is present in the world too—drawing the world into communion. It is important for the bishop to study the world and to know and understand the forces at work and the people behind them. The bishop is therefore willing and able to speak the language of their mission context. They are able to proclaim a vision of the Gospel of Good News of Salvation to their people, in a language and using symbols and images they understand. The bishop speaks as one of the people and is able to move the hearts of men and women for the work of ministry.

The future bishops will accomplish this work because they will support all the baptized to be sure. This bishop, though, must be connected in ways unseen since the early days of the Church. They are known, and they know their people, and those who minister to them. They are able to be continually in touch, and through this connection, build-up the wider community. The bishop is a unifying pastoral presence for the people entrusted to their care. Through the network of relationships, with the bishop as the hub, the internal life and ministry of the church, its members, the secular leaders, and those who are seeking are all connected into a much broader family of God which is greater and stronger than any particular group that gathers on any given Sunday morning. It is in this way that the bishop is able to marshal support for those who need it, those without a voice, and those without a community. The bishop of the future

Church will no longer be given authority or be considered a prince of the church because of station. The bishop of the future Church will be the chief servant of all, the friend of many, and will receive leadership because of her humility and careful guiding hand. The bishop of the future Church is seen as the shepherd and spiritual guide of her people. This will all be done, not by lording power over those in their care, but rather by working with them.

Likewise, the role of the priest of the future Episcopal Church goes through a tremendous transformation.[648] The priests of the future will be more connected to their people. Not unlike the bishop's ability to be among the people the priest now has a much larger capacity to be in touch with his/her parishioners. The priests are connected to them and able to pastor them in ways that participate more in their life than any time since the turn of the previous century. The amplified human will have the crowd on the shoulder, and so does the priest and she will call that crowd her parish. This will redefine what it means to care for a congregation. No longer will that be simply a building and the people who attend on any given Sunday, the future priest now connects in various ways with people across the Christian community and across her mission context making real world connections between church and what the past church called secular persons.

The priest of the future will to be a teacher. The priest standing in front of a congregation will no longer be the predominant way of teaching. The future Church calls forward priests who connect people with resources and with other people, so that the self-learner can make their own learning pilgrimage. The priest will be a guide, a mentor in the process of self-learning and discovery that offers support to the pilgrims that come in and out of the community. Think about the young girl that Mitra gets to be the "grandmother" to the children learning DNA sequencing. The priest will be that grandmother for the many who are looking to connect with God and learn about God. Today you get a degree that is the paper that enables your credentialing for ministry. Degrees in the wider university field are fading in importance as courses of study and continuing education opportunities allow students to specialize. In the future Church the licensing of individuals will be based more on their particular gifts and unique studies than a degree. I imagine that in many cases licensing will come after apprenticeship. Therefore the local priest will be responsible in the future for making sure the community is connected to best resources and tools for discovery. Constantly working with the theocurious, the priest is aware of their longings and desires, and so helps make the broader network come alive with people and conversation.

The priest of the future will continue to take their place with other priests in the councils of the Church. Like everything else, the nature of governing will have changed. (We will look at the changing face of the overall organization in a future chapter.) The future councils of the Church will have a few characteristics worth mentioning now. They will not require the time, effort, and financial support that they do today. The business of Church to be conducted in ever-smaller units, compared to the mammoth amount of unnecessary administration that occurs in the present Church. The councils of the Church will be more connected globally. There will be an ever-growing overlap of networks and relationship nodes that allow the future Church to gather in ever greater conversations across boundaries—building mutual learning and support cadres for mission. Finally, the way in which the mind of the Church is unified beyond any contextual division will be the sign that the future Church has returned to mission (service, evangelism, stewardship, and formation) leaving conflict behind. Yes, the future priest will take their place in the councils of the church but the councils will have been remade.

The future priest understands that her work is to preach. She will do this in all manner of forms. She will use the pulpit, small group settings, web, text conversations, by uploading talks and videos, by sharing ideas throughout her network, and by every evolving means possible. Long gone are the days when proclaiming the gospel was the work of Sunday morning from a pulpit. The priest is to proclaim the Gospel of God in Christ Jesus, and will do so by pushing out into the connected world words, images, and music. The art of preaching will be the art of sharing stories and having conversations throughout the community. Like the first followers of Jesus who offered the story of Jesus to people in poor houses, in prison, on the roadside, and in the marketplace, the priest will be ever ready to proclaim the Gospel by sharing the story of their own pilgrim journey and connecting with others.

The future priest is ready to forgive. The future priest talks about brokenness, sin, and falling away from God. She does it in such a way that she is clear that there is always plenteous grace and redemption. The priest offers forgiveness for the brokenness in the world. She is known for offering a *message of grace* to all in the community. The future Church is ushering in a new time of grace and forgiveness for all. There is, in this new Christian community, a wisdom about the complexities of life and the brokenness of human endeavors. The honesty of having our failings and flaws will be understood to be part of human life. It is also the seat of creativity, initiative, and growth. The future priest understands that when people fall and hurt themselves, others, and the environment, they need access to someone who will listen, understand, and give God's forgiveness to them; so that they may use these opportunities of greater self-awareness to direct their own amendment of life. The past Church is notorious for telling people they are sinful. The future Church will be known as an honest Church, one that faces the reality of the human condition, but is ready to forgive.

The priest of the future blesses people. The present church has worked hard to control its blessing of people, families, life, and the world around them. The priest of the future Church is in the midst of the community context. Throughout the Church and the world, the priest is blessing people and their relationships. The future Church will have moved beyond the present-past Church's diatribes into a time where it generously blesses people. The future Church is less controlling about the priests' ability to bless and be a part of people's lives. We will move away from an overly legal way of dealing with these issues. Such a law based approach to the priest's pastoral ministry has empowered both ends of the spectrum who want to continue to fight over social issues—bullying one another with legislation and litmus tests. No longer are the blessings controlled but instead the priest is trusted to do the good thing, the best thing. This trust will be built not by following canons, but by the relationship the priest has with their bishop. It will be this new connected relationship that will allow the priest the freedoms needed to be out and about in their community context preaching, teaching, forgiving, and blessing.

The priest of the future will be about the work of administering the rites of initiation for those who find their way into community. No longer will the baptismal rite be imprisoned in the church on Sunday morning. The future priest baptizes all the time and anywhere baptism is desired. The priest understands that baptism has had many forms throughout its history, and uses every opportunity and every form to baptize, as the self-directing pilgrim (like the eunuch in our earlier story) directs that they are ready. It will no longer be a baptism that is given by God and the Church when the priest decides the person is ready. That is old thinking. The priest of the future understands that baptism is about the work of Christ that has already been done, and it is for each person to decide when he or she is ready. The future priest knows that they are responsible for being prepared to baptize and so will baptize people in Church on Sunday, in prison, at the hospital, and by the roadside and everywhere a person may choose. The future Church is so invested in front door evangelism, in communication throughout its network, and in formation as a lifelong process, that it practices open baptism anytime anywhere for all people.

The priest will also be the chief sacramentalist for the community, celebrating and administering the Holy Eucharist. The priest of the future will celebrate on Sunday as they do today; and on sacred days and holidays. The future priest, though, will take the sacrament out of the Babylonian captivity where it resides today, at altars behind closed doors. The priest of the future Church takes the bread and wine and goes out into their mission context—out into the world—and celebrates the Eucharist. The local priest will work with other priests to ensure that all communities and congregations receive the sacrament as well—no matter how small or where it gathers: peoples' homes, nursing homes, community centers, in the back of an office, or in hospitals. They understand that not everyone can come to the church, and so sacraments (like formation) are taken out into the world. The Eucharist will be celebrated in just about every location imaginable; the present Church's idea that this happens in one place on Sunday morning is dismantled in favor of expanding the Eucharistic reach of the fellowship of believers. I do not believe the future Church will officially open the sacrament

beyond a believer's meal for the baptized. I do not think the future Church will change its canon on this. However, the future Church will not police it, because the future Church knows God is so much bigger than canon and custom. The priest will be clear that baptism is the rite of entrance into community and about the boundaries of the Eucharist. Remember how important this is to the digital native— they want to know what the boundaries are. However, the priest of the future knows that God is at work here and wherever bread is broken and wine is shared, God is in the process of working and gathering his people. Some may be baptized and some not. The priest, who is a forgiver and a blessing to others looks upon all those who come to Christ and raise their hands, and gives them bread and wine—no questions asked. The priest knows that God is an abundant God. God is an all -powerful and all -encompassing God. God is gracious and a lover of souls. God is reaping and sowing, sowing and reaping.

The future priest will pattern his life after the life of God in Christ Jesus. This means that the priest will be out and about in the world. Jesus was an itinerant preacher, teacher, and sacramentalist. He made community wherever he went. Then he sent his followers out to do the same. He called them with their many vocations and taught them how to go. Go, go, go. He sent them out to meet every kind of person, and to heal and forgive and bless. Jesus said do not sweat it if they do not want you...move on. He inspired a sense of hope and a positive future for those who followed AND for the whole world. He wanted those who used his name and the name of God to be people who went out with good news to every place and every people and to share what they had discovered. In the present- Church, we can get distracted by politics and piety and start believing that patterning our lives after Christ is about sex and holiness. The pattern of life that Jesus taught was pretty simple: love God, love your neighbor, do not hurt people, do not worry, and go. The priests of the future is humbled, knowing that like all the vocations of the church, it is notabout *them*. It is forever and always about connecting people with the creator of the world. The future priest goes. The priest will not be known as a person who sits inside their office or tied to their PC. The mobile ability to have office and connections in your car, coffee shop, or in other people's homes and workplaces, means that the priest will be un-tethered from the church property; thereby, making all priests itinerant preachers, teachers, guides and sacramentalists. The priests of the future Church will work with many other priests and deacons to connect to the people in the community. They will go out and do their work. Some will have communities that are like churches today. Some will have several small communities in people's homes and workplaces. Still others will minister as priests within work environments as missionaries to businesses, neighborhood community centers, hospitals, public schools, and communities designed for aging people. The priest will be connected to people out in the world and not primarily be associated with only one geographical location—the church building. Some will manage large communities, with complex layers and disbursed smaller congregations connected to it. The priests will inhabit many roles, in many places, and find that like Christ, they will simply go.

The deacon is a servant in the future Church, as they are in the Church today. I will always remember that a friend once told me that by The Middle Ages the deacon's primary responsibility was to read the gospel for the old decrepit bishops in the liturgy. In the last century, the role of the deacon has been confined inside the church. It happened in large part because of the great socialization of government and the exporting of service ministries to NGOs. The deacon once had an incredible job of leading the church in service by caring for the people in the community who were in need. The deacon of the future Church must return to an essential role in connecting the Church's gospel message with the community and its needs. Yes deacons will serve all people, particularly the poor, the weak, the sick and the lonely.[649]

The deacons of the future will serve in ever-new ways. The future deacons will be skilled at community organizing both for the sake of the local church and the sake of the community. They will be involved in creating new congregations and Christian Communities, where the Church is not already present. Deacons will preach and teach on behalf of the church with a special focus on service of others. The deacons will start new Christian communities in places where the poor are left without advocates, where the weak need help, and the sick and the lonely are in need of aid and companionship.

The deacon will help with connecting and organizing the community to help it become healthy and well. The Church's concern for the community will lead the deacon of the future Church to connect members of the Christian community with members of the local context to meet in home groups and to discuss the community needs. He or she will use all the connectivity and network power of the greater Church to bring resources to work with the local neighbors to resolve conflicts, set aside green space, make the neighborhood accessible, find means to clinics and preventative health care, and clean up the community.

The deacons will work to connect the needs of the people (inside the community and outside the community) to the leaders of the church (lay and ordained) so that those needs may be engaged. The community of believers in the future will be connected to the needs of the community. The future Church, in large part because of the deacon's connectivity, will be known as a community that cares. The deacons will model the spirit of Christ and the first disciples, who understood that the work is always to love neighbor and to serve neighbor—it is here that the Church will be always put in the mind of Christ as a community. We have already said the work of the future Christian community will *not* be to build new systems of toxic charity. The role of the deacon is one that is about real relationships, real people, real needs, and real concerns. In this way the old models of throwing money at issues (as the present-past Church has done) will be set aside for new models of mutual engagement.

People who serve in the church will be of every age. While there is a resurgence in ordinations of young people, there will continue to be older clergy ordinations. Longer and healthier life spans and the trend towards second careers and multiple avocations will continue to have a strong affect. The bishops, priests, and deacons of the future Church will be full time, part time, and non-stipendiary. The greater numbers will be part-time and non-stipendiary. There will be deacons and priests who are doctors, lawyers, mechanics, waiters, and hairdressers. There will also be vocations that are full time and serve in greater capacities to undertake the wider church organization. In the future Church, the full time ministers will be far outnumbered by the part time ones. This will be true not because of a small and shrinking Church. It will be this way because the Church has removed its hold on vocations, and is growing. It no longer puts large amounts of money into the employment of a vast number of clergy, instead using those dollars for local ministry impact. Our future is not that we will grow and then return to a full time professionalized clergy and jettison these innovations. The church *will* always have professional full time clergy and pay them, but the new variety is here to stay and it will not regress. Without this diverse model of vocations the mission of the Church is jeopardized.

Christian communities will be of many and varied types. This means that clergy will work in a variety of contextual settings. In a suburban community, the future church may be organized with a full time priest serving with several non-stipendiary priests, who help with the wider sacramental and pastoral responsibilities of the growing community and its multiple sites. Meanwhile in the same parish community, a non-stipendiary priest and several deacons might be out starting new communities in underserved areas, and creating service connections throughout the surrounding neighborhood. In an urban context we might find a non-stipendiary priest and deacon working in a slum, or poorer part of town, to build up a Christian community around an organized project like a community garden to provide fresh fruit and vegetables in the middle of a food desert. They might be sponsored and connected with a larger community like the one mentioned above or they might be stand-alone. A large urban parish may have several full time priests and deacons, an army of non-stipendiary clergy, a host of lay preachers, pastors, and administrators, who oversee multiple mission sites, and a variety of small congregation/communities across the whole city. Still, a small community congregation may have a full time priest or be served by an urban or suburban non-stipendiary leader. All of these scenarios of the future Church will share resources and build ministry capacity by sharing administration and overhead. There will be bishops who have several dioceses that they help to oversee. Non-stipendiary and part-time bishops will join them to help increase the pastoral reach. Gone are the days of concern over numbers of bishops representing dioceses. Missionary bishops working in teams and sharing episcope will replace the "full-time one bishop to a diocese" model. Bishops will raise up and call forth a diverse clergy and lay population focused on the mission of the new church. There will be bishops who hold positions as heads of congregations and large urban communities. There will be bishops who travel, and make as their vocation the support of new ministry contexts where various creative and innovative styles of leadership are needed to propel ministry forward. There is *no* one solution or idea with which the future Church carries out its ministry. It does all things necessary for the sake of the God's mission of reconciliation.

In the fourth century, the Church of Milan did a crazy thing. It elected an unbaptized Christian as their bishop because that particular individual was exactly who the church needed in order to fulfill God's mission. The Church of Milan was made up of cities of many different sizes that included Liguria and Emilia. Milan had several monuments and was a populous city. There were imperial palaces and a complex of wealthy Roman homes with a thriving population.[650] It was a region of great commerce and the center of Roman authority for the region. The urban Christians of the time met in all kinds of places from synagogues, and homes, to public spaces. It was a time of great growth and expansion. There was a growth in the formalization of Christianity as we have discussed. It was also a time of numerous clergy and large communities. The diocese was, by this time, a large geographical area. This thriving diocese, with growth and commerce and political power, did this crazy thing—they elected a man called Ambrose to be their bishop. Today we call him St. Ambrose.

St. Ambrose was a Roman citizen. He grew up sometime around 340 AD. His father was a prefect of Gaul and his mother was a devoted Christian. Ambrose, like his father before him, was educated and studied literature, law and rhetoric.[651] He made his way into politics and eventually became a prefect or "governor" himself. He was to oversee Liguria and Emilia on behalf of the Roman state from his headquarters in Milan.

We might imagine that from an early stage in life, his mother, too, had an influence on him. We know that he was participating in the catechumenate while in Milan.[652] You might remember from our earlier discussion, that the catechumenate at this time was a lengthy process. He found himself in the middle of the Arian controversy— the controversy of the day.[653] As governor, he had to deal with the disruption as it played out in the civic world too, for church and politics are siblings that have never gotten along particularly well. In the middle of this furor the Bishop of Milan, who was an Arian, died. We can imagine that Ambrose as a neophyte and as governor went to a meeting where they were to elect the bishop's replacement out of pure religious and political curiosity. He may have even hoped that as governor he might be able to keep the different parties from devolving into violence. People on both sides of the controversy turned to Ambrose and decided to elect him as their bishop.[654] Evidently everyone thought this might bring peace including, the emperor, Valentinian II. The problem was of course that Ambrose was not a baptized Christian.

Ambrose pleaded that the orthodox canon did not allow neophytes to be ordained. He was put under house arrest, and eventually conceded. The bishops agreed to put aside the canons and to make room for Ambrose's ordination.[655] He was baptized. The Christian historian Paulinus, in his book, *Life of Ambrose*, records what happened next. Evidently, the bishops were willing to set aside the requirements for ordination but not the preparation. Therefore, Ambrose, following his baptism, spent each day fulfilling all of the varying ecclesiastical offices. This means that Ambrose spent time serving in every church grade from doorkeeper to priest.[656] It turns out that Ambrose was just what the church needed at that time. He had the gifts and was able to lead the church through a difficult and trying time.

The goal of the future Church will be to find and work with individuals of every kind who already work well and are committed to the positive future of the Church. Regardless of education, credentials, jobs, and pay, the future Church sees everyone as a missionary of God's reconciling work. It is not a church where clericalism is disguised as the ministry of the baptized. The Church, though, does clearly understand the different responsibilities of each order and its work.

In the ancient models, leadership was neighborhood-oriented. This meant that you found the leaders in the people who were connected to your family, your business, or invested in your community. The future Church finds its leaders from every part of society, regardless of background, and time within the community. The future Church builds collaborative leadership across geographical boundaries, and is not limited to one on one relationships, but amplifies them through electronic means. In our "back to the future" models we will have more Ambrose type leaders.

The ancient Church and its leadership were wise enough to figure out how they were going to enable the person with the gifts needed by the church to serve. This will be the way of the future Episcopal Church.

CHAPTER TWENTY-ONE
Self-learners and their Learning Communities

*"I'm completely library educated... I discovered me in the library. I
went to find me in the library. Before I fell in love with libraries, I was
just a six-year-old boy. The library fueled all of my curiosities, from
dinosaurs to ancient Egypt. When I graduated from high school in 1938, I
began going to the library three nights a week. I did this every week for almost
ten years and finally, in 1947, around the time I got
married, I figured I was done. So I graduated from the library when I was
twenty-seven. I discovered that the library is the real school."*
— Ray Bradbury, *The Art of Fiction No 203 Interview*

The future Episcopal Church will form Christians in new ways
and train its clergy in new ways. The re-formation of education will
have a profound impact on seminaries, which have occupied a
premier place in priestly training for the last several centuries. In
fact, the shifts currently underway have already affected seminaries.
Because of these shifts, we have been asking what it will take to keep
seminaries alive. How many seminaries are needed? Who will
survive? How much money will it take? The question for the future
Church is really quite a different one: what kind of organization will
we need to help self-learning vocations succeed in the new mission
context?

I enjoyed the documentary written and directed by Penn Jillette
and Teller entitled *Tim's Vermeer*. It was shortlisted for the Oscar in
2014. It is a story about Texas inventor Tim Jenison. I was attracted
to the film because I was a fine art student in college and enjoy
painting. Johannes Vermeer, who lived in 1632 in Delft, Netherlands,
was one of the thousands of artists I studied. I was always captivated

by the beauty and detail found in his work. Generally known as a master who painted with light, Vermeer has captured the imagination of art lovers for centuries. While in school we were introduced to the idea that Vermeer possibly used a camera obscura. (Figure 7) In this way, he possibly was able to paint exactly what he saw. Philip Steadman and

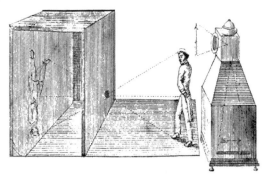

Figure 7: A camera obscura uses light to capture an image. Earliest evidence of a similar device dates to China in 470 to 390 BCE.

British artist David Hockney (a personal favorite) have offered insight on the use of optics such as the camera obscura by artists over the centuries.   Tim Jenison, after getting Hockney's book for Christmas, decided to investigate this a bit more.

Jenison specializes in hardware and software video imaging tools for personal computers. He looked at Vermeer's work, and knew Hockney and Steadman were onto something. He said in an interview, "I happen to know this because I'm a video guy, and I understand the limitations of human vision. This is a tough argument—most people think they can see pretty well—but when I saw that, I thought, 'Vermeer must have used something to get those colors right. You just can't see that; you can't paint it.'"[657] Over Vermeer's lifetime he painted about twenty paintings in forty years. Jenison decided he would try to paint a Vermeer. What he did was to actually recreate Vermeer's *The Music Lesson*. His goal was not to paint it but to paint exactly what Vermeer painted exactly as Vermeer painted it. It took him over 5 years in which he painted for 130 days. Jenison built a room exactly like the room in which Vermeer painted. He got everything correct. From the light, to the fabrication of an exact duplicate of the harpsichord in Vermeer's painting, everything was precisely as Vermeer would have seen it. He then used a lens (which he ground himself) and a mirror device he believed to be similar to Vermeer's, to create exactly the same painting scenario as the grand master. The result is stunning. While Jenison is not a painter by trade, the work he created and the process by which he took to create it make him one. While some might argue that Jenison was simply a machine, what he created is beautiful and he captured the light and the color in a miraculous way.

Jenison did not go to school to learn to paint like Vermeer. He did not have a private tutor teach him how to paint. Out of fascination with process Jenison learned to paint and then accomplished an amazing thing. He is not a carpenter, yet he built chairs, tables, and windows for the room. He is not a glazier, but he fabricated the window panes. He is not someone who has served an apprenticeship for years to learn how to make a viola, but built by hand a working *viola de gamba*. He is not a painter, but painted a beautiful piece of art. The art critics and blogosphere are on fire with rage and interest over what he accomplished and if it has meaning. I think most of the conversation misses the point. Jenison out of interest, passion and obsession (the hallmarks of any artistic muse) taught himself to be an artist. He is a self-learner who went through extraordinary steps to accomplish an extraordinary thing. Self-learners will do almost anything to become proficient at an art or even a ministry.

Seminary makes a particular claim as to its importance in the process of forming clergy. Seminaries, like their counterpart ivory towers, work on a common and shared understanding of how their educational institution fits in the overall social context. In institutions of higher education, they believe that "basic research yields scientific knowledge, this leads to generating technology, than then leads to practical applications, that then leads to economic growth and other benefits."[658] The investment by society and business in the university's research will provide a general benefit to the populace. People enjoy the benefits of this research throughout their lives. This is called a Baconian linear model after the philosopher of science Francis Bacon.[659] Scientist and biochemist Terence Kealey offers this notion that "academia leads to applied science and technology and technology leads to practice.[660] Nassim Taleb agrees with Kealey and argues, this "model may work in some very narrow but highly advertised instances."[661] What is interesting, they say, is that there is no scientific or rigorous evidence that it is true or that it works.[662] In other words this is a bias—we assume it is true without much evidence because it is our experience and therefore normative. In fact, Taleb argues, the whole thing may be an "illusion."[663]

Taleb offers a parable for us to consider that illustrates his point. A collection of researchers at an Ivy League school gather to lecture birds on how to fly. They put a few birds in a room and offer a lot of important information about flight, equations, measurements, and pictures that illustrate their equations about the certainty of flight. The birds leave the room and fly. The researchers then record what took place and offer a thesis through the department of ornithology "that mathematics leads to ornithological navigation and wing-flapping technologies."[664] This news is repeated in lectures to other students. Researches fail to study the quantity of birds that fly without the institution's aid. Taleb says, "So the illusion grows."[665] While he can be snarky, the point here is not anti-education or anti-learning, and it is not dismissive. It is in fact quite the opposite. Taleb's point is pro-learning. It is pro self-learning and encourages the proper place of mentors in the process. Taleb believes that the individual should be in charge of the learning process and the institutions or learning communities need to be responsive to the learner. He is arguing for experienced based and need based learning—not unlike the ministry preparation of the early church.

Taleb says that more often than not the skills and ideas that are gained while doing, failing, and doing, or those that are naturally ours, are believed to have come from books and teachers.[666] These ideas that the institution and its professors are necessary to the success of life, business, and the economy are "narrative fallacies" and "confirmation fallacies."[667] Narrative fallacies are "created because humans have a limited ability to look at sequences of facts without weaving an explanation into them."[668] Confirmation fallacies are when individuals string together unproven and disconnected facts without research to confirm a pattern that is not there. We are blind to unconventional methods or the role of unorthodox practices in success.[669] Taleb offers, instead, this loop of thinking: random tinkering (antifragile) leads to heuristics (technology) leads to practice; or, apprenticeship leads to random tinkering (antifragile) that leads to heuristics (technology) that leads to practice and apprenticeship.[670]

My contention is that seminary makes the case that: classroom study of the past produces knowledge about the present which then leads to an understanding about ministry, and the tools for ministry (technology); which leads to practical applications in real ministry situations, ;which then leads to growth, health, and vitality of the church. The problem is that is not what is happening. Therefore, we are creating many narrative fallacies to explain the situation. Our n bias is that seminary is essential in its current form, and so we do not examine it. Instead, we continue to make up our own story about why ministry is struggling. We are misusing a perfectly good resource like the seminary, and we are not addressing the issues that really face the Church.

We might ask: is it possible that what worked in the 200 years of the church's most rapid growth might work better than our current practice? The future Church will allow people to do ministry (antifragile), to tinker with the church. Where the minister needs knowledge, information, or tools, they find them: in mentor relationships, by taking seminary classes, and by studying other models. This leads to real world heuristics—ministry technologies. The future Church will create a new pattern and make available apprenticeships. This will in turn lead to random tinkering and building communities, and new kinds of thinking around connection. This will lead to different ways to do service and evangelism, and new possibilities for stewardship and formation. This then leads to new technology and ways of doing and being church. In turn, this creates new heuristics and leads to more practice and tinkering and apprenticeship. This is what this chapter is about—exploring the future of self-learners in community.

The Christian church has not always formed clergy through seminaries. In the chapter on formation we discussed the changes in baptismal preparation practices from the first centuries to today. The same shifts are apparent with the history of the formation of clergy. We accept that ordination and its process of selection, study, and rite are normative.

During the first four centuries after the resurrection of Christ we see, a steady progression of formalization of practice. In the beginning, there is no evidence of any kind of formal training for those who are to lead the small and growing Christian communities. Church historians believe that there was a great focus on the gifts of the Spirit, evident in the writings of St. Paul. There is also some evidence in the *Didache* that apostles, prophets and teachers are gifts given by the Spirit. [671] Historians believe that the earliest organization depended primarily upon the gifts of the Spirit for discerning Church leadership.[672] At the same time, the *Didache's* approach to the prophets of this era seems questionable to say the least. The Didache, as we have seen in previous chapters, is a pinpoint in the development of the Church into a more formalized, organized community. By the second century that leadership appointed by the Holy Spirit with the discernment of the community begins to take on a different face.

The rise of the bishop brought with it control and organization— as we have seen previously. The bishop was the central figure from whom all other clerical practices emanated. The bishop was himself the emblem and the practitioner of all other duties of the clergy. They shared his work. (1 Tim. 3. 13) Harold Rowden, in his excellent work on the history of theological education says this, "In practice, many of these were discharged by presbyters, deacons, and those in the increasing number of minor orders, under the close supervision and guidance of the bishop, father-in-God to the clergy as well as the laity. This intimate personal association of the bishop with his clergy was a source of inspiration and direction to untried clergy."[673] What historians surmise is that from the time of the first Epistles in the New Testament, and letters from the second century, there is a "subdivision" of orders. Like the story of Ambrose, we see that people move from office to office in a "stepping stone" sequence.[674] Keep in mind that Roman society itself was organized with similar hierarchies. These appear to be adopted by the Church. By the third century there seems to be some evidence that there was an examination.[675] Due to debates over theology, control was essential for the budding church.[676]

These theological debates are indispensable if you want to understand the rise of theological education. At the time philosophical schools within Roman society were normal. These philosophical schools and their students put pressure on the Christian movement to make sense within the contemporary standards of reason. School models were adopted by some early Christian communities like the Gnostics (later ruled heretics). The early Church, because of some of these debates, was developing a set of authorized scriptures. These reasons caused the Church to get organized in its teaching ministry. For the most part, bishops turned a lot of this over to others—though there is evidence of the great philosophical minds among early bishops. The apologist was born out of necessity. These were individuals who had the responsibility of educating seekers and new believers. They too were essential to the instruction of future Church leaders.[677] Thus, we have in our Christian evolution, the creation of the Catechetical School of

Alexandria, which grew and had a profound impact upon the church (circa 170).

The Catechetical School in Alexandria prepared individuals for interaction with the culture in which the church found itself. It was at its greatest point under the leadership of Origen the Church's first systematic theologian—later a heretic.[678] The school provided its students with an understanding of the mission field (through courses on the profane sciences). It educated its students on the differences between secular philosophy and religious moral and philosophical perspectives. It also had a course on Christian theology to prepare those who attended for apologetic discourse with the secular philosophers. Origen developed the school with an eye to the Alexandrian and Jewish schools of the day. This was not education for education's sake. The sole purpose of the school was to prepare individuals to go out and make a case for Christianity in a pluralistic world. It was a school for the future leadership of the Church and for its missionaries.[679]

This was not a school like ours today. It was a group of disciples sitting with a master in a home. It was a personal model of formation. J. Lebreton and J. Zeilier, authors of an *Encyclopedia of Early Church History*, write, "[the teacher] transformed his disciples still more by his personal influence than by his scholarship. He was not a lecturer who merely appeared from time to time before an audience; he was a master and tutor who lived constantly with his disciples."[680] Schools grew up in many of the major Christian hubs of the ancient world: Alexandria, Caesarea, Antioch, Edessa, and Nisibis. The school in Nisibis was discontinued after it was decided they were heretics and the school in Edessa took some 800 of their students.[681] These were large schools by the end of the second century and necessary for forming leadership in the new and thriving Church organization.

The Church and its theological schools emerged from this time period as a jewel in the crown of the Roman Empire. However, 500 years after the resurrection of Christ, they had new pressures. By the time they reached The Middle Ages, but before the Protestant

Reformation, they had a completely different missionary context. The hordes of invaders had dismantled Roman society, and with it, many of its organizational tendencies. The Church had to survive—exposed because of the fall of its protective Empire. It also had to deal with a whole new people to whom an introduction of Christianity was needed—the barbarians. They were nothing like the Roman citizen schooled in philosophy.[682] It was during this time that we see the rise of monasticism. The monasteries provided an incubator for the next stage in theological education. It was from these centers of thinking that there was a rise of new missionary zeal. Beginning in the fourth century, from St. Basil of Caesarea and the Cappadocian Fathers, there was a clear movement to a more scholastic approach.[683] Irish monks and scholars prepared a whole new generation of missionaries that travel all over Western Europe and the British Isles. In turn they set up other monasteries and sent out more missionaries. The monasteries trained missionaries in how to share the monastic tradition. The Commune of Vaison (529) instructed "every monastic priest to take a child under his care, teach him the Psalter, liturgical rites and Christian morals 'to put him in the way to succeed him'."[684]

Theological schools organized by the local bishop (sometimes called bishop schools) continued to be a part of the theological education environment throughout The Middle Ages. The schools in Gaul, Canterbury and York taught Greek, Latin, music, astronomy for the Church calendar, ecclesiastical law, and liturgy to its pupils. The ninth century saw a requirement that every cathedral also have a school. Also, bishops had the duty of ensuring that their clergy received training. At the Council of Toledo in 675, bishops were to require clergy whose knowledge was deficient to remedy such deficiency.[685] This seems to indicate that theological education was not necessarily a prerequisite but that ordination could precede it.

By the end of The Middle Ages, the Church and Empire were once again united in the ruling of the state. Monasteries and schools were the primary places for priestly instruction. By the Fourth Lateran

Council in 1215, a bishop was still responsible for the training of clergy. However, the actual training had now moved on to the purview of universities. The rise of the university in the fourteenth and fifteenth centuries saw the first foundations of schools that look like our seminaries today. Moreover, the shift of duties by the bishop to affairs of state resulted in the handing over of priestly preparation to universities. These were primarily general programs that could include canon law and politics. Theology was post-graduate. The style of study was by then predominately lectures given by a community of teachers under the supervision of a warden or head of school.[686] Evangelism was in large part the domain of the brothers—the Dominicans and Franciscans who were focused on the un-churched and pastoral care for the people.[687] Scholasticism and formal education were the standard for most regular priestly formation.

The Protestant Reformation period reinvigorates theological education. By this time some form of formal education prior to ministry is the norm. The focus is upon preaching and teaching brought about by a Biblical Humanism. The rediscovery and focus upon biblical studies experienced resurgence. There are attempts at general examinations. The reformers took their task of reformation seriously and schools under John Calvin and Martin Bucer's direction were important centers for the movement. Preference in the reformed communities was given to ministers coming out of these schools; therefore, their influence across Europe was profound. On the now Roman side of the church there was the creation of a two-seminary model of preparation. The lesser seminaries, or local seminaries, were focused upon general theological education—the basics plus reading and writing. The greater Roman seminaries were to provide in-depth ministerial training in order to keep up with the Protestant reformers.[688] For example Claudio Acquavia, the Superior General of the Society of Jesus, 1581, wrote out a curriculum for Jesuit seminaries that was derived from Calvin's academic regulations.[689] General studies were done in lecture hall formats and more advanced studies were undertaken through a tutorial and self-learning style curriculum. Regardless of Church, Roman or Protestant, the universities were the primary seat of training for ministry. Rowden quotes the statutes of Sidney Sussex College, Cambridge, founded in 1596. The college is intended to be "with its regard for the Church, a kind of seminary in which we want only the best seeds to be planted, and these, when planted, watered by abundant showers from the branches of the sciences, until they have grown to such maturity that they may be thence transferred into the Church, so that it may by feasting richly upon their fruit grow into the fullness of Christ."[690] And, we never looked back.

During the American colonial period clergy were trained overseas and sent to America. Some concern grew in local congregations about the training of ministers for the new mission context. There was concern that the university model, with its classes and tutorial traditions, were creating some "gaps" and lack of consistency for graduates and practitioners. [691] Once again the mission context dictated that change was necessary. In 1808 the Massachusetts Congregationalists founded Andover Theological Seminary. Other denominations soon followed. This was the first seminary in the U.S. Our own Episcopal tradition founded General Seminary in New York in 1817, Virginia Theological Seminary in 1823, Yale Divinity School in 1854, and The Philadelphia Divinity School in 1857.

Most everyone agrees that today there is growing gap between the church and the seminary. Many students are new to Christianity and so do not have the basics of the faith, or a familial rooted understanding of their inherited faith. Therefore, students often have to begin with basic teaching about the Episcopal Church. Many potential missionaries and students find three-year residential programs inaccessible for many reasons and not all of them financial. Ethnic shifts in the broader culture are creating a strain on seminaries to prepare a diverse population of "culturally competent leaders" when most faculty themselves are not ethnically diverse.[692]

Michael Battle, former President of Interdenominational Theological Seminary, and current Ambassador to the African Union, said, "The church is necessary for the seminary, but the seminary is not necessary for the church."[693]

The issue is "theory-induced blindness."[694] We have accepted a theory that our current manner of formation tied to seminary education is the only tool for ministry preparation. Consequently, we have not known how to fix it and are blind to the new tools at our disposal. At the end of the day, the Church does not need seminaries that train clergy for the present-past, or look as they have for the last two hundred years. Seminaries training in old models, with old tools, behind self-imposed walls, and disconnected from the new mission context are seminaries preparing students for a church that is not going to exist in the future. These kinds of seminaries are not necessary to the formation of clergy for the future Church. Those graduating from seminary today, with the capacity to serve for 30 years, will be ministering in a world that will span to 2045.

The future Episcopal Church has a mission and that mission has to have missionaries. We have selected and formed missionaries for every age and this age is no different. The future Church will train leaders in a variety of settings, using a diversity of means. It will do so because the future Church will exist in a multi-dimensional world of varying contexts and needs for ministry. Standardization on the current large industrial platform does not work any longer. In some cases the future church, like the early church, will train clergy on an apprentice model—attaching future clergy to adept clergy. The future Church will increase its number of local theological schools, or bi-vocational schools, to train ministers. The future Church will demand that seminaries prepare students to be able to be adaptable and prepared for varying mission contexts. The future Church will want training entities to be adaptable themselves to diocesan needs and to the particular self-learner's demands. This will mean a disbursement system with satellites for easier, broader access.

Seminaries are a part of higher education in this country. As such they are tied to the shifts and movements taking shape. Author Anya Kamenetz is a writer for *Fast Company* magazine and a columnist for *Tribune Media Services.* She published a book entitled *DIY U.* In an Institute for the Future conference devoted to the future of higher education, she shared her views on the landscape. Today education is exorbitantly expensive to begin with. It is not accessible to people. And, education in its current form is not relevant. [695] The issue is that "in a knowledge economy, there's just a need for more and more education."[696] Kamenetz asks then, "Is the stuff that we're learning and the ways that we're learning it really relevant to the world we live in?"[697] The landscape of education includes The Khan Academy, which is a nonprofit, training anyone anywhere school. There is also P2PU, an online university that is peer-to-peer learning. Stanford University has launched Algorithms: Design and Analysis, part I. This is a free online course taught by Tim Roughgarden. In the class, you learn several fundamental principles of algorithm design: divide-and-conquer methods, graph algorithms, practical data structures (heaps, hash tables, search trees), randomized algorithms, and more.[698] This is all free to the online user. As we have seen in the previous chapter on formation there are emerging trends in self-learning with shifts in content, social networking, and accreditation. Like the themes in this book, IFTF suggests that students are in-between where we have been and where we are going. Marina Gorbis who was also at the conference said, "young people today are caught in the transition between two worlds—the world of institutional production of education and a new world of possibilities for highly personalized on-demand continuous learning."[699] The same is true for the seminary. As we move into a new missionary era, seminaries,- will be challenged to become the kind of seminaries the future Church needs. They will be challenged to become the kind of training school that students are familiar with.

Kamenetz says that universities will need to respond. Universities should "re-appropriate their existing infrastructures toward technology-forward [tools] with open resources for students."[700] This would include mapping out individual curricula in conversation with the student in order to amplify what they already know—giving credit for previous experience. The same is true for the seminary of the future. With the growth of bi-vocational schools, this is especially true for seminaries. How will the future seminary train through distance learning and create more accessible Anglican course curricula for both distance learners who are on an ordination track and laity working in a Christian Community? Seminary is not going away. The three-year residential program will not go away. But it must change. The seminary of the future has a responsibility to God and to God's church to prepare people for the future mission and its context. No matter how much money a seminary has or does not have, no matter how many students are enrolled, it is obligated by the very nature of serving God to lead into the future. Seminaries must provide cheaper, more accessible, and more relevant tools for training missionary leaders.

In her book, *The Nature of the Future*, Gorbis tells the story of a young man who taught himself architecture- Andy Rhimes.[701] Rhimes had been accepted into one of the finest architecture schools in the country. However, after one year, he decided to take some time off. He felt that he was doing work that was irrelevant. He had spent his teenage years excitedly collecting information and self-learning architecture. He found school disconnected with the excitement. On his own he had discovered Frank Gehry, Gaudi, Koolhouse, I. M. Pei— some of the greatest architects of the modern era. Rimes felt that he did not have time to think while in school. He left school after seven months and got a job working at a fast food restaurant. A friend told him about Socrates 2.0. This was a new platform that connected students with mentors in their desired fields. Rhimes found a mentor and went back to school—this time on his own terms. He was connected to others who were studying with his particular mentor. There was conversation and sharing of resources. He connected with museums, community colleges, and public lectures. Through the program, he learned about an app called ArchGenius that allows him to point his smart phone at an architecturally interesting building and get its history and details so he can literally learn on the street. Socrates 2.0 keeps track of his learning progress and helps him gain points towards his architect certification.[702] Rhimes is not alone in the growing number of students taking charge of their education.

Gorbis believes that we have, "like other areas of our economy, created an education system that is optimized for massive scale."[703] The future, Gorbis says, will be higher education that is easy to access, individualized, highly contextualized, ubiquitously free content, community driven, and has intrinsic rewards for meaningful learning.[704] This is the new currency with which seminaries must deal..

While the seminary has dominated our preparation for ministry for hundreds of years, their range of influence is shrinking. I do not believe, as do many that the seminary or the university will go away. I am more hopeful. The need for human conversation and personal interaction are essential in the learning process. Some of the most important conversations that take place are those outside the classroom where students and professors can engage in one on one self-directed study and thoughtful conversation. The foundations of this model are changing, and like every other area of the church there is a new ecology emerging and that ecology is the seminary of the future.

The future seminary will be a seminary that has moved from "episodic learning to learning flows."[705] The new reality is that people can learn all the time and everywhere. The idea that learning only takes place at the seminary in a classroom with a specialized theologian lecturing is an idea of the past. Handheld devices and an interconnected, Wi-Fi-available world will mean that people will have access to content, as they need it. How many times recently have you been in a conversation and you wanted to know more about something and you picked up your smart phone and found the answer? This new norm means there is a new content commons that spans human knowledge. It also means accessibility and networking will allow for collaborative platforms. The future seminary will be about providing continuous learning opportunities for the church— for laity, deacons, priests, and bishops. The seminary of the future will be the new learning hub offering resources of quality to those who need it when they need it. While this has been the domain of the wider Church organization and the diocese, the future seminary must take this up as their particular and unique voice within the wider community.

Another learning shift the future seminary will take is that it no longer will be focused on an exchange of resources.[706] Instead, the future seminary will be involved in collaborative work with self-learners to attract them into a learning community where the resources of the seminary are placed at their fingertips. The seminary of the future will have a new goal that is to have the best education *commons* available to entice learners into their particular setting. The seminary of the future will market its online information, its courses (online and in person), access to mentors and specialists, and participation in learning labs. The future seminary will live in a world that is diverse and where the amplified individual navigates from real world experience to Internet learning. This person will expect, as will the future Church, the seminary to adapt to a multiplatform engagement to prepare individuals for mission.

The future seminary will no longer be a conveyor of content only.[707] Instead the seminary of the future will be a curator of content for the church. The Internet is filled with information. This massive amount of theological information without any mentor/guide to evaluate and access is simply static. The seminary of the future will be focused upon making sense of the environment. The seminary will become a place (online and in person) where individuals know that the offered information is curated well. It will be easily accessible, easy to sort, easy to find, easy to consolidate, and easy to deliver.[708] The ability to deliver in any form the right information resources at the right time and in the right mission context will be a leveraging point that differentiates the seminary of the future from the past. The goal will be to build capacity, church-wide, by providing (for example) a brilliant lecture on missiology to students in the room, to students online, and to thousands and thousands of interested church members trying to sort out their context.[709] This means that the seminary is curating information and sharing in a variety of forms for a variety of purposes. Nothing is wasted or lost as the seminary of the future multiplies its reach through modules, courses, and widely available tools.

The future seminary will understand that it is no longer working at one scale, but up and down the scale.[710] The seminary of the past is physically built for large scale. New technology creates a whole new scale. A small classroom now has the potential for huge scale. Sebastian Thrun at Stanford University taught a class in artificial intelligence to 150,000 online students.[711] The seminary of the future will consistently work at scales larger than any it saw in its previous history. The seminary of the future will then be able to offer personal courses of study and avenues for learning creating the ability to reach students from all over the church and many different countries.

In recent years seminaries have moved away from fieldwork requirements, where students worked in congregations. I believe this trend will reverse and more field work and tinkering around mission will become a part of the fabric of learning. The students will be challenged to use their studies in local congregations, new communities, and new service work. Trinity Seminary, Ambridge, Pennsylvania is doing this work well as it integrates teaching and church starts. It also trains people for ministry through their distance-learning program. Meanwhile, other Episcopal seminaries have lagged behind despite encouragement and grants. Practicing ministry and studying are an important part of the learning process and fits in the mentor/learner model.

Currently, the seminary of the present past is focused on offering degrees. The seminary of the future must make a shift from awarding degrees to reputation metrics.[712] There will still be a place for the awarding of degrees, but this will not be the main focus, the main money maker, or the most needed prize that the seminary offers the future Church. Instead, the seminary of the future will understand that what is needed is a multiplication of learning platforms. In the world outside the seminary walls today, there are a variety of ways in which people share opinions, views, review products, and institutions via Yelp, Facebook, Urbanspoon and the like. Recently a poll taken through one of these services (oDesk) asked individuals to rank the reasons they chose a contractor. In their ranking criteria the possession of a degree was at the bottom of the list. At the top of the list was the individual's performance on a task.[713] What this illustrates in a microcosm is the wider shift in the culture to the performance and product that is delivered as more important than the degree a person holds. The future Church will already know that what is important is the mission, and that this mission can be, and has been, undertaken by all kinds of people with all kinds of backgrounds, and with all kinds of education. The future Church will be hyper-focused on mission and so it, too, is looking for individuals who can do mission. The future seminary will place all its energy in aiding these future leaders to be successful. It will continue to offer residential programs and degrees. The seminary of the future will also offer weekend programs and non-residential online learning certificates. This is an intentional transaction change from gaining money through fulltime residential student enrollment for future priests to overall engagement with missionaries, of every kind, in providing resources and classes for success.

The future seminary will move from a grade-centered curriculum to a continuous feedback loop.[714] The growing ability to gain analytical information and to build reputation through assessment is changing the way in which individuals reflect upon their work with mentors. The future seminary will use tools that better create an evaluation of the individual based upon the mastery and performance of skill, rather than the one (sometimes questionable) grade. The seminary of the future will improve student learning by providing continuous feedback on their work overall. These kinds of metrics are already present in Socrates 2.0 and The Kahn Learning Academy. Anyone who has participated in an online course for credit knows how the new metrics are being used to gauge class participation, for instance. The seminary of the future will use everything in its power to create better, more self-reflective tools for students, as opposed to simply giving grades and writing a letter to the bishop telling them of their student's progress.

General Ordination Exams (GOE's) and other standardized tests will go the way of the large lecture halls. Individualized and diverse mission contexts will call for a variety of reflective tools to show preparedness for ministry. This diversity alone will push the future seminary into a learning community where intake of information and output of information are no longer the standards of success. The future seminary will know that providing continuous feedback platforms for those participating in their community are necessary in order to have the best performance in the mission field. This will not end with their studies. Remember, the future of learning is lifelong learning.

Imagine a person listens to a seminary professor give a talk on the origins of the Christian Church via their Facebook page. They continue to pull seminary presentations from a variety of schools while they grow in their faith through local ministry. After being licensed to preach they are taking classes online and starting a new community. They take their first official class at the seminary while they are in their discernment process. Then they take their first year online while working at their job and continuing their ministry. They take a mix of classes while in residence and online throughout the rest of their studies amplifying skills they already have and investigating new areas of Christian thought with which they are not familiar. After graduation the self-learning priest continues with online courses (and from time to time in person short courses) to sharpen their preaching and communication skills. Continuing education will have a whole new meaning and the seminary of the future will be its hub.

The future seminary must invest in providing collaborative spaces.[715] There will be a shift in the physical space of learning. We can already see this in new business space designs. There is a need for collaborative space where students can plug in, hook up, and connect with one another in person and online. There is a need for more small group and one-on-one spaces for mentoring and working with apprentices. Smaller home/local school type environments like the first and second century will be present throughout the geography of the future seminary as it looks at making such space available in a building or in a chat room online. Classroom flipping will become more normative in the future seminary. This is where individuals view lectures online at home, while in person, the students spend time in conversation, collaborative projects, and learning labs.[716] The seminary will also be a provider of hacker and maker spaces. This is where members of the wider church and the public can participate in the learning pilgrimage. The future seminary becomes a host to theocurious individuals, who are interested in learning more about the church or helping with a particular mission context issue.

The seminary of the future will focus on training both lay and ordained for mission. Providing a new learning ecology online with inexpensive tools, and new ways of creating learning space and collaboration will all be the hallmarks of the future seminary. The seminary will understand that there is a new wave of makers who are invested in seeing the future Church alive and flourishing. The makers are willing to do what they need to do, and the future seminary is ready to help empower them, raising the best spiritually and theologically prepared missionaries. Regardless of whether or not the student is to be bivocational or full time, the seminary of the future will help to ensure that the future missionary is undergirded with sound Biblical scholarship, healthy ministry practices, and a wealth of resources to form unabashed Episcopalians.

There are some artifacts of the future seminary in our midst. Over ten years ago Mary MacGregor and I, and a few others, gathered in a room and came up with a theological school concept for training laity and clergy. MacGregor did the lion's share of the work and brought life to The IONA School. The Diocese of Texas created a way to train bi-vocational clergy who could not leave their homes and their employment for three years to attend residential seminary. The Rev. Sam Todd joined the effort and put together a brilliant faculty to teach. The team is largely made up of PhDs who are adjunct or retired seminary/university faculty members. Today, thanks to the innovation of The Rt. Rev. Dena Harrison, and collaboration with the Seminary of the Southwest, in Austin, the school has spread to over 10 dioceses. This is a great example of how seminaries can redefine themselves and serve as a learning hub for the wider Church. The future of the school will be dependent on how well it begins to multiply itself online and create real time community between the different schools for mutual and shared learning. Other dioceses are starting local schools also. These are smaller, regional collaborations which are more pliable than the former seminary type structures. Trinity School for Ministry was an early adopter of online training in our denomination; others are following. This is a place where seminaries could learn from one another and share their experiences in order to improve accessibility across all of the seminaries. There are numerous lay programs popping up across seminary campuses. These tend to be regional and largely inaccessible to people who do not live in the local area. How well the seminaries open up these programs online will gauge their long-term participation in the future seminary movement. There are also seminaries experimenting with new models of library accessibility like the eBook reader project in the province of South Africa. There is a shortage of librarians to take care of the massive number of discarded and aging theological texts filling libraries that remain largely inaccessible to students in the vast areas of Africa. The Rt. Rev. Dr. Thabo Makgoba has launched a project that will give access to students of the great theological and other libraries of the world.[717] In 2014, Virginia Theological Seminary held an *eformation* conference that shared formation media rich formation tools. They held the gathering as a learning lab. Acting as a resource, the seminary offered a vision of how cultural shifts are changing the way individuals engage the spiritual journey.

L. Gregory Jones is Vice President and Vice Provost for Global Strategy and programs at Duke University, where he is also professor of theology in the Divinity School. In the magazine *The Christian Century*, he writes to the present day seminaries and their leadership, "Incremental changes are insufficient."[718] The changing missionary context is causing "tectonic" shifts.[719] He lists: "the digital revolution; the emergence of a 'multinodal' world of complicated ethnic relationships and cultural dynamics, both within the United States and globally; changing patterns of denominations and new forms of congregating; the questioning of—and cynicism about—institutions; economic stresses on Christian organizations that challenge old business models and press issues of sustainability; shifting vocations of laypeople; and the lure of cities."[720] Jones calls for "clarity about why theological education is important and a willingness to experiment—and to experiment in ways richly connected to the best of our traditions."[721]

The future Church will require its seminaries to be part of the education of the larger population of DIY missionaries. These are the amplified Christians who are eager to innovate, design, modify, and make things on their own and in collaborative groups for the sake of God's mission of reconciliation.[722] The future seminary, like its church, must value open collaboration. It will tap into networks and platforms that enable self-organizing structures for local adaption. The future seminary will be characterized by openness to the future, self-learning, continuous reflection and adaptation based upon the needs of the mission field. It will invest in capacity-building, and in bringing down the cost of learning by multiplying access and participation. The future seminary will empower community building. It is focused upon the ultimate goal (not of educating clergy) of building Christian communities of health and wellness throughout the world.

The future Episcopal seminary must reclaim the meaning of being a missionary organization. What Gorbis writes about higher education goes for the future seminary as well. Its promise is to "bring passion, self-direction, and social connectivity into our lives and into our work. At its best, social structuring creates a promise to turn what has been directed and ordained by institutions into a labor of love. It is about turning education into a highly personalized and socially embedded experience."[723] The success of the future seminary will be measured on how well it understands the mission focus of the future Church it aims to serve.

CHAPTER TWENTY-TWO
Future Diocese, Future Wider Church

*"No body of knowledge needs an organizational policy. Organizational policy
can only impede the advancement of knowledge. There is a basic
incompatibility between any organization and freedom of thought."*
— *William S. Burroughs, Ali's Smile*

At the core of a missionary Episcopal Church is a bishop serving
God's people and undertaking service and evangelism for the sake of
reconciliation. The only reason to have a diocese is to help organize
the mission of a particular area, and to stay out of the way of a living
Church making its missionary journey. The only reason to have a
wider church organization is to organize the mission for a particular
region. Everything else is extra. This has been the essence of our
structure and it continues to be so today. Sure, we can add a lot of
other things to it. Those who are the elite power brokers in the
organization will tell us that their parts are also essential. This is not
true, though. It is a lie one leader tells its Church citizens in order to
maintain their place in power. The Church would continue to make
its way in the world without all that we pretend is necessary. Our
structures have been and forever will be a utilitarian exoskeleton for
the real work of God's Holy Spirit. What we know today is that this
skeleton and all its scaffolding and framework which we have so
labored to construct no longer works. It no longer protects us. It no
longer enables us to be agile in the culture. It no longer supports the

mission efforts of our Church. The present church is organized to operate in a context that no longer exists. The same pressures that all major manufacturing companies and institutions face in this time period are the same pressures the church faces. Companies as large organizations for a single purpose have existed to minimize transaction cost. They were created in order to buy at quantity and buy down cost of production. Their mission was to create a smoother transaction and delivery. Their massive mechanical production lines cut down on mistakes and saved time. Every cog had a wheel, every wheel had a person to man it, and the machine was well oiled, competition was low, and life in the corporate world was good. Over the last ten years though, the corporate world has been restructuring. Vision and mission work in the boardrooms have been undertaken to rethink whole companies. Mergers and acquisitions, increased resource sharing, and building mammoth organizations, were all for the sake of increased control and decreased risk. The world of business and the machine of the company have radically changed in the new world of communication and technology. The shift from manufacturing things to an information economy, and the rise of local makers in their garages, where the hobbyist competes with the professional, has changed almost everything. The legacy of the twentieth century is the last vestige of a modern machine era with companies and organizations that look like and work like the era from which they came. They have too many interests and too much capital tied up in the wrong things to make the shift easily. So these modern companies are struggling with purpose and they are not easily finding their place in the market around them. The church organization (diocesan and church wide) is no different.

Frederick Hayek was an Austrian born British economist who lived through most of the twentieth century. He argued that the centralized economy could not exist because of the impossible need to control things. Not unlike Nassim Taleb, he understood that the health of society was not dependent on large organizations that are actually more fragile, but on smaller ones that enable a better more disbursed economy. In part, Hayek simply believed in the freedom of individuals to create, market, sell and disburse goods in a much more efficient and free manner. The centralized organization and economy required too many controls over the whole economic and social state. He used a term called *catallaxy* to describe a "self-organizing system of voluntary co-operation" as the primary means of economic vitality. The Nobel Committee used his argument for self-organizing systems in their press statement awarding him the Nobel Prize in 1974.[724] Hayek believed in a spontaneous order within economics that was not unlike the development of language within society. Centrally planning an economy is impossible because society itself is inherently decentralized, and would need to be brought under control. While Hayek was looked at as having missed the boom in large corporations and the economic entanglement of government and business in the middle of the last century, he is now being turned to again as the new information economy and maker movements are beginning to mimic his catallaxy theory.[725] What Hayek intrinsically knew is that the power of innovation in the hands of the people will beat the centralized organization.[726]

We are today departing the mechanistic age that brought with it huge complicated bureaucracies.[727] Margaret Wheatley writes, "We now speak in earnest of more fluid, organic structures, of boundary-less and seamless organizations."[728] The Church is a whole system. It is a network of individuals who are seeking and learning—it is a learning organism. People in their basic nature are self-organizing.[729] They do it in different ways but they connect and create society naturally because we are meant to live in community with one another. The foundations of the new infrastructure for the Church will be built upon the self-organizing, self-learning, socially structured mission context in which we find ourselves.[730] The reorganization will be a *catallaxy*.

The reorganization will be brought about by a mutual adjustment of the meet-ups, un-conferences, community websites, and crowds that make up the future Church.[731] Because of our innate ability to have our own biases within the structure, it is difficult to see this self-organizing as anything other than fringe movements. However, they are quickly becoming the mainstream. The Church will have to make a conscious shift to engage at the many levels where it finds its citizenry. The mission organization of the future no longer outsources to a structure or bureaucracy the work that individuals can do for themselves. The professional elite mission organization is now in the hands of a new citizenship that is eager to innovate for the sake of the Gospel of love and reconciliation.[732]

The present church is just now taking its first messy steps upon the new journey that is leading to the future organization. Everyone has a part in the change. The change is happening, and as the reorganization begins the question is: how will each person act and react in the midst of variation from the norm, chaos, information overload, entrenched behaviors, and new ways of doing Church? The Church is a vessel of a wily Holy Spirit that is moving and creating. The Church is an organism characterized by probabilities and potential. It is an organization to be sure, but organizational thinking in the past has tended towards a mechanistic and deterministic strategy. In today's culture such organizations are fragile and failing. It is weakened by the VUCA world around it. The future Church will be a Church that possesses tremendous tensile strength, a capacity to grow, to be autopoietic, and to adapt to its new mission context. It must do this because it is always and everywhere made up of people who are not living in a diaspora, but in the midst of the mission context itself.[733]

The Episcopal Church is organized by diocese, and it also has a church-wide structure. We have a way of doing mission together—an economy. Aristotle was the first to use the word economy. He used it to describe "the art of household management."[734] Aristotle was trying to explain the way markets worked and drew parallels between the smallest organization and the largest. Originally the term diocese itself (Gr. *dioikesis*) meant the economy or management of a household.[735] In Roman law, a diocese was a geographic region dependent upon a city for its administration.[736] We might remember here how Ambrose was the governor of the area that included Liguria and Emilia, but he lived in Milan. This is an example of how a diocese is dependent upon its city for administration in the Roman system. Circa the end of the third century, Emperor Diocletian designed twelve dioceses, twelve great divisions, and established them in the empire, and over each he placed a *vicarious* or vicar.[737] It was into this Roman society and form of government that Christianity grew— adopting its terms and organization.

In the beginning there were no particular rules for the organization of the church. It was autopoietic in nature. It was in fact a self-organizing system of communities that were created by the movement of the Holy Spirit, and the spreading of the good news of God in Christ Jesus. The first organization we see deference to the Apostles and their successors. As the Church grew there seems to be some further deference given to the local apostles or apostolic connections. For instance, we see early on James, the brother of Jesus, who is connected with the church in Jerusalem. Most likely the first communities were connected with Jewish communities and synagogues in the cities. They would be organized as such until being kicked out sometime after 70 C.E. There were also societies and other rural movements, as we have previously discussed. The new gentile Christians created communities of their own. We see evidence of this throughout the New Testament. A new Christian might then join a neighborhood community nearby. Most scholars believe that during this nascent beginning of the Christian movement, there was not a lot of organization to be administered. An Apostle during this time or apostolic leader would have simply overseen the community life— this would have been his domain of authority. Like St. James in Jerusalem, we see Ignatius of Antioch and Polycarp of Smyrna emerge by the end of the first century as having some organizational authority over the Christian community in these townships. At this time we still don't have any formal authority over a jurisdiction or its administration. The diocese in these first years does not really exist. The mission of the Church is purely an act of an apostolic leader and growing community. The church is like a grape vine. Christ is the stem, the people are its branches and it is bearing much fruit. (John 15.1-8) There was a great dependence upon the Holy Spirit and its movement upon the Church of the day. We should not overly organize the metaphor that Christ gives us, because for over one hundred years the church quite literally was not much of an organization, and was much more an organism.

In the Church's second century, as we have already seen in discussions about the *Didache* and the *Apostolic Constitutions*, there is a growing set of rules and expectations about the ministry of the Church and a natural turning to the apostolic authority (the bishop) for the oversight of how people come into faith, the administration of the sacraments, and the general teaching of the Church. By the middle of the third century each Christian community of any means had a bishop at its center. At least in the East, these places with Bishops in residence were called the diocese.[738]

We also know that these bishops and their dioceses seem to have grown up around communities of size and in urban areas. There were bishops in the country districts as well and in smaller towns. These were rural bishops called *Chorepiscopi*.[739] They would eventually be merged into the then more formalized diocese as time passed.[740] In Egypt alone by the fourth century there were over one hundred bishops and jurisdictions. This was seen by the list of bishops attending the Council of Alexandria.[741] At the same time, the western and northern regions had fewer bishops, and they were more spread out with wider dioceses to oversee.[742] By the fourth century (about the same time as the Diocletian changes) the diocese and its supervision more closely resembled the Roman government structure. Most cities had a bishop and a territory with boundaries. Not everyone thought this was how it should be. St. Innocent, in 415, did not share the idea that the Church should follow the exact boundaries of the state. Nevertheless by the Council of Chalcedon in

451, the local bishop operated within a diocese that closely resembled the same boundaries defined by the state. The bishop was responsible for the economy of the church for that region. When it was changed by the Roman state, the Church would respond by making modification.[743]

After settling into this habit of mimicking state geography and organization, dioceses remained largely unchanged. The bishop was supported by a host of presbyters/priests and deacons. New churches were founded and bishops were put in place to oversee their growth and ministry. The evolution moved from every church having a bishop to the bishop having oversight of priests and deacons, overseeing the local work at the church where the bishop was not present. The role of the bishop shifted from being a leader of a single church to being a geographic apostolic representative.[744] It is clear, throughout the writings of the pre-Reformation period, that the purpose of the bishop and the diocesan organization were for the mission of the Gospel.

When the Roman Empire fell at the feet of the invading armies, much of the society turned to the organized Church for support. Bishops Leo I in the fifth century, and Gregory I in the fifth century, were statesmen and public administrators, raising armies, taxing, and overseeing the mission and teaching of the Church. The civil society in the east was stronger politically, and so the bishops did not take on the same powers as in the west. In the west this trend of bishops as a mix of religious and civic authority continued. In many western states the bishops served as chancellors and heads of the court. When we think of the theological education throughout this time period, it is not surprising that the clergy tended to be well educated. The Lord Chancellor of England was almost always a bishop up until the dismissal of Cardinal Thomas Wolsey by Henry VIII.

How a diocese was created, the purpose of the diocesan structure, and the administrative work of the bishop were in large part the same throughout the time of the Reformation and into the post-Reformation period. The Church of England, among other churches, sent clergy over to the new colonies to oversee the mission work and to serve as chaplains to the colonists.

Prior to the American Revolution, The Church of England in the colonies was linked to the diocesan leadership of the Bishop of London. The tradition imparted to the colonies was largely one of an established Christian culture and society where the domain and control of the bishop with his clergy was seen as an ordinary part of both religious and civic society (this being an artificial boundary that they would not have understood). The work of the church was to help govern, to oversee the moral discipline of the people, and to help generally improve society.[745] After 1702, the Society for the Propagation of the Gospel in Foreign Parts (SPG) began missionary activity throughout the colonies. On the eve of the American Revolution, about 400 independent congregations were reported throughout the colonies, with over 300 clergy—most of whom were loyalists to the British Crown.[746]

After the American Revolution the English Church pulled back its mission efforts and the Church looked towards other countries for support. It is important to understand that in this time period the Church of England in the Americas almost died. Because of the varying kinds of churches that had been created across the colonies, the DNA of the American Episcopal Church was not yet set. There were small conventions that met. They gathered local congregations and their leadership together to discuss the issues of mission and organization. There were no bishops. These conventions argued over the importance of having bishops, the nature of the church, and the importance of clergy. In the end, the Episcopal Church in Connecticut elected Samuel Seabury as bishop in 1783. He sought consecration in England but because of The Oath of Supremacy[747], he could not be ordained. So the Church turned to Scotland, and he was ordained in Aberdeen on November 14, 1784.[748] Seabury was to be "the first Anglican bishop appointed to minister outside the British Isles".[749] One year later, the American Episcopal Church was ordaining its own clergy.

The fledgling Episcopal Church gathered representatives in its first General Convention in 1789, with representative clergy from nine dioceses meeting in Philadelphia to ratify the Church's initial constitution, thereby becoming the first Anglican Province outside of the British Isles.[750] The Church took on governance that mimicked the new country, and ordered itself in a democratic federalist structure. The church was to be, for the purpose of mission, a constitutional confederacy of interdependent dioceses.[751] It was to be called the Domestic and Foreign Missionary Society and it began its first foreign mission in Texas and the West. The challenges in governance in this new era were unity in the face of major differences on liturgy, and tensions between clergy and lay authority. The new Church also struggled with the creation of a prayer book and specifically how were bishops to relate in the wider Church organization. It also faced an important goal of spreading the Gospel across the western frontier. It would resolve most of these differences becoming a strong, powerful, and influential church by the twentieth century. It was the self-organizing of the new Americans that sought to establish and continue the practices of the Church of England in this newly formed country. In the absence of a hierarchy and structure, the people gathered and organized themselves for mission.

America grew and changed over the next century, and the Episcopal Church changed with it. The industrial revolution had a profound impact upon business and corporations. It had an impact upon the Church as well. There was a mutual shared leadership between the wider society and the Episcopal Church. Membership included J. P. Morgan, Astors, Vanderbilts, Harrimans, and Henry Ford.[752] These were not always the best examples of Episcopal citizenry. The Church was intermingled with the largest number of leaders in business and banking across the U.S. with its influence continuing into the twenty-first century.[753] The twentieth century would be the peak of the Episcopal Church's self-confidence. It focused its governance on becoming the unofficial national church—

all the while it was engaging in mission in Haiti and all over the world. It was the height of the industrial age, and so the Episcopal Church with its industrial leaders formed itself through further governance standardization. It was concerned with the work of the modern corporation that was command and control, centralization of mission and ministry. The growth of program and administrative bureaucracies would be the hallmarks of this period of organizational change. After all, the Episcopal Church had become one of the largest protestant denominational churches. Membership grew from 1.1 million members in 1925, to a peak of over 3.4 million members in the mid-1960s.[754] This included the dioceses in the U.S. and a multinational mission field that stretched across the globe. In 1930s the Church went through an organizational change, and prayer book revision. The organizational change placed within its governance structures the denominational paradigm of big church with a franchise approach to mission both domestic and foreign.[755]

By the 1960's the Church had moved into a central Church Office and had a Presiding Bishop CEO model. While the church focused upon racial equality and social justice, the model of governance shifted, as did the governance structures of large successful corporations, and the state, to a form of regulatory agency.[756] Cultural upheavals, disagreements about women's ordination, the ordination of gay and lesbian clergy, and continued liturgical revision marked this period. The end of the era, when the world listened to the Church, has meant a lot of time spent at every level continuing legislation in convention that goes largely unheard in wider cultural circles and social context. The new media environment has tended to keep the dysfunction and disunity of the Church on the front page, while the profound impact it is having in terms of social engagement and service is relegated to the back page, if covered at all.

The Episcopal Church, like every large denomination, has decreased in numbers and programs, while not drastically reorganizing for the new mission context or evolving needs of the church and mission it is meant to serve. The bishops and their clergy are inundated with organizational requirements that are artifacts of a bygone industrial era. The focus on hierarchy, structure, and governance that is modeled on a corporate reality that is now over 80 years old no longer works. There is a growing disconnect between those who lead and the grass roots movements of lay mission and service. The Church is still mired in culture wars, wringing its hands over shrinking attendance, and trying to save itself by better budgeting in the wake of shrinking resources. The present past Church organization that exists today continues to look back in an attempt to sustain aging structures, force uniformity over unity, and create diversity by legislation at conventions.

The Task Force on Reimaging the Church (TREC) was created to help guide the church through a new time of reorganization for mission. They released this statement regarding the current state of Church governance: "Yet this 'national church' ideal did not stand the test of time, and reductions in the centralized staff and program began in the early 1970s. Since then, The Episcopal Church (like many denominations) has sought to exert influence over congregations and dioceses through church wide regulations, even as the trust that once bound Episcopalians together across structures has eroded."[757] TREC then posed these questions: What does a 21st century missionary Episcopal Church need from its church-wide organization? What functions and activities should best take place at the church-wide level, rather than regional or local levels? What should be funded through a centralized budget? What should be mandated for all congregations and dioceses, and what should best be left to local discernment and discretion? Who should participate in what kinds of decisions? What primary challenges can a church wide organization help The Episcopal Church address?"[758]

The organization at the diocesan level and the church-wide level does not serve the new mission context well. In the Diocese of Texas, we recently embarked on a time of reflection and thinking through of our diocesan canons. The unified voice of the committee was summed up in the words of Bishop Harrison who said to our

Executive Board, and to me, "The canons describe a Church I no longer recognize."

The problem with our current situation is that we can see on the one hand that our organization does not work. On the other hand we are invested in how it works now. The problem remains that what we are most afraid of is how change will affect us as individuals, our power, and our authority. Michael C. Jackson, in his text *Systems Approaches to Management*, writes, "The things we fear most in organizations—fluctuations, disturbances, imbalances—need not be signs of an impending disorder that will destroy us. Instead, fluctuations are the primary source of creativity."[759] With an understanding that the church-wide organization and the diocese have always found a creative way to undertake its mission, we look from the past into the future.

Let me introduce you to the Coasean ceiling, the Coasean floor, and scalability. Every, and I mean *every*, organization and institution has operating costs. The church has an economy, an operating cost that is real—time, money, and energy. The Coasean ceiling is the point above which the transaction costs of managing a congregation, a diocese, or a church-wide organization prevent it from working well. The Coasean floor is the point below which the transaction costs of a particular type of activity, no matter how valuable to someone, are too high for the congregation, diocese, or church-wide organization to pursue. Nobel Prize winning economist Ronald Coase, in his 1937 paper "The Nature of the Firm" introduced the world to this key to economic viability.[760]

The Dutch East India Company was chartered in 1602. It is truly the first organization of its type to figure out how massive scale creates an ability to work between the floor and ceiling. By keeping prices managed within the market, so they are not too high for people to actually purchase merchandise, while at the same time lowering operational cost, the institution itself can increase profits and share of the economy. The Dutch East India Company did just that. They created organizational structures that managed the operational cost between the floor and ceiling.[761] As other companies followed suit, and their industry grew, new corporate models of the church went along too. Recently, I read the book by Simon Winchester entitled *Krakatoa: The Day the World Exploded.* In it, he made a side comment about how the missionaries followed the trade industry. The growing corporation model influenced the Church, along with its missionary movement of the nineteenth and twentieth centuries. Accessibility, scalability, and manageability were all part of the diocesan infrastructure concerns for the church as they were with any business. Intentionally or subconsciously, the church has been, for the most part of the last two hundred years, managing to keep its diocese—its economy—within the floor and ceiling Coase describes.

Managers manage the corporate model by helping to build scalability within the organization. Scalability is when the corporation is increasing its reach while doing so at a minimum cost, thereby increasing profits. It is the way of the corporate model. We cannot imagine a Church organization that does not think in terms of managing its economy. We are consistently managing salaries, income, and service to members and to the world. We are managing the Coasean floor and ceiling. When you sit at a vestry meeting, talking about the budget with a Starbucks coffee in your hand you are an example of how this model has affected both industry and the Church.

In his book, *Life Inc,* Douglas Rushkoff makes the case that "corporatism" has colonized everything. The corporate DNA has saturated our language, our institutions, our non-profits, and our media.[762] The Church in the mid-twentieth century with its mission expansion, growth in programing, growth in staffing and growth in average Sunday attendance was an era of scalability. It was a time when the Church, like every other organization, grew. While many will claim a lot of reasons for the shrinking size of the Episcopal Church in our time, the reason may be as simple as the fact that we have not changed our organization to match the changing missionary context, thereby keeping our economy operating between the floor and ceiling. Technology leader, lecturer, and consultant Clay Shirky points out that it is the same for everyone. It happens all the time. "[Every] institution lives in a kind of contradiction: it exists to take advantage of group effort, but some of its resources are drained away by directing that effort. Call this the institutional dilemma—because an institution expends resources to manage resources, there is a gap between what those institutions are capable of in theory and in practice, and the larger the institution, the greater those costs."[763] Our dilemma came when we did not keep our focus on the mission, and instead shifted our focus to the organization itself. We have tried to manage ourselves out of the current situation by shrinking our budgets and doing less with less. We turned inward and tried to accomplish keeping everything the same but just doing it for less. Meanwhile the growing cost of doing business kept rising.

The nation's economy affects everything from the salary of clergy, the giving of parishioners and the budget of the congregation. We looked at these economic effects in chapter two but it is important to have a quick review as we examine the interplay between local congregation and wider Church organizations. What we know is that an overall picture of inflation reveals an average annual inflation rate of 3.22%. This has essentially doubled every 20 years in the last 100. Therefore, an average congregation in the Episcopal Church operating between the Coase's floor and ceiling has to maintain 64 people every Sunday and an average pledge of $2,491. It cannot lose any members (or their pledges) *and* it has to add one individual/family every January, which immediately pledges the average amount in order to keep up with the operating cost on a pure inflation model. If a pledging member dies, gets angry, or moves away, then the church must replace two pledgers. This is an impossible task given the shrinking average Sunday Attendance and budgets over the last 50 years. Now add to your mental picture of this difficulty the increase in diocesan and church-wide askings.

Historically, the bishop and the organization have been responsible for the administration of the Church's mission. The local diocese and church-wide organization has not paid any attention to the congregations' operating revenues, and their floor and ceiling. Instead they have continued to increase the cost of doing business. Yes, the money has increased, but it is inflationary. The percentages of the diocesan and church wide askings have increased too. Having built program staffs, ministries, committees and commissions, the dioceses also have faced financial crises. This has affected the wider Church organization. We have seen percentages of shared giving up to as high as 21% of income from parishes. This has drained money from the local mission field and moved it up to the wider church structures. No business continues to increase its overall revenue while shrinking the cash in hand to do its work at a local level.

Think of franchising for a minute. The franchise model works this way: You pay an upfront fee for the organization's business strategy, marketing strategy, operations strategy, and the use of its name. That's pretty much what franchising is—you are establishing a relationship with a successful business so you can use its systems and capitalize on its existing brand awareness in order to get a quicker return on your own investment. You are using its proven system and name, and running it by its rules. You are getting supplies with a recognizable name at a lower cost because the franchise itself manages the floor and ceiling for you. You are allowed to put your franchise in a location where the franchise believes you will do well and where there will be customers. I say all of this because it is important to understand one very basic fact: the diocese and wider church are to do everything it can to make their local churches successful given their missionary context. Any organization that continues to take more and more income in the face of less and less money with higher cost of doing business is essentially cannibalizing its own organization. Since the 1960's the Episcopal Church, and almost every other denomination, operating in the present past, has effectively mismanaged the Coasean floor and ceiling of its economy.

In order to do its work in the current mission context, it is the responsibility of the mission institution (the diocese and wider Church) to create a shared ministry model that is focused on the local Christian community and its efficient and effective mission work. Over the last 30 or more years, diocesan and wider church leadership have continuously abdicated their responsibility and scapegoated congregations as the primary reason for the failure of mission. In an Episcopal model, it is the responsibility of the Bishop in conversation with the wider Church, to lead the change needed to affect new mission revitalization. The future Church must understand its responsibility, theologically and historically, for the economy of the spiritual household, and must be engaged in a dynamic local partnership with its clergy and congregations / communities.

The future Church will invest in the mission success of its congregations. It will lead with vision and build unity by understanding the shared interests and needs of the organizations under its care. It will create processes and procedures that are limited to the needs and success of the local mission context. Always remembering that the local Christian community exists purely for the sake of the reconciling mission of God, the diocese and wider Church will be there to support and help. The future Church must understand that it has to support the local community by doing those things that only the local community cannot do for itself. Many diocese and church wide organizations believe that this is an additive process. The local church cannot do something, so the diocese will do it, and we can all participate. Here is an example: The local church cannot support the program of the lollipop guild, so the diocese picks it up and supports it and budgets for it by using gifts from all the churches/communities for its underwriting. This is well and good in a program model. This is how it worked in the present past Church. The future Church will ask if the lollipop guild is necessary for the success of the mission in the local context and if it is, the wider church underwrites it, and if it is not necessary for the success of local mission, the wider church will not fund it. The future Church must understand it is responsible for multiplying and spreading efforts on the ground that effectively enhance the mission of service and evangelism. If the ministry does not directly enhance the local mission, it will not be taken on by the wider diocese and not funded.

The future Church will be fully aware of the trends we have been talking about and will focus on creating Christian communities that engage the amplified individual. The structures and the governance of the overall organization will be attuned to the trajectory of the "personal empowerment" trends.[764] The customization that all individuals are used to will be the same customization the diocesan structure must be attentive to. There will be an expectation that a one size fits all program model is not acceptable. The future diocese is aware that interactive media (from Facebook to games like Call of Duty), conscious economic social power (online giving and tweet donations), new commons for shared experiences (foreign missionaries and flash mobs) are all key ingredients to the new amplified church citizen's world. Just as they are constantly placing themselves and their experiences out in the world, they too expect the organizations they are part of to give them space for mass conversation that participates in organizational direction. These are qualities that are expected from the organizations they interact with—both big and small.[765]

The qualities that have emerged in our discussion about the culture and mission context are: self-agency, self-customization, self-organization, and self-learning. We are clear that we are in midst of a massive shift from digital vs. physical, to the digital and physical becoming enmeshed. We know that everything will be tagged so that amplified individuals will be able to find and discover the world around them. These digital natives are our parishioners and our neighbors.[766] We know that The Occupy movement and the Arab Spring are only two examples of how amplified individuals and super connected communities will mobilize for the common ideals in the future. Self-organizing mobs are going to become more and more common. Whether networking for politics, to raise disaster relief funds, clean up the community, build something, or discuss a book. Such connectivity will bring with it the power to shape economic markets, politics, and relationships within real-time communities.[767] The future Church organization will be accustomed to dealing with how the amplified individuals meet-up and accomplish tasks and set goals. The future Church will know that regular swarms and mobs are the new teams. It will be immersed in and uses the crowd list/friend list and has discarded the Rolodex. It must be aware of how quickly "dark mobs" might emerge and move against the best interest of the organization; therefore, it will be prepared to deal with this eventuality through communication strategies that link the diocese, parishioners and their broader networks together. The Church will understand that such eventualities are an opportunity to be grasped and not something that can be prevented. These are going to happen and the Church must be ready to use these as a teaching moment. The future diocese will engage in the merger of art, gaming, and social structures across physical and digital space—using this as only one of the many mission contexts in which it dwells. It will be involved in creating navigation tools for the complex media environment, personalizing technologies of cooperation and networking, and leading/pushing communication of information and knowledge. Community commons building and connections to any place, any time, learning hubs will be part of the diocesan work.

The church hierarchy in the present church will be challenged to understand that people are directing their own gatherings, and that they are not necessarily going to show up because a program is offered. Gathering is now an option that comes when like-minded individuals create a common space to achieve a common goal. The future church will have to grasp the idea of ministry *with* people instead of *to* people. The future diocese will aid congregations to become savvy *swarm* and *mob* builders, intimately linked to the broader community and the community conversation. With new technologies evolving, the future church will take the opportunity to better network around skill sets, gifts, and leadership traits across *friend's lists*. The future church will returned to an era of being a link, a connection, and a bridge, in a society which values connecting interests with real world tasks and needs.

The future Church must take advantage of the new networking potential of a socialstructured world in order to catapult itself forward into the new missionary age. Yes, like every other modern organization, our economy has been disrupted. The prime cause is the new advent of a self-organizing world—the same thing that is our link to the future. The socialstructured world changes everything, and it changes the possibilities—redefining floor and ceiling of our household economy. Social tools drastically reduce transaction costs. The new tools will be used by the future Church to capitalize on loosely structured groups, to build cohesive strategies where it can no longer afford to have oversight by the full-time ordained.[768]

In other words the future Church will beat the Coasean floor by allowing loosely structured groups to self-organize without the transaction cost associated with the large program church of the past. By harnessing the interest of its membership, the future church must figure out that it can structure and govern itself more effectively, thereby leaving dollars in the local context for mission. It can do this by having clear boundaries around the community and the mission projects. It will make joining and participating in the work of the church easy, ensuring that the work that is being done is providing some form of personal value for the individuals involved. The future Church will use these self-organizing groups across the community, building cells of support for congregations and communities. This subdivision and multiplicity of small working mission groups increase the antifragility of the overall organization. Shirky says, "In systems where many people are free to choose between many options, a small subset of the whole will get a disproportionate amount of traffic (or attention, or income), even if no members of the system actively work towards such an outcome. This has nothing to do with moral weakness, selling out, or any other psychological explanation. The act of choosing to spread widely enough and freely enough creates a power law distribution. This explains, among other things, the dynamics (and ultimately the success) of tools like *wikis* where there is a disproportionate amount of participation by an extremely small percentage of the overall users, while the vast majority contribute little or nothing."[769] Essentially what the future Church will do so very well is to build an overall collective intelligence in every area of mission, such that there is energy, innovation, and collaboration across the whole network of members and neighbors, thereby harnessing the power of a large group of individuals.[770]

The future Church will have, diocesan leaders, structures and a church wide support system that are essentially built upon the people's interests and talents that it seeks to serve. The network of the baptized and their neighbors is the network that undertakes the ministry of organization. James Surowiecki points out, in his book *The Wisdom of Crowds,* that "large groups of non-experts are capable of coming up with wiser solutions those small groups of experts.[771] We, as Episcopalians, believe in the movement of the Holy Spirit and the ministry of all people to work together to accomplish God's mission. This is a piece of our non-negotiable understanding of what it means to be an Episcopalian. Surowiecki's research reveals that in fact this belief is not simply a unique Episcopalian-ism but is the very nature of society. Study after study reveal that "naïve" or "unsophisticated" individuals can and will organize in order to accomplish complicated, jointly advantageous goals, though in the beginning they may not be unified or have clarity about the goals themselves. Human beings, regardless of background, can gather and self-organize and move towards a common goal adeptly and quickly.[772] The future Church must believe this to be true theologically and must enact it throughout its structure and governance. Holding on to one of the most essential DNA ingredients to our Episcopal way of undertaking our mission—the collaboration of the people of God, the future Church has undermined the specialist theology now gripping the church, and will free itself to once again take on the work of God's people together.

Did you know that over 10 billion people participate in the creation of a "living earth simulator?" The idea of Swiss scientist Dirk Helbing, the simulator uses the wealth of crowd support to understand how the world works and avert potential crisis. The project website (www.futurict.eu) states: "The ultimate goal of the FutureICT project is to understand and manage complex, global, socially interactive systems, with a focus on sustainability and resilience. The living earth simulator uses information from scientists, techno files, and others to build a real-time understanding of the world."[773] This is one of the most amazing projects I have encountered in my research, and it illustrates how complexity is not limited by crowd participation. The better-known Wikipedia uses about 150 people and thousands of volunteers to build its database. Yes, as it has problems with facts, its accuracy continues to grow and its wealth of information is astonishing. These platforms are creating projects and hubs within the wider information network that engage and enable greater participation by interested people. They reach far greater numbers of people with their participatory commons. These creative commons, Gorbis writes in *The Nature of the Future*, enable organizations to be guided by their leadership and those who are members of the community in ever-new ways.[774]

The future church will depend upon its leadership, and whole community, to help minimize transaction cost of planning and coordinating activities, by using crowds. These crowds will have some particular qualities to them. The crowd structure will be made up of friends of Jesus, and collectively united around the Episcopal Church vision. The future Church will be technologically savvy. It will develop a standard of quality that reflects the context standards of the day. The future Church will be engaged in helping manage supply chains. It will be collaborative in all things. The future Church structures will be an enmeshment of hardware, software, and people—it will be amplified like its users. It will be characterized by antifragility through a structure that is at once unified, but more often characterized by the diversity of networked communities. It will be focused tightly on the ability, need, and goals of the local congregation. The future Church will be reflective and continually seeking knowledge about its performance and how it can improve its mission support at the local level; and, where it is in error, it will reform itself. Finally, it will have the characteristic of affiliation rather than obligation.

There really are only a few things that a future church will need from its diocesan or church wide structure. The local Christian community will need support for their clergy and leaders to help them lead and undertake their mission locally. The local mission will need the unifying voice of the wider Church to help produce and expand the vision and mission of the Episcopal Church, so that seekers may find representative materials that direct and connect individuals with communities. The local mission will need the purchasing power of the wider Church. The local congregations will need client support for basic business services. Local leadership will help in navigating health, wellness, and insurance in a new age of health care. The wider Church will keep resources locally by spending appropriate resources on governance and structure.

The structures of the future will be judged based on how well they support the local leadership—clergy and laity. The wider church structures will be tasked with making formation at every level accessible, shareable, and useable. Formation is a lifelong process for every person. In the self-learner world, the church must recognize that it needs infrastructure enabling the self-learners to discover more about God, themselves, and the Episcopal community around them. The diversity of types and sizes of communities across the Church will mean that it will be the Church structure's responsibility to help build the technological infrastructure for this work.

Accessibility for all members and their neighbors will be essential. The information must be shared freely. The present past has certainly been characterized by an age of suspicion and a lack of desire to share widely. The future Church is not only known for its ability to find good quality information but is also known for its willingness to share with others. This will require pushing the edge of translation and provision of information about our church in multiple languages. Useable information at the local context is essential for the first two ingredients to be of any use. The present past church is consistently looking at providing information *it* believes is important to share. Frequently, this is not the kind of information people need and it is rarely laid out in a way that is useable. The future Church must build a useable fount of information which can be searched, sorted, and retrieved, and of a high quality so that it is desirable to share. No single church can provide this platform; therefore, it falls to the structure of the local diocese and wider church to provide it, because it is essential to everything— service, evangelism, stewardship, and connection. You can see this already at work in the LOGOS project. (vimeopro.com/epicentervideos/logos/)

The future Church will have more of these projects built and organized for church wide use.

The future diocese will lead in communication strategy. The present past diocese and church wide structures spent money on program ministry offices and groups, the future diocese and structure use the lion's share of their dollars to fund communication. They will be the leaders in software and network tools. They will be the leaders in providing Internet driven means for pushing information and shaping stories. They are also watching for the cutting edge in communications. The diocese of the future is constantly testing new communication tools and seeing what will work the best for individuals. It will provide training in communication and will help the amplified members of its congregations become better communicators. Money must be spent on front facing websites and technologies that will help connect seekers to local congregations.

The future Church will be responsible for creating training for its clergy and leadership that meets the characteristics above. It will be the leadership's responsibility to make training available for all people in accessible languages for the raising up of a crowd of Church workers who are eager to take on the mission of God in their local community. The future diocese will be responsible for helping fund, and hold accountable the training organizations and institutions that prepare ministers. Where there are none, it will work with crowds to source and create needed training. Where it exists, the future Church will hold it accountable to producing clergy and leadership at the local level. Resources will shift quickly over the next ten years to an investment in local training of every kind. It is the future diocese and the wider church's responsibility to provide localized clergy training, so that time and energy are not taken out of the mission field. Moreover, the training for the laity on how to do the work of the church will be essential. The future Church must have: in its tool bag videos and online classes on how to be a pastoral visitor, a lay reader, Eucharistic visitor or chalice bearer, how to run small groups of various kinds, how to serve on a vestry, vestry best practices, how to start up a service ministry, and a host of other raw materials that take the pressure off the local congregation when it comes to providing quality training. This will free up time at the local level to do ministry and allow further lay involvement in the teaching and sharing of the Gospel at every level.

We have talked about the work of unity and having a unifying vision of the future Church and its beliefs. A key piece of the work is for the wider Church and the local diocese to construct platforms for the sharing of this information. It is the wider church's responsibility to nurture the network nodes and hubs, for better crowd and self-organizing tendencies of the new mission context. Gorbis wrote, "Organizations are: building social production platforms to reinvent themselves, extend their capabilities … expand[ing] internal pipelines, generating engagement, reaching out to new markets and audiences"[775] The future diocese and wider Church structures will figure out how to crowd source everything from discernment for future leaders, placement of future congregations and communities, to planting of new service ministries. The future diocese especially will use the vast wealth of energy, talent, and on-the-ground information to guide its mission strategy. No longer is it a bishop, or maybe a priest, looking out and seeing that something needs to be done. The future Church will multiply its ability to move and grow and respond by increasing participation on a grand scale. The present Church has spent the last decade building connections. The future Church must harness those connections for the purpose of God's mission.

The operating costs of doing present past church are far beyond the ceiling, and stewardship no longer covers much of what we can do, so we have turned inward. Outer mission of service and evangelism has all but dried up in the present past Church. Today new life and many new models of community are beginning to emerge. They are using different capital and budget processes to fund mission—bring down the cost. It is the work of the future diocese to create further an operational economy for the business side of the mission model. This means that the future diocese will build purchasing cooperatives for electricity, office products, technology, and computers. The future diocese will ensure that every parish is plugged in with touch screens and high tech cable optics to provide accessible online connection between church leaders, communities, and resources.

The Rt. Rev. Brian Prior, of Minnesota, did just that in his diocese, working out a grant process and deal with Best Buy (a locally owned corporation) to wire the diocese. Every diocese of the future will be released from people's cast-off 5-year-old computers, and will use the most up-to-date cloud technology and hardware to present material and resources to their people and neighbors. The diocese of the future will figure out new economic models for starting congregations, allow for bi-vocational planters, and find more diverse community start up strategy. We know what the future looks like in terms of church plants. It is the future diocese that will take those models and create easy to use plans, strategies, and step-by step manuals. Every community can begin another community. Every community can begin a service ministry with their neighbors. Every community can rethink its connection to the community. The future diocese provides the guiding support for this work. The diocese will bridge the gap for the start-up's space needs: by negotiating for the new community public space usage, finding office space and build-to-suit leasing options, by decreasing the cost of erecting a first building (like the new model church in the Diocese of Texas which costs $500,000 and seats 190 people), and by networking diocesan-wide crowd funding. The future diocesan and church wide structures will use their collective power to buy down operating cost for the purpose of increasing mission dollars.

The future diocese will be a clearinghouse for congregational leadership support regarding business services. The cost of doing business, and the complexity of business with banks and auditors, are expensive. Meanwhile, transparency and higher standards of reporting will increase. It is my belief that in the future, the Church will have to prove its non-profit status to the government for purposes of showing that it contributes to the community. We already see these battles taking place. On an annual basis in Texas, hospitals have to show that their community benefit is equal to or greater than their tax relief in order to maintain their nonprofit status. I think the same types of reporting will increase across the country for any organization wishing special options regarding tax status. Fraud within the non-profit community is also raising standards, and even Congress is concerned about governance issues within the non-profit sector. The future diocese will provide client services to its member churches and communities by building capacity through shared business service applications. It will build banking templates for budgeting a congregation's finances. It will negotiate and build unified accounts with payroll companies that ensure all employees are paid through the same service at a cheaper rate. It will create unified investing co-ops, enabling larger, more complex investment strategies for large and small endowments. It will deploy a unified audit so that congregations of different sizes can have excellent governance regarding their funds. The future diocese will centralize services for banking, and deploy advocates from diocesan centers that can help run the business part of a local church's operations. It will provide coaching that is provided online, via real-time video, and onsite that will improve the best business practices of any given congregation. This will free up time and money at the local level for mission work. Fund management is one of the most vulnerable places within the overall financial system of the Church, and the smallest congregations are some of the *most* vulnerable. Liability and legal counsel will be part of the service work of the wider Church, as will disaster response and crisis management. Similar to the financial client service packages, these too, will be areas where collaborative networking of resources will benefit the whole organization, if successfully underwritten by the whole and then shared.

We already do joint health insurance coverage on a diocesan basis. The last few decades have been marked by the increase in the cost of health care. Most of the focus has been on providing inexpensive coverage to clergy and their families. This has been done, in large part, by sharing cost with the clergy, and building larger pools of the insured in order to diversify the actuarial tables and create a less vulnerable health care cost pool. The future diocese must recognize that tinkering with formulas and money are not the only way to have a healthy and effective clergy and leadership team. Therefore, the diocesan-wide structures will work to create well communities of clergy, their families, and all individuals under their care. Church wide leadership has to help the individuals it employs to maintain a healthy lifestyle. This will mean advocating for rest, time off, and sabbaticals. It will mean working to ensure regular check-ups, exercise, and nutrition.

The future diocese and church wide structure will also deal with the issues of governance. The present past church is heavily invested in governance. In my opinion, too much money, energy, and time is spent on ineffective governance and outdated structures of the church. We spend an inordinate amount of time passing resolutions created by a few people, and then voted on by a few people, which in the end has little or no effect in the halls of government. Our governance is today ineffective at bringing about social change at the highest levels of our society, and we continue the masquerade that these resolutions that impact social change. Meanwhile, we have abdicated our real work at the local level of service and evangelism. Regardless of how much we like winning legislative debates, these debates and the policies and unfunded mandates that often accompany them, do not create changed hearts. In fact they make more fragile systems with a false sense of uniformity. They don't serve the mission of reconciliation well.

We have the best scientifically managed system of governance that you can buy—if you live in the nineteenth century. The last reform of our governance structure was undertaken in 1930 under the leadership of Episcopalian George Thurgood Marshall—and it failed. Robert Haas, former CEO of Levi Strauss, describes the potential of our world of governance as an opportunity for change. With semblance of hope he offered, in a 1990 interview, "We are at the center of a seamless web of mutual responsibility and collaboration, a seamless partnership, with interraltionships and mutual commitments."[776] To do governance as a seamless partnership is to undertake the true Episcopal ideal of mutual and collaborative work on behalf of our neighbor. This is to do real justice work hand in hand with others, around shared and potentially transformative service ministry. Sir Isaac Newton's science, and later the Industrial Revolution, created an opportunity for entrepreneurs to give birth to a governance structure that mimicked what they saw in the mechanical innovation of their time and in the science of their age.[777] Wheatley writes, in her book *The New Science*, "Marrying science with the art and craft of leadership was a way to give more credibility to this young and uncertain field. (This courtship continues today in full force, I believe from the same motivation.)"[778] Wheatley believes that the new science of quantum theory teaches us that the self-organized system is one that is playful and free. It is a system where everyone has a chance to participate and have a voice. Self-organization is a key ingredient to all life. Yet, instead of creating chaos, organisms have a peculiar kind of life together that is mutually supportive and communal. Humanity can work the same way—its governance structures can work the same way.[779] This is of course the model for an antifragile style of governance. Gorbis in *The Nature of the Future* writes, "Our technology infrastructure, the new levels of data and information at our disposal, and our urgent need to create new patterns of governance in line with today's level of scientific knowledge make it possible...to restore the democratic process to 'we the people,' to make the policy process more deliberative, more democratic, and more transparent."[780] The task for structures in the future will be less about command and control and more about invitation and making space for freedom and creativity. Success will be gauged on how well the structures return the work to the people at all levels of the organization—broadening participation. Future Church governance will have been transformed from the work of the few on behalf of the many to the work of the many.

CHAPTER TWENTY-THREE
Deliberate Governance for an Amplified Age

"The City is what it is because our citizens are what they are."
— Plato, <u>The Republic</u>

After Jesus was resurrected, the apostles began to meet. They met in an upper room, they met in Jerusalem, and they met and met. People, like Paul, attended these meetings and asked the apostles' opinion about subjects like the mission of the church, and the apostles deliberated, and sent them back out to do the work. The second century bishops and leaders continued to meet after the age of the apostles was over. They convened whole church councils to argue over the issues of the day: the Bible, liturgy, theology, and the basic business practices of the church. The councils of the church, Roman, Orthodox and Reformed, have forever dotted our historical timeline and will continue to do so for many years to come.

The leadership of the Episcopal Church of the future will take their place with deacons, priests, and bishops in the councils of the Church. Like everything else this will have changed. The councils will not require the time, effort, and financial support that they do today. The governance of Church to be conducted in ever-smaller units compared to the mammoth amount of unnecessary administration that occurs in the present Church. The Councils of the Church will be more globally connected. There will be an ever-growing overlap of networks and relationship nodes that will allow the future Church to gather in greater conversation across boundaries—building mutual learning and support cadres for mission. Finally, the way in which the mind of the Church is unified, beyond any contextual division, will be the sign that the future Church has returned to mission (service, evangelism, stewardship, and formation), leaving conflict behind.

The old model of governance has been a response to the machine age. We have built a representative machine-like organization that outsources our church citizenship to a group of specialists. We elect a group (sometimes for decades) to learn a unique system of governance and we empower them to make decisions on our behalf. Then routinely, every three years in the case of General Convention, and every year in the case of local conventions, the people complain about what these specialists did, how they went about doing it, and how much money was spent doing it.

The Episcopal Church is now considering the future of governance. It is considering ways in which to change and deal with a cumbersome governance structure. Attempts to change the overall length of the General Convention, to focus and prioritize legislative agendas, reduce legislative committees, and ease the rules of the house are among suggested ideas. I believe that when we focus on these things we miss the important ideals set by our Church's founders, which is to have a corporate model where the laity and clergy participate in governing the mission of the wider Church. I want to focus our attention beyond the present tinkering with the system and look at an overarching self-organized model which will better suit a church of amplified human participation.

There are a variety of self-organized models of governance that are now being experimented with across the country. One of the largest is the Agora model in California that allows citizens to make decisions together. It is modeled after the agora in ancient Greece where citizens rotated through the city council. It works on a system of crowd learning and then shared decision-making—not unlike a jury system. Individuals are tasked with helping to sort out major issues facing their communities. Citizens in New Zealand used crowd sourcing to make major decisions after the earthquake of February 2011 in Christchurch.[781] The U.S. Navy engaged crowds to help work on solving the issue of piracy.[782]

James Fishkin is a professor of communications and the Director of the Center for Deliberative Democracy at Stanford University, and has written a book entitled *When People Speak*.[783] The people at the Center have worked to build deliberate polling and governing processes, enabling citizens to have a greater voice in governance in the U.S., China, Australia, Bulgaria, and Northern Ireland. Gorbis' writing introduced me to their work. She writes, "The process brings together groups that mirror the demographics of larger populations in their states, regions, or countries and puts them through a process of learning, discussing, and debating issues that affect them but that under normal circumstances are decided by power elites, either technocratic or political or both. Fishkin and his colleagues have found that average citizens are able to make good decision in areas as complex as local budgets, regional integration, criminal justice, and tax policy."[784]

The future Church must use tools such as these to empower its members church-wide to engage in the work of the diocese and wider church. Doing so will mean that the future Church has a membership that is more engaged. They will understand the diversity of the issues, and are more often likely to change their minds. They will be interested in how to participate in local action that helps to transform their community. They will make better, more informed, more effective decisions together. All of which will be oriented towards mission at the local level.

The future Episcopal Church will govern itself using rich and open data. It will share strong and diverse information to educate its membership. The Church will share it freely, and accessibly, and it will enable an ever-larger group to take part in the decision-making. Governance will no longer be the purview of the general convention elite. The reality is that General Convention deputies are people who either do not work, who have a job with a minimum of two weeks' vacation a year, or who can afford to lose two weeks' pay. While we pretend that it is a representative form of government, it is not because it excludes individuals who cannot afford to attend from taking part in governance. In the same way that Gorbis talks about government, future Church governance will harness "sophisticated decision-support tools for exploring in crowds alternatives and uncovering complex interdependencies."[785] The future Church will move away from a limited representative form of governance to a richly diverse participatory form of governance. It will do this by creating and developing "engagement platforms" similar to those being deployed in countries today, which enable wide citizen participation and discernment. The future church will move away from elite forms of group decision making and small board participation to "rich micro participation" models, allowing for church citizens to be part of the wider discussions for the Episcopal Church and the global Anglican Communion.[786]

The key to making the shift is in understanding where our blindness lies in the current system. Throughout the last fifty years, the Episcopal Church has believed that in order to make decision-making representative we needed processes of governance to create discussion with a diverse group of voices. This created a new elite. Democracy is actually the creation of a wider distribution of decision-making power and not a smaller one.[787] What happened to the General Convention, and all diocesan conventions, happened to most U.S. led corporations in the same time period—they became the epitome of "bureaucratic sclerosis."[788] Surowiecki, in *The Wisdom of Crowds*, says that this, in turn, created a hierarchical organization that had many layers of management. The effect of this was actually disempowerment of the individuals in the system, focus on financial budgets instead of on-the-ground contextual mission, and as with U.S. companies, this has been a costly mistake.[789]

How will the future diocese and church wide leadership get to this new reality? With the future in mind, the church will continue should continue its course of reform. Here I want to make a case, not for the particular changes needed, but for the goals of a new deliberative and networked form of governance for the Episcopal Church. Given all we know about the future Church, and if we are to set our minds at re-forming governance for the future Church, we will have to remember what Church governance is about. The goal of the future Church governance is always and everywhere to support the local congregation in undertaking God's mission of reconciliation in the world. Our goal is to ensure that this work is done faithfully and mindfully.

Here are some "rules for engagement" in reforming the structures of church governance. The organization must be focused on issues that affect the local context the most, and engage the most people. The work must be to "harvest the wisdom in disagreement" through the development of localized contextual discussions across a diocese or the wider church.[790] Move into group discussions (online or face to face) and use guides to help the conversation through non-partisan materials, printed resources, well designed interactions, and follow-up reports that will help manifest a sharing of information throughout the system.[791] The key feature here is utilizing methods of gathering people beyond the elites, for discussions that are important to the local members, not just those issues that are dictated by the an elite group of representatives. This will help to improve attitudes toward governance in general.

Regardless of where you stand in any political arena today, there is a sense of democratic disempowerment. In a church with a "representative" system, we are affected by the same attitudes as the rest of the culture. The future Church will not only gather and better inform its people, it will involve them in the overall processes. This will help to empower them and make for a more effective vocalizing of issues facing the diverse church. What is lost currently is the ability to honor the diversity of voices and contexts. The future church, knowing this, will work to improve community relationships. It is about the local mission, after all.

Councils and conventions must be focused on building strong community relationships, decreasing polarization, and helping to focus public engagement at a local level where there is value.[792] This deliberative styled governance counters typical hostility towards the *other* by broadening the individual's interaction with others.[793] The work of governance and those who govern will be to foster listening, and understanding, and to enlarge individual horizons, so that they can realize both our interconnectedness and our interdependence — so that in the end, even governance is building affection between people. Deliberative self-governance processes depend upon the ability of people to have good will towards one another, and communicate across barriers.[794] When this happens, self-interest is balanced with the interest of the overall community, by ideas like the common good. When governance moves out of the realm of a specialized few, doing specialized work, for a few weeks every three years, the church achieves something it has not had since its beginnings—it achieves the creation of a reflective process that is reattached to the people doing work in the field.

The future Church will remember that the work of the organization (whether it be at board meetings, in the office, or at a convention) is everywhere and always to increase the mission work of service and evangelism by connecting people to one another and with their neighbor. A decentralized and more deliberative style of sharing governance increases the network of conversations, and in the end has a result of building concern for the local communities in which the Church finds itself. When deliberative processes connect people to good information, bring them together for effective conversation, and build hubs for the work of governing, people's attention to local concerns grow, as does their action and interaction.

In 2006, David Mathews, former Secretary of Health, Education and Welfare wrote, "There are some things that only governments can and must do, but there are other things that only citizens outside government can do—change political culture, modify human behavior, transform conflicts."[795] He called this the "great eye-opener" of twenty years of study of the process of democracy that he undertook with the Kettering Foundation.[796] The Church is connected to the local community in every place where it is doing ministry. It is part of the work of governance to keep its attention there so that it can respond. The goal of good governance is not to make the trains run on time and to get massive amounts of legislation passed/defeated in a short amount of time, with the least amount of financial drain on the institution. The work of good governance is to help keep people working in the world and undertaking God's mission. So when the Church returns to a more deliberative and localized work of governing and becomes aware of local issues, it is also more apt to work with their neighbors to deal with those issues.[797]

Our particular way of being Church is one that has a goal of involving people in the work of governance; therefore, we are still going to have to make decisions together. If we take the preceding goals in mind and look at our governance at the diocesan and wider church levels, we see an opportunity to do better. If we engage more people, educate/inform them, invite them into the process, focus their attention on local issues and problems, create new venues for understanding one another, and have actionable deliberations we will have greater impact. The result will be that board rooms, executive committees, standing committees, councils, and conventions will become better connected to the people whom it is the church's goal to serve. This connection and involvement in the Church wide citizenry in the end makes for stronger deliberation and better decisions. This is true in the wider world and it is true in our own context.[798] The future Church will engage in deliberation that ranges from public forums, networked meet-ups (online and face to face), leader engagement with questions and answers, problem solving hackathons, focused web forums and discussions, and feedback loops. This is the empowering work of a self-organized system governing itself. In the end leaders (both clergy and lay) are better connected to those they represent and better attuned to the issues and complexity of the diverse ministry context which the Church inhabits. Together, there is a better focus of attention on ministry and less focus on issues that do not affect everyone but have a tendency to polarize and disenfranchise one another.

The shift that the future Church must make in its governance is an essential one, and one that is not a surprise given the theme of this book. The shift will be a deliberate move, rethinking the participants in church governance. The Church citizen of the future will no longer be just an inhabitant of a pew, uneducated in church affairs, a once a year voter, consumer of Church, and from time to time volunteer. Instead, every citizen of the future Church is a co-governor of his or her own community. They will be conveners and participants in deliberative governance that helps build community action for the transformative common good of the society. The Church citizen of the future is a partner, a self-educator, an organizer, a person who shares information and gathers neighbors together. He or she is involved in making change occur and ensuring that the local concerns are part of the wider church conversations. The Church citizen of the future will engage the structures with reforms and remake them, and is empowered to do so by an interested and connected leadership.[799] This work is an essential ingredient in the work of creating a truly participatory governance structure for all the baptized. The future Church must understand that institutional decision making at every level is not the final consequence of an ecclesiological democratic tradition. Instead, the future Church will recognize that the governance, the councils, and conventions are only a few of many tools for engaging the local Christian community in transforming the world outside its doors.[800] Governing is never the end and purpose of the Church. It is always and everywhere a means by which the work of God in Christ Jesus is supported; and where it is not it must be changed and reformed.

A miraculous future Church moment happened at General Convention in 2012. There was a diverse group of networked individuals, a large part of whom were digital natives, who were tweeting and communicating about the meeting. They were frustrated and concerned about a variety of things. Mostly, they seemed frustrated with the lack of understanding that what the convention was engaged in was not at all productive or focused on those issues that they felt were important. They continued to communicate electronically, and then they called for a meet-up. They met to discuss the possibility of nominating a person for one of the high offices. They decided on a candidate, and others that they wanted to vote for, and designed a strategy for continuing their goals of amplifying their voice within the convention. It worked. They came close to electing their candidate, who came in second. They were able to shape a large part of the discussion around restructuring. They were, all in all, successful given their desire to communicate, gather, and affect the proceedings. Imagine what would have happened if they had organized at the local level? Think about the different kind of power they would have had if they had networked their interest across the church and then raised up leaders to be on the floor at the General Convention. Think about what would have happened if they had followed a pattern of deliberate self-governing, and built a strong political force that shifted General Convention, and elected the change agents they thought best for the Church. I think it will not be long before this happens. These digital natives are on the right track. The problem is, and will be, how the public office (even in the Church) settles the newly elected into the power structure of an age-old system that is no longer effective. Even if they had elected the person they wanted they would have been put into the old system. I am hoping better for my digital native brothers and sisters. The Church is even now counting on them to take their place in the councils and lead those councils into the future.

CHAPTER TWENTY-FOUR
Ch-ch-ch-Changes (and face the strain)

"Here's to the crazy ones.
The misfits. The rebels. The troublemakers.
The round pegs in the square holes.
The ones who see things differently.
They're not fond of rules.
And they have no respect for the status quo.

You can praise them, disagree with them, quote them,
disbelieve them, glorify or vilify them.
About the only thing you can't do is ignore them.
Because they change things.
They invent. They imagine.
They heal. They explore. They create. They inspire.
They push the human race forward.
Maybe they have to be crazy.

How else can you stare at an empty canvas and see a work of art?
Or sit in silence and hear a song that's never been written?
Or gaze at a red planet and see a laboratory on wheels?
While some may see them as the crazy ones, we see genius.

Because the people who are crazy enough to think they can change the
world, are the ones who do..."

— Jack Kerouac, Apple "Think Different" Campaign, 1997

So, how will this all happen? What are the ways in which we go about making these changes? How do we lead into the future now that we have some ideas about its potential and possibility? There have been two important leadership moments in my life when a friend and coach has looked at me and said (essentially), "You are a leader and you will do it. It is what we need from you." Perhaps this is a little raw, a little tough, but the reality is that we will make our own future—or not. It is up to us, the vast number of Episcopalians, to step into our role as citizens of the Church and make this future happen. That being said, I think we need to be mindful of one another. We need to be mindful of how we go about engaging our future strategically. We need to be mindful of the ethics involved in the work that is before us. Finally, we will need to be mindful of our pastoral responsibilities to those who are in our care.

The way we have typically gone about the process of change over the last one hundred years goes something like this: We see an issue. We write a resolution or canon. We propose it to our local diocese and it is passed. Then we send it along to the provincial level in order to build support and it is passed there as well. Or, we have a committee that decides it is important and so it makes a proposal. Either way, it makes its way into the bowels of the General Convention process. If it makes it out on the other side, the presiding officers will assign a manager to be in charge. They in turn make it their own, and stamp it, and gather around some supporters. They then ramp up the goals even more, and in a closed-door room, define the strategy and outcomes. They may have some way of measuring the results—though this typically is not part of our charism in the Church. Regardless, people in power put other people in power to direct the strategy and remake the machine/redesign the program, or do whatever it is supposed to do according the resolution. Then there is an attempt to implement the idea. What happens next is that it typically works for a few years and then is forgotten. Out of disinterest or neglect, it lies fallow and when it is brought up that we were supposed to do this, then blame is assigned to the appropriate person or persons. Even if the project is the brainchild of a bishop (I have had a couple of these myself) we do the same thing. We come up with an idea to tinker with the machine and put some people on it and when the tinkering is done it had little or no effect.[801] We are mechanics.

This is how change works in the mechanical world. You find a problem. You come up with a solution. You fix the solution. When that doesn't work you figure out why and you either fix it again or abandon the project. What I have learned, though, is that we really have a limited idea of why things work or do not work. We have a limited view of all the interconnecting parts. We have a norm, a mean, which we perform above and which we perform below, but seem to hover out there no matter what we do. We redo vision statements, we set new goals, we assign more hierarchies, and build new programs to fix things. But the fixing does not happen, and we are running out of people to blame. Margaret Wheatley points out that this is not the way that *life* works.

Wheatley offers to us a different model that we can apply to life in the organism of the Church. The model goes something like this: Some portion of our community, our organization, experiences *something* that is wrong. This does not require the church to vote on it. It does not have to be a large majority. The *something* could be anything. The small group, the few people, or the large group, decide that this *something* needs attention. They need to learn more about this *something*, so the individuals gather up all the information, good, bad, and indifferent, about the "disturbance" and circulate it throughout the network of relationships it has. Other individuals grab on to it and have the same reaction. They amplify it by sharing it. The information is itself changing at this point. It is being interpreted. It is growing. The group (which is larger now) understands it better, and it has more meaning than it did. The relationship of the disturbance with the overarching organization is clearer, more understandable. The Church as a whole must now deal with the disturbance. It is forced by the meaningfulness of the information, and it is willing and able to let go of a previous understanding of how the organization's experience of the world was ordered. It is able to rethink or change structure, habits, and systems. Yes, this does create some confusion and some chaos. Wheatley says this part is always the most uncomfortable and the most painful. She writes that it is a "state that always feels terrible."[802] So let us be disturbed!

It is in this moment that the future Church becomes apparent. As the old is passing away, the new becomes more visible. The future Church lets go of the present past and steps into a new way of doing things. This is messy, to be sure. But the future Church operates on process and adaptation and it begins to reorganize using all the new information about the disturbance. Like a ghost in the machine, the Holy Spirit continues to work and move within the church making it new even as the old passes away. The future Church continues to change and make its way into new habits, new ways of governing, and new ways of doing mission. The future Church is different because it understands the world and the world's disturbances differently. The future Church and its citizens understand something now that every other living system understands and lives by, and that truth is that it changes because that is the only way to preserve itself.[803] In the movie *Lucy*, Morgan Freeman, in the role of a scientist, tells students that natural living cells choose either immortality or reproduction depending upon its ecosystem. [804] This is a popular example of what Wheatley is saying about organizations. Living systems in nature transform themselves in order to adapt to their environment. This is what the ancient Church always did and it is what the Church must do as it makes its way into the future. The future Church is even now acclimatizing to the new cultural ecosystem and reproducing and replicating the living parts that will survive the present past Church.

In order to do this, the Church will have to exhibit several essential behaviors as a community. The future Church, as an organism, must find within itself individual members who share the belief in a living Church. They will be unabashedly Episcopalian and believe that the mission of God in Christ Jesus is more important than the existent power structures and our place in them today. Some within the organism will not find the same "shared significance."[805] It will not be a failure if some of the present day citizens do not participate in the future Church. It will be because they are tied to the present past Church and they do not hold the ultimate mission as the highest mission. This is okay and is natural. The only thing to be aware of here is that they will continue to believe that other disturbances are of more importance. With close examination, shared information, that is representative and widely distributed, will reveal in the end, that actually the disturbance they are experiencing is a disturbance for a Church organism that no longer exists. The future Church will understand this creative freedom, but will be no less focused on the shared significance and the goal of a living mission.

The future Church will understand and will enact participation with its citizens. It will know that "participation is not a choice." For organizations, it is the nature of their mission context.[806] The future Church will network and organizes itself in a wide conversation, both to gather information and to share it. "Life," Wheatley says, "insists on participation."[807] There are no shortcuts. As a bishop, I have learned the hard way that no matter how much easier I think it would be if people would just do what I want them to do, this shortcut is never actually a shortcut. I have come to understand that what Wheatley says is true—people want to participate. The work of the future Church and its leadership is to create broad based networking, communication, and gatherings that enable participatory leadership. What I know about life in the diocese and with her people is that they never obey—they only and always react. What the future Church is interested in is, "loyalty, intelligence, and responsiveness."[808] To have those qualities in the life of the future Church, the leadership must share information and build reaction and shared attention towards common work. This is how it will multiply, and deal with the disturbances it experiences.

The leadership of the future Church knows that its citizens are constantly interpreting their own reality and experience. Wheatley tells us that different parts of all living organisms may experience different sensations or different realities. The organism does not normally lack an idea of what it needs to do, but instead unifies around a common response. The future Church does the same. Just as there is value in the organism of the future Church for sharing our stories, there is value in acting and working together. When the future Church works together it will be able to build commons and amplify its impact in the local mission context, despite the diverse experiences everyone is having. The focus on mission –service and evangelism—helps continue an organizational life that values individuals who either do not have the same shared story or have a competing or different story than the majority of the community.[809] All are valued, all are part, and all are enabled to do the work of God in Christ Jesus. Lastly, the future Church must connect, connect, and connect. The work of connection is so essential because it amplifies the story, it amplifies the work, and it amplifies the essential ingredient of what it means to be Church—connecting to God and one another. The future Church will thrive in its new environment, because it has absorbed the idea of working with people's own tendency to self-learn and self-govern.

One of the ways that we are going to get from here to there is by navigating the future with attention to the areas of shifting change we have already discussed. This means that the present church will begin to make changes that integrate the amplified human into the overall structure and ministry of the church. The present Church will explore and then amplify how current tools are already doing this. What are the ways in which we are already making connections with people, and how do we create and enhance what is already working, while at the same time creating new ways of integrating life in and outside the church?[810] Another way that the present Church will take a step into the future is by continuing to focus on the local, and supporting the work that is taking shape there. The broader Church organism must be attentive to and support the local citizens in their work to establish mission. Any time, the wider Church structures pull away from this focus on the *local* it further disenfranchises the service and evangelism efforts that are having the greatest cumulative effect on transforming the community.[811] The present Church will need to begin to use "digital mirrors" to reflect on itself and its current place within the broader cultural narrative. It will do this in order to better understand where it can place its self within the broader mission environment so that seekers can more easily find it. This is more than simply finding out where "Episcopal" is mentioned online. Of greater value will be the work of understanding where our Episcopal identity may best fit within ongoing conversations online and in the world around us. Where is it that the Episcopal Church has an opportunity, by being itself, to impact and affect local community dialogue in a positive and transformative way?[812] We have to do this in a way that is simplified and decreases the walls currently existing between perspective members and existing communities. Accessibility and simplicity will be key words to gauge how well we are making inroads into the wider world of online communication and networking. Lastly, we need to build and construct social networks that will amplify our organization within the lives of its citizens and their neighbors. Most of this may in fact be the manipulation of current and new technologies. Nevertheless, it will be important to connect people through thoughtful and intentional means. Adding to this, the collection and the interpretation of data that is important to the organization, and freely sharing it, will be an utmost priority.[813] This is seen clearly in the chapter on formation.

I believe that we will need to figure out how to hold one another accountable to the work that is before us. We are coming out of an age where we measure everything. "You can't manage what you can't measure," said the statistician and popular engineer Edwards Deming. Number crunching is the venue of mangers, and we have used them to try to figure out what is happening in the present Church. The problem is that we are only measuring things we think we see. We then make conclusions about what we see and we create stories—narrative biases. The question that Wheatley raises is a good one and one worth asking ourselves whenever we get into a room and start going over the numbers: "What are the problems in organizations for which we assume measures are the solution? Assumedly, most managers want reliable, quality work. They want people to perform better: They want accountability, focus, teamwork, and quality."[814] This is true. I think we would all say, on our best day, "We want an effective missionary vessel for God's reconciling love." We might add more to that, but that is the guts of it all. We want well communities that are positive additions to their neighborhoods, and involved in the lives of the people who live there. Yes, we want to be accountable and we want focus. We want to work together, and we want people and God to think we are giving our best quality effort. Wheatley then continues, "If you agree that these are the general behaviors you're seeking, ask whether, in your experience, you've been able to find measures that sustain these important behaviors over time?"[815] Measurements do not change performance. Throughout this book we have seen a constant theme of connection. Therefore, I suggest that the present Church set about a different kind of measurement. We know that it is the feedback loop that creates reflection and adaptation. So, it is in the feedback loop that we will need to find our critical way of judging progress towards the future Church idea.

The Church is a reflective organism created by God to reflect God, and God's reconciling love out into the world. This is how the Church gives glory to God—by undertaking God's mission through service and evangelism. Therefore, the future Church will invest in receiving feedback from throughout its networks of real relationships. It will understand that each context is different and that feedback from any particular place is self-determined, and important to that part of the church. This feedback must be valued. In a numbers approach, it is one size fits all, and criteria are imposed and individual contextual ministry is devalued. For example, when we look at the growth in the urban/suburban church movement based on statistics we devalue the great work being carried out in small communities. The future Church will invest in hearing feedback from all over and from any segment. A numerically focused church categorizes everything so that some information can be dismissed. The future Church must value what the local church values, and relishes the experiences (no matter how small or how great) that are new, surprising, and essential to life and vitality. It will do this because it knows that creating an environment that is predetermined, predictable, and routine is one that is ultimately pretty for a while, but in the end fragile, and will come tumbling down. The future Church will value adaptability, innovation, and wellness rather than stability and control. It must understand that in a VUCA world strength is gained by engaging in the context outside the church community, and to do so is going to create action and reaction, that in turn will build a better more sustainable community.

The future Church will be looking for revelation throughout its communities. It knows that revelation is deeply connected to the incarnation and the people of God. Revelation is found in creation and co-creation. Revelation is found in gardening and harvesting. Revelation is found in sharing stories with one another. The future Church values those opportunities and experiences where revelation has potential and will shy away from stable, controlled, and static meaning. Finally, the present past Church is a system that adapts to measurement. It looks at numbers, and bases all of its action on patterns of statistical behavior. The future Church, while on the one hand will take care of its household economy, will also be a Church that is eager to adapt and change, based upon the change and shifts in its context.[816]

Let me say here a word about the pastoral work that is before us. Harvard Business School is a leader in thinking around organizations, and the competitive edge corporations need to have in order to succeed in the new millennium. The ideas generated by the authors and thinkers there have transformed the world of business that we have today. One in particular is worth mentioning here. Clayton M. Christensen came up with a descriptive phrase to help understand how leaders are supposed to act when doing the same thing that brought success in the past is now the wrong thing to do in the new business climate: "the innovator's dilemma." He offered this to the business community in 1997 and quickly followed with the idea that the solution was "disruptive innovation."[817] There is even a competition for disruptive innovation, and a list of this year's most disruptive technologies in *Forbes Magazine*.[818] We might think of the evolution of records to eight tracks, to cassettes, to CD's and now to mp3s as a great list of disruptive technologies that brought to market cheaper replacements and completely colonized the economy. Do you remember Beta and VHS? This is exactly what we are talking about here.

Jill Lepore, in a recent *New Yorker* article on disruptive innovation wrote, "Much more disruption, we are told, lies ahead. Christensen has co-written books urging disruptive innovation in higher education (*The Innovative University*), public schools (*Disrupting Class*), and health care (*The Innovator's Prescription*). His acolytes and imitators, including no small number of hucksters, have called for the disruption of more or less everything else. If the company you work for has a chief innovation officer, it's because of the long arm of *The Innovator's Dilemma*. If your city's public-school district has adopted an Innovation Agenda, which has disrupted the education of every kid in the city, you live in the shadow of *The Innovator's Dilemma*. If you saw the episode of the HBO sitcom *Silicon Valley* in which the characters attend a conference called TechCrunch Disrupt 2014 (which is a real thing), and a guy from the stage, a Paul Rudd look-alike, shouts, 'Let me hear it, DISSS-RUPPTTT!,' you have heard the voice of Clay Christensen, echoing across the valley."[819] Disruptive innovation is a theory that propagates the notion that one organization in business outdoes another organization by out-performing and producing a product that in turn puts the less desirable item out of business. Lepore, in her article, shows numerous examples of why Christensen is wrong in his assertion that this is actually what is happening or that this is what is best for civilization. The debate on this particular topic is hot and divisive within the wider Harvard community. The Church is not interested in disruptive innovation and I do not believe that it is the best example of how life works.

Yes, Christensen has compared this theory to the nature of evolution. I agree with Lepore that he does not quite have it right. The Church is an organization that has lasted over thousands of years, and the future Church is even now becoming a transformed and transforming agent within the wider culture. It has had this longevity and will continue to adapt into the future, not because it is disrupted, dies and something takes its place; but, because it is a "dissipative" system that is constantly in touch with its environment, and so ever adapting and changing to its mission context.[820]

Remember earlier we talked about Ilya Prigogine who coined the phrase "dissipative structures" first putting forth the idea of *dissipation theory*.[821] This is the idea that the self-organizing system is changed, and transformed, as it interacts with its environment. Disorder disrupts and causes the organization to in turn experience a fluctuation, and adapt. We are not a cannibalizing organism that eats its own in order to manifest a new something. The present past Church is not destroyed by the future Church. Instead, here we have the metaphor of resurrection. Just as Jesus is bodily transformed in the resurrection, so the church as a dissipative organism, and is transformed as it enters this new mission context. Some cells fall away, some cells stay, and some cells adapt and change adding new colors and identity to the ever growing and changing Church body.

This is important because the Church does not turn over one way of doing things, leave everyone behind, loot the organization and move on. Just as the first disciples, faced the transition brought about by Pentecost, and the new mission to the gentiles, first took care of the widows and orphans so too the church is always mindful that it lives with many generations all together in one house. The Church exists today with my dear friends, my mentors, and those who invited me to consider ministry but are part of a Church that in many ways does not exist. I have friends and even family who are part of, and devoted to, the Church of the present past. The Church does not leave anyone behind. True, there are some who have departed and decided not to go along with us on this journey, and that makes me sad. But the Church has both the capacity and the responsibility to care for those who faithfully have supported the mission of the church in their age. It is perhaps for this reason that change and transformation within the organism is slow and at times painfully so.

Phyllis Tickle transformed the thinking of several generations when she offered her now essential text on the future Church entitled *The Great Emergence.*[822] In it she offers a history that highlights how every 500 years the Church goes through a "rummage sale," and cleans out the old forms of spirituality and replaces it with new ones. This does not mean that previous forms become obsolete or invalid. As in a dissipative organism, the old forms lose pride of place as the dominant driving forms and new ones emerge as essential for navigating the mission context. She talks about Constantine in the late 4th century, early 5th, the Great Schism of the 11th century, the Reformation in the 16th century, and now the postmodern era in the 21st century as having been points of reference for these changes. One can in fact go back further through the great history of the predecessor Jewish community, of which Christianity is a part, and see similar trends. She has said on many occasions that what is giving way right now is Protestantism, in the form that we know it, and what is appearing is a new form of Christianity, what she is calling "The Great Emergence." Tickle is not sure whether the new Christianity will emerge in a kind of tribal form, an individualistic form, a social form, or a combination of all of these. She is convinced that Protestantism in all its denominational forms is losing influence and is giving way to a disruptive form of Christian expression. Coming out of a modern philosophical trajectory, it is difficult to imagine not having only one thing; for example Protestantism or a something else. My perspective is a post-modern one, and tends to be at home with *both/and* visions of reality rather than *either/or* visions. This is a characteristic typically found in those generations born in the late sixties and beyond. Because of this particular hermeneutic[823] I then have no problem believing in and imagining a different future completely. The Meta narrative has been deconstructed and we have been living in a time of great fragmentation. Tickle's work captures this reality well. I believe we are now seeing glimpses of the future. We are now entering a new time of writing, through mission, a new narrative. Schrödinger's Cat can be thought of as both alive and dead. Our Church can be seen as both dead and alive. The Episcopal Church can be both the Protestant Church of the past and the new Church of the future.

I believe the Episcopal Church is itself a dissipative organism that is even now evolving. It will exist with all its many previous forms but it will also include tribal like communities, the self-formation practices of a populace, wanting to imprint everything themselves, and societies or collectives of like-minded, service oriented believers. The future Episcopal Church is a strong and healthy member of Protestantism and the growing home of many self-organized amplified future Christians. What is essential though, and why I like Tickle immensely (besides the fact that I credit much of my own thought pilgrimage on her influence, kindness, and willingness to speak) is this—the church is having a rummage sale. This is exactly right!

The present past Church is selling off the idea that uniformity is unity. It is selling off the idea that it is of value to the mission of the church that the second largest democratic meeting in the world (next to the parliament of India) is the Episcopal Church's General Convention. It is setting down its idea that liturgy must in all places be one. It is discarding the idea that sending money is all you have to do to make a difference in the world. It is shedding the mantle that Sunday morning attendance and Sunday School attendance is the only requirement for good discipleship. It is selling off at a bargain basement price the notion that every church works on the same model, looks the same, and has the same ministries. It is letting go of the model of leadership that says one paid priest to one congregation.

It is giving up its unused residential seminary programs that no longer train people for the future Church. The church is selling off the idea that a monthly paper newsletter counts as communication. It is setting aside the idea that mission is best funded through large bureaucratic institutions centralized for optimal control. It is an immense rummage sale. Perhaps you will have some ideas about what else should be added to the list. At the end of the day all the refuse of the past church will have to go as the future Church is remade. One of the things that the Gospels are clear about is that the fishermen immediately dropped their nets, they let go of their past, and they followed Jesus into their future. (Mark 1.14ff) The future Church is making its pilgrim journey down the road to meet Jesus and lightening its load, casting off those things that hold it back from becoming the Kingdom of God.

Here we might now venture a word of caution before we proceed about the future; lest you think I am not taking my own medicine. I know that our "sense making machinery" wants to see the future just as it sees the past.[824] Our brains lead us to believe if we do x, y, and z, it will all work out. We have no control over the future. The illusion that we do is comforting, and I am all about comfort. Our anxiety and fears may be assuaged if we just believe that if we do what we need to do, we will be all right in the end.[825] We are completely dependent on the Holy Spirit—we are not the ones in control. There is no guarantee, no matter how much our brain tells us this is good stuff and it will work, by golly! Businessmen and women will try and beat the odds and illustrate how they outperformed everyone else. For the Christian, our task has been clear over the centuries: believe in God, believe in Jesus, believe in the power of the Holy Spirit to bring about the Kingdom of God, and believe that God's mission will be successful, and do our work of leadership faithfully and honestly.

Is there a shadow side to our life as Church? Is there a shadow side to the future Church? Carl Jung, psychotherapist and founder of analytical psychology, believed that every person had a shadow side. It is that part of you that on the one hand is the seat of creativity and also can be the seat of projection. If it remains unconscious, it can even be a source of evil, for what is unknown to us still plays a role in our choices and values, and sooner or later spills into the world from us.[826] If the person or organism is not aware of the shadow, it is left to cause trouble and chaos in the background; and, because it is unconscious, often it is justified by blaming or shaming others for its failings. The Church as an organism also has a shadow side. It is the source of all of its creativity and it is also the place from which scapegoating emerges.

Part of the reason the Church, past and present, has wounded so many people, is that it has been unaware of its shadow nature and in so doing has become at times a "terrible monster."[827] What happens is that the church, being that great magnet for projection, often accepts the projections of spiritual parent from its parishioners. At times it even plays the scolding punitive parent. Individual leaders may unwittingly collude with this projection to gain power. At its worst the church's goal has too often been to be an organization that doles out prescriptions and controls for the navigation of life. This typically leads to the burning of heretics, puritanism, and scores of walking religiously wounded. At its theological and psychological worst, what the church may do is keep its parishioners in an eternal childhood state.[828] If we never allow God's people to grow up, they will be forever dependent upon the church as mother/father. But God intends people to grow up spiritually. God intends the Church to help them in this process. The Church offers a deeply freeing gospel, one that engages the self-learner and pilgrim in each of us. The Church does this through a gospel shared by means of ritual—connection to God through the mystery of the sacraments. It also does this by means of sharing story and symbol.[829] This can be transformational for the pilgrim.

This is why the future Church rejects all kinds (conservative, liberal, biblical, liturgical, and moral) of fundamentalism. The enlightened Church knows that whenever it seeks to convince people that all they need to do is stop questioning and believe what the

Church says, they are only fostering co-dependence and spiritual immaturity. On such occasions, such a church locks out creativity, innovation, and the Holy Spirit that revitalizes a living organism.[830] The Episcopal Church believes in living into the questions, and does not shy away from paradox and the challenges of scholarship—when it is at its best. The world, with its considerable knowledge and its pluralism, needs a Church that offers more than henotheism. It is looking for just such a church as we have it in our power to become. So the Church has to both accept the centrality of faith as the core of its identity, while remaining open to the animating, generative Spirit.

Accepting a new model of mission will inevitably bring a sense that this possible church is the new normal—a new standard. We may be all too eager to say, "If you are not doing church this way then it isn't the future church." This is exactly the kind of behavior that will shut down the creativity and life that are needed and sought. It is precisely this diverse conversation between traditions and versions of the Episcopal Church in mission that energizes. The future Church cannot be afraid of this profound energy that dwells in the shadow. Instead of pretending to hide and proclaim we all believe the same thing in the same way, the future Church will say, "Come along with us on this spiritual journey. We have a lot of questions, but God seems to be here in this stew, and we are all working hard to listen to the variety of voices God is using." The future Church is not a new standardized program, though it will be our tendency to make it so. It is not a way of taking away creativity and visions of what Church might be. This is not some new ministry offering a new postmodern fundamentalism of futurist ideas.

The future Church must be aware of its shadows, and will resist its desire to stay put and hide from the world. It will be aware that it likes fostering a diaspora and an unhealthy one at that. It will know that it will want to codify and take power away from those who are all too willing to project it upon a new adopted parental figure. The future Church will know that it is always willing to tell others how to do it right. It will be aware that it wants to reject complexity. It will be aware that at its worst it has a great potential to be an exploitative religious structure. Moreover, it will always lean towards this attitude when it thinks it is one with the spiritual Christ. The more the Church claims to know the mind of God, the more it is ego-driven and confessing its shadow side. The more it abandons mystery for certainty the more it moves away from God. It is easy for the church to stay focused on law, punishment, and righteousness/cleanliness. This is the church and religion which Jesus rejects and says, rather, serve our brothers and sisters. (Mark 2.23, Matthew 5, John 5, 9; Paul speaks about death by this law in Romans 5.12ff) In this *false imitatio Christi* the Church will always become amoral and a law unto itself.[831]

Instead, the message of Jesus and the message of the living future Church are congruous. It is a message of love, grace, reconciliation, and service of others. It is always in the bringing of the shadow into the light that redemption and transformation happens. The creative work of living the life that Christ led is the goal of the Church. *Imitatio Christi* is doing what Christ did, but it also summons each of us to live life as authentically as Christ did in his time. Thomas A. Kempis, a fourteenth century theologian and spiritual father, wrote, "Now, there are many who hear the Gospel often but care little for it because they have not the spirit of Christ. Yet whoever wishes to understand fully the words of Christ must try to pattern his whole life on that of Christ."[832] The Church lives into sacrament and service (the outward and visible signs of its spiritual life) acting out in its life the life of Christ. We are also called to be a church that is authentically itself—in our time and context. The past Church has argued over these two approaches. The future Church engages a both/and *imitatio Christi*—it seeks to live its mission in the way Christ lived life and as authentically as Christ lived.

The future Church must invest its whole being in connecting people to God and not to itself. It is about the real work of religion. *Religion* means to connect that which is disconnected. The future Church will take those sacraments, stories, and symbols, and create a healing balm for the sin-sick, disconnected soul, and will go out into the world to undertake God's work there.[833] At the same time it will be constantly reflective, and submit itself to the on-going work of repentance and reconciliation with God and its people, confessing whenever or wherever it uses denial and projection to gain power.

The Church is becoming that ever-refined vessel of God's love. The future Church will not be a program for gaining converts. It will not be about winning back the powers of the world that it has lost.[834] The church will become the sacrament that reveals God's love and grace in the world. This is the work of Christ and it is the work of each Christian.[835] The future Church will lose itself in the world by giving itself over completely to it.[836] It is ever becoming less of itself, more of the mysterious Christ in the world, so as to manifest and propagate Christ's self-giving love throughout society.[837] The future Church will believe that God, as Trinity, is at work in the world, and so it will seek God there, hoping to join in and participate.

You may say this is a daunting challenge. It is uncomfortable and chaotic. You may say that we do not have the wherewithal to accomplish it. You may say that we have shrunk beyond our ability to recover. Or, you may say we do not have enough funds. The ancient Church has shown repeatedly its ability to adapt, create and innovate without resources. So I do not buy it. It is not money or size that makes the difference.

Simon Sinek reminds us, in his important book *Start With Why*, that the Wright Brothers had no support and no money but they were focused on flight and that is why they beat Samuel Langley to the air. Unlike the Wright brothers, Langley had the money, the backing of the government, private investors, and was known across the country. Everyone thought that Langley would be the first to fly but it was the Wright Brothers who remembered *the why* and so they stayed focused on flight—and were the first. Sinek says that innovators Steve Jobs and Steve Wazniak of Apple, Dr. Martin Luther King, Harley Davidson, Disney, Southwest Airlines, and John F. Kennedy are all examples of people and organizations who were successful because they remembered *why* and begin everything with *why.*[838]

The leaders of tomorrow's Episcopal Church remember *why* we do what we do—God's mission of reconciliation. It is not money and it is not size or strength that drives us. It is our unity around the mission of God to reconcile God to the world through acts of love that pulls us together to build a community that is at work in the world, serving and sharing the Good news of God in Christ Jesus. Our 20th Episcopal Presiding Bishop, Henry Knox Sherrill said, "The joyful news that He is risen does not change the contemporary world. Still before us lie work, discipline, and sacrifice. But the fact of Easter gives us the spiritual power to do the work, accept the discipline, and make the sacrifice."[839]

This is the time to dream dreams. We would do well to remember the moment the Holy Spirit came down upon God's people, "All were amazed and perplexed, saying to one another, "What does this mean?" But others sneered and said, "They are filled with new wine." And Peter said, "These are not drunk, as you suppose, for it is only nine o'clock in the morning. No, this is what was spoken through the prophet Joel: 'God declares, that I will pour out my Spirit upon all flesh, and your sons and your daughters shall prophesy, and your young men shall see visions, and your old men shall dream dreams.'" (Acts 2.17ff) This is not a time to stay small and on our island. This is not a time to remain sweet and precious. It is not a time to remain quiet. This is not a moment in which the church can or should work on legislating a pretty future. The future Episcopal Church needs people who get off the island and get messy in the world around us.

The future Church is depending on us to speak up and out. We are called to be bold. The future Church is hoping the present Church will engage the chaos around us. Let us rely on our historical dissipative nature and discover the changes and evolutions that await us in the mission field. In order to accomplish this, we are going to have to be willing to mess up and do it wrong. We as Christians know that our strength is in our honest vulnerability and we will not be successful if we are bold, but do not openly accept when we are weak. It is okay to feel weak and it is okay to feel fear. People will ridicule us and people will try to shame us for daring greatly. But daring greatly is the call.

Daring greatly may be all there is. In the face of certain suffering, confusion, and even death there is life. After all, daring greatly is the man on the cross and the man in the arena. Daring greatly is resurrection. Daring greatly is the attitude of the future Church.[840] Brené Brown introduced me to this brilliant quote from Theodore Roosevelt. It reminds me that it is not those on the sidelines who offer slurs and barbs that make a difference. It is not the critic who counts. It is the one in the arena.

It is not the critic who counts; not the man who points out how the strong man stumbles, or where the doer of deeds could have done them better. The credit belongs to the man who is actually in the arena, whose face is marred by dust and sweat and blood; who strives valiantly; who errs, who comes short again and again, because there is no effort without error and shortcoming; but who does actually strive to do the deeds; who knows great enthusiasms, the great devotions; who spends himself in a worthy cause; who at the best knows in the end the triumph of high achievement, and who at the worst, if he fails, at least fails while daring greatly, so that his place shall never be with those cold and timid souls who neither know victory nor defeat.[841]

God is praying that laborers will go into the fields for the harvest is great and laborers are few. Our call is to step forward as leaders committed to a future Church engaged in the mission of God. We are the ones to see the artifacts of the future church around us today, and to harness them for the missionary work of service and evangelism. We in the Episcopal Church must raise a loud shout and respond to God's prayer, affirming, "Our Church is alive! And, Here I am, Lord send me."

EPILOGUE
Criticism, Questions, and Further Thoughts

I had a great group of pre-readers. They were critical partners. Many of their suggestions helped to shape the text in its final form. They also challenged me. I think challenging my ideas is important and it helped me think about a response. In the service of continuing the discussion and provoking more conversation I have pulled several pieces of criticism, questions, and further thoughts together in this epilogue.

Schrödinger's Church Cat

In speaking with a few friends who are scientist and physicists they pointed out that the idea that the Schrödinger's Cat experiment is trying to illustrate is more than simply that the cat is dead or alive. Schrödinger found himself in the middle of a debate where the Newtonian physicists were arguing that Quantum Physics could not measure anything. Quantum Physics was not deterministic enough and therefore should be set aside for the more exacting Newtonian laws. Schrödinger's cat illustrates scientifically that Quantum Physics with its probability is actually quite accurate. Moreover, we participate as the observer in the probability.

It became clear in our discussions that what is important in this addition to the metaphor is the idea that we no longer live and work in a deterministic Church. The Church in fact is a Church of probabilities. We have an opportunity to participate in these probabilities. The frustration and anxiety we feel is that we continue to use the mechanistic Newtonian world view which hopes for a deterministic outcome. We arrive at the end of our work having found that the VUCA world has worked its magic on our designs. A probabilistic approach, which I think I am arguing for in this book, offers a more pliable, adaptable, innovative, and creative organism called the future Church.

Another insight that came in discussions about Schrödinger's Church Cat is the image that the Church, like the cat, is made up of both the past and the future. Of course this image hearkens to the old phrase, now discarded, the "Church Militant" and the "Church Triumphant." In large part these words have been discarded because of their association with war and poor mission practices. The image of a church that is both the past and the future though is helpful. The Church of the past and present is a Church that is very real. It has accomplished great things and has a very real history. The Church today is groaning towards its completion even now. It is impacting the lives of millions of people. The Church of tomorrow will undertake its work. We are always our past, our present, and our future.

I embrace this reality and actually believe this is why the history of our Church and its ancient practices are so important. They remind us that we haven't always "done it this way." Our looking back gives us ideas about how we might undertake our future mission. It also reminds us that the Church of the past has always been rooted in its context trying to figure out how best to be faithful. Someone once asked me what I hope people would say about our time together as bishop and diocese. I replied, "I hope they would say we were faithful." Yet, I would hasten to add that faithfulness means figuring out what our mission dictates we do in order to be successful at the work that God has given us.

Let us Organize the Organism

It was pointed out in reflections on the text that I spend a lot of time on the idea that the Church is an organism and not an organization. Is not the Church an organization with real powers, authorities, hierarchies, budgets, and policies? The answer is, "Yes, of course the Church is an organization." Sometimes in making our case we err on one side more than the other. So, let me offer a little balance and a challenge to the Church Organization.

The problem that we face as a denominational Church is that we always think of the Church as an organization. We think of it as a particular organization with habits and ways of being. I believe these happen to be deterministic and based on a Newtonian model, but yes it is an organization. A great example is The Reimagining the Episcopal Church task force (TREC) that was charged to help think about the Episcopal Church of the future. Their recommendations have been predominately to tinker with the existing organization and its structure. Instead of asking the bigger question that I ask in the chapter on Church wide governance about how to involve as many people in governance as possible, TREC got stuck on the mechanics of executive officers, reporting, and efficiencies. It got stuck in the old machine model and tried to figure out how to better build a better machine by adjusting the cogs. The same thing happened in the Anglican Church of Canada and in the Methodist Church, among others. Their attempts at structural reform failed. If we do not force ourselves to use a different language, with different metaphors, and look for different ways of organizing and leave behind organization frames we will continue to sit in stagnation.

It is not too late of course for TREC and the Episcopal Church. The question remains can the future Episcopal Church become a Church of the Future using the tools of its cultural context to do governance, mission, stewardship, service, and evangelism. The future of vocations and how we raise up a true community of the baptized are before us. The answer is in moving out of a mechanistic and deterministic machine approach to organizational theory and move intentionally into a self-organizing, probabilistic, innovative, participatory, autopoietic community.

Change is coming. People are self-organizing. People are figuring out new ways to be Church and become Church. The governing bodies and leaders must decide how painful that change is going to be. Continuing the organizational path that is before us will create an ever more painful change metric for the people and institutions involved. Choosing to embrace a new way of being and thinking will be painful. All change is. But I promise you embracing the future Church that is even now making itself known in our midst will be less painful. I think it will be exciting and thrilling.

Do You Really Mean That We Have To Like Them?

In the chapter on reconciliation I have proposed that our unity in Christ is our fundamental obligation. One of my pre-readers has said that I have "dodged a very tricky question." The challenge is: if we do not tolerate those who do not support the civil rights of African Americans then why do we tolerate those who do not support the civil rights of gays? We might say, we would not have a racist in leadership. Why would we have someone homophobic in leadership? So what do we do?

I think this is difficult because we are going through a cultural upheaval on many issues—sexuality is only one. We could argue that the issues of immigration and our continued racist attitudes in the U.S. remain flash points for the church. We are working out our theology on marriage and on blessings. At the core of that issue in the public sector is the issue of justice, the freedom of Americans making contracts with other Americans, and the ability to control our assets and our health. All of these issues get tied up in theology as well— perhaps more with marriage than with other issues. But I doubt it in the end. I think there was a good deal of theological support for slavery which served as a bulwark against what was right.

I would say on the one hand the Episcopal Church has to be clear about who it is and what the boundaries are going to be. We need to choose leadership wisely. I think we need to be clear about what are the healthy ways we remain in community. I think this will be difficult. In part I say this because we have not quite decided yet how all of this is going to work out. So the vast majority of Episcopalians have been at the whim of the winning 25% on right or the winning 25% of the left. In the last three decades we have lived through massive swings while the great moderate Episcopal Church has been under represented.

Let me say this about who we are, and this comes from my history in Texas. We had a bishop who was opposed to the 1979 prayer book. He did let congregations use the experimental liturgy. He was really tough on these issues that included women's ordination. Some say he was the only one to vote against the new prayer book in the House of Bishops. But to him our charism as an Episcopal Church was clear. When we as a church decided something we decided it. That was that. He ordained women and he allowed the use of the 1979 Book of Common Prayer. Let me say this about divorce. When the Episcopal Church began to allow for remarriage a lot of room was given to those bishops who would not do it. I am pretty sure that the Episcopal Church has actually had racists in the Episcopate and in leadership—after the Civil War and throughout the 1960s. I am not looking at the past with rosy glasses or pretending that any of those previous times of great disturbance were not very difficult and painstaking to move through.

I say all of this because I think there is a piece of who we are as Episcopalians that we have forgotten. We are people who have fought with one another on the floor of councils and conventions, we have voted against one another, we have believed that our neighbor was incredibly wrong. But we have, in the past, remained friends in Christ. We have given each other room to learn from one another. We have in the past had a great tolerance for the thorn in our brother and sister's flesh or side because we had enough humility to know that we probably had a greater thorn in our own being. Leaders and loud voices have attempted to change this in the church and attempted to make us into a more fragile church by the exclusion of others. People will know we are Episcopalians by our unbearable tolerance for one another. I would argue that our church has some work to do on this. We have intentionally excluded gays and lesbians and we have intentionally excluded conservatives. It is time that we move on. It is time we work more on keeping people together than dusting off our feet and walking away.

In my mind there is a great difference between saying, humbly: we have made this decision. We are setting new standards of behavior. We want everyone to stay and we will treat everyone the same even if they do not agree. Everyone is welcome here—even those who disagree with me. Then if people drift or decide their spirit is enlivened elsewhere, then so be it. Let us bless them with kindness and mercy. Let us ask them to pray for us sinners. Let us vow to hail each other on the road with friendship.

It is not the Episcopal Church's charism to cut people off, kick them out, or give them what they deserve. God does not do that with us and we are not to do so with others. We do well to remember the unjust servant in Matthew chapter 18 beginning at verse 21. The master of the household forgives the servant a great deal of money, the servant then went to a co-worker who owed him money and threw him into prison until his family could repay the debt. It is not a good ending I fear once the master of the house finds out about it all. We are to forgive and try and start over all the time. Forgive, forgive, forgive, and forgive as we are forgiven. Jesus never says forgive them when they get it right. Jesus never says forgive them when they figure it out or when they finally agree with you. Jesus does not send his disciples out to gather in the likeminded and those who are on my side. At least, that is not the gospel I read.

Let me say this is very hard work. I do not get it right much of the time. It is complicated especially when people's churches are involved. I think the leadership of our church (on both sides) has done irreparable damage to the other in the name of justice and orthodoxy. It is time for us to move towards one another and be reconciled to Christ and one another. I am clear that God wants all of us to enter the kingdom of God. Jesus came to save the whole world— I figure that means everyone. No lost causes. At least, that is what I am counting on. As my friend reminds me: when it is all said and done, when I am waiting for my redeemer, 100% forgiveness will be what matters.

I Love Mission Trips

The chapter on service makes a strong case that we need to be careful not to do toxic charity. A number of the quotes are harsh commentaries on mission trips. One pre-reader reminded me that there is in fact literature that supports the mission trip. A friend of his in Tanzania has even said, "If you have $5,000 to give to the church in Tanzania, please give us half and use the other half to come and visit." The pre-reader challenged me that check book giving alone is too cold; the relationship is important.

In the chapter on stewardship another pre-reader challenged me to think of ways in which the micro-contributor participates in the community.

Both of these are very important truths and I want to parse them out a bit here. I am making the case that we need to be very careful about how we might be affecting, in a negative way, the people and communities that to which we direct funds. Lupton and others make a good case for accountability, for insuring we are not demeaning the individuals we give money to, and to think creatively about how we give. We want to invest in transforming the community and creating well communities. The Episcopal Church and others are not trying to create co-dependent communities. The critics of the modern mission trip make a good point and I understand and I believe they are correct.

So, what I would say is let us call the trip what the trip is: a visit. We are making a visit to our brother and sister Anglicans. We are going to x-land in order to meet people and learn from them about life. We are making a pilgrimage because we hear that God is at work in their community. We are interested in getting to know them and be in relationship with them. This is what we are doing. We are making communion visits.

When the missionary society called The Compass Rose began to raise money for global communion work, it created a boundary. Before it gives it has to make a visit to that place. In this way they are able to listen and hear from the people. I think this is the point of the chapter on service.

My point is that if we want to give money or join people in a local project we can. Figuring out what is a good project is going to take a bit more work in the future. It will take cultural humility. It will be a cautious work to make sure that we are not actually hurting people by trying to do good. The same rules go for the community outside our church.

We have done the same thing in our local context. We have in many cases reached out to do good and created more problems for the people we were trying to serve. A great example is a church that created a breakfast program. It is a really cool program. It feeds a lot of people. It has fed a lot of people. It also pulls a very need population away from the centers of town where they can receive the most help. It requires them to use energy to get all their stuff down to the church. They have to use two tokens/tickets to use public transportation to go back and forth. Sometimes they give clothes detergent or shampoo but no place for people to wash clothes or take a shower that is available elsewhere. The truth is that the program is really wonderful on the surface. People feel good working there. I have felt good working there. But if we ask seriously: is this the best program for this group of people, and in the right place? We probably would answer no.

I love mission trips but let us call them communion visits. Let us call them pilgrimages. I want to be honest about the fact that these trips are more about us than the people we serve. And, let us invest in the relationship by all means. This is what keeps micro contributors and others from the cold practice of just giving. Let us get people together to build new economics around service with dignity for all the people involved. Let us change the world by giving without being demeaning. Let us change the world through a web of relationships.

Everything is Bigger In Texas

The critique often comes that this is all easy for me to talk about because the Episcopal Diocese of Texas is a wealthy diocese. The reality for everyone else is very different and I just do not understand the difficulty of starting new communities without funds. This argument is also usually accompanied by the idea that we need to continue to send money to the Church Wide office so they can help plant congregations in underserved areas of the Church.

Yes, I would say it is nice to have money. I believe that the mission of Christ necessitates starting new communities. When I first began as bishop I thought to myself that it would be great to have sixty million dollars to plant churches. I began work on creating just such a foundation—The Great Commission Foundation (GCF). Today the GCF has one hundred and thirty million dollars. You know what I discovered? It is not enough. It is nice—do not get me wrong! I love it! It is awesome. But it is not enough.

If we believe in planting new communities to reach the unattached Church population, there is not an economic formula wherein the established present Church can fund all the Churches needed. Across the 57 counties of the Episcopal Diocese of Texas we need to plant more than 50 new communities to reach the people who live within our geographic area. We have a plan for 15 in five years. But I am telling you we have to have more than that. The economic model of one priest, on one piece of property, with a building and 120+ people is not economically feasible if we accept that church/community planting is essential to the mission of God.

We have mechanisms to start these churches and communities. We have the missionary work force to start these churches. Using innovative and disbursed models of theological training we can raise cadres of leaders in every diocese to plant new communities. We have the ability to license lay people to be evangelists, pastoral administrators, and preachers. We license people to take the sacrament to a few people—why not 25 people or more. Imagine a community of 200 people serving as a hub church with 10 different communities attached all run by the laity. Bi-vocational clergy attached to the congregation work with the deacons there to help the rector pastorally care for the attached communities. We believe in the ministry of the baptized but we are so locked in the ministry of the clergy we cannot see the potential of rewriting an organic church planting economic model.

Should not the Church Wide office at 815 Second Avenue New York help by collecting money from the local diocese and then redistribute the monies into areas that are underserved? The Episcopal Diocese of Texas was a mission diocese funded in large part by the women's auxiliary of the day which collected for church mission. We were also supported by gifts from congregations in the East and in London. The Episcopal Church also sent out money and missionary bishops. The Church Wide structure works best to start new dioceses or to help missionary dioceses grow. This I think is a good model. It is a model I would support.

I do not think that collecting money from dioceses to start one expensive church in another diocese is a good use of funds. The reality is asking dollars/assessment dollars can be best directed by local churches in conversation with their diocesan leadership. No organization cannibalizes the local congregations in the way we do as a wider church. In a time of overarching organizational crisis with whole dioceses on the economic brink, the wider Church and diocese are wise to leave as much money at the local congregation as possible.

My point is that at the end of the day money is not what keeps us from creating new communities and new churches. What keeps us from starting new communities is having a vision of a God who wants to spread God's reconciling love lavishly across the earth—believing that God has the Episcopal Church to start those communities. We must unleash the sleeping power of our laity to truly do the work of the baptized which is to give thanks to God by undertaking transformative service in the world and by creating new communities of every kind in every place.

It's Good To Be The King

"You are advocating for a disbursed church rather than the current hierarchal one. What about bishops, priests, and deacons?" Let me take this in two parts. First let me say that what is important is to understand that I put the vision piece first because it dictates, in my unabashedly Episcopalian opinion, some nonnegotiables. I am not in favor of a congregational church or a church that is without the three-fold order of ministry (or four-fold if you want to add in the laity). I think if we do not have an unabashed vision of who we are as Episcopalians, we might as well be someone else. We could be Unitarians, we could be Presbyterians, Lutherans, or Methodists. But we are not those kinds of Churches. (Those are great Churches by the way. I love my brothers and sisters in those churches and I want them to be very happy there. And, I want to work with them and their unique style of doing ministry to grow the kingdom of God.) We Episcopalians have a very particular nature where each order does certain things.

I think we think of this nature as hierarchical because as Episcopalians we value the sacraments, we value ordination, and we value liturgy. Those values tend to mean we over value the people in our community who do these things. On top of that is the overlay of business. We are an organization, and we have organized ourselves. We have chosen to place our bishop diocesans as the CEO's and Chairs of the Board. This corporate overlay also creates a hierarchy of a sort. Though this may be a more dangerous thing given the amount of business, leadership, and management expertise our bishops actually have. One person quipped that people elect bishops for pastoral reasons and then give them a CEO job. I do not think it is quite that bad but there is a lot of business—even in small diocese.

What I am arguing for in this book is a rethinking of those orders of vocation for a new time and a new context. We need to face the fact that serving as bishop, priest, and deacon doing the same things we have done for the last 50 years is not getting us anywhere. We need to re-envision and become the leaders needed at this time. Moreover, I think that those orders need to be disbursed throughout the community. And, if we are going to refer to the laity as a separate order with certain work—then we need to empower them and unleash them to go and do that work. Even when doing so looks as though it threatens the current order of things.

I Prefer Bowling Alone

One pre-reader noted that he believed that what we are experiencing in the United States is the "gradual unfolding of Robert D. Putnam's book Bowling Alone." Putnam's must read points out that urban, suburban living (which is where the majority of people are) is so exhausting and hard, folks want to be entertained effortlessly (so restaurants, movies do well). At the same time these overworked exhausted people do not want to be part of anything that requires organization and is regular. Putnam believes that this trend is seen everywhere—freemasons are in trouble, so is Rotary, so is Amateur Dramatic organizations, so is everything. The Church is an organization that requires something from folks and this is not popular.

The pre-reader then says that the Church might respond to this problem by creating effortless ways of participating. We can envision more services that cater to every taste —and cyber church, and flexible ways of attending are the way forward. We can see here that in this way there is overlap with my vision, but a slightly different foundation. The reader goes on to say, "Of course the other response is to say that discipleship isn't meant to be effortless and therefore the Church will be a counter cultural witness to community in an age that is too tired to have community."

My response is that there is real evidence that human beings are created with a need to be in community. We are made to love. We are made to be loved. We have a desire, fulfilled or unfulfilled, to be part of a community. I am not trying to negate the experience of individuals who want to live a life of solitude. Our own Church may have stories of such people who are sainted. We can look throughout the emerging work on societies and see this reality being illustrated in case statement after case statement. For my purposes the work of Brené Brown is the most insightful, in part, because it is based upon thousands and thousands of research hours. She believes we are created to belong. David Eagleman, a neuroscientist at Baylor College of Medicine, actually believes the brain is healthier when in relationship with others. My point is that we are meant for community—we are built for it. This does not mean that we naturally all need or want to go to church and we just have not found the right one yet.

I am offering the idea that because we are made for community and in many respects are healthier when we are in community with others that we as human creatures make community. We naturally form it. One minute it looks like we are playing a video game called Warcraft and the next thing you know we have designed it so we can be in community with others playing the same game. We create a dating site and the next thing you know we are part of one of the largest electronic communities ever imagined—Facebook. As human beings we are and will continue to look for community, make community, design community, and search out community.

I do not believe that left to their own devices we will self-organize an Episcopal Church. Though how awesome would that be! What I am saying is that when those individuals want help in making community, when they are looking for community, and when they discover community—The Episcopal Church needs to be there. We need platforms and webs of relationship (electronic and real) where they can find us. Setting up shop, having an open door, and hoping they will find us are going to be an every shrinking way in which a generation of digital natives find community.

I would also add that I am not in favor of an easy discipleship. I am in favor of walking with individuals as they discover their own discipleship path. Discipleship is hard work. But our beloved Episcopal Church has a pedagogical model of nineteenth century education in mind for formation. You come to our church and we will bless you by imparting information about liturgy, vestments, and clergy with a little reformation history thrown in for good measure. Ta dah! You are an Episcopalian. We have to reinvent and rethink how we nurture discipleship. I think we need to stop fooling ourselves that we have some kind of higher discipleship model and the culture just does not like it. We have to nurture people and help them curate their spiritual journey. This is going to take a whole different kind of thinking.

I hasten to add that the future Church will become a true sanctuary for the Amplified Human. It will be a place of spiritual disciplines, quiet reflection, and sanctuary away from the overscheduled and over produced world. It will be a place of sacramental mystery, transcendence, and transformation. I believe the Church of the future will be one of the few places that individuals will be able to find the divine the wholly/holy other. However, the Church will be a remote inaccessible place if it does not embrace the amplified mission culture. In other words: people will not be able to find the sanctuary they need if it is not discoverable within the context of the digital native.

I think when we get to this part of the discussion we want to try and make this easier for ourselves. I do not think this is the pre-reader's point but it is worth mentioning here. Our brain short circuits when it is faced with a very complex set of issues, variables, and types of people, add in a good mix of organizational change brought on by economic and cultural shifts in a VUCA world. What we do, physically, is our brain answers and looks for broad sweeping answers to questions that were not asked. We actually have a lazy brain. (You can read more about this in Daniel Kahneman's work.)

I say this because I think the old mechanical/deterministic church is looking either for the program to fix everything, or the old church wishes to dismiss the culture because it just does not want what we have. I think we have to really look and think deeply and creatively about how to engage the digital native and the other new generations well. We dismiss a lot of great opportunities by thinking that it is an either or proposition. There are as many versions of the Episcopal Church as there are communities, contexts, cultures, groups, individuals, and desires to find the divine. The future is filled with multiple probabilities—not just two. The future is so bright you have to wear shades!

To Seminary or Not To Seminary?—That is the Question

Let me say about seminaries that I am completely (COMPLETELY) a believer in their work and their future. I had hoped to point out that everything is changing. The Church needs are changing, the economy of seminary is changing (from a fulltime resident student model to a more flexible one), the students themselves are changing, and the way we think about education is changing. This is a lot.

Here is the first significant difficulty all my seminary leaders face: Accreditation. This is an actual problem. The reality is that while everything is in flux the authorities are trying to safeguard a quality education experience. Meanwhile, public colleges are becoming more flexible, and on-line oriented. There is a huge move away from doing research within the institution because of the huge takes from the larger institution. Research dollars are shrinking to 40% of their take because of university overhead. So, let us say—it is a mess.

Our seminaries are trying to do the best they can. These are my friends. They are trying to create good priests. They take seriously their charge. They work hard. They are responsive and responsible to the wider church—except in this time of great flux the Church cannot make up its mind either. So our seminaries and their leadership need prayer and support—and we need to be part of the conversation in navigating the future. We will help the seminaries help us, while at the same time navigating tricky waters with accreditation and their governing authorities. This does not lessen my belief that radical change is in order for these institutions too.

We have all had some very good discussion in two areas worth exploring. The first is in the area of future vision itself. The second is in the area of the self-learning student. Let us begin with the area of vision. One pre-reader offered this example of the danger of vision. He said, speaking ecumenically (but it is all true in TEC seminaries as well), twice in the last fifty years the "futurists" predicted what would happen to theological education. Those institutions that got on the bandwagon and tried to live into the trends that were anticipated, are either out-of-business or a shadow of their former selves. The seminaries that have bucked those trends and lived-into the future as it arrived rather than trying to second-guess it, are still here and in most cases stronger than ever. It does not mean the latter group is not innovative and up-to-date, it means they changed from a position of stability and strength, not from a position of survival and fear.

I would say of course we want to work from a position of strength. But not all seminaries have an endowment large enough to guarantee survival, not all seminaries have an owning diocese to help it along, and not all seminaries are attached to a major university. So, we have to realize that some of the cost of not changing is also being born by structures without which survival would be impossible.

I also want to say that failure was not brought about by looking towards the future alone. Failure was brought about by a variety of contributing sources. One of which is the shrinking enrollment of students in seminaries. The wider community of theological education has known for some time that we have too many seminaries. Over a decade ago, the leaders of these seminaries were having this conversation. So, closures are brought about by a lot of factors.

I am not saying that my views about seminaries should not be examined critically. I think they should. What seminaries have been doing is not leading and leaning into the future but holding back and I think that is my concern. If I am right, and maybe I am not right, the following is true: 1. It costs more today to run seminaries. Buildings, staffing, maintenance, requirements, insurance, electricity, and salaries for professors cost more today than they did four decades ago. 2. There are as many seminarians today as there were at the high water mark of the Episcopal Church. This is true. It is also true that they are not all attending Episcopal seminaries. Therefore, due to the number of seminaries, the number of students receiving training elsewhere (in part due to expense and in part due to family economies where someone needs to work) and through the expansion of less expensive more accessible models, the economy of running a seminary based on residential three year student tuition is not financially sustainable. This is true unless you have some other way to cut the cost. 3. Students themselves are changing. They are looking for other ways to get training and to do the work that they wish to do. The amplified human who is a digital native is not only going to seek inexpensive ways of getting certified, they are not going to continue to pay the high cost of education. (Take a look at the documentary *Ivory Tower* to see how this is shaking up major universities.) This trend will affect seminaries. 4. If the mission is

THE most important thing. And, I think it is, then dioceses need more lay and clergy who are trained well, but inexpensively, and without leaving home for three years. I believe we are just at the beginning of a seminary shake up.

I would argue for the seminary. I argue that it is the seminary that needs to respond to the church and say, "Yes." You need more accessible training for laity: we are going to get it for you. You need people who can get trained in the field: we will get it for you. You need programs on the weekends and at night so you can take shifts with the family at home or keep down a job: we will get it for you. We will get materials multiplied in a variety of languages because you need it. We will build and create a new economy of scale and diversity that is not dependent upon the three year residence e but complements it. The seminary will help you raise and train pastoral leaders, lay preachers, and lay administrators. The e seminaries have a ton of resources, people, knowledge and know-how, and we will help you. It will be sacrificial. It will be hard work. Everyone has to work hard and everyone has to change as we walk into this future.

The seminary that says to the Church we see what you need and we are here for you.: those are the seminaries that are going to be around in three decades. My message is deal from a place of strength. If you have enough students, if you currently have enough money, if you are attached to a university, or if you have an owning diocese(s), then by all means deal from a place of strength. The future Church historians will have a chapter on seminaries to be sure. They will look back at this time and they will talk, not about the ones that survived, but the ones that led and carved out and built up the new seminary of the future.

The second good issue brought to my attention regarding theological education is around the idea that "everyone is eager to learn." It seems in my book that my case for self-learners assumes a self-motivated person who wants to have a richer experience. This particular pre-reader retorted that lots of people once they are ordained never read a book again. This, of course, is an exaggeration but the point is well taken.

I think we could probably write a whole other book just on the nature of human beings. I believe that people in general have a desire to survive. I think I could make a pretty good case this is true and it is what has brought us to this point of history as a global civilization. I believe we were given and have an ability to reflect. It is one of the amazing things that makes us human and separates us from other species we have observed. This ability to reflect, think, refine, practice, learn, and try again is one of our strengths. In short, I believe we are self-learning self-organizing creatures.

The truth is that people are self-educating right now. They are learning about the Episcopal Church with the help of the internet. There are other people who are taking theology classes right now that are of a very high quality just because they want to be better lay ministers. There are people currently looking for God and the divine and spirituality on their own.

We cannot pretend that people are not constantly looking up and trying to learn and understand the world that they live in. Statistically it just is not a true statement that people are not invested in learning for themselves. We can debate the quality of that learning to be sure. The scientific reality is that retention rate for a self-learner is higher than rates for those who are forced to memorize information or take classes because the system requires it.

People are self-learners and they are self-learning about God and they are self-organizing around their ideas about God. Part of my point is that we can wait for these self-learners to walk in our door someday or we can be a part of their self-learning experience. If we are not out there and on the Internet, then we will be harder to find. How do we help seekers and self-learners find us?

Book learning and higher forms of education and formation are part of a very complex learning society. They are necessary. I think we agree on this point. All of that being said, I would quickly add that it is highly possible that the church, in order to be successful in its mission, does not need every priest to be trained in a certain way, tested for the same knowledge, and having marked certain scholastic boxes in order to be a good priest. But this is the model we are currently using as the standard of training. I am inviting seminaries to figure out how to achieve a new standard of training. I would remind us that seminaries have not always offered master degrees. That is a relatively recent phenomenon. Today it has become the assumed norm.

We need clergy who are philosophers. We need clergy who are historians. We need clergy who are business people. We need clergy who understand the history of liturgy. We need clergy who are really good at taking care of the dying. We need clergy who are entrepreneurial and innovative. We need clergy who are traditional. They do not all need to have a three-year residential seminary experience and learn all the same things so they can practice and be a good clergy person and accomplish God's mission. I think that is my point.

People need to learn some things in order to do ministry. Where and how they learn those things are up for discussion right now. I want clergy who serve in my diocese to love the Episcopal Church, know its tradition, and pass along its faith. My goal is to work with the seminaries of the Church to help me get that done. The fact is that I need more missionaries and more church planters and more lay leaders than we have time or money to train. So, we all have to come together (seminaries and dioceses) to help us accomplish the mission that is before us. It is necessary and it is urgent. I am looking (and believe I have) seminary partners who want to help.

I Don't Trust Futurists—But I Like You

Only a dear friend would voluntarily read 500+ pages of my writing. Only a dear friend would then tell me the truth, "I'm always anxious about books that attempt to say something about the future, especially the future of the church. When futurists speak, one of three things happens: (1) their words become a self-fulfilling prophecy, usually in the direction of their most negative predictions; (2) people believe them and work to create their imaginary future (no matter how well-trended) and that usually turns out disastrously; or (3) people listen, critique, and prepare carefully for what is coming as it comes, remaining strong and focused in the meantime, but not with head in the sand. It is anticipating with patience so we can sort out the trends that will be manifest from those that were a futurist's fantasy, no matter how well informed."

Let me begin by saying, "Thank you to all my pre-readers." I know now that you love me! You have proven yourself. I should treat you and JoAnne (my first editor) to a very fine steak dinner with fine wine. You all deserved it. I love our conversation. I love your challenges—even though some were hard to hear. I think it is in the conversation where the healthy energy lies and where our probable future is most given life.

I am a bishop and our diocese is involved in three great seminaries. We have 400 clergy and families depending upon the diocese for their livelihood. We have thousands of employees who depend on their positions in our churches. We have a pastoral responsibility to over 70,000 Episcopalians in the Diocese of Texas alone. The things in this book will challenge my own existing policies. The things that I say will cause us as a diocesan family to think about how we do things. I have challenged myself. I am a bit scared. After all, the fiscal responsibility alone is titanic in scale. I am aware and mindful; and, I take that interconnected relationship and responsibility very seriously. I have even wondered: should I publish the book? We must indeed do this work with a great deal of discernment. We must, "listen, critique, and prepare carefully for what is coming as it comes, remaining strong and focused in the meantime, but not with head in the sand."

Yet at the same time we must dare. We must dare to build a Church in which a Noah like journey might bring all to a new land. We must dare to listen and speak to burning bushes. We must find the words when all we have are fear and anxiety. We must turn to our closest friends when we are weak of heart. We must risk going up against mighty forces outnumbered and without preparation. We must believe that the light of God will last even though all of our resources look as though they are depleted. We must drop our old ways of doing things and follow. We must dare to go out on our own and do things like heal people, start communities, and share good things—even though some of us have never done those things before. We must venture out against the stormy sea and row away from the safety of the shore to the other side. We travel into lands where they do not know the God of whom we speak.

We have been chosen for just such a time as this. You see, we do these things, not because we can always do them from a position of strength. We do these things not because they are safe. We do these things not because we believe we will be successful. We risk it all and we do things because of the God in whom we believe. This is our sacred story.

BIBLIOGRAPHY

The Alban Institute. *The In-Between Church*. Bethesda, MD: The Alban Institute, 1998.

The Alban Institute. "Raising the Roof." http://www.alban.org/raisingtheroof/changingSize.asp

Ambrose, Stephen E. *Undaunted Courage*. New York: Simon & Schuster, 1996.

Anderson, Chris. *Makers: The New Industrial Revolution*. New York: Crown Business Press, 2012.

Aristotle, *Nicomachean Ethics*. Trans J. A. K. Thomson. New York: Penguin Classics, 2004.

Augustine of Hippo. *The Confessions*. Grand Rapids, MI: Baker Book House, 2005.

Ayres Jr., B. Drummond. "The Episcopalians: an American elite with roots going back to Jamestown." *The New York Times.* December 19, 2011.

Bader-Saye, Scott. "Bonds of Affection: The Transformational Possibilities of a Platitude." The Conference, 2014.

Balge, Richard D. "A Brief History Of Evangelism In The Christian Church." Synod-Wide Convocation on Evangelism, Wisconsin Lutheran College, Milwaukee, Wisconsin. August 15-17, 1978. http://www.wlsessays.net/files/BalgeBrief.pdf

Banks, Adelle M. "Survey Finds Vitality in Multisite Church Model." Religion News Service. March 11, 2014. http://www.washingtonpost.com/national/religion/survey-finds-growth-vitality-in-multisite-church-model/2014/03/11/7affef86-a944-11e3-8a7b-c1c684e2671f_story.html

Barna, George and Hatch, Mark. *Boiling Point: Monitoring Cultural Shifts in the 21st Century*. Ventura, CA: Regal Books, 2001.

Barna Group. "45 New Statistics on Church Attendance and Avoidance," March 3, 2008, https://www.barna.org/barna-update/congregations/45-new-statistics-on-church-attendance-and-avoidance#.Uh8552TXgVk

Becker, Howard S. *Outsiders: Studies in the Sociology of Deviance.* New York: Macmillan, 1963.

Becker, Howard S. *Art Worlds.* Oakland, CA: University of California Press, 1982.

Bellah, Robert. "At Home and Not At Home: Religious Pluralism and Religious Truth," The Christian Century, April 19, 1995, 423-428.

Bellah, Robert. *Habits of the Heart.* Oakland, Ca: University of California Press, 1996.

Bellah, Robert. *The Broken Covenant.* Seabury Press: 1975.

Berry, Wendell. "It All Turns on Affection," Awards and Honors: 2012 Jefferson Lecture. http://www.neh.gov/about/awards/jefferson-lecture/wendell-e-berry-lecture

Bird, Warren. "Today there are more than 8,000 multisite churches." LeadNetLeadNet. http://t.co/IWsq4bj5k3

Bly, Robert. *The Sibling Society.* New York: Addison-Wesley Publishing, 1996.

Boyte, Harry C. "Reframing Democracy: Governance, Civic Agency, and Politics." *Public Administration Review 65.* 2005.

Brand, Stuart Brand. "Founding Father." Wired. September 2003. http://archive.wired.com/wired/archive/9.03/baran_pr.html

Brewer, Priscilla. "Demographic Features of the Shaker Decline, 1787–1900," Journal of Interdisciplinary History 15.1. Summer 1984: 31–52.

Brown, Brené. *Daring Greatly.* London: Gotham Books, 2012.

Bryson, Bill. *A Short History of Nearly Everything.* New York: Random House, 2005.

Bryson, Bill. *At Home*. New York: Anchor Books, 2010.

Bullock, F. W. B. *A History of Training for the Ministry of the Church of England and Wales from 1800 to 1874*. St. Leonards-on-the-Sea, Budd & Gillatt,1955.

Bush, Vannevar. "As We May Think." *The Atlantic Monthly*. July 1, 1945. http://www.theatlantic.com/magazine/archive/1945/07/as-we-may-think/303881/

Capra, Fritjof. *The Turning Point*. New York: Bantam, 1983.

Carcasson, Martín. "Core Principles for Public Engagement." Thataway. www.thataway.org/files/Core_Principles_of_Public_Engagement.pdf

Carcasson, Martín. "Beginning with the End in Mind: A Call for Goal-Driven Deliberative Practice." Occasional Paper / no.2 / 2009. http://www.publicagenda.org/files/PA_CAPE_Paper2_Beginning_SinglePgs_Rev.pdf

– *The Catholic Encyclopedia*. New York: Robert Appleton Company, 1909. http://www.newadvent.org/cathen/05001a.htm

The Church Hymnal Corporation, Prayer Book and Hymnal (New York: Church Publishing, 1979).

– *The Cloud of Unknowing and other works*. Trans. A. C. Spearing. New York: Penguin Classics, 2001.

Coase, Ronald. "The Nature of the Firm." *Economica 4, no 16* . 1927.

Cox, Harvey. *Religion in the Secular City: Toward a Postmodern Theology*. New York: Simon and Shuster, 1984.

Davies, Stella. *History of Macclesfield*. Didsbury, Manchester: E. J. Morten Publisher, 1961.

Dawkins, Richard. *The Selfish Gene*. 1989. Doi: http://books.google.com/?id=WkHO9HI7koEC&pg=PA192

Dawkins, Richard and Williams, Rowan. "Nature of human beings and the question of their ultimate origin." Oxford University, 2013. http://www.youtube.com/watch?v=jzqa6VMI0UQ

Dix, Dom Gregory. *The Shape of the Liturgy*. London: Dacre Press, 1964.

– "Domestic Racial and Ethnic Membership report for 2009. " Episcopal Church. http://library.episcopalchurch.org/sites/default/files/episcopal_d omestic_racial-ethnic_membership_2009.pdf

Dobbs, Betty Jo Teeter and Jacob, Margaret C. *Newton and the Culture of Newtoniansim*. New Jersey: Humanities Press, 1995.

Dozier, Verna J. *The dream of God: A call to return*. Cambridge, MA: Cowley Publications, 1991.

Duggan, Maeve and Smith, Aaron. "Cell Internet Use 2013." Pew Research. September 2013. http://www.pewinternet.org/2013/09/16/cell-internet-use-2013/

Dunagan, Jake. "Design: Post Newtonian Governance," in 2009 *Ten-Year Forecast: The Future is a Chance to Be New*. Palo Alto, CA: Institute for the Future, 2009.

Johansen, Bob. "2008-2018 Map of Future Forces Affecting the Episcopal Church." Institute for the Future. Presented at The Consortium of Endowed Parishes meeting at St. David's, Austin, TX 2008.

Johansen, Bob. *Get There Early: Sensing the Future to Compete in the Present*. San Francisco, CA: Berrett-Koehler Publishers, Inc., 2007.

Johansen, Bob. *Leaders Make the Future*. San Francisco: Barrett-Koehler Publishing, 2012.

Kingston, Anne. "Get Ready for Generation Z: They're smarter than Boomers, and way more ambitious that Millennials." Macleans. July 15, 2014. Doi: http://www.macleans.ca/society/life/get-ready-for-generation-z/?utm_content=bufferb8101&utm_medium=social&utm_source=twitter.com&utm_campaign=buffer

Loader, William. "First Thoughts on Year C Epistle Passages in the
 Lectionary." Pentecost 15. Murdoch University, Uniting Church in
 Australia,.
 http://wwwstaff.murdoch.edu.au/~loader/CEpPentecost15.htm

Meister, Chad. *Introducing Philosophy of Religion*. Nashville, TN: Abingdon
 Press, 2009.

Eames, Robin et al. *The Windsor Report*. 2004. Doi:
 http://www.anglicancommunion.org/windsor2004/index.cfm

Eagleton, Terry. "Postmodernism,." *Presis* 6. 1987, 7-24.

– "Episcopal Ministry: The Report of the Archbishops' Group on the
 Episcopate." London: Church House Publishing, 1990.

Finn, Thomas Macy. *Early Christian Baptism and the Catechumenate*.
 Collegeville, MN: Liturgical Press, 1992.

Foley, Edward. *From Age to Age: How Christians Have Celebrated the
 Eucharist*. Chicago: Liturgy Training Publications, 1991.

Friedman, Thomas. *The World Is Flat*. New York: Farrar, Straus & Giroux,
 2005.

Friedman, Uri. "12 Maps That Changed the World." *The Atlantic*.
 http://www.theatlantic.com/international/archive/2013/12/12-
 maps-that-changed-the-world/282666/

– "The Future of Everything Summit of Ideas and Digital Invention," March
 2013, Manchester, UK. http://futureeverything.org

Gladwell, Malcolm. *The Tipping Point: How Little Things Can Make a Big
 Difference*. Boston: Little, Brown and Company, 2000.

Gorbis, Marina. *The Nature of the Future: Dispatches from the Socialstructured
 World*. New York: Free Press, 2013.

Gortner, David. "Up to the Task: Clergy Leadership for the 21st Century,"
 Virginia Theological Seminary. January 2014.

Hill, Christoper T. "The Post Scientific Society," *Issues in Science and Technology*. Fall 2007.

Hall, William P. and Nousala,Susu. "Autopoiesis and Knowledge in Self Sustaining Organizational Systems." 4th International Mulit-conference on Society, Cybernetics and Informatics. June 2010. Orlando, FL.

Harvey, David. *The Condition of Postmodernity*. New York: Wiley-Blackwell, 1989.

Hauerwas, Stanley, Milbank, John and Bretherton, Luke in Conversation. "Theological Reflections on Being a Theologian and the Task of Theology." Faith & Public Policy Forum and SCM Press. King's College, London. October 18, 2010. http://podcast.ulcc.ac.uk/accounts/kings/Social_Science/Milbank_Hauerwas_Bretherton.mp3

Hayek, F.A. *Law, Legislation, and Liberty*, Vol. 2. Chicago: University of Chicago Press, 1978.

Hayes, Richard. "The Word of Reconciliation." Faith and Leadership. July 20, 2010. http://www.faithandleadership.com/sermons/the-word-reconciliation

Hein, David and Shattuck Jr., Gardiner H. *The Episcopalians*. New York: Church Publishing, 2004.

Heisenberg, Werner. *Physics and Philosophy: The Revolution in Modern Science*. Lectures delivered at University of St. Andrews, Scotland, Winter 1955-56.

Heisenberg, Werner. "Critique of the Physical Concepts of the Corpuscular Theory," Trans Carl Eckhart and Frank C. Hoyt. *The Physical Principles of the Quantum Theory*. 1930.

– "The History of Work." Readers' Digest Australia. http://www.readersdigest.com.au/history-of-work.

Hotchkiss, Dan. "Searching for the Key: Developing a Theory of Synagogue Size." Congregations 27, no. 1. January–February 2001.

Howard, Robert. "Values Make the Company: An Interview with Robert Haas." *Harvard Business Review*. September-October 1990.

– "Identity and Vision—Draft." Reimagine The Episcopal Church Task Force. http://reimaginetec.org/identity-and-vision-draft

Institute for the Future. "The Future of Persuasion." Summer 2010, http://www.iftf.org/uploads/media/SR-1321_IFTF_FutureofPersuasionReport-1.pdf

Institute for the Future. "Extreme Learners." 2014. http://www.iftf.org/our-work/global-landscape/learning/extreme-learners

Institute for the Future. "From Educational Institutions to Learning Flows." 2013. http://www.iftf.org/uploads/media/SR-1580-IFTF_Future_of_Learning_01.pdf

Institute for the Future. "Future Work Skills 2020." 2011. http://www.iftf.org/uploads/media/SR-1382A_UPRI_future_work_skills_sm.pdf

Institute for the Future. "The Internet Human." http://www.iftf.org/internethuman/

Institute for the Future. "Knowledge Tools of the Future." 2008. http://www.iftf.org/our-work/people-technology/technology-horizons/knowledge-tools-of-the-future

Institute for the Future. "Learning: 2020 Forecast." 2013. http://www.iftf.org/our-work/global-landscape/learning

Institute for the Future. "Young People in the World of Abundant Connectivity." June 2001. http://www.iftf.org/our-work/people-technology/technology-horizons/networks-in-use-young-people-in-the-world-of-abundant-connectivity

–   "International/Christian History." Christianity Today. http://www.christianitytoday.com/ch/1998/issue57/57h026.html

Jackson, Michael C. *Systems Approaches to Management*. New York: Springer Science & Business Media, 2000.

Jankiewicz, Darius. "A Short History of Ordination." April 5,2013.
http://www.memorymeaningfaith.org/blog/2013/04/history-ordination-part-i.html#_edn1

Jeffries, Adrianne. "2nd Annual Film Festival Hints At Just How Disruptive
Kickstarter Could be." Betabeat, July 2011.
http://betabeat.com/2011/07/2nd-annual-film-fest-hints-at-just-how-disruptive-kickstarter-could-be

Jones, L. Gregory and Jones, Nathan. "Deep trends affecting Christian
institutions." Faith and Leadership.
http://www.faithandleadership.com/content/l-gregory-jones-and-nathan-jones-deep-trends-affecting-christian-institutions

Jones, L. Gregory. "Something old, Something New: Innovation in Theological
Education." *Christian Century*. Feb 10, 2014.
http://www.christiancentury.org/article/2014-01/something-old-something-new

June, Williamson. "Urban Design Tactics for Suburban Retrofitting." Build A
Better Burb. http://buildabetterburb.org/11-urban-design-tactics-for-suburban-retrofitting

Jung, C. G. *Psychology and Religion: West and East*. Princeton, NJ: Princeton
University Press, 1958.

Kawasaki, Guy. "A Practical Blog For Impractical People, The Art of
Evangelism." January 12, 2006.
http://blog.guykawasaki.com/2006/01/the_art_of_evan.html#ixzz363laECaM

Kahneman, Daniel. *Thinking, Fast and Slow*. New York: Farrar, Straus and
Giroux, 2011.

Kinder Institute. "Kinder institute 32nd Annual Report." Rice University,
2012.
http://has.rice.edu/uploadedFiles/Houston_Area_Survey/FINAL%20-%202013%20KIHAS%20Report.pdf

Koester, Craig. *Hebrews. Anchor Bible Commentary vol. 36*. New York:
Doubleday, 2001.

Kreit, Bradley. "Investing in Local Communities to Improve Health." Institute for the Future. November 7, 2011. http://member.iftf.org/node/3989

Krauss, Michael E. "Keynote-Mass Language Extinction and Documentation: The Race Against Time." 2007.

Lasn, Kalle. *Culture Jam*. New York: Eagle Book, 1999.

Lewis, C. S. *The Four Loves*. New York: Houghton Mifflin Harcourt, 1991.

Leadership Network. "Multisite Scorecard." March 11, 2014. http://leadnet.org/available-now-the-leadership-networkgeneris-multisite-church-scorecard/

Lebreton, J. and Zeilier, J. *A History of the Primitive Church, IV*. New York: Collier Books, 1948.

Lepore, Jill. "Disruption Machine: What the gospel of innovation gets wrong." *The New Yorker*. June 23, 2014.

Lerner, Jonathan. "Pop-Up Urbanism to Build Community Health: Street Makeovers Put New Spin on the Block." *Pacific Magazine: The Science of Society*. January 16, 2012. http://www.psmag.com/magazines/news-and-options/street-makeovers-put-new-spin-on-the-block-38926

Littlejohn, Stephen W. and Domenici, Kathy. *Engaging Communication in Conflict: Systemic Practice*. Thousand Oaks: Sage Publications, 2001.
Lodge, Carey. "Connecting churches and schools." *Christianity Today*. February 10, 2014. http://www.christiantoday.com/article/connecting.churches.and.schools.on.education.sunday/35774.htm

Lupton, Robert D. *Toxic Charity: How Churches and Charities Hurt Those They Help*. New York: Harper Collins, 2011.

Macquarrie, John. *A Guide to the Sacraments*. London: SCM Press Ltd, 1997.

Macquarrie, John. *Principles of Christian Theology*. London: SCM Press, 1966.

Macy, Gary. *The Hidden History of Women's Ordination: Female Clergy in the Medieval West*. New York: Oxford University Press, 2008.

Maslow, A.H. "A theory of human motivation." *Psychological Review*, 50(4), 1943. http://psychclassics.yorku.ca/Maslow/motivation.htm

Mathews, David. "Community Politics: A Lens for Seeing the Whole Story of Kettering Research." *Connections.* Winter 2006.

Mattingly, Terry. "Backsliders and the unchurched equal the Nones." November 4, 2013. Patheos. http://www.patheos.com/blogs/tmatt/2013/11/backsliders-and-the-unchurched-equal-the-nones

Mayfield, Ross. "Weblog: Market's Technology & Musings." October 13, 2008. http://ross.typepad.com/blog/2005/08/web_of_verbs.html

McCracken, Kristin. "Inventor or Artist?" *Huffington Post Blog*, December 9, 2013. http://www.huffingtonpost.com/kristin-mccracken/inventor-or-artist-an-int_b_4399366.html

McGehee, J. Pittman and Thomas, Damon J. *The Invisible Church: Finding Spirituality where You are.* Santa Barbara, CA: ABC-CLIO Publisher, 2008.

McIntosh, Gary. *One Size Doesn't Fit All.* Grand Rapids, MI: Revell, 1999.

Meeks, Wayne. *First Urban Christians.* New Haven, CN: Yale University Press, 1983.

Merton, Thomas Merton. *New Seeds of Contemplation.* New Directions Publishing: New York, 1972.

Michalski, Jerry. "Thriving in the Relationship Economy: What is the Relationship Economy? How is it different from what went before? How do you thrive in it? What do you need to learn & do?," Institute for the Future. August 31, 2013. http://prezi.com/3igqdq90g-y0/thriving-in-the-relationship-economy

Milbank, John, Catherine Pickstock, and Ward, Graham, et al. *Radical Orthodoxy.* Routledge: London and New York, 1999.

Milbank, John and Oliver, Simon, et al. *The Radical Orthodoxy Reader.* Routledge: London and New York, 2009.

Mitra, Sugata. "Build a School in the Cloud." TED. TED 2013.
https://www.ted.com/talks/sugata_mitra_build_a_school_in_the_cl
oud

Mitra, Sugata. "Kids can teach themselves." TED. TED 2007,.
http://www.ted.com/talks/sugata_mitra_shows_how_kids_teach_th
emselves/transcript#t-1183000

Miyaoka, Osahito, Sakiyama, Osamu and Krauss, Michael. *The Vanishing
Languages of the Pacific Rim.* Oxford: Oxford University Press, 2007.

Moyo, Dambisa. "Dead Aid." Fordham.
http://www.fordham.edu/economics/mcleod/Dambisa_moyo_Dea
dAidForward.pdf

Naisbitt, John. *Megatrends.* New York: Time Warner Books, 1982.

Nations, Tim. "What 7 Rapidly Growing Churches Are Learning About
Multisite." Lead Net. May 15th, 2014. http://leadnet.org/what-7-
rapidly-growing-churches-are-learning-about-multisite/

Newton, John. "Front-door Evangelism theology." Resources for
Invite/Welcome/Connect. Episcopal Diocese of Texas.
http://www.epicenter.org/newcomer

Newton, John. *New Clothes.* New York: Church Publishing, 2014.

Nunes, Paul and Downes, Larry. "The Five Most Disruptive Innovations."
Forbes. January 10, 2014.
http://www.forbes.com/sites/bigbangdisruption/2014/01/10/the
-five-most-disruptive-innovations-at-ces-2014/

Oliver, Edmund H. *The Social Achievements of the Christian Church.* Toronto:
Ryerson Press, 1930.

Payne, Claude E. *Reclaiming the Great Commission.* San Francisco: Jossey
Bass, 2000.

Peter, Laurence J. *Peter's Quotations: Ideas for Our Time.* New York: Bantam
Books, 1977.

Pelikan, Jaroslav. *The Vindication of Tradition: The 1983 Jefferson Lecture in
the Humanities.* Yale University Press: New Haven, 1986.

Pew Research Center. "Political Polarization in American Public: Political Polarization and Personal Life." June 12, 2014. http://www.people-press.org/2014/06/12/section-3-political-polarization-and-personal-life/

Prichard, Robert. History of the Episcopal Church. New York: Church Publishing, 1999.

Prichard, Robert. The Anglican Communion: A Brief History Lesson. http://www.livingchurch.org/anglican-communion-brief-history-lesson

Prigogine, Ilya and Stengers, Isabelle. Order out of Chaos. New York: Bantam Books, 1984.

Piepkorn, Arthur Carl. Profiles in Belief: The Religious Bodies of the United States and Canada. New York: Harper & Row, 1977.

Rainer, Thom. "Seven Reasons Why Church Worship Centers Will Get Smaller." December 9, 2013. http://thomrainer.com/2013/12/09/seven-reasons-why-church-worship-centers-will-get-smaller/

Reed, James E. and Prevost, Ronnie. Education in the Apostolic Age. Nashville: Broadman and Holman, 1993.

– "Research and Statistics." Episcopal Church. http://www.episcopalchurch.org/page/research-and-statistics

– "Meet Generation Z: Forget everything you learned about Millennials," produced by New York City advertising agency Sparks & Honey. June 17, 2014. Doi: http://www.slideshare.net/sparksandhoney/generation-z-final-june-17

Richardson, Cyril C. "Didache." Early Christian Fathers. New York: Touchstone, 1996.

Roberts, Alexander and Donaldson, James. "Apostolic Constitutions." The Ante-Nicene Fathers, Volume VII. Edinburgh: T. & T. Clark, 1967.

Robinson, Ken. "How Schools Kill Creativity." TED. http://blog.ted.com/2006/06/27/sir_ken_robinso

Roosevelt, Theodore. "Citizenship In A Republic." Sorbonne, Paris, France. April 23, 1910. http://www.theodore-roosevelt.com/images/research/speeches/maninthearena.pdf

Rothauge, Arlin. Sizing Up Your Congregation. New York: Seabury Professional Services, 1986.

Rowdon, Harold H. "Theological Education in Historical Perspective." *Vox Evangelica*, vol. 7, 1971.

Ruff, Richard. "Active listening—a forgotten key to sales success." Sales Training Connection. September 16, 2011. http://salestrainingconnection.com/2011/09/16/active-listening-a-forgotten-key-to-sales-success

Runcie, Robert. "Opening Address: Lambeth Conference," *The Truth Shall Make You Free*. London: Church House Publishing, 1988.

Rushkoff, Douglas. *Life Inc: How Corporatism Conquered the World and How We Can Take It Back*. New York: Random House Trade Paperbacks, 2011.

Ryrie, Charles. *Balancing the Christian Life*. Chicago: Moody Press, 1994.

Satterlee, Craig Alan. *Ambrose of Milan's Method of Mystagogical Preaching*. Collegeville, MN: Liturgical Press, 2002.

Schaff, Philip and Wace, Henry et al. *The Nicene and Post Nicene Fathers of the Christian Church*. Grand Rapids, MI: Wm. B. Eerdmans Publishing Company, 1989.

Schmemann, Alexander. *For the Life of the World*. Crestwood, NY: St. Vladimir's Seminary Press, 1973.

Schwartz, Barry. and Ward, Andrew. "Doing Better but Feeling Worse: The Paradox of Choice." Swarthmore College. http://www.swarthmore.edu/SocSci/bschwar1/Choice%20Chapter.Revised.pdf

Sebastian, David. "Trends in Theological Education in North America." Anderson University School of Theology, Anderson, Indiana.

Shirky, Clay. *Here Comes Everybody*. New York: Penguin, 2009.

Sinek, Simon. *Start With Why*. New York: Penguin, 2009.

– "Smart Cities and Smart Citizens," *Sustain Magazine*, Posted May 1, 2013, http://sustainmagazine.com/smart-cities-smart-citizens

Smith, Philip. *Dictionary of Greek and Roman Biography and Mythology*, Boston: Little, Brown and Company, 1867.

Stark, Rodney. *The Rise of Christianity: A Sociologist Reconsiders History*. Princeton, 1996.

Stetzer, Ed. "Starting, Staffing, and Supporting a Multisite Church." Christianity Today. March 17, 2014. http://www.christianitytoday.com/edstetzer/2014/march/startin g-staffing-and-supporting-multisite-church.html

Stevens, R. Paul. *The Other Six Days: Vocation, Work, and Ministry in Biblical Perspective*. Carlisle: Paternoster Press, 1999.

Stiehm, Judith Hicks and Townsend, Nicholas W. *The U.S. Army War College: Military Education in a Democracy*. Philadelphia, Pa: Temple University Press, 2002.

Surowiecki, James. *The Wisdom of Crowds*. New York: Random House, 2004.

Thompson, Barkley. *Elements of Grace*. Marion, AR: Trinity press, 2013.

Taleb, Nassim Nicholas. *Antifragile: Things That Gain from Disorder*. New York: Random House, 2012.

Taleb, Nassim Nicholas. *Black Swan*. New York: Random House, 2007.

Task Force For Reimagining The Episcopal Church, Identity Paper. September 19, 2013. http://reimaginetec.org/identity-and-vision-draft

Taylor, Charles. *A Secular Age*. Cambridge, MA: The Belknap Press of Harvard University Press, 2007.

Tellier, Luc-Normand. *Urban World History*. Québec: Press de l'Université du Québec, 2009.

Tickle, Phyllis. *The Great Emmergence: How Christianity is Changing and Way*. New York: 2008.

Tillich, Paul. *Shaking the Foundations*. New York: Charles Scribner's Sons, New York, 1955.

Villanueva, John Carl. "Electron Cloud Model." August 25, 2009. Universe Today. http://www.universetoday.com/38282/electron-cloud-model/#ixzz33vq8ipk1

Warburg-Johnson, Bettina. "Anya Kamenetz Tells What's in Store for Education." Institute for the Future. August 14, 2012. http://www.iftf.org/future-now/article-detail/do-it-yourself-university-style-anya-kamenetz-tells-whats-in-store-for-education/#sthash.RsdKXK1h.dpuf

Westerhoff, John H. Westerhoff. *Will Our Children Have Faith?* New York: Morehouse Publishing, 1976.

Wilford, John Noble. "The World's Languages Dying Off Rapidly." New York Times, September 18, 2007. http://www.nytimes.com/2007/09/18/world/18cnd-language.html?ex=1347768000&en=faaeb910e26d6ba8&ei=5088&partner=rssnyt&emc=rss

Williams, Peter W. *America's Religions: From Their Origins to the Twenty-first century*. Chicago: University of Illinois Press, 2008.

Whaples, Robert. "Hours of Work In U.S. History." Wake Forest University. http://eh.net/encyclopedia/hours-of-work-in-u-s-history

Wheatley, Margaret. *Finding Our Way*. San Francisco: Berrett.-Koehler Publishers, 2005.

Wheatley, Margaret. *Leadership and the New Science*. San Francisco: Berrett-Koehler, 2006.

White, Edwin Augustine and Dykman, Jackson A. et al. *Annotated Constitution and Canons*. New York: Church Publishing Incorporated, 1985.

Winchester, Simon. *The Man Who Loved China*. New York: Harper Perennial, 2008.

Yankelovich, Daniel. *Coming the Public Judgment*. Syracuse, NY: Syracuse University Press, 1991.

Zscheile, Dwight. "Episcopal Church in context, Episcopal structure in Context, Rethinking Church wide organization in a New Apostolic Era. " Doi: http://www.provinceiv.org/images/customer-files/ZscheileSynod.pdf

INDEX

T

END NOTES

[1] Bill Bryson, *At Home: A Short History of Private life*, (New York: Anchor Books, 2010), 7ff.

[2] *Ibid*, 3.

[3] *Ibid*, 5.

[4] Nassim Nicholas Taleb coined the phrase "antifragile" in his essays and book by the same name.

[5] Quantum is the smallest amount of physical quantity. Quantum studies is about measuring and understanding how the smallest parts of the universe work.

[6] I first heard of Schrödinger's cat and superposition from Bill Bryson's book entitled: *A Short History of Nearly Everything* (New York: Random House, 2005), 191.

[7] *Ibid.*

[8] Howard S. Becker, *Outsiders: Studies in the Sociology of Deviance* (Macmillan: New York, 1963) 9.

[9] *Ibid*, 179.

[10] Howard S. Becker, Howard S, *Art Worlds*, (University of California Press: Oakland, 1982) xv.

[11] Margaret Wheatley, *Leadership and the New Science* (San Francisco: Berrett-Koehler, 2006), 68

[12] *Ibid*, 70

[13] Paul Zahl, Episcopal Diocese of Texas Clergy Conference, 2012, on the doctrine of imputation.

[14] Bob Johansen, *Leaders Make the Future* (San Francisco: Barrett-Koehler Publishing, 2012), 34.

[15] Pronounced LEMhigh. This image was first used in my Diocese of Texas Council Address in 2010. I was first published in my essay in the book *Who We Shall Become*, Church Publishing, 2013. It is expanded here.

[16] Stephen E. Ambrose, *Undaunted Courage*, (New York: Simon & Schuster, 1996), 266.

[17] *Ibid*, 266.

[18] *Ibid*, 267.

[19] *Ibid*, 266.

[20] We cannot downplay the catastrophic collision about to take place between cultures, nor undertake some new kind of spiritual colonialism.

[21] We must be careful to avoid "manifest destiny." The persecution and manipulation that came with the discovery were lessons hard learned and rarely repented from. We do not want to make the same colonial mistakes in regard to this new missionary

movement.

[22] Johansen, *Leaders*, 6.

[23] Wheatley, *New Science*, 28.

[24] Judith Hicks Stiehm and Nicholas W. Townsend, *The U.S. Army War College: Military Education in a Democracy*. (Temple University Press, 2002) p. 6.

[25] Bob Johansen, *Get There Early: Sensing the Future to Compete in the Present* (San Francisco, CA: Berrett-Koehler Publishers, Inc., 2007).pp. 51–53.

[26] Two authors Margaret Wheatley and Marina Gorbis survey the world around us and they see that our culture is filled with organizations that are using outdated models of community life to find their way in the emerging millennia in which we find ourselves. See The New Science and The Nature of the Future.

[27] Wheatley, *New Science*, 7.

[28] *Ibid.*

[29] *Ibid.*

[30] Jake Dunagan, "Design: Post Newtonian Governance," in 2009 Ten-Year Forecast: The Future is a Chance to Be New (Palo Alto, CA: Institute for the Future, 2009). As quoted in Marina Gorbis, *The Nature of the Future: Dispatches from the Socialstructured World* (New York: Free Press, 2013), 99.

[31] Gorbis, 99.

[32] Thomas Friedman *The World Is Flat* (New York: Farrar, Straus & Giroux, 2005).

[33] Gorbis, 99.

[34] "45 New Statistics on Church Attendance and Avoidance," Barna Group, March 3, 2008, https://www.barna.org/barna-update/congregations/45-new-statistics-on-church-attendance-and-avoidance#.Uh8552TXgVk "Unattached- people who had attended neither a conventional church nor an organic faith community (e.g., house church, simple church, intentional community) during the past year. Some of these people use religious media, but they have had no personal interaction with a regularly-convened faith community. This segment represents one out of every four adults (23%) in America. About one-third of the segment was people who have never attended a church at any time in their life."

[35] *Ibid.*

[36] *Ibid.*

[37] *Ibid.*

[38] The Apostle Paul was a tentmaker and an evangelist. A popular way of referring to clergy who make their living at a different job than working full time for the church is "tentmaker priest."

[40] The Rt. Rev. Ian Douglas is the first person I heard use this phrase, "God has a mission, God's mission has a church."

[41] Adapted from Brené Brown, *Daring Greatly* (London: Gotham Books, 2012), 63.

[42] *Ibid.*

[43] *Ibid*, 64.

[44] *Ibid.*

[45] Adapted from Peter Sheahan's quote in Brené Brown's *Daring Greatly*, 65.

[46] *Ibid*, 65.

[47] *Ibid*, 64.

[48] *Ibid*, 64.

[49] This is a footnote for those who either didn't watch TV in the 1960's or you were born after the 80's. There is no other excuse. Gilligan's Island is a popular American sitcom that aired for three seasons, beginning in 1964. It is a story about five passengers who set sail in a boat named *The Minnow* on a three-hour tour. Their tiny ship is tossed by rough weather and the fearless crew saves the day. *The Minnow* eventually lands on the shore of an uncharted desert island. They are marooned on the island: Gilligan, Skipper, the millionaire Thurston Howell III and his wife (Lovey), Ginger the movie star, the Professor, and Mary Ann. Of course, no one can find them and they are lost in the midst of a great ocean. You can watch it on Netflix.

[50] Bob Johansen, *Leaders*, 50.

[51] *Ibid.*

[52] *Ibid*, 51.

[53] Priscilla Brewer, "Demographic Features of the Shaker Decline, 1787–1900," Journal of Interdisciplinary History 15.1 (summer 1984): 31–52; Stein, *Shaker Experience in America*, 337–70.

[54] Wheatley, *New Science*, 19

[55] Augustine of Hippo, *The Confessions*, (Grand Rapids, MI: Baker Book House, 2005), 216ff doi: 978-0-8007-8762-2

[56] Bob Johansen, *Get There Early*, 21.

[57] Institute for the Future, "2008-2018 Map of Future Forces Affecting the Episcopal Church" (Presented at The Consortium of Endowed Parishes meeting at St. David's, Austin, Tx 2008).

[58] Bob Johansen explains these ideas well in *Leaders Make the Future*. These ideas are also present in Guy Kawasaki and Clay Shirky's work.

[59] Wheatley, *New Science*, 12.

[60] *Ibid.*

[61] Nassim Nicholas Taleb, *Antifragile: Things That Gain from Disorder* (New York: Random House, 2012), 151.

[62] Johansen, *Leaders,* 32.

[63] An acculturated church is one that has adopted the behavior patterns of the surrounding culture as opposed to one that uses the behavior patterns to serve the spread of the Gospel.

[64] German philosopher Karl Jaspers first used the term *axial age, axis age* or *axial period* (Ger. *Achsenzeit*, "axis time") to describe 800 to 200 BC. Jaspers believed that

during this time there was a revolution in thinking across all of India, China and the Occident. Jaspers, in his Vom Ursprung und Ziel der Geschichte (The Origin and Goal of History) identified a number of key thinkers all of whom influenced future philosophies and religions. There is also during this time period similar identified common characteristics in each area. Jaspers saw striking parallels without any obvious direct transmission of ideas from one region to the other. Having found no recorded proof of any extensive intercommunication between these regions/cultures Jaspers held up this age as unique. Further he believed that the rest of the human history grew and stemmed from this important time period. Chad Meister, *Introducing Philosophy of Religion* (Nashville, Tn: Abingdon Press, 2009), 10.

[65] Thomas Merton, *New Seeds of Contemplation* (New Directions Publishing: New York, 1972) 143.

[66] The Church Hymnal Corporation, *Prayer Book and Hymnal* (New York: Church Publishing, 1979), 531.

[67] Robert Bellah is author of many books, including *The Broken Covenant* (New York: Seabury Press 1975) and, with others, *Habits of the Heart* (Oakland, Ca: University of California Press, 1996).

[68] Robert Bellah, "At Home and Not At Home: Religious Pluralism and Religious Truth," *The Christian Century*, April 19, 1995, 423-428

[69] Fingarette keeps this from becoming stale in mission as the culture of *home* comes into contact within new contexts. He writes: Yet we must retain an openness to experience such that the dark shadows deep within one vision are the mute, stubborn messengers waiting to lead us to a new light and a new vision ... We must not ignore the fact that in this last analysis, commitment to a specific orientation outweighs catholicity of imagery. As quoted in Bellah, "At Home."

[70] *Ibid.*

[71] Robert Bellah in his essay returns to the work of Paul with the Athenians and offers us a sense of both the difficulty of what we must do and a challenge to reengage our mission: ...[I]n order to preach Jesus Christ and him crucified to the biblically illiterate Athenians, Paul must convince them of the fundamentally Jewish notion of a creator God who is Lord of all and who will bring the world to an end in a last judgment. Only in that context does the incarnation, crucifixion and resurrection of Jesus Christ make sense. Even though Paul abrogated the Jewish ritual law for the gentiles, he still, in a critically important sense, had to convert them to Judaism before he could convert them to Christianity. That is as much the case today as ever and is evidenced by the fact that the Hebrew Scriptures are canonical for Christians.

[72] This passage is mentioned by Augustine and Aquinas, and is even the answer of Dante when he arrives in Paradise. Craig Koester, *Hebrews*, Anchor Bible Commentary vol. 36 (New York: Doubleday, 2001), 478.

[73] These images were used in sermons preached in the Fall of 2013 and a portion of these reflections were written into the Forward for Dean Barkley Thompson's book

Elements of Grace (Marion, Ar: Trinity press, 2013).

[74] Paul Tillich, *Shaking the Foundations* (New York: Charles Scribner's Sons, New York, 1955), 11.

[75] "First Thoughts on Year C Epistle Passages in the Lectionary," Pentecost 15, William Loader, Murdoch University, Uniting Church in Australia.
http://wwwstaff.murdoch.edu.au/~loader/CEpPentecost15.htm

[76] Bella, *Christian Century*. He also states: "It would confirm the suspicion of the Athenian philosophers about Paul: "He seems to be a proclaimer of foreign divinities" (Acts 17:18). Indeed, today much missionary work carried on by Americans or Western Europeans in the non-Western world, emphasizing individual salvation rather than a transformed way of life." This means that what a lot of people offer as evangelism is only the proclamation of just another foreign divinity.

[77] *Ibid.*

[78] *Ibid.* Bellah again challenges my thinking: "This Trinitarian complex of remembrance of Christ, appeal to the Spirit, and thanksgiving to the Father is not simply one aspect of the church's life; rather, it is the very act of the church's life, the act in which the church's koinonia is realized. The church is that community whose common life is a lively remembrance of Jesus Christ, in the power of the Spirit, to the glory of God the Father. And it is in this way that the communion of the church in history becomes a living sign of the eschatological reconciliation of the world with God."

[79] *Ibid.*

[80] As quoted in Bella, *Ibid.*

[81] Bellah, *Christian Century.*

[82] *BCP, 531.*

[83] *BCP,* 816.

[84] Jaroslav Pelikan, *The Vindication of Tradition: The 1983 Jefferson Lecture in the Humanities,* (Yale University Press: New Haven, 1986) 65.

[85] Wheatley, *New Science,* 21. If a living system can maintain its identity, it can self-organize to a higher level of complexity, a new form of itself that can deal better with the present.

[86] *BCP,* 847.

[87] *Ibid.*

[88] *Ibid,* 304.

[89] *Ibid,* 358.

[90] Task Force For Reimagining The Episcopal Church, *Identity Paper* (September 19, 2013) sec II. http://reimaginetec.org/identity-and-vision-draft

[91] *Ibid.*

[92] *BCP,* 850.

[93] *BCP,* 526 and 853.

[94] *Identity Paper.*

[95] *Ibid.*

[96] Charism means a gift or a particular work given to a person.

[97] *BCP*, 518.

[98] *BCP*, 531.

[99] *BCP*, 562.

[100] John Macquarrie, *A Guide to the Sacraments* (London: SCM Press Ltd, 1997), 6.

[101] *BCP*, 543.

[102] *Ibid.*

[103] *BCP*, 857ff.

[104] *BCP*, 859.

[105] Psalm 31, *BCP*, 129.

[106] *Identity Paper.*

[107] *Ibid.*

[108] I was glad the TREC Identity Statement recognized this when the group articulated: "The Episcopal Church is not the only tradition to hold these individual values, but their combination and dynamic interplay foster our church's uniqueness and vitality." Having worked on this project I have to say that a great deal of the writing responsibility truly goes to Dwight Z... for his work on this section. *Ibid.*

[109] My friend the Rt. Rev. Ian Douglas does a fine job describing in brief the Episcopal Church history. You can find it in a book in which we both have essays: "W(h)ither the National Church--Revisited: Changing Mission Structures of The Episcopal Church" in Winnie Varghese *et al, What We Shall Become: The Future and Structure of The Episcopal Church* (Church Publishing, 2013).

[110] *Identity Paper*, sec III.

[111] Edwin Augustine White and Jackson A. Dykman *et al, Annotated Constitution and Canons* (New York: Church Publishing Incorporated, 1985), 4. It was not entered into the Preamble until 1964 and ratified in 1967.

[112] Henry Knox Sherrill was the last bishop to serve both a diocese and as Presiding Bishop. He led the Church during its high watermark and appeared on the cover of Time Magazine on March 26, 1951.

[113] Robert D. Lupton, *Toxic Charity: How Churches and Charities Hurt Those They Help* (New York: Harper Collins, 2011).

[114] Simon Sinek, *Start With Why* (New York: Penguin, 2009) 225.

[115] *Ibid.*

[116] Wheatley, *New* Science, 18.

[117] *Ibid.*

[118] *Ibid*, 20

[119] From the Baptismal Covenant: Celebrant: Will you proclaim by word and example the Good News of God in Christ? People: I will, with God's help. *BCP*, 305. Also see Matt 8.23-27.

[120] Milton Richardson was the fifth bishop diocesan of Texas.

[121] *Ibid.*

[122] *Hymnal* (New York: Church Publishing, 1982), 525.

[123] I do not imply here a neo-latitudinarianism. I believe this freedom is only manifest within a community that proclaims a monotheistic faith in God as creator and Jesus as the incarnate Son who fulfills salvation history. It is only without faith in a Trinitarian God and the basic of the faith that you get latitudinarianism; that is, those who offer the practice of religion without doctrine.

[124] Robert Prichard has an excellent paper on the nature of our communion relationship entitled: The Anglican Communion: A Brief History Lesson. You may read it here: http://www.livingchurch.org/anglican-communion-brief-history-lesson

[125] BCP, 858.

[126] BCP, 360.

[127] *Ibid.*

[128] Robert Runcie, "Opening Address: Lambeth Conference," *The Truth Shall Make You Free* (London: Church House Publishing, 1988), 16.

[129] Robin Eames *et al, The Windsor Report* (2004), 37. Doi: http://www.anglicancommunion.org/windsor2004/index.cfm

[130] Richard Hayes, "The Word of Reconciliation," Faith and Leadership, July 20, 2010, http://www.faithandleadership.com/sermons/the-word-reconciliation

[131] Alexander Schmemann, *For the Life of the World* (Crestwood, NY: St. Vladimir's Seminary Press, 1973), 99.

[132] Scott Bader-Saye, "Bonds of Affection: The Transformational Possibilities of a Platitude," The Conference, 2014. Also see, C. S. Lewis, *The Four Loves* (New York: Houghton Mifflin Harcourt, 1991), 31ff. Bader-Saye introduced me to this idea that affection is a key ingredient to Christian communities.

[133] *Ibid.*

[134] *Ibid.*

[135] "Political Polarization in American Public: Political Polarization and Personal Life," Pew Research Center, June 12, 2014. http://www.people-press.org/2014/06/12/section-3-political-polarization-and-personal-life/

[136] Bader-Saye.

[137] *Ibid.*

[138] *Ibid.*

[139] *Ibid.*

[140] Wendell Berry, "It All Turns on Affection," Awards and Honors: 2012 Jefferson Lecture. http://www.neh.gov/about/awards/jefferson-lecture/wendell-e-berry-lecture

[141] Gorbis,174.

[142] *Ibid.*

[143] *Ibid*, 176.

[144] Thom Rainer, "Seven Reasons Why Church Worship Centers Will Get Smaller," December 9, 2013 http://thomrainer.com/2013/12/09/seven-reasons-why-church-

worship-centers-will-get-smaller/. Also see: Ed Stetzer, "Starting, Staffing, and Supporting a Multisite Church," Christianity Today, March 17, 2014, http://www.christianitytoday.com/edstetzer/2014/march/starting-staffing-and-supporting-multisite-church.html; Tim Nations, "What 7 Rapidly Growing Churches Are Learning About Multisite," Leadnet, May 15th, 2014, http://leadnet.org/what-7-rapidly-growing-churches-are-learning-about-multisite/; and Adelle M. Banks, "Vitality in Multisite Church Model," Religion News Service, March 11, 2014, http://www.washingtonpost.com/national/religion/survey-finds-growth-vitality-in-multisite-church-model/2014/03/11/7affef86-a944-11e3-8a7b-c1c684e2671f_story.html

[145] Here is the report everyone was talking about:http://leadnet.org/available-now-the-leadership-networkgeneris-multisite-church-scorecard/

[146] *Ibid.*

[147] *Ibid.*

[148] "Mobile Technology Fact Sheet," Pew Research, January 2014, http://www.pewinternet.org/fact-sheets/mobile-technology-fact-sheet/

[149] "Social Networking Fact Sheet," Pew Research, January 2014, http://www.pewinternet.org/fact-sheets/social-networking-fact-sheet/

[150] "Internet Use Over Time," Pew Research, January 2014, http://www.pewinternet.org/data-trend/internet-use/internet-use-over-time/

[151] Maeve Duggan and Aaron Smith, "Cell Internet Use 2013," Pew Research, September 2013, http://www.pewinternet.org/2013/09/16/cell-internet-use-2013/

[152] This paragraph comes from a conversation with The Rev. Joe Chambers.

[153] A. H. Maslow, "A theory of human motivation," *Psychological Review*, 50(4), 370–96. http://psychclassics.yorku.ca/Maslow/motivation.htm

[154] Brené Brown, *Daring Greatly* (Gotham Books: London, 2012) 10ff.

[155] "The Internet Human," IFTF, http://www.iftf.org/internethuman/

[156] *Ibid.*

[157] *Ibid.*

[158] Gorbis, 25.

[159] *Ibid*, 26.

[160] *Ibid.*

[161] Chris Anderson, *Makers: The New Industrial Revolution* (New York: Crown Business Press, 2012), 191ff.

[162] Just in case you don't know what Lego are you need to put this book down, dust off your Tandy TRS-80 and search the *Internet-webs* for Lego and see what you have been missing.

[163] IFTF, *2008-2018 Map.*

[164] *Ibid.*

[165] *Ibid.*

[166] Fritjof Capra, *The Turning Point* (New York: Bantam, 1983), 76-77. As quoted in

Wheatley, *New Science*, 3, 5-6.

[167] Wheatley, *New Science*, 5ff

[168] Werner Heisenberg, *Physics and Philosophy: The Revolution in Modern Science* (1958) Lectures delivered at University of St. Andrews, Scotland, Winter 1955-56.

[169] Werner Heisenberg, "Critique of the Physical Concepts of the Corpuscular Theory," trans Carl Eckhart and Frank C. Hoyt, *The Physical Principles of the Quantum Theory* (1930), 20.

[170] Daniel Kahneman, *Thinking, Fast and Slow* (New York: Farrar, Straus and Giroux, 2011), 201.

[171] Wheatley, *New Science*, 6.

[172] Capra.

[173] Wheatley, *New Science*, 6.

[174] Bill Bryson, *At Home*, 25.

[175] Wheatley, *New Science*, 101ff.

[176] *Ibid.*

[177] Nassim Nicholas Taleb, *Black Swan* (New York: Random House, 2007), 8.

[178] A procrustean bed is a standard that is enforced uniformly without regard to individuality. Procrustes was a mythological figure who cut people down to size to fit in an iron bed.

[179] Taleb, *Antifragile*, 106.

[180] Kahneman, 87.

[181] *Ibid*, 85.

[182] *Ibid*, 86.

[183] *Ibid*, 202.

[184] Wayne Meeks, *First Urban Christians* (New Haven, Cn: Yale University Press, 1983), 76.

[185] *Ibid*, 75.

[186] *Ibid*, 77.

[187] *Ibid*, 78.

[188] *Ibid*, 80.

[189] *Ibid*, 80.

[190] *Ibid*, 82.

[191] *Ibid*, 83.

[192] The customary is a list of usual practices for a community.

[193] Edward Foley, *From Age to Age: How Christians Have Celebrated the Eucharist* (Chicago: Liturgy Training Publications, 1991), 39

[194] *Ibid*, 63.

[195] *Ibid*. 87.

[196] Bryson, *Home*, 322 and 475ff.

[197] Charles Taylor, *A Secular Age* (The Belknap Press of Harvard University Press: Cambridge, 2007) 775.

[198] *Ibid*, 774.

[199] *Ibid*, 542.

[200] *Ibid*, 543.

[201] Harvey Cox, Religion in the Secular City: Toward a Postmodern Theology (Simon and Shuster: New York, 1984) 159.

[202] If you are interested in further reading the following texts are suggested: *The In-Between Church* (Bethesda, Md: The Alban Institute, 1998); contributions by Dan Hotchkiss to the article, "Searching for the Key: Developing a Theory of Synagogue Size," Congregations 27, no. 1 (January–February 2001); a recent work by Gary McIntosh, *One Size Doesn't Fit All* (Grand Rapids, Mi: Revell, 1999); and some preliminary findings from the National Congregations Study (NCS) headed by Mark Chavez at the University of Arizona. "The tipping point" has become a household term because of Malcolm Gladwell's book, *The Tipping Point: How Little Things Can Make a Big Difference* (Boston: Little, Brown and Company, 2000).

[203] Arlin Rothauge, *Sizing Up Your Congregation* (New York: Seabury Professional Services, 1986).

[204] Wheatley, *New Science*, 65.

[205] *Ibid*

[206] Margaret Wheatley, *Finding Our Way* (San Francisco: Berrett.-Koehler Publishers, 2005) 68.

[207] *Ibid.*

[208] *Ibid.*

[209] *Ibid.*

[210] "Raising the Roof," Alban Institute, http://www.alban.org/raisingtheroof/changingSize.asp

[211] Capra, *Turning Point*, 96, 99. As quoted in Wheatley, *New* Science, 20.

[212] Uri Friedman, "12 Maps That Changed the World," The Atlantic. http://www.theatlantic.com/international/archive/2013/12/12-maps-that-changed-the-world/282666/

[213] *Ibid.*

[214] *Ibid.*

[215] *Ibid.*

[216] *Ibid.*

[217] Wheatley, *New Science,* 34.

[218] "Smart Cities and Smart Citizens," Sustain Magazine, Posted May 1, 2013, http://sustainmagazine.com/smart-cities-smart-citizens

[219] *Ibid.*

[220] *Ibid.*

[221] *Ibid.*

[222] Smart citizens live in smart cities. This is a way of networking people into a platform that generates participatory community life. Smart citizens are connected

with one another and the population within a city. For example the Amsterdam Smart City project seeks to connect government officials, citizens, and academics to build government e-services.

[223] *Ibid.*

[224] *Ibid.*

[225] *Ibid.*

[226] *Ibid.*

[227] *Ibid.* IFTF pulled these ideas together from the "The Future of Everything Summit of Ideas and Digital Invention," held on 21-24 March 2013, Manchester, UK. Further info can be found at: http://futureeverything.org

[228] *Ibid.*

[229] June Williamson, "Urban Design Tactics for Suburban Retrofitting," Build A Better Burb, http://buildabetterburb.org/11-urban-design-tactics-for-suburban-retrofitting/

[230] *Ibid.*

[231] *Ibid.*

[232] *Ibid.*

[233] *Ibid.*

[234] *Ibid.*

[235] *Ibid.*

[236] *Ibid.*

[237] *Ibid.*

[238] Kinder Institute 32nd Annual Report," Rice University, 2013, http://has.rice.edu/uploadedFiles/Houston_Area_Survey/FINAL%20-%202013%20KIHAS%20Report.pdf "When asked a slightly different question this year, half of the respondents (by 50% to 48%) said they would prefer to live in "an area with a mix of developments, including homes, shops and restaurants," rather than "a single-family residential area." Figures have been consistent across the years in rejecting basically a 50/50 split since 2007, the first time that question was asked." They go on to say, "Among the survey participants in the nine surrounding counties, 43% said they would choose the opportunity to live in an area with a mix of developments, rather than in a single-family residential area. These are remarkably high numbers for this sprawling, car-dependent city, further underscoring the substantial demand for more urban alternatives that now cuts across the entire metropolitan region."

[239] *Ibid.*

[240] *Ibid.*

[241] Terry Mattingly, "*Backsliders* and the *unchurched* equal the *Nones*," November 4, 2013, Patheos, http://www.patheos.com/blogs/tmatt/2013/11/backsliders-and-the-unchurched-equal-the-nones

[242] *Ibid.*

[243] "45 New Statistics on church Attendance and Avoidance," The Barna Group, March

3, 2008, https://www.barna.org/barna-update/congregations/45-new-statistics-on-church-attendance-and-avoidance#.Uh8552TXgVk "With Americans pursuing a growing number of "church" options, some of the traditional measures of church health are being redefined. According to a new study released by The Barna Group, which has been studying church participation patterns since 1984, popular measures such as the percentage of people who are "unchurched" - based on attendance at a conventional church service - are out of date. Various new forms of faith community and experience, such as house churches, marketplace ministries and cyberchurches, must be figured into the mix - and make calculating the percentage of Americans who can be counted as "unchurched" more complicated."

244 Ibid. "Six out of ten adults in the Unattached category (59%) consider themselves to be Christian. Even more surprising was the revelation that 17% of the Unattached are born again Christians... A significant proportion of the Unattached engages in traditional faith activities during a typical week. For instance, one-fifth (19%) read the Bible and three out of every five (62%) pray to God during a typical week."

245 See ISH-BCM fMRI research here: http://ish-tmc.org/fmri-study-on-the-effects-of-prayer/

246 Ibid. "Homebodies- people who had not attended a conventional church during the past month, but had attended a meeting of a house church (3%). Blenders- adults who had attended both a conventional church and a house church during the past month. Most of these people attend a conventional church as their primary church, but many are experimenting with new forms of faith community. In total, Blenders represent 3% of the adult population.

Conventionals- adults who had attended a conventional church (i.e., a congregational-style, local church) during the past month but had not attended a house church. Almost three out of every five adults (56%) fit this description. This participation includes attending any of a wide variety of conventional-church events, such as weekend services, mid-week services, special events, or church-based classes."

247 Ibid.

248 Kinder Institute, 32 Year Report. You can go to the general Kinder Institute page here: http://has.rice.edu/

249 Ibid.

250 Ibid.

251 Ibid.

252 Ibid.

253 "America's Coolest Cities," Forbes, (August 12, 2014) http://www.forbes.com/pictures/emeg45kmll/introduction-12/ "Using [Bert] Sperling's Diversity Index, which measures the likelihood of meeting someone of a different race or ethnicity, favoring cities with greater diversity. And we factored in age, drawing on U.S. Census Bureau data and favoring places with a large population of people aged 20-34." You can read more about Sperling's diversity index here:

http://www.bertsperling.com/2012/08/21/americas-coolest-cities

[254] "Domestic Racial and Ethnic Membership report for 2009," Episcopal Church, http://library.episcopalchurch.org/sites/default/files/episcopal_domestic_racial-ethnic_membership_2009.pdf

[255] William P. Hall and Susu Nousala, "Autopoiesis and Knowledge in Self Sustaining Organizational Systems, 4th International Mulit-conference on Society, Cybernetics and Informatics, June 2010, Orlando, Fl. This paper challenges the idea that there is ever a closed system sociologically or molecularly. Systems are always porous to their surroundings.

[256] *Ibid.*

[257] *Ibid.*

[258] *Ibid.*

[259] *Ibid.*

[260] *Ibid.*

[261] Here is more information about Paul Baran on the Rand website. Paul worked for Rand Corporation, which used to be focused on military solutions. Today Rand is a firm doing analysis and consulting. http://www.rand.org/about/history/baran.html

[262] *Ibid.*

[263] *Ibid.*

[264] *Ibid.* See the actual report here: http://www.rand.org/content/dam/rand/pubs/research_memoranda/2006/RM3764.pdf

[265] *Ibid.*

[266] Stuart Brand, "Founding Father, " Wired, September 2003, http://archive.wired.com/wired/archive/9.03/baran_pr.html

[267] *Ibid.*

[268] Barna, *Boiling Point*, 250.

[269] *Ibid*, 252.

[270] SimCity was a popular game that allowed people to build communities online.

[271] *Ibid*, 251.

[272] Flash mob Eucharist is a large public gathering where people have a Eucharist – organized by means of social networks.

[273] *Ibid*, 25. The Barna Group calls these Boutique Churches: "these are congregations with one ministry: worship, discipleship, fellowship, community service."

[274] *Ibid*, 252.

[275] Learn more about Episcopal Service Corps here: http://episcopalservicecorps.org

[276] Barna, *Boiling Point*, 252.

[277] *Ibid.*

[278] *Ibid*, 253.

[279] *Ibid*, 253.

[280] Warren Bird, "Today there are more than 8,000 multisite churches,"

LeadNetLeadNet,
http://t.co/IWsq4bj5k3
[281] Wheatley, *New Science*, 20.
[282] *Ibid.*
[283] *Ibid.*
[284] *Ibid.*
[285] Wheatley, *New Science*, 21. Wheatley is getting her information from the landmark paper by Prigogine and Stengers, published in 1984.
[286] Wheatley, *New Science*, 4.
[287] Simon Winchester, *The Man Who Loved China* (New York: Harper Perennial, 2008).
[288] Needham's book is worth a look at and Simon Winchester's The Man Who Loved China is excellent. A short list of the inventions is found in a well documented wiki article here: http://en.wikipedia.org/wiki/List_of_Chinese_inventions
[289] Winchester, *China*, 236.
[290] I think it is important to point out that Sheldon Cooper of *The Big Bang Theory*, named his cats after all the members of the Manhattan Project, including Feynman. One he named Zazzles because he was "so zazzy." I also have a cat named Zazzles. Episode entitled *The Zazzy Substitution*.
http://bigbangtheory.wikia.com/wiki/Sheldon's_Cats
[291] John Carl Villanueva, "Electron Cloud Model," August 25, 2009, Universe Today, http://www.universetoday.com/38282/electron-cloud-model/#ixzz33vq8ipk1 While thinking about how to begin this chapter The Rev. Patrick Miller and I were at the Latin church site in the Holy Land where they remember the Ascension of Jesus. He mentioned in passing that Quantum physicists used clouds as a way of describing their work. So I looked it up.
[292] *Ibid.*
[293] *The Cloud of Unknowing and other works.* Trans. A. C. Spearing (New York: Penguin Classics. 2001) ch 6.
[294] Taleb, *Antifragile*, 32.
[295] *Ibid.*
[296] Casuistry is the application of theoretical rules to particular situations.
[297] *Ibid*, 26.
[298] Optionality is the multiplicity of investment opportunities that only come after the initial investment.
[299] Narthex is the front porch of the church. It is the anteroom before you enter the nave, where the people sit, and then the sanctuary – where the altar resides.
[300] That is correct! The separation of Church and State was not normative until 1833. The Constitution is referring to a national church, but at the time it was assumed that local churches would be supported by the government for their charity work.
[301] Charles Ryrie, *Balancing the Christian Life* (Chicago: Moody Press, 1994), 86.
[302] In the writings of Aquinas, Milbank, and Pickstock. John Milbank and Simon Oliver,

The Radical Orthodoxy Reader (Routledge: London and New York, 2009) 17.

303 *Ibid.*

304 William T. Cavanaugh, *Radical* Orthodoxy, John Milbank, Catherine Pickstock, and Graham Ward, et al (Routledge: London and New York, 1999) 185.

35 Bader-Saye.

306 *Ibid.*

307 Berry.

308 *Ibid.*

309 *Ibid.*

310 Jerry Michalski, "Thriving in the Relationship Economy: What is the Relationship Economy? How is it different from what went before? How do you thrive in it? What do you need to learn & do?," IFTF, 31 August 2013, http://prezi.com/3igqdq90g-y0/thriving-in-the-relationship-economy/

311 *Ibid.*

312 *Ibid.*

313 Gorbis,197.

314 Mchalski.

315 *Ibid.*

316 *Ibid.*

317 *Ibid.*

318 *Ibid.*

319 Gorbis, 41.

320 *Ibid,*188.

321 For more on stewardship see Episcopal Diocese of West Texas Stewardship site: http://www.dwtx.org/department-ministries/stewardship/year-round-stewardship/. And, Vital Practices article on year round stewardship: http://www.ecfvp.org/vestrypapers/wholehearted-stewardship/liberating-stewardship/

322 Gorbis, 46.

323 ScholarMatch as quoted in Gorbis, 59.

324 Gorbis, 60

325 *Ibid.*

326 *Ibid.*

327 Kickster article with facts about movie and pledges: https://www.kickstarter.com/projects/559914737/the-veronica-mars-movie-project/posts/777894

328 Adrianne Jeffries, "2nd Annual Film Festival Hints At Just How Disruptive Kickstarter Could be," Betabeat, July 2011: http://betabeat.com/2011/07/2nd-annual-film-fest-hints-at-just-how-disruptive-kickstarter-could-be/

329 Information on Episcopal Relief, http://www.episcopalrelief.org

330 "Research and Statistics," Episcopal Church,

http://www.episcopalchurch.org/page/research-and-statistics
[331] Gorbis, 62.
[332] *Ibid.*
[333] Gorbis, 62. Gorbis writes, "Elizabeth Dunn, a professor of psychology, and her colleagues at the University of British Columbia showed that spending more of one's income on others predicted greater happiness. Dunn's studies also show that participants who were randomly assigned to spend money on others experienced greater happiness than those assigned to spend money on themselves. Her work and other studies suggest that beyond the point at which people have economic security, happiness doesn't scale with money, even very large amounts of money. We are more happy spending money on social experiences than on buying things."
[334] Gorbis, 64.
[335] Edmund H. Oliver, *The Social Achievements of the Christian Church* (Toronto: Ryerson Press, 1930), 30.
[336] Tertullian, *Apologeticus 39*. As quoted in Ibid, 29.
[337] Clement, *2 Clementine* 16.4. As quoted in Ibid, 31.
[338] Oliver, 75.
[339] *Ibid*, 75.
[340] *Ibid*, 87.
[341] *Ibid.*
[342] *Ibid*, 136.
[343] *Ibid*, 147.
[344] *Ibid*, 176ff
[345] *Ibid*, 177.
[346] BCP, 302ff.
[347] Dambisa Moyo, "Dead Aid," Fordham:
http://www.fordham.edu/economics/mcleod/Dambisa_moyo_DeadAidForward.pdf
[348] *Ibid.*
[349] Lupton, 5.
[350] *Ibid*, 2
[351] *Ibid*, 4.
[352] *Ibid*, 34.
[353] *Ibid*, 8.
[354] *Ibid* 139.
[355] *Ibid*, 139.
[356] *Ibid.*
[357] *Ibid.*
[358] *Ibid.*
[359] *Ibid.*
[360] *Ibid.*
[361] *Ibid.*

362 Gorbis, 29.

363 *Ibid.*

364 *Ibid.*

365 The World Health Organization's definition of Health found in the preamble of its constitution http://www.who.int/about/definition/en/print.html

366 IFTF, *2008-2018 Map.*

367 *Ibid.*

368 Bradley Kreit, "Investing in Local Communities to Improve Health," IFTF, November 7, 2011: http://member.iftf.org/node/3989

369 *Ibid.*

370 *Ibid.*

371 These goals are taken from a yearlong study of how to reinvigorate service ministry in health in the Diocese of Texas. Visioning, research, and community study led the staff and board of The Episcopal Health Foundation to adopt this broad framework. I believe it is a hallmark of defining the future of service that truly meets real need in our communities.

372 Adapted from the Episcopal Health Foundation Strategic Plan.

373 *Ibid.*

374 *Ibid.*

375 *Ibid.*

376 *Ibid.*

377 *Ibid.*

378 Jonathan Lerner, "Pop-Up Urbanism to Build Community Health: Street Makeovers Put New Spin on the Block," Pacific Magazine: The Science of Society, January 16, 2012 http://www.psmag.com/magazines/news-and-options/street-makeovers-put-new-spin-on-the-block-38926/

379 *Ibid.*

380 *Ibid.*

381 "Complete streets," Wikipedia, http://en.wikipedia.org/wiki/Complete_streets

382 *Ibid.*

383 *Ibid.*

384 *Ibid.*

385 *Ibid.*

386 Johansen, *Leaders,* 55.

387 *The Encyclopedia of Early Christianity*, 2nd ed, s.v. "Christianity."

388 *Ibid.*

389 *Ibid.*

390 Rodney Stark, *The Rise of Christianity: A Sociologist Reconsiders History* (Princeton, 1996) as quoted in Christianity Today, s.v. "International/Christian History." These estimates are based on 40 percent growth per decade, and roughly correspond with figures found in early church documents:

http://www.christianitytoday.com/ch/1998/issue57/57h026.html
391 Richard D. Balge, "A Brief History Of Evangelism In The Christian Church,"
Synod-Wide Convocation on Evangelism, Wisconsin Lutheran College, Milwaukee,
Wisconsin,
August 15-17, 1978: http://www.wlsessays.net/files/BalgeBrief.pdf
392 *Ibid.*
393 *Ibid.*
394 *Ibid.*
395 *Ibid.*
396 *Ibid.*
397 *Ibid.*
398 *Ibid.*
399 *Ibid.*
400 *Ibid.*
401 *Ibid.*
402 For more on "generous evangelism," see the author's series of evangelism lectures
given in November 2011, www.adoyle.libsyn.com/webpage/2011/11
403 Guy Kawasaki, "A Practical Blog For Impractical People, The Art of Evangelism,"
January 12, 2006:
http://blog.guykawasaki.com/2006/01/the_art_of_evan.html#ixzz363laECaM
404 *Ibid.*
405 *Ibid.*
406 *Ibid.*
407 *Ibid.*
408 Richard Ruff, "Active listening – a forgotten key to sales success," Sales Training
Connection, September 16, 2011,
http://salestrainingconnection.com/2011/09/16/active-listening-a-forgotten-key-to-
sales-success The ideas in the paragraph are summed up well in the above article. I
learned most of this in Clinical Pastoral Education and in Transformative Mediation
training at George Mason. This is a good short article on the basics.
409 *Ibid.*
410 *What about Bob?* 1991 movie in which a successful psychotherapist loses his mind
after one of his most dependent patients, a manipulative, obsessively compulsive
narcissist, tracks him down during his family vacation.
411 Kawasaki.
412 *Ibid.*
413 *Ibid.*
414 John Newton, "Front-door Evangelism theology," resources for
Invite/Welcome/Connect. Episcopal Diocese of Texas,
http://www.epicenter.org/newcomer
415 *Ibid.*

[416] *Ibid.*

[417] *Ibid.*

[418] *Ibid.*

[419] "Vision Statement," Diocese of Texas, http://www.epicenter.org/diocese/about-the-diocese/vision

[420] Newton.

[421] *Ibid.*

[422] "The Future of Persuasion," IFTF, Summer 2010, http://www.iftf.org/uploads/media/SR-1321_IFTF_FutureofPersuasionReport-1.pdf

[423] *Ibid.*

[424] *Ibid.*

[425] *Ibid.*

[426] *Ibid.*

[427] *Ibid.*

[428] *Ibid.*

[429] *Ibid.*

[430] *Ibid.*

[431] *Ibid.*

[432] *Ibid.*

[433] *Ibid.*

[434] *Ibid.*

[435] *Ibid.*

[436] *Ibid.*

[437] *Ibid.*

[438] *Ibid.*

[439] *Ibid.*

[440] *Ibid.*

[441] *Ibid.*

[442] *Ibid.*

[443] *Ibid.*

[444] *Ibid.*

[445] *Ibid.*

[446] *Ibid.*

[447] Barry Schwartz and Andrew Ward, "Doing Better but Feeling Worse: The Paradox of Choice," Swarthmore College, http://www.swarthmore.edu/SocSci/bschwar1/Choice%20Chapter.Revised.pdf

[448] IFTF, "Persuasion."

[449] *Ibid.*

[450] *Ibid.*

[451] *Ibid.*

[452] Kalle Lasn, *Culture Jam*, (New York: Eagle Book, 1999) 3ff.

[453] Luddites were a reform movement that destroyed machinery in mills because they thought that the technology threatened their jobs – 1811.

[454] "The History of Work," Readers' Digest Australia, http://www.readersdigest.com.au/history-of-work.

[455] Robert Whaples, "Hours of Work In U.S. History," Wake Forest University, http://eh.net/encyclopedia/hours-of-work-in-u-s-history

Table 1
Estimated Average Weekly Hours Worked in Manufacturing, 1830-1890

Year	Weeks Report	Aldrich Report
1830	69.1	
1840	67.1	68.4
1850	65.5	69.0
1860	62.0	66.0
1870	61.1	63.0
1880	60.7	61.8
1890		60.0

Sources: U.S. Department of Interior (1883), U.S. Senate (1893)
Note: Atack and Bateman (1992), using data from census manuscripts, estimate average weekly hours to be 60.1 in 1880 — very close to Weeks' contemporary estimate. They also find that the summer workweek was about 1.5 hours longer than the winter workweek.

[456] *Ibid.*

[457] Dom Gregory Dix, *The Shape of the Liturgy* (London: Dacre Press, 1964), 744-5.

[458] *Ibid.*

[459] David Harvey, *The Condition of Postmodernity* (New York: Wiley-Blackwell, 1989), 7.

[460] Terry Eagleton, "Postmodernism," *Presis 6 (1987, 7-24).* As quoted in *Ibid,* 8ff.

[461] Harvey, 7ff

[462] *Ibid.*

[463] These are rounded numbers. The National Institute for Health has specific data: http://www.nimh.nih.gov/health/publications/the-numbers-count-mental-disorders-in-america/index.shtml

[464] Robert Bly, *The Sibling Society*, (New York: Addison-Wesley Publishing, 1996), 44ff.

[465] *Ibid.*

[466] The Shallows is a 250-page book by writer Nicholas Carr, published in the US, which is part of the growing debate. Carr wrote an essay for the Atlantic magazine entitled "Is Google making us stupid?" He writes that there is "the uneducating of Homo sapiens," and a rewiring of neural pathways and networks that may yet deprive the human race of the talents that drove our journey from caves to PC terminals.

[467] *Bly.*

[468] Richard Dawkins and Rowan Williams, "Nature of human beings and the question of their ultimate origin," Oxford University, 2013,

http://www.youtube.com/watch?v=jzqa6VMI0UQ

469 "Meet Generation Z" Sparks and Honey. Doi: http://www.slideshare.net/sparksandhoney/generation-z-final-june-17

470 *Ibid.*

471 "Young People in the World of Abundant Connectivity," IFTF, June 2001, http://www.iftf.org/our-work/people-technology/technology-horizons/networks-in-use-young-people-in-the-world-of-abundant-connectivity

472 *Ibid.*

473 *Ibid.*

474 *Ibid.*

475 *Ibid.*

476 *Ibid.*

477 *Ibid.*

478 The Rev. Joe Chambers helped me with this paragraph and offered the ideas and examples.

479 *Ibid.*

480 *Ibid.*

481 *Ibid.*

482 *Ibid.*

483 *Ibid.*

484 *Ibid.*

485 *Ibid.*

486 *Ibid.*

487 *Ibid.*

488 *Ibid.*

489 Trainspotting, 1996 film.

490 You can watch this on YouTube Trainspotting (9/12) Movie CLIP - Colonized By Wankers (1996) HD.

491 Ken Robinson, "How Schools Kill Creativity," TED, http://blog.ted.com/2006/06/27/sir_ken_robinso

492 Verna J. Dozier, *The dream of God: A call to return* (Cambridge, Ma: Cowley Publications, 1991), 67.

493 John Newton, *New Clothes* (Church Publishing: New York, 2014) 137.

494 Richard Dawkins, *The Selfish Gene* (, 1989), 192. Doi: http://books.google.com/?id=WkHO9HI7koEC&pg=PA192, "We need a name for the new replicator, a noun that conveys the idea of a unit of cultural transmission, or a unit of imitation. 'Mimeme' comes from a suitable Greek root, but I want a monosyllable that sounds a bit like 'gene'. I hope my classicist friends will forgive me, if I abbreviate mimeme to meme. If it is any consolation, it could alternatively be thought of as being related to 'memory', or to the French word même. It should be pronounced to rhyme with 'cream'."

[495] Dawkins and Williams debate.

[496] John Noble Wilford, "The World's Languages Dying Off Rapidly," New York Times, September 18, 2007, http://www.nytimes.com/2007/09/18/world/18cnd-language.html?ex=1347768000&en=faaeb910e26d6ba8&ei=5088&partner=rssnyt&emc=rss

[497] Michael E. Krauss, "Keynote-Mass Language Extinction and Documentation: The Race Against Time," 2007. As quoted in Osahito Miyaoka, Osamu Sakiyama and Michael Krauss, *The Vanishing Languages of the Pacific Rim* (Oxford: Oxford University Press, 2007), 3–24.

[498] Dix, 55.

[499] Here is a great website with source material on early Christian writing http://www.earlychristianwritings.com/

[500] There is an excellent scholarly article on reading and writing in ancient periods at the Oxford Biblical Studies website. http://www.oxfordbiblicalstudies.com/resource/scribal.xhtml

[501] James E. Reed and Ronnie Prevost, *Education in the Apostolic Age* (Nashville: Broadman and Holman, 1993) 73.

[502] *Ibid,* 75.

[503] Jonathan Draper, "The Didache" (Gospel Perspectives v. 5) 269. Cited http://www.earlychristianwritings.com/didache.html

[504] Cyril C. Richardson, "Didache," *Early Christian Fathers* (New York: Touchstone, 1996) 128ff.

[505] *Ibid.*

[506] Reed and Prevost, 113.

[507] Alexander Roberts and James Donaldson, "Constitutions', *The Ante-Nicene Fathers,* Volume VII (Edinburgh: T. & T. Clark, 1967), 389.

[508] *Ibid,* 475-476.

[509] Thomas Macy Finn, *Early Christian Baptism and the Catechumenate* (Collegeville, Mn: Liturgical Press, 1992), 43-47.

[510] You may have seen this section while surfing the BCP during a boring sermon. It really is worth a read. "Concerning the Catechism." BCP, 844.

[511] Encyclopedia Britannica, s.v. "Robert Raikes," http://www.britannica.com/EBchecked/topic/489694/Robert-Raikes "The son of a printer and newspaper publisher (the Gloucester Journal), Raikes succeeded to his father's business in 1757. He joined in such humanitarian causes as prison reform and hospital care. Noting the unsupervised behaviour of Gloucester children on Sundays, Raikes engaged in 1780 a number of women to teach reading and the church catechism on Sundays. The experiment was so successful that he could record in the Gloucester Journal (Nov. 3, 1783) that the district had become "quite a heaven upon Sundays." The Sunday-school movement spread rapidly to all parts of the country. In 1785 the Sunday School Society was formed. The Sunday School Union (1803) was a

direct result of Raikes's work."

512 Carey Lodge, "Connecting churches and schools," Christianity Today, February 10, 2014, http://www.christiantoday.com/article/connecting.churches.and.schools.on.educatio n.sunday/35774.htm

513 Stella Davies, *History of Macclesfield* (Didsbury, Manchester: E. J. Morten Publisher, 1961), 219–225.

514 "Episcopal Church Calendar, Holy Women Holy Men," Episcopal Church, http://satucket.com/lectionary/WAMuhlenberg.htm

515 *Ibid.*

516 *Ibid.*

517 John H. Westerhoff, *Will Our Children Have Faith* (Morehouse Publishing: New York, 1976) 5.

518 I first saw these comparisons in a handout I received at a Leadership Academy for New Directions conference. The handout was created in 1993 by Thomas K Ray then Bishop of Northern Michigan.

519 Wheatley, *Finding,* 1.

520 *Ibid.*

521 *Ibid,* 2.

522 *Ibid.*

523 *Ibid,* 3.

524 *Ibid,* 5.

525 *Ibid,* 25.

526 *Ibid.*

527 *Ibid.*

528 Stanley Hauerwas, John Milbank & Luke Bretherton in Conversation "Theological Reflections on Being a Theologian and the Task of Theology," Faith & Public Policy Forum and SCM Press, King's College, London, October 18, 2010 http://podcast.ulcc.ac.uk/accounts/kings/Social_Science/Milbank_Hauerwas_Brethert on.mp3

529 I am adapting here ideas from Sir Ken Robinson's TED talk on the future of education to highlight how creativity will play a key role in our work of formation. Ken Robinson, TED Talk, http://blog.ted.com/2006/06/27/sir_ken_robinso/

530 *Ibid.*

531 *Ibid.*

532 *Ibid.*

533 Laurence J. Peter, *Peter's Quotations: Ideas for Our Time* (New York: Bantam Books, 1977), 25.

534 Robinson.

535 *Ibid.*

536 *Ibid.*

[537] *Ibid.*

[538] *Ibid.*

[539] Sugata Mitra, "Kids can teach themselves," TED, TED 2007,
http://www.ted.com/talks/sugata_mitra_shows_how_kids_teach_themselves/transcript#t-1183000

[540] *Ibid.*

[541] *Ibid.*

[542] *Ibid.*

[543] *Ibid.*

[544] *Ibid.*

[545] Sugata Mitra, "Build a School in the Cloud," TED, TED 2013,
https://www.ted.com/talks/sugata_mitra_build_a_school_in_the_cloud

[546] *Ibid.*

[547] *Ibid.*

[548] Mitra, *Kids Can Teach.*

[549] *Ibid.*

[550] "Knowledge Tools of the Future," IFTF, 2008, http://www.iftf.org/our-work/people-technology/technology-horizons/knowledge-tools-of-the-future/

[551] *Ibid.*

[552] *Ibid.*

[553] Vannevar Bush, "As We May Think," *The Atlantic Monthly*, July 1, 1945,
http://www.theatlantic.com/magazine/archive/1945/07/as-we-may-think/303881/

[554] *Ibid.*

[555] Gorbis, 161.

[556] John Naisbitt, *Megatrends* (New York: Time Warner Books, 1982), 32ff.

[557] IFTF, *Knowledge Tools.*

[558] *Ibid.*

[559] Christoper T. Hill, "The Post Scientific Society," *Issues in Science and Technology*, Fall 2007, 78-84.

[560] *Ibid.*

[561] *Ibid.*

[562] *Ibid.*

[563] Ross Mayfield, "Weblog: Market's Technology & Musings,"
October 13, 2008, http://ross.typepad.com/blog/2005/08/web_of_verbs.html

[564] "Extreme Learners," IFTF, 2014, http://www.iftf.org/our-work/global-landscape/learning/extreme-learners/

[565] *Ibid.*

[566] *Ibid.*

[567] *Ibid.*

[568] *Ibid.*

[569] *Ibid.*

[570] *Ibid.*

[571] *Ibid.*

[572] "Learning: 2020 Forecast," IFTF, 2013, http://www.iftf.org/our-work/global-landscape/learning/

[573] *Ibid.*

[574] *Ibid.*

[575] *Ibid.*

[576] Gorbis, 76.

[577] *Ibid,* 79.

[578] *Ibid,* 82.

[579] *Ibid,* 83.

[580] *Ibid.*

[581] *Ibid.*

[582] IFTF *Learning.*

[583] *Ibid.*

[584] *Ibid.*

[585] *Ibid.* We have got to rename this!

[586] *Ibid.*

[587] *Ibid.*

[588] *Ibid.*

[589] *Ibid.*

[590] *Ibid.*

[591] *Ibid.* IFTF calls these sousveyors.

[592] *Ibid.*

[593] Gorbis, 84.

[594] *Ibid.*

[595] *Ibid.*

[596] For more information on BioCurious see: http://biocurious.org/about/

[597] Gorbis, 84.

[598] Gorbis, 91. I am adapting Gorbis quote regarding the future of education: "Social structured education actually brings us back to a future envisioned by Socrates, Rousseau, and Dewey, but with a whole new set of tools... These tools and platforms make it possible for us to pursue education that is individually paced and intrinsically motivated. We can use these tools to make the dream of Socrates, Rousseau, and Dewey a reality. We can create the kind of rich, meaningful, de-institutionalized education they envisioned."

[599] Darius Jankiewicz, "A Short History of Ordination," April 5,2013, http://www.memorymeaningfaith.org/blog/2013/04/history-ordination-part-i.html#_edn1

[600] *Ibid.* The exact phrase reads: *nec quemquam in ordinem legit, nisi quem ipse bene scisset.* Historia Augusta, vol. 1 (Cambridge: Harvard University Press, 2000), 159.

[601] *Ibid.*

[602] *Ibid.* Ignatius Magnesians 6.4, in Staniforth, 88.

[603] *Ibid.* Jerome Dialogus contra Luciferanos 21, in The Nicene and Post Nicene Fathers of the Christian Church, ed. Philip Schaff and Henry Wace (Grand Rapids: Wm. B. Eerdmans Publishing Company, 1989), 6:331.

[604] *Ibid.* Schillebeeckx, 38-41; the ontological distinction between ordinem et plebem that had already appeared in Tertullian, and was eventually accepted by Christian thinkers, made this development inevitable. Cf., Vinzenz Fuchs, Der Ordinationstitel von seiner Entstehung bis aug Innozenz III (Amsterdam: P. Shippers, 1963), 280; R. Paul Stevens, The Other Six Days: Vocation, Work, and Ministry in Biblical Perspective (Carlisle: Paternoster Press, 1999), 151; Gary Macy, The Hidden History of Women's Ordination: Female Clergy in the Medieval West (New York: Oxford University Press, 2008), 27.

[605] Apologetics is an argument justifying religious doctrine.

[606] David Gortner, "Up to the Task: Clergy Leadership for the 21st Century," Virginia Theological Seminary, January 2014

[607] *Ibid.*

[608] *Ibid.*

[609] *Ibid.*

[610] *Ibid.*

[611] *Ibid.*

[612] *Ibid.*

[613] *Ibid.*

[614] *Ibid.*

[615] *Ibid.*

[616] *Ibid.*

[617] *Ibid.*

[618] *Ibid.*

[619] Ian Morrison, *The Second-curve* (New York; Ballantine Books, 1996), 7.

[620] *Ibid.*

[621] *Ibid.*

[622] Wheatley, *Finding*, 251.

[623] *Ibid*, 252.

[624] *Ibid.*

[625] *Ibid.*

[626] "Future Work Skills 2020," IFTF, 2011, http://www.iftf.org/uploads/media/SR-1382A_UPRI_future_work_skills_sm.pdf

[627] *Ibid.*

[628] *Ibid.*

[629] *Ibid.*

[630] *Ibid.*

[631] *Ibid.*

[632] *Ibid.*

[633] *Ibid.*

[634] *Ibid.*

[635] *Ibid.*

[636] *Ibid.*

[637] *Ibid.*

[638] *Ibid.*

[639] *Ibid.*

[640] *Ibid.*

[641] *Ibid.*

[642] *Ibid.*

[643] *Ibid.*

[644] *Ibid.*

[645] *Ibid.*

[646] BCP, 517ff. Adapted.

[647] A cathedra is the bishop's chair in the cathedral

[648] BCP, 531ff. Adapted.

[649] BCP, 543ff. Adapted.

[650] Luc-Normand Tellier *Urban World History* (Québec: Press de l'Université du Québec, 2009), 274.

[651] Philip Smith *Dictionary of Greek and Roman Biography and Mythology*, s.v. "St. Ambrosius" (Boston: Little, Brown and Company, 1867),139–40.

[652] Craig Alan Satterlee, *Ambrose of Milan's Method of Mystagogical Preaching* (Collegeville, Mn: Liturgical Press, 2002), 47.

[653] The Arian controversy describes several controversies between a one clergyman and theologian Arius and a bishop and Athanasius related to Christology. The controversy divided the church from before the Council of Nicaea in 325 to after the Council of Constantinople in 381. It dominated Church politics for over fifty years. It had to do with the nature of God, Jesus, and the Holy Trinity.

[654] Smith.

[655] Satterlee.

[656] Paulinus, Vita Ambrossi, 9 (Novoni) 62. As quoted in Smith.

[657] *Ibid.*

[658] Taleb, *Antifragile*, 217.

[659] *Ibid.*

[660] *Ibid.*

[661] *Ibid.*

[662] *Ibid.*

[663] *Ibid.*

[664] *Ibid.*

665 *Ibid.*

666 *Ibid,* 217.

667 *Ibid.*

668 *Ibid.*

669 *Ibid.*

670 *Ibid,* 218-219.

671 Harold H. Rowdon, "Theological Education: A Historical Perspective," *Vox Evangelica,* vol. 7, 1971,75-87.

672 J. Lebreton and J. Zeilier, *A History of the Primitive Church,* IV (New York: Collier Books, 1948), 971.

673 Rowdon.

674 *Ibid.*

675 Cyprian, *Epistles XXIX.*

676 Rowdon.

677 *Ibid.*

678 *Ibid.*

679 *Ibid.*

680 Lebreton and Zeilier.

681 Rowdon.

682 *Ibid.*

683 *Ibid.*

684 *Ibid.*

685 *Ibid.*

686 *Ibid.*

687 *Ibid.*

688 *Ibid.*

689 *Ibid.*

690 F. W. B. Bullock, *A History of Training for the Ministry of the Church of England and Wales from 1800 to 1874* (St. Leonards-on-the-Sea, Budd & Gillatt,1955), 4. As quoted in Rowdon.

691 David Sebastian, "Trends in Theological Education in North America" Anderson University School of Theology, Anderson, Indiana.

692 *Ibid.*

693 *Ibid.*

694 Kahneman, 277.

695 Bettina Warburg-Johnson, "Anya Kamenetz Tells What's in Store for Education," IFTF, August 14, 2012, http://www.iftf.org/future-now/article-detail/do-it-yourself-university-style-anya-kamenetz-tells-whats-in-store-for-education/#sthash.RsdKXK1h.dpuf

696 *Ibid.*

697 *Ibid.*

[698] See class description here: https://www.coursera.org/course/algo

[699] Warburg-Johnson.

[700] *Ibid.*

[701] Gorbis, 69ff.

[702] *Ibid.*

[703] *Ibid*, 75.

[704] *Ibid.*

[705] "From Educational Institutions to Learning Flows," IFTF, 2013, http://www.iftf.org/uploads/media/SR-1580-IFTF_Future_of_Learning_01.pdf

[706] *Ibid.*

[707] *Ibid.*

[708] *Ibid.*

[709] *Ibid.*

[710] *Ibid.*

[711] *Ibid.*

[712] *Ibid.*

[713] *Ibid.*

[714] *Ibid.*

[715] *Ibid.*

[716] *Ibid.*

[717] Read more about it here: http://www.anglicannews.org/news/2014/01/southern-africa-archbishop-launches-africa-e-reader-project.aspx

[718] L. Gregory Jones, "Something old, Something New: Innovation in Theological Education," Christian Century, Feb 10, 2014, http://www.christiancentury.org/article/2014-01/something-old-something-new

[719] *Ibid.*

[720] Ibid. Jones suggests for future reading: "Deep trends affecting Christian institutions," by L. Gregory Jones and Nathan Jones at faithandleadership.com: http://www.faithandleadership.com/content/l-gregory-jones-and-nathan-jones-deep-trends-affecting-christian-institutions

[721] *Ibid.*

[722] Gorbis, 133. Adapted.

[723] *Ibid*, 203.

[724] ." Nobelprize.org. September 10, 1974.

[725] Anderson, 143.

[726] *Ibid.*

[727] Wheatley, *New Science*, 15.

[728] *Ibid.*

[729] *Ibid.*

[730] Gorbis, 210.

[731] Gorbis, 210. Hayek's means are listed by Gorbis in *The Nature of the Future*. The

nature of Catallaxy used here is from Hayek's work. Hayek, F.A. Law, *Legislation, and Liberty*, Vol. 2, (Chicago: University of Chicago Press, 1978), 108–9.

[732] Gorbis, 210. Adapted from Gorbis' thoughts on the new economy and organization.

[733] Wheatley, *New* Science, 15. Adapted.

[734] Aristotle, *Nicomachean Ethics*, trans J. A. K. Thomson, (New York: Penguin Classics, 2004) 32.

[735] *The Catholic Encyclopedia*, s.v. "Diocese," (New York: Robert Appleton Company, 1909). http://www.newadvent.org/cathen/05001a.htm

[736] *Ibid.*

[737] *Real-Encyclopädie der classischen Altertumswissenschaft*, s.v. *"vicarious"* (Stuttgart, 1903) V, 1, 716.

[738] Op cit. "The Apostolic Canons (xiv, xv), and the Council of Nicæa in 325 (can. xvi) applied this latter term to the territory subject to a bishop. This term was retained in the East, where the Council of Constantinople (381) reserved the word diocese for the territory subject to a patriarch (can. ii). In the West also parochia was long used to designate an episcopal see. About 850 Leo IV, and about 1095 Urban II, still employed *parochia* to denote the territory subject to the jurisdiction of a bishop. Alexander III (1159-1181) designated under the name of *parochiani* the subjects of a bishop (c. 4, C. X, qu. 1; c. 10, C. IX, qu. 2; c. 9, X, De testibus, II, 20)."

[739] *Catholic Encyclopedia*, s.v. "Chorepiscopi" (New York: Robert Appleton Company, 1913).

[740] *Ibid.*

[741] *Ibid.*

[742] *Ibid.*

[743] *Ibid.*

[744] *Ibid.*

[745] Dwight Zscheile, "Episcopal Church in context, Episcopal structure in Context, Rethinking Church wide organization in a New Apostolic Era, " doi http://www.provinceiv.org/images/customer-files/ZscheileSynod.pdf

[746] David Hein and Gardiner H. Shattuck Jr., *The Episcopalians* (New York: Church Publishing, 2004), 52.

[747] An American, Seabury was not willing to take an oath to be loyal to the king.

[748] Robert Prichard, *History of the Episcopal Church* (New York: Church Publishing, 1999), 88.

[749] Arthur Carl Piepkorn, *Profiles in Belief: The Religious Bodies of the United States and Canada* (New York: Harper & Row, 1977), 199.

[750] *Episcopal Ministry: The Report of the Archbishops' Group on the Episcopate*, (London: Church House Publishing, 1990), 123.

[751] Zscheile.

[752] Peter W. Williams, *America's Religions: From Their Origins to the Twenty-first century* (Chicago: University of Illinois Press, 2008), 264ff.

[753] B. Drummond Ayres Jr. "The Episcopalians: an American elite with roots going back to Jamestown," The New York Times. December 19, 2011.

[754] Prichard, 313.

[755] Zscheile.

[756] *Ibid.*

[757] "Identity and Vision – Draft," Reimagine The Episcopal Church Task Force, http://reimaginetec.org/identity-and-vision-draft

[758] *Ibid.*

[759] Michael C. Jackson, *Systems Approaches to Management* (New York: Springer Science & Business Media, 2000), 77.

[760] Ronald Coase, "The Nature of the Firm," *Economica* 4, no 16 (1927): 386-405. As quoted in Gorbis, 32.

[761] *Ibid*, 33.

[762] Douglas Rushkoff, *Life Inc: How Corporatism Conquered the World and How We Can Take It Back*, (New York: Random House Trade Paperbacks, 2011). As quoted in Gorbis, 33.

[763] Clay Shirky, *Here Comes Everybody*, (New York: Penguin, 2009), 21.

[764] *2008-2018 Map.*

[765] *Ibid.*

[766] *Ibid.*

[767] *Ibid.*

[768] Shirky.

[769] *Ibid.*

[770] Gorbis, 30.

[771] James Surowiecki, *The Wisdom of Crowds* (New York: Random House, 2004). As quoted by Gorbis, 30.

[772] Surowiecki, 137.

[773] Gorbis, 110.

[774] *Ibid*, 113.

[775] *Ibid*, 30.

[776] Robert Howard, "Values Make the Company: An Interview with Robert Haas," *Harvard Business Review*, Sept.-Oct. 1990, 133-144.As quoted in in Wheatley, *New Science*, 158.

[777] As quoted in by Wheatley in NS, 159. Betty Jo Teeter Dobbs and Margaret C Jacob, *Newton and the Culture of Newtoniansim* (New Jersey: Humanities Press, 1995).

[778] *Ibid.*

[779] *Ibid.*

[780] Gorbis, 118.

[781] *Ibid*, 101.

[782] *Ibid.*

[783] *Ibid*, 100.

[784] *Ibid*, 101.

[785] *Ibid*, 102.

[786] *Ibid*.

[787] Surowiecki, 232.

[788] *Ibid*.

[789] *Ibid*.

[790] Stephen W. Littlejohn & Kathy Domenici, *Engaging Communication in Conflict: Systemic Practice* (Thousand Oaks, CA: Sage Publications, 2001), 48.

[791] Martín Carcasson, "Beginning with the End in Mind: A Call for Goal-Driven Deliberative Practice" (Occasional Paper / no.2 / 2009). http://www.publicagenda.org/files/PA_CAPE_Paper2_Beginning_SinglePgs_Rev.pdf

[792] *Ibid*.

[793] *Ibid*.

[794] Daniel Yankelovich, *Coming the Public Judgment* (Syracuse, NY: Syracuse University Press, 1991), 224.

[795] David Mathews, "Community Politics: A Lens for Seeing the Whole Story of Kettering Research," Connections (Winter 2006): 4.

[796] *Ibid*.

[797] Corcasson.

[798] As quoted in in Corcasson. "The work of public administration scholars such as Matt Leighninger, Archon Fung, James Creighton, John Nalbandian, & Lisa Bingham, as well as organizations such as the International Association of Public Participation, the Institute for Local Government, and the National League of Cities, clearly reveals that there is a movement within institutional structures that is realizing the poor quality of much public participation and are seeking new and more productive ways of interacting with the public." See also the recently released "Core Principles for Public Engagement" available at www.thataway.org/files/Core_Principles_of_Public_Engagement.pdf.

[799] Harry C. Boyte, "Reframing Democracy: Governance, Civic Agency, and Politics." Public Administration Review 65 (2005): 536. Related concepts include collaborative governance, used by the Weil Program on Collaborative Governance at Harvard University, as well as collaborative public management, used by Lisa Bingham & Rosemary O'Leary in their recent Big Ideas in Collaborative Public Management (M.E. Sharpe Inc., 2008).

[800] Corcasson.

[801] Adapted from Wheatley, *Finding*, 84.

[802] *Ibid*, 86

[803] *Ibid*, 86.

[804] *Lucy*, directed by Luke Besson, Canal, 2014.

[805] Op cit, 88.

[806] *Ibid*.

[807] *Ibid*, 89.

[808] *Ibid*, 91.

[809] *Ibid*, 92.

[810] Adapted from Gorbis, 199.

[811] *Ibid.*

[812] *Ibid.*

[813] *Ibid.*

[814] Wheatley, Finding, 156.

[815] *Ibid*, 157.

[816] *Ibid*, 158ff. Adapted from Wheatley's distinctions between "feedback" and "measurement."

[817] Jill Lepore, "Disruption Machine: What the gospel of innovation gets wrong," *The New Yorker*, JUNE 23, 2014.

[818] Paul Nunes and Larry Downes , "The Five Most Disruptive Innovations," Forbes, January 10, 2014, http://www.forbes.com/sites/bigbangdisruption/2014/01/10/the-five-most-disruptive-innovations-at-ces-2014/

[819] Lepore.

[820] Wheatley, *New Science*, 21.

[821] Ilya Prigogine and Isabelle Stengers, *Order out of Chaos* (New York: Bantam Books, 1984). As quoted in in Wheatley, *New Science*, 21.

[822] Phyllis Tickle, *The Great Emmergence: How Christianity is Changing and Way* (New York: 2008).

[823] One's hermeneutic is one's underlying perspective.

[824] Kahneman, 204.

[825] *Ibid.*

[826] C. G. Jung, *Psychology and Religion: West and East* (Princeton, Nj: Princeton University Press, 1958), 76.

[827] J. Pittman McGehee and Damon J. Thomas, *The Invisible Church: Finding Spirituality where You are* (Santa Barbara, Ca: ABC-CLIO Publisher, 2008), 38.

[828] *Ibid.*

[829] *Ibid.*

[830] *Ibid*, 40.

[831] Jung, 293.

[832] Thomas A. Kempis, *Imitation of Christ*, Leadership University, doi: http://www.leaderu.com/cyber/books/imitation/imitation.html

[833] *Ibid*, 44.

[834] John Macquarrie, *Principles of Christian Theology* (London: SCM Press, 1966), 393.

[835] *Ibid.*

[836] *Ibid.*

[837] *Ibid.*

[838] Sinek, 11ff.

[839] Henry Knox Sherrill, "Easter Address," *The Outlook*, March 1952.

[840] Brown, 59ff. Adapted.

[841] Excerpt from Theodore Roosevelt's Speech "Citizenship In A Republic" delivered at the Sorbonne, in Paris, France on 23 April, 1910. http://www.theodore-roosevelt.com/images/research/speeches/maninthearena.pdf. Brené Brown first introduced me to this speech in *Daring Greatly*.

Made in the USA
Middletown, DE
18 May 2015